PRAISE FOR

Feeling Our Way: Embracing the Tender Heart

"Regina is issuing a plea and a challenge for us: to accept our innate sensitivities as the gift that they are and not as a burden to be covered up, ignored and lamented. Through the use of her auto-biographical description of her own healing and work, she is showing us that this acceptance is not only the first step in our own healing, but opens the reception of a revolutionary and evolutionary new paradigm for our world—one where the heart is in charge of our enormous power to manifest and create what we choose to make. The wounds, individual and collective, are all out in the open for all who have eyes to see. This book is a contribution to the deepening discussion of 'What now?'"

~ **JONATHAN M. GOLDMAN**, M.Ac,, author of *Gift of the Body: A Multi-Dimensional Guide to Energy Anatomy, Grounded Spirituality and Living Through the Heart*

"Interwoven with myths, scientific research, energetic interpretations, spiritual reflections and personal sharing, *Feeling Our Way: Embracing the Tender Heart* offers the reader a very readable (hard to put down) format for understanding the empathic experience—i.e. our abilities to sense the inner states of others. Dr. Bogle presents an exquisite interpretation of Donna Eden's and Jonathan Goldman's work to provide a more accessible avenue for emotional healing through the integrative doorway of energy medicine. I believe this book will become the quintessential text book not only for empaths but for nursing, mental health, and energy medicine professionals, and all those wanting to more deeply understand, work with, and appreciate the value of feelings in our lives."

~ **MELANIE MOFFAT**, RN, LMT, CHTP, EEM-AP

"I have been learning from Dr. Regina Bogle for years and celebrate her new book, *Feeling Our Way: Embracing the Tender Heart,* which has something important to say to all healing professionals and those on a journey toward wholeness. With a tender heart, Dr. Bogle does a masterful job integrating traditional modalities of healing, mythology, spirituality, physiology, and energy medicine while telling the story of the Empath."

~ **JULIE A. COOK,** MAPC, Pastoral Counselor, Marriage and Family Therapist, (retired), Spiritual Director

"Our world stands at the crossroads. Our feelings offer us information regarding the choices which face us but in order to choose wisely we need to understand what we feel. Will we create a future shaped by love or ignorance? Will we sensitively reach out to others or numb ourselves in fear? Will we allow ourselves to trust our hearts for guidance or yield to societal expectations that the future will repeat the past? For millennia, sages have known that our most authentic way forward is through love and a deep understanding that we are one, all the while recognizing that our individual journeys contribute to the whole. As Dr. Regina Bogle states so clearly in her seminal book, *Feeling Our Way: Embracing the Tender Heart:* 'Oneness is heart consciousness.'

"I encourage you to journey with Dr. Bogle as she explores the wisdom of the tender heart and its capacity to embrace the feeling and empathic aspects of our human nature—both within ourselves and others. Her work is a gift to the world and places us one step closer to not just surviving as a species, but thriving."

~ **DR. VICKI MATTHEWS**

"*Feeling Our Way: Embracing the Tender Heart* offers a unique approach to the understanding of empathy and the difficulties and challenges that we face on a daily basis. Dr. Bogle's synergistic combination of traditional psychological perspectives, energy medicine and energy psychology presents a more cohesive and compassionate picture of our sensitivities and responses to life's stressors. The depth and insights within the pages of *Feeling Our Way* are like a compass that so many of us need. Having a compass does not dictate the route we take in life but helps us to keep going in the right direction no matter how circuitous the path. This work promotes personal empowerment through an honoring of feelings and a deepening of love. In this way we can then transform what may have been a liability into a treasure. This is truly a book written from the heart."

~ **CELESTE M. SAUNDERS,** MD, FACEP

"Written by the most insightful person I have ever met, this book is Dr. Bogle's gift to the world. Anyone who reads it will receive much understanding of themselves and others and be opened to a deeper compassion for all. May her experienced and enlightened heart touch yours."

~ **LINDA TYRIE,** D.C.

"In *Feeling Our Way: Embracing the Tender Heart,* Regina Bogle gently proclaims a new and liberating perspective for those who identify with the archetype of 'Empath.' Bogle describes in a beautifully poetic way how the tender and sensitive soul, whose gifts may have been a double-edged sword for years, can soar in freedom with the reassurance that our emotions—even when negative and confusing—play a major role in the journey to spiritual health and wholeness."

~ **JO-ELLEN DARLING,** MS, Writer and Christian Contemplative

"'It is wisdom to know others; it is enlightenment to know one's self.' (Lao-Tzu). In this courageous work, Dr. Bogle inspires us to understand ourselves more deeply by creatively synthesizing a variety of ancient and modern teachings. As a natural outflow of this understanding, tenderly embracing oneself as a feeling human being naturally becomes easier. Simultaneously poetic and practical, this work offers insight into ways to appreciate and rewire our responses for increased well-being and the possibility of healthier relationships with ourselves and others. Brava!!!"
~ **SARAH FINNERTY,** MD, MPH, FACEP

"Both for the lay person and for those involved in all facets of the healing arts, *Feeling Our Way: Embracing the Tender Heart* gifts the reader with an opportunity to explore and understand the multifaceted dimensions of being human and, in particular, empathic. Beautifully presented with simplicity and clarity, this integrative work offers a great reference for appreciating the multi-dimensional ways we humans are able and continually invited to receive informational stimuli and make a response.

"As an empath, I found myself reading a bit at a time, and then reflecting on what I'd read as it related to my ongoing questions: who am I and who are you? *Feeling Our Way* has helped me understand why I am always asking these questions. Now that I am able to appreciate the layers and systems at play within us, I realize that the process of unraveling the true and authentic self is complex as well as simple.

"In summary: What does it mean to be an empathic human being, in this body, with such sophisticated physiology, living now? I found *Feeling Our Way: Embracing the Tender Heart* a meaningful guide for answering this question, now, for myself."
~ **PATRICIA H. MORRIS,** Heart Break To Happiness Coach and Feng Shui Consultant

FEELING OUR WAY

EMBRACING
The Tender Heart

FEELING OUR WAY

EMBRACING
The Tender Heart

REGINA BOGLE, M.D.

Feeling Our Way: Embracing The Tender Heart
© 2016 Regina Bogle, M.D., EEM-AP
www.reginaboglemd.com

All rights reserved worldwide. No part of this publication may be reproduced, distributed, or transmitted in any form or by any means, electronic or mechanical, including photocopy, recording, or any information storage and retrieval system, without written permission from the author except in the case of brief quotations, embodied in critical reviews and certain other noncommercial uses permitted by copyright law.

Exceptions: Figures 5-2 ("Triple Warmer") and 16-1/18-1 ("Kabbalistic Tree with Flaming Sword") were adapted by the author from Public Domain images on Wikimedia Commons under the Share Alike license. The details of this license and the availability of these illustrations for future use may be found via the respective links in the Reference Section of this text.

Attributions: Figure 3-7 ("The Limbic System") was adapted from the work of Blausen.com Staff; Figure 5-2 ("Triple Warmer") was adapted from the work of Depak Muniraj; Figures 16-1/18-1 were adapted from Morgan Leigh's "File:Tree of Life wk 02.jpg."

Special thanks for permission to use the image for Figure 3-5: The Heart's Electromagnetic Field. Image courtesy of the HeartMath® Institute – www.heartmath.org.

The information provided in this book is designed to provide helpful information on the subjects discussed. This book is not meant to be used, nor should it be used, to diagnose or treat any medical, psychological, or psychiatric condition. For diagnosis or treatment of any medical or psychiatric problem, consult your own physician. The publisher and author are not responsible for any specific energetic imbalances, physical or mental health concerns, or allergy needs that may require professional supervision or attention and are not liable for any damages or negative consequences from any treatment, action, application or preparation, to any person reading or following the information in this book. References are provided for informational purposes only and do not constitute endorsement of any websites or other sources. Readers should be aware that the websites listed in this book may change.

Publisher's Cataloging-in-Publication Data

Names: Bogle, Regina.
Title: Feeling our way : embracing the tender heart / Regina Bogle, MD.
Description: Yachats, OR : Wild Ginger Press, 2016. | Includes bibliographical references and index.
Identifiers: LCCN 2016952992 | ISBN 978-1-943190-09-6 (pbk.) |
    ISBN 978-1-943190-10-2 (ebook)
Subjects: LCSH: Energy psychology. | Energy medicine. | Sensitivity (Personality trait) | Alternative medicine. | Mind and body therapies. | BISAC: BODY, MIND & SPIRIT / Healing / General. | BODY, MIND & SPIRIT / Parapsychology / General.
Classification: LCC RZ999 .B54 2016 (print) | LCC RZ999 .B54 (ebook) | DDC 615.8/52--dc23.

Ordering Information:
If you are interested in quantity sales for your organization, please contact Regina Bogle at reginaboglemd@gmail.com.

Wild Ginger Press
www.wildgingerpress.com
Book & Cover Design by Bobbi Benson
Illustrations by Regina Bogle

Dedication

To

Sacred Love

and

The Beautiful Heart

with

Gratitude

for

All Your Many Manifestations

CONTENTS

Table of Illustrations xiii

Acknowledgments xv

Foreword xxi

Introduction xxix

Part I: The Resilient Heart

Foundations 1

    Chapter 1: What Does It Mean to Be an Empath? 3

    Chapter 2: Who Is an Empath? 19

    Chapter 3: Our Empathic Brains 39

    Chapter 4: The Empathic Stress Response 63

    Chapter 5: Our Responsive Energy Systems 77

    Chapter 6: The Empathic Aura 103

    Chapter 7: The Holistic Human Being 129

Part II: The Compassionate Heart

Healing 149

    Chapter 8: Child Development and Empathy 151

    Chapter 9: The Inner Critic and the Broken Heart 173

Chapter 10: The Healing Heart 195

Chapter 11: The Role of Consciousness in Healing 219

Chapter 12: Learning to Love Oneself 241

Chapter 13: Energetic Coping Techniques
for the Empath 259

Chapter 14: Deep Healing and the
Empathic Experience 279

Part III: The Spiritual Heart

Purpose 295

Chapter 15: The Longings of the Soul 297

Chapter 16: The Empath and Spirituality 325

Chapter 17: Appreciating Ancient Wisdom 349

Chapter 18: The Ethics of Care for Self 377

Chapter 19: The Ethics of Care for Others 401

Chapter 20: The Spiraling Path Continues 421

Conclusion: A New Story for the Empath 437

References 443

Index 453

About the Author 461

TABLE OF ILLUSTRATIONS

Part I: The Resilient Heart
Chapter 2: Who Is an Empath?
  Figure 2-1: A Three-Dimensional Schematic for Empathic Sensitivity, Processing, and Response 37
Chapter 3: Our Empathic Brains
  Figure 3-1: The Divisions of the Nervous System 44
  Figure 3-2: Cell Membranes Responding to Hormones and Neurotransmitters 47
  Figure 3-3: Schematic for the Distribution of the Vagus Nerve .. 49
  Figure 3-4: The Sino-Atrial Node of the Heart 53
  Figure 3-5: The Heart's Electromagnetic Field 54
  Figure 3-6: The Anatomical Parts of the Brain 56
  Figure 3-7: The Limbic System 59
  Figure 3-8: The Insula 59
Chapter 4: The Empathic Stress Response
  Figure 4-1: Mirror Neurons in the Brain 67
Chapter 5: Our Responsive Energy Systems
  Figure 5-1: The Meridian Flow Wheel 87
  Figure 5-2: Triple Warmer Meridian's Pathway 90
  Figure 5-3: Spleen Meridian's Pathway 95
Chapter 6: The Empathic Aura
  Figure 6-1: Layers of the Aura 106
  Figure 6-2: Central and Governing Meridians 112
Chapter 7: The Holistic Human Being
  Figure 7-1: The Holistic Model of Human Consciousness and Its Correlation with the Five Levels of Soul 132

Part II: The Compassionate Heart

Chapter 8: Child Development and Empathy

Figure 8-1: The Power Point and Its Proximity to the Vagus Nerve 154

Chapter 10: The Healing Heart

Figure 10-1: The Seven Major Chakras 197

Chapter 13: Energetic Coping Techniques for the Empath

Figure 13-1: The Main Neurovascular Reflex Points 269

Figure 13-2: The Five Rhythms Model 271

Figure 13-3: Chart of Correlation between Meridians, Yin/Yang Qualities and Emotions 273

Figure 13-4: The Five Rhythm Neurovascular Reflex Points... 274

Part III: The Spiritual Heart

Chapter 16: The Empath and Spirituality

Figure 16-1: The Ten *Sefirot* of the Tree of Life 334

Figure 16-2: The Crossroad of the Horizontal and Vertical Paths and Its Protection 345

Chapter 17: Appreciating Ancient Wisdom

Figure 17-1: The Three Worlds of the Vertical and Horizontal Paths 359

Figure 17-2: The World Tree 371

Chapter 18: The Ethics of Care for Self

Figure 18-1: The Ten *Sefirot* of the Tree of Life 394

Chapter 19: The Ethics of Care for Others

Figure 19-1: Ways of Caring for Self and/or Others 417

Acknowledgments

AS I CONTEMPLATED how I might express my deep gratitude for all those who have assisted me during this writing journey, the popular expression, "It takes a village to raise a child" came to mind. I realized that it also takes a village to write a book. Throughout this process I have felt very much like a conduit for something larger, wiser, and more caring than anything I might ever imagine or hope to be. The nature of the topic and the timing of its publication seem linked with forces in the web more intentional than I can fathom. I have played my small part thanks to the Love in this web and to the many individuals who have responded to that Love so as to play their part as well.

My gratitude also extends in three directions: past, present, and future. My life experience to date has contributed enormously to the content presented, and in my quest to understand it I must thank all those authors who have befriended my soul by sharing their wisdom and guidance. Many of them have been cited in this work, but not all. Also, my teachers have offered all sorts of gifts in the course of their sharing: some of them stood in front of a classroom; some have participated in the classes I have taught; a few of them sat in the healer's chair; many sat across from me in my consultation room. I would specifically like to acknowledge the foster children and parents with whom I've worked—they have taught me how love truly does exist in the darkest of places, and that healing is always possible.

I also give deep thanks to my family members, older and younger, who have both provoked and healed some of those shared darker places during our time together on Earth. Particularly I thank my parents, Michael and Myra, who gave me life and did their best to pass on more than they themselves received. I am also grateful to my son, Anthony, for deepening my heart and for allowing me to play a role in the deepening of his. In their ways, they have taught me much about love, the giving and receiving of it, and how it extends beyond lifetimes.

I want to thank Francesca, and Jim, Justin, Sandra and Carol, Dave, Jon, Jenn and Joyce for their efforts to negotiate the complexities of human love with me. I also hold deep gratitude for my soul friends who have traveled the depths with me, blessing our interwoven paths with love and support. Acquaintances and strangers have occasionally revealed something precious in golden moments as well—they will likely never know how much I thank them.

In the present, I want to acknowledge my deepest gratitude to all those who have offered their encouragement and assistance as related to the writing of this book. Some played a very valuable role in giving this manuscript its form and I would like to specifically acknowledge them here:

To my sister and lifelong companion, Mick Katch, who has made this publication a reality in the most practical of ways through her heartfelt intention to "take the pressure off" and make it possible for me to "pursue my dream."

ACKNOWLEDGMENTS

To my publisher, Bobbi Benson of Wild Ginger Press, for her generous advice, flexibility, and guidance throughout the entire process of making this manuscript into a book; her creative eye, technological wizardry, and gracious receptivity made the cover and the illustrations a reality. And to Mary Montanye, who guided me to Bobbi during our pilgrimage to Chartres!

To the early readers of my manuscript, especially to Trish Bogle, Vicki Matthews, and Barbara Sussman, for their courage and kindness in saying the hard things, which made a huge difference in the structure and presentation of the manuscript; and to Zulma Alvarez, Laurel Leland, and Linda Tyrie, whose suggestions, support and validation early on mattered just as much. Also, I extend a sincere "thank you" to Barbara Sussman for helping me to more deeply appreciate Kabbalah in our studies together.

To those who read the manuscript in its final stages, specifically Julie Cook, Jo-Ellen Darling, Sarah Finnerty, Jonathan Goldman, Melanie Moffat, Trish Morris, and Celeste Saunders, for their reflections which touched my heart.

To those whose unique gifts supported this publication in significant ways: for professional editing, Janet Gelernter; for her website expertise, Lori Kats; and for the author photograph on the cover, Martha Doerr.

To David Feinstein, not only in his role as teacher and colleague, but also for providing technical guidance during the initial stages of my writing, and for facilitating the accurate representation of Donna Eden's work at its conclusion. In this context, I also extend my gratitude to Michelle Earnest, current Director of Education for the Eden Energy Medicine Certification Program, who so generously gave her time, efforts, and helpful suggestions regarding the Eden Energy Medicine and Innersource Handouts citation review.

To the HeartMath® Institute and to Ryan Dana who so generously coordinated copyright permission to use the image "Magnetic Field of the Heart" for Figure 3-5. I am also grateful to *Wikimedia Commons* for the public domain use of several "Gray's Anatomy plates" and other images that served so well as models for many illustrations in the text.

To Jennifer Bradley, Dondi Dahlin, Marcella Kraybill-Greggo, Jim Licaretz, Marie Perkins, Shannon Ransom, Heidi Rausch, Anthony Smock, Judith Van Buskirk, and Barry and Louise Young for their practical assistance, helpful reflections, and heartfelt encouragement regarding the intricacies of this book's publication.

To Mary Cameron for asking the provoking, pivotal question that specifically directed my consciousness toward the deeper meaning of empathy and helped all the seemingly incongruous facets of my life converge; and to Eagle Skyfire for her behind-the-scenes support along this journey.

To Karina Yanku whose interest in the topic led to an interview about this work on her radio show, "The Healing Artist," in February 2015.

To the participants in my Healing Mondays classes, my sincere gratitude for their soulful questions and reflections, faithful support, and ongoing commitment to developing their gifts to make this world a better place.

I also want to acknowledge my dear Macrae, unconditional love on four legs, who often curled himself in my lap as I typed or insisted that I take breaks to play with him, all the while reminding me that love and laughter matter—a lot!

ACKNOWLEDGMENTS

Finally, as I contemplate the future, I want to thank all those who are making the effort to honestly explore their feeling sensitivities so that they may heal themselves and share their wisdom for the betterment of our world.

May the Divine Mother who has entrusted me with the writing of this manuscript bless all who read it. Amen.

FOREWORD

EACH MORNING as dream slides into waking, I wonder what mystery will reveal itself before my next nightly surrender to sleep. One such morning, cool and crisp amidst the flaming colors of autumn, I took my Westie, Macrae, for our daily walk. This particular mystery began on the way home when a smaller brown dog came bounding down the street. Without leash, collar, or any identification, he gestured to play with Macrae who responded in kind for a moment or two until, overwhelmed, Macrae signaled his need for rescue. The little brown dog—obviously wet from some unknown activity—placed his front paws on my knees, seemingly wanting me to pick him up as well. His eyes held a sweet, relational gaze as they met mine. He clearly had an owner who loved him. I wanted to reunite them, knowing I would long for such a reunion with Macrae should he ever be lost to me. My arms were full, however, and I guess our little brown friend decided that freedom felt more desirable, as he sprang down the street at a gallop.

With gratitude for Macrae in my arms and sadness for the owner of the brown furry fellow, I returned Macrae to street level and we continued our walk in the same direction as our friendly freedom-seeker but far, far behind him. At my inquiry, the parents and children waiting for the school bus at the next corner acknowledged they had seen the dog run full tilt past them. They thought they knew his residence, but at this point he was nowhere in sight. Macrae and I continued our walk, but I felt sad and concerned. I uttered a prayer into the universal web of Love that he be found and returned to his home.

Every time I passed the apartment-above-a-garage where I thought he lived I uttered the same prayer. Not seeing anyone to query during our walks, I remained clueless as to where he actually came from or whether he ever made it home. On the fifth day, not far from where I had first spotted our runaway, a nicely dressed man with a foreign accent asked, to my surprise, if I knew anything about a little brown dog. He told me that a teenage girl had been inquiring about the furry fellow at his church several blocks away and only later did he realize that his friend had found a dog of that description. He didn't know where the girl lived, so he was asking everyone he met on his walk in hopes of finding her. I gladly said, "Please come with me!"

We knocked at the door of the garage/apartment and two young girls responded. I asked if they had lost a dog and the elder said no, but their neighbors had. She and her sister took us next door to a similar residence where she knocked, but got no answer. She told us that the dog really belonged to her neighbor's sister, who lived out-of-state. In his excitement, her pet had broken free of the rope that confined him to the porch. His owner was heartbroken: "Noz was her baby," the girl told us. The man said he would return and tape the name and phone number of his friend who now had Noz on the door. With gratitude for this amazing encounter, Macrae and I returned home and I continued to utter my prayer that all would turn out well.

Days passed before I saw the girls—all four of them from both garage apartments—waving to me as they made their way to their bus stop. I asked if Noz had made it home. He had! With smiles abounding, we all parted company to pursue our respective adventures.

This sweet little story unfolded amidst all the ravages and tragedies of our current world. Caring people experienced separation, loss, likely some anger and guilt, helplessness, uncertainty, determination, persistence, trust in strangers, and the joy of reunion. Only the last of these feelings felt good. All the other emotions and the decisions they sparked required a measure of endurance for the uncomfortable. The odds were stacked against the owner ever holding her brown, furry "baby" again. In fact, when I saw him he was running in the opposite direction from where he was found—at least a six-block difference! Given the many possible outcomes, some of them tragic, how amazing that it ended as it did. All those of us involved were just feeling our way, but our hearts played a major role in this joyful reunion as well.

Unfortunately, feelings do not always make their way to our hearts. Especially when our feelings carry pain, when they bring an ache or any kind of upset to the heart, many of us tend to find some numbing agent or behavior to avoid the experience. When we do so, we deprive that wound of the love the heart can also offer. Yes, our beautiful, tender hearts can be hurt, but they can also heal us. It is these opposite qualities in fact that make our hearts tender. The dictionary definitions for the word "tender" include soft, delicate, vulnerable, caring, caressing, and—in law—an offering. Our hearts embody all of these qualities. They bear a sensitivity and a delicacy that can easily be hurt. They also accept what they see, welcome what they enfold, forgive readily, and love us into wholeness. Our hearts are tender by design: their offering of tenderness serves a beautiful, healing purpose.

Yet we sometimes deal with an aching heart by placing a wedge in it to isolate the hurting part, to numb it. That wedge makes for a broken heart, dividing it in two; thus, the healing part can't help the hurting part. We often incorporate this divide as a coping mechanism, but it really never works, certainly not for long. The insertion of this pseudo-protective defense often springs from the unconscious and not until we become conscious of it can we restore the fullness of the heart's experience. We need our hearts whole—their natural state. They offer us an amazing, multi-dimensional opportunity to connect to our deeper selves, to other people and creatures on the planet, to our souls, and with the Divine. Feelings—which differ from the heart in their origin and purpose—offer the heart much information about its many connections. It is the heart, when open and involved in life experience, that embraces and transforms our feelings as it guides us to manifest love. When our hearts have been broken, however, we in our consciousness must first embrace the heart, the whole of it, so that its healing love can flow anew.

Our world is suffering—from violence, climate change, economic downturns, and myriad pollutions of the environment—and consequently we all suffer as well. We have been educated in a patriarchal paradigm in which Charles Darwin's principle known as "survival of the fittest" is taught as a fact of nature. When we see the world through our *thinking* mode, we may falsely apply this to society as well. When we *feel* the implications of this, however, we know pain and suffering must accompany this viewpoint. The dark implications of the quip "only the strong survive" are becoming more difficult to ignore. Yet a shift in consciousness, subtle only in the slowness of its pace, is occurring in our midst.

In ancient days, a matriarchal paradigm held human consciousness with its awareness rooted in the earth, the power of the Feminine, the body, feelings, community, and the mother. As our brains evolved and we developed egos and the ability to discern differences, we moved into the patriarchal paradigm of the Masculine, the mind, productivity, the individual, and the father. As our consciousness continues to evolve we will wed these two polarities. We will remain conscious as individuals while also recognizing that we are one. Oneness is heart consciousness: we will know it not just because we *think* it, but because we *feel* it. Our minds must come to realize that feelings carry important information. As our consciousness evolves we must educate our minds to listen to our feelings and value what they offer.

World events support this growth by inviting each of us to notice our feelings, to accurately identify what sparks them, and to better discern what they mean both for ourselves and the world around us. Rather than view sensitivity and all its expressions—such as tearfulness, anxiety, ecstasy—as weakness, we would do better to understand their triggers. Rather than admonish the sensitive to "put a good face on it," in effect silencing them, it is far better to listen to what they feel, appreciate the deeper truth underlying their feeling, and seek wisdom in an attempt to resolve the matter. Similarly, we must apply these suggestions to ourselves. How often do we ignore what we feel? Or say to ourselves, I'll deal with that later? When "later" never comes, we likely have surrendered to the fear that Darwin's principle will triumph. We have learned that love and sensitivity do not mesh well with this old paradigmatic need to be strong. In truth, "survival of the fittest" is killing us. We are being invited to seek another way.

As I have sat in my psychiatrist's chair across from the many, many souls who found their way to me, I now realize with amazement that so many of them were empaths unconsciously protecting their hearts from further pain. Their very gift of sensitivity caused them considerable hurt and shame, followed by anxiety and depression as they tried to fit into an insensitive world. They had been diagnosed with disorders and numbed with medications without ever realizing the power and importance of their gifts. Their capacity for love was enormous, but buried so as to protect them from a world that has not recognized, and therefore not validated, the strength of their love. They knew well how to survive, despite the depth and intensity of feeling that besieged their inner world more often than not. Their capacity for endurance on the emotional plane rivaled that of any athlete on the playing field. Despite these strengths, however, they often perceived themselves to be weak, defective, and at fault for almost everything. Without their redemption, an enormous life-saving resource for our planetary and species survival will be wasted.

Hope for our world lies with those who are sensitive. It rests with those who can read the subtleties of imminent dangers before they manifest overt disaster. As experienced by the many people who responded with care and effort to the escapades of our furry brown emissary, these nuances reveal themselves in day-to-day conversations, the small decisions of the individual which impact more individuals, with a movement into the collective that can change everything. But this sensitivity can only help us if we honor it as valuable. As the stakes progressively heighten, hiding one's sensitivity to those subtle distinctions or numbing one's capacity for such awareness, will not help us survive. We live amidst paradox now: a focus on survival will kill us; a focus on vulnerability will save us. Evolution, by its very definition, changes in response to all sorts of circumstances. Darwin's principle may have been correct when he formulated it, but we are evolving into a new paradigm where love marks the difference between life and death.

Thus we are challenged to change, to heal, to grow. Can we begin, as a society, as a culture, as a species, to recognize the importance of the newly evolving paradigm? Can we begin to acknowledge and validate the power of love and the strength of our tender human hearts that serve as love's transmitter? What if we dared to pay attention to what goes on in the minds *and* hearts of those with whom we converse, blog, work, travel, and live? Each singular, seemingly tiny shift in the collective psyche (as described by Carl Jung) or the morphogenetic field (as depicted by Rupert Sheldrake) adds to the power of the new paradigm. Courage is an important ingredient for this transition, but not the only requirement. We need some guidance and some options so as to discover which path is best for each of us individually. We also need help and support—and not just from the earth plane—for this life-saving journey.

Love has many faces as it penetrates the dualisms and diversities of incarnated life. This book will delve deeply into how that love manifests through feelings when received and honored by an awakened, tender heart. It will also offer guidance for how to embrace a tender heart that has been broken. From this newly envisioned perspective of strength, we will not battle anything—not even violence and hatred. We will not—empathic people *cannot*—ignore these painful experiences, but we need not war against them: "…love will never be taught and understood through severity and fear."[1] Love will be taught through sensitivity and through love itself.

What follows is in part a story of my own unfolding but, more importantly, it presents the lessons I have learned along the way about being an empath. I have imparted these insights in a general way to clients in my work as a psychotherapist and they have found them to be consistently helpful. I now share these understandings and healing methods with the reader as an invitation to better appreciate our capacity for empathy, no matter what its degree; to respect that quality in others who may have more or less of it than we do; and to use this gift to build a new energy in the collective that will shift the paradigm toward not just our survival, but our thriving. While this may sound overly optimistic and idealistic to some, I have experienced this shift personally and I witness it daily in my practice. People hunger for this healing and we need it without delay.

I now invite the reader to stretch a little and journey with me into the healing of our sensitivity and our capacity to love, in the hope that we will each choose to honor our unique gifts so as to make the world a better place—not only for ourselves, but for future generations.

Namaste.

---

[1] Anonymous, *Meditations on the Tarot: A Journey into Christian Hermeticism,* trans. Robert Powell (New York, NY: Jeremy Tarcher/Penguin, 1985), 181.

Introduction

ASCENDING FROM THE STAIRWELL of a busy New York subway one Friday morning in November 2009, I gazed upon a sea of legs walking in opposite directions along the crowded sidewalk. The clatter of heels on concrete blended with the low-pitched drone of subways and the honking horns of street traffic to create a cacophonous greeting. Scents of people, foods and gasoline added to the mix and my sensory system paused. An ethereal armor came over me as I made my way into the fray.

I found myself reflecting upon the speed of everything around me, the blur of intent faces more sure of their directions than I. Each of those faces had a story, none of which I would ever get to know. In that moment a sea of souls, each with a personal history and a real-time agenda, surrounded me, while my pressing intention was to arrive at a hotel on time. Perhaps my stressed facial expression matched theirs as we unconsciously negotiated the New York streets together. In any case, my whole sensory system revved up several notches—a feeling I didn't particularly enjoy.

I had no idea then that I am an empath. I only knew that I managed life better if I gave myself enough alone time, budgeted my exposure to turmoil and chaos, and continued to read and explore anything that might help me understand why my inner state seemed to respond so differently from those I knew and loved. Now that I recognize myself as an empath, I can retrospectively appreciate why relationships, life circumstances, and developmental hurdles felt so enormously overwhelming. Fortunately, as a spiritual seeker and persistent sojourner in search of healing, I have also learned many wonderful healing modalities along the way.

Having preferred to hide in the shadows most of my life, I hadn't planned to share much of my story. Yet, by working with other empaths over the past few years, I have come to realize that sharing our stories softens the sense of isolation. As I now reflect upon my life, I see that several stories rest one upon another. I will share some of these layers here by way of introduction.

My Visible Life

Upon superficial review, my life presents as fairly conventional by today's standards. As the eldest of three children born to my Italian father and my English/Scottish/Irish/Welsh mother, I absorbed the lessons of caring for others and keeping the peace. Witnessing my mother care for her very ill parents before their deaths when I was six years old deeply influenced my later decision to become a physician. I attended Catholic schools through college, followed by medical school and a psychiatric residency. I then married, had a child, divorced, lived as a single mom for several years, remarried, negotiated blended family issues as best I could, and divorced again. After residency I also worked as a psychiatrist in various settings (hospitals, outpatient clinics, schools, and private practice) with different populations, prescribing medications and holding on with

INTRODUCTION

all my strength to what has become a dinosaur—providing psychotherapy as a psychiatrist. Since 1984 when I completed my residency, the changes in insurance coverage for mental health services have dramatically altered the practice of psychiatry. The restriction of the psychiatrist's role to medication management and treatment overview, often time-limited to fifteen minutes, simply never worked for me.

Over the past several years my practice has completely shifted. I no longer prescribe medications at all, but not because I am opposed to them: in my experience they serve a life-saving purpose at times, and I do work with clients who take psychotropic medications prescribed by other practitioners. Now I prefer to practice Energy Medicine, Energy Psychology, and psychotherapy. If I were to both prescribe medications and practice Energy Medicine, liability issues would demand that medication management be the priority. Furthermore, pharmacy regulations, paperwork requirements, and ever-changing insurance restrictions have complicated and interfered with the practice of a specialty I had chosen for its soulful qualities. The hours required for the empathic, healing connection with a client which I so value have lost their priority in our modern world. I could not sacrifice my values, derived from my empathic resonance with others and a deep desire to heal, to the political and financial agendas of others not sitting in the therapy room with us. Over time, it became increasingly evident to me that I had to make a choice: in 2012—without regret—I chose to integrate insight-oriented psychotherapy with Energy Medicine.

My Invisible Life

On a deeper level, using information one would never glean from archives, my story begins with the considerable anxiety I experienced as a child. By the age of twelve I was able to consciously appreciate that depression made me feel more grounded, providing a deep, reliable—albeit painful and inaccurate—sense of identity and place in the world. This sometimes gloomy, often despairing emotional state colored my high school, college, medical school and residency years. Few people knew this, however. Despite—or perhaps in response to—the heavy emotional pain of my teens and twenties, I developed a strong will, reliable endurance, and a deeper perspective regarding life's hardships and heartaches. The pain others experienced found a resonant home within me. Somehow they must have sensed this, as many would share their intimate stories with me. Not only did I feel honored by this, but my supervisors were amazed by how much detail I discovered about my clients. I considered my clients' stories sacred and over time learned to appreciate the subtleties of diagnosis through my evolving compassionate filter.

During my early college years, a co-worker introduced me to the deeper layers of astrology and before long I had learned to calculate and construct birth charts on my own. I devoured the writings of famous astrologers, seriously trying to understand myself in a more meaningful and compassionate context than that offered by psychiatric diagnostic labels. Consequently, my psychiatric training privately included astrological perspectives regarding the integration of opposites and resonance with energies beyond the self. These reflections helped me translate the traditional, polarized concepts of health and illness into more broad, even soulful dimensions.

Once my medical/psychiatric internship began in my mid-twenties, I finally surrendered to my need for more face-to-face assistance and found a professional who served as my mentor and psycho-

INTRODUCTION

therapy-focused psychiatrist. His sensitivity and wisdom helped me discern the difference between the emotional blur of my inner world and the boundaries of life's practicalities. Additionally, over the course of the next five years, astrological writings led me into the realm of Feminine archetypes and the work of Carl Jung. After six years of a cognitive behavioral approach to my psyche's dilemmas had instilled a reliable sense of grounding, five more years of Jungian analysis guided me through the deeper aspects of my inner world. The revelations in my dreams and their panoramic vista of symbols allowed me to reconnect with the Spirit-seeking roots of my childhood.

That longing for sacred sharing reawakened even more intensely during a pilgrimage to Chartres Cathedral in May 2014, followed by an Energy Medicine tour of ancient sites in England. Several months later, life offered me an opportunity to explore a path of spiritual sisterhood and sacred creativity in the Way of Belle Coeur.[2] These journeys have afforded me a deeper sense of the Divine not unlike that described in the Upper, Middle and Underworlds of ancient myths—my discoveries regarding these will unfold in the later chapters of this book. Prior to and in the course of all this, I had the benefit of learning and practicing Energy Medicine. I had stumbled upon Reiki in 2001, the practice of Eden Energy Medicine in 2008, and the work of Jonathan Goldman in 2015. These practices not only resonated with something deep in my soul, they helped me appreciate an amazing, previously foreign level of our human being-ness and guided me into a whole new dimension of healing. The practices of Energy Medicine and Energy Psychology have provided the thread

---

[2] Sybil Dana Reynolds, *Ink and Honey* (Chandelles Press, 2012).

of connection into a universal web of seemingly different yet vitally intertwined experiences. Energy has revealed itself as the missing link between the psychology and psychiatry ideals I have studied and the spirituality I have loved.

Healing My Life

Based on the expectations of my anxious childhood and depressed young adult years, I could never have predicted or even imagined the life I currently lead: my inner state could never have borne it gracefully. The internal intensity and sense of vulnerability that continuously thwarted my inner peace demanded that I direct all my energies toward quelling that torment. Well into my twenties I lived in an emotional prison of overwhelming reactivity to stimuli I could not always name, predict or control. My internal responses to life circumstances melded into an overarching judgment that I was somehow defective, unable to keep pace with life's demands, and lacking the wherewithal to define any purpose or meaning to my experience.

From my teens through my mid-twenties I lost all hope, living a life of secret inner torture from which I could see no escape. I'm not sure why I continued to place one foot in front of the other. I felt called to study the perspectives of astrological writers who described human experience with acceptance and as an opportunity to become conscious of our purposeful place in the world. Perhaps the compassionate perspective of these authors accessed and harnessed the deep spirituality that continued to flow in the underground recesses of my being. I could not have named it at the time, however. Instead I quietly described my unwillingness to completely give up as "my perverse curiosity" and dared to wonder, could it possibly get worse? Even more unlikely, could life possibly get better? In my pursuit of answers, I decided to honor those life threads that felt meaningful and to follow wherever they led. I had nothing to lose and possibly something to gain.

I now reflect upon my life as an amazing adventure with meaningful lessons abounding. Yet no amount of healing will change my nature, I realize. I have simply accumulated tools to maintain a resilient baseline, to return to that baseline after life throws its curve balls, and to deeply heal the old wounds caused by reacting strongly to people's moods, behaviors, beliefs and ensuing life events. My convictions about myself, others, their intentions toward me, and life itself have required major re-visioning. Eden Energy Medicine, Energy Psychology, and Jonathan Goldman's work with sacred Light have provided an effective and simple doorway to access these many layers of self and bring balance and healing where possible. It has given me enormous joy to witness these modalities being effective for others as well.

I now realize that true healing happens in the deep, mysterious caverns of our psyches. Even as a child, my empathic sensitivities, muddled and confused as they were, recognized the limitations of what I now professionally identify as ego. The soulful essence of us, filtered through our heart experience, nurtures and guides a deeper process that resides in the realm of Mystery. Finding a way to understand this experience and to name a meaningful life purpose transformed my emotional and psychological healing into a spiritual quest. Journeying with shamans, re-examining my religious origins, studying Torah and Kabbalah with a friend, and numerous other pursuits eventually offered a more congruent understanding of why I live with an empath "nature" amidst the significant social and worldly turbulence and suffering on this planet. As my path continues to evolve, this learning reveals deeper and deeper layers of life's Mystery.

Using This Book

Autobiographies traditionally describe the outer events of a person's life, but my inner life has offered considerably more riches for pondering. This book, then, is not so much an autobiography, but offers the story of my own inner healing journey presented in a more thematic, less chronological way. With enormous gratitude to the individuals who have assisted me in this healing—which didn't always feel good at the time—I offer this book for all those who feel *and* who want to better understand what they feel and why. We will also explore the deep impact empathic abilities can have upon our self-concept, how we can begin to heal, and what purpose our capacity for empathy may serve. It is my hope to offer the reader a guidebook of sorts for healing our hurts and redeeming our empathic experience. To this end I will share what I know about interventions that have helped me and others with whom I've worked as they negotiated their own empathic journey.

To explore these issues in a meaningful way, this book is organized into several sections. The first two chapters directly address the questions, "What does it mean to be an empath?" and "Who is an empath?" The next two chapters describe our neurology: how our bodies receive information, what our brains do with that information, and how our nervous system copes with the resulting confusion or cohesiveness that shapes our life experiences. Next we will address our energy systems: what they are and how they encode the information entering our energy field in ways that extend beyond, yet still affect the physical part of our being. We will then explore the psychological aspects of how our cells and energies contribute to our sense of self in the world, shaping our personalities with coping styles and defenses. Oddly, these self-protections may or may not truly reflect who we are at core, and they may or may not actually help us feel safe. While they seemingly developed in order to shield and protect the broken tender heart, we eventually discover that an awakened heart needs no such defense.

Later chapters further address our healing and our developing appreciation for the blessings of living with empathy from a heart-centered perspective. Once we have specifically identified the roots of our difficulties and their resulting wounds, we will explore in greater depth the role of consciousness in this healing journey, along with restorative options offered by Energy Medicine and Energy Psychology. Healing is referenced throughout this work, but will be given even greater emphasis as we turn to the ancestral wisdom of myths and fairy tales to help us more deeply understand the issues, and the practical as well as spiritual guidance these stories offer. We will also, I hope, come to appreciate the sacredness of healing and the opportunities arising directly out of empathic experience. Finally, we will integrate all this to discover the many valuable, necessary, and ethical contributions heart-centered, empathic people can make to those in their personal and larger webs of connection.

The reader will find within these pages the simple techniques that can be easily shared in a book, while there are many others too complicated for this format that only a well-trained professional can offer. Whatever the path chosen, I encourage empaths to seek an honest mirror to all that lies within them. Owning ourselves, with all our strengths and vulnerabilities, is an essential aspect of redeeming the empath within. Identifying what does not belong to us is critical as well; the release of other people's "stuff" accumulated from years of living a relational life may require professional assistance to provide the needed grounding as a new, more authentic sense of self takes hold. Having an empathic guide may make all the difference, especially to those who have suffered a great deal of emotional pain and confusion regarding their personal boundaries. For others, validation of what they have deeply suspected may be all that is needed.

Finally, it is important to note that the experience of empathy lies on a continuum. Thus, while this book will certainly address the concerns of highly empathic people, anyone with any degree of sensitivity to the feelings and concerns of others can benefit from what lies within these pages. Those who might not think of themselves as empathic may still discover new ways to understand and appreciate themselves and those they love. Additionally, psychotherapists, nurses, teachers, Energy Medicine practitioners, and spiritual seekers may find this work of value. Because this offering is integrative in nature, each reader may find some of the subjects familiar, but be less well versed in others. Consequently, I have tried to write in a fashion that explains the basics while simultaneously stimulating further thought as the threads of connection between these seemingly separate fields of endeavor reveal themselves.

This book appeals to our desire to leave the closed circle of the familiar and routine, and to spiral into new territory. It sometimes poses more questions than answers, serving as a map or guide. In truth, the answers we seek do not reside on a map, nor does a tour guide do our traveling for us: the answers reveal themselves as we engage in the journeying. They wait for each of us to discover them and make them our own. The reflections I offer in the following pages come from my own journey as an empath, but I want to acknowledge that we are all on a journey, seeking our own treasure. Each of us contributes in our own way to a greater whole, and the lessons we learn, the fruits we bear, enrich all of us, past, present and future.

I knew a shaman whose prayer for our circles began with: "May our lessons be gentle." I suspect that to some degree we can make choices about that. While the greater All may simply want us to learn and to share information, *how* we learn and *what* we learn is up to us. To my way of feeling and thinking, life is really one huge lesson about Love. I wish for us all that our lessons be gentle.

PART
I

The Resilient Heart
Foundations

CHAPTER 1

What Does It Mean to Be an Empath?

THERE COMES A POINT IN LIFE when one begins to wonder why things have unfolded the way they have, for what purpose one was born, and how one can live the rest of one's days meaningfully. Many writers and philosophers attribute this questioning to the "mid-life crisis," but I suspect such ponderings can happen to anyone at any time and maybe they come to most of us more than once. I also wonder if these questions come early and often to those who are sensitive, who feel deeply, and who struggle to make sense of their often troubled inner terrain. As one of their number, I have been privileged to meet many such individuals, particularly in the course of my work as a child psychiatrist. We tend to ask these questions, especially the one about life purpose, early in life. If our well-meaning parents are not able to recognize this gift of soulful searching they may think we're strange in some ways. While this misunderstanding can hurt, we may discover that, in the cosmic scheme of things, it offers just what we need to further us along the healing path of the soul.

With this in mind, I often wonder what purpose so much sensitivity and so much consequent heartache can serve. Is it leftover personal karma? Or ancestral karma? Or a planetary need to which many souls have responded? In any case, most of us come to this incarnation clueless about the gifts of our sensitivities. For some reason, we have to suffer them first and redeem them later. Unfortunately, there are few guidebooks explaining how to do this meaningfully, and our culture expects quick fixes to get those troubled feelings gone without ever making the effort to understand why they arose in the first place. In the midst of all this, the soul must speak loud and clear if we are to notice and listen to her. Much stumbling in the dark occurs, which in itself invites us to notice what hidden inner light or force refuses to surrender to despair. In essence, we are "feeling our way."

Empaths are beautiful people who live at various stages of awareness regarding all the issues facing us. Most human beings have empathy, but many learn that their feelings, be they physical or emotional, may get them into trouble with a society that emphasizes efficiency, productivity, and control. Our culture focuses on the supremacy of the ego and of the individual, whereas feeling-connections journey into the realm of community and of soul. As human beings on Planet Earth in the early twenty-first century, we live in a time of enormous transition. Our consciousness is experiencing a huge paradigm shift and many are feeling a quiet, if not turbulent, challenge to all they have known as secure. These disruptions can rattle the most courageous and bring despair to those who cannot envision life beyond ego agendas and personality needs. For those anchored in something deeper and more profound, however, this transition brings an opportunity for welcome transformation, and those sensitive to its nuances can facilitate a gentler passage.

Dedicating the time and attention necessary to understand ourselves and our feelings sets us on a journey of personal healing and spiritual exploration. These feelings, we come to realize, serve as invitation: we have been given the glorious opportunity to awaken our empathic hearts. And by so doing we can become even more consciously and courageously empathic. However, we must first understand what it means to be an empathic person. To explore this issue in detail I will begin by sharing more of my personal story, but my hope is that each person will bring wonder to their own story, what has led to this moment, and where this moment can lead. This book is a call to all those who are willing to feel more consciously. It is time for us to recognize our gifts, accept our challenges, develop our strengths, discover our purpose, and engage in life fully as the meaningful, powerful, gentle, and compassionate people we are. The Earth and her people—all living beings—need us NOW!

My Process of Discovery

Without recognizing what it meant to be an empath at the time, my own journey began as an anxious child whose memories of respite revolved around my maternal grandmother. My parents were good people who did their best to raise three children amidst life's hardships. Sadly, my grandparents' deaths six months apart when

I was six years old plunged all of us into a state of grief which at my young age I could not name. No one realized how much the empathic anchor of my grandmother's love had stabilized my inner world, nor how its absence had upended it. Not until I turned twelve did I recognize that depression felt more grounded than the steady presence of anxiety—although then I had no words for those feeling states. No one seemed to notice; outwardly, I functioned well.

Depression served as my constant companion until my late twenties when I finally had the courage to seek help, and the mental wherewithal to use it well. Unfortunately, leaving the depression behind and retrieving a state of inner peace meant that I had to retrace my steps and re-experience my early anxiety. While definitely unpleasant it was only temporary, I discovered. The resources I had lacked as a child were now available to me as an adult and were enormously helpful. That healing phase involved discovery of the Feminine and my realization that feelings matter. The door opened for my essence to peek through and gradually venture out of my protective, yet self-imprisoning closet.

While my sojourn through medical training and psychiatric residency offered much by way of technical information, physiologic understanding, mental health labels and treatments, the expectation that I maintain a detached professional stance, develop my logical assessment skills, and organize information and my life according to the demands of the medical community did little to validate or support my intuitive and feeling-based strengths. Fortunately, during my third year in medical school, one of my psychiatric supervisors conducted an empathic interview with a very distressed man, and because of it I chose psychiatry as my specialty. This choice shocked everyone, including myself, yet looking back I can see that he modeled an empathy I longed to experience, as well as a caring I intuitively knew I wanted to share. I simply hadn't realized that it had value to others in the medical profession, or that I could offer this myself.

Four years later I encountered another supervisor, someone I could trust with my interest in astrology. I will never forget one particular supervisory session during which I hesitantly described how working with a family left me feeling even more depressed than my usual state; he suggested I was sensing the depression of the family members as a group. I was both shocked to realize that such a thing might be possible and relieved to think I wasn't crazy. He named my gift and reflected back to me the beauty of my sensitivity. Because of this experience, I was eventually able to integrate what I had learned during my medical and psychiatric training through so much effort with the deeper, more naturally flowing and more important knowing of who I am. I will forever be grateful to both these supervisors. Their support of the non-traditional aspects of my essence has not only contributed to this work, but literally saved my professional and emotional life. These two supervisors initiated my healing process by showing me how to honor and redeem my sponge-like, sensitive, empathic gifts.

Only more recently, as I engaged in the work of processing the loss of each of my parents, did I realize that my memories of childhood were not only much more visual than auditory, but they were heavily laden with feeling. As I teased these apart with deeper reflection, I came to appreciate how those feelings were often empathically derived, not necessarily or primarily originating within me. One such memory involved my father driving me to an orthodontist appointment: I sat behind him in the car and visually took in the rainy day. The feeling was one of "yuck"—all my life I attributed that feeling to rainy days. Yet during the last year of his life he used to say, "Rain makes you beautiful!" and during a trip to Scotland, while out on the land in pouring rain, I felt no "yuck" at all. I have since come to wonder if that remembered feeling of "yuck" on a rainy day derived from my sensitivity to his sullen emotional state at the time. Given his difficult circumstances at that point in his life—providing for his wife and children, responsibilities for his own business, financial concerns, and extended family issues—this makes sense to me now. It has also released the "yuck" of the memory and given me a new sense of gratitude for rainy days!

This awareness and many others have given me a much deeper appreciation for how a child's empathic abilities impact his or her development. As a psychiatrist working with children, I have witnessed the many ways sensitive young people respond to life. Even those with autism have shared their stories, their concerns, and their hearts with me, so I can write about the experience of being an empath with the confidence of knowing there are many of us "out there." In my quest to help these children, and of course to understand myself, I pursued various avenues of study and exploration. As it turns out, the spirituality that so passionately held me as a child now clearly presents itself as the ultimate avenue to true healing. It gives meaning to life's heartaches, and invites us into a state of genuine and deep joy. Spirituality involves a deeper connection, a conscious connection with one's soul. Interestingly, I have found that those who are willing to own their empathic abilities readily agree that spirituality is a very important part of their lives.

So as one thread of the web led to another, I found my way to Donna Eden and David Feinstein, Ph.D., in 2008. Still without realizing I am an empath, Eden Energy Medicine and Energy Psychology helped me truly change the embedded patterns within my own energy systems and, over time, those of interested others. I discovered that anxiety need not last, so fear no longer restricts me from trying new experiences. If my mood slides into a depressed state, I can readily shift it as I explore its triggers and restore balance with energy interventions. When painful memories arise, I process them such that new perspectives can energetically replace the scenes previously stored in my brain, thereby healing old wounds. As my own energies flow more freely, I can more easily open my heart, live more fully, explore opportunities with greater courage, and feel the amazement of an adventure I never dreamed I'd be able to manage. Life still has its challenges and heartaches, but they now need not be feared or avoided. Self-criticism is no longer the huge tyrant that once ruled my life. Gratitude, self-acceptance, and compassion become the lessons and opportunities of each day.

Amidst these many healing experiences, the recognition that I am an empath came in a flash when the co-facilitator at a Celtic gathering in 2013 asked, "Is anyone here willing to teach a class about empaths?" In that moment, all the pathways of my life converged. I finally appreciated my sensitivity as a gift and an even deeper healing proceeded from that awareness. Now, realizing that I so readily sense the feeling states of others, I know in my core that I am part of something huge, intangible, and intentional. As a participant in this communal flow, I become a conscious co-creator. I recognize that being an empath holds meaning.

Empathy

When I mention the topic of "empaths" to people, invariably someone asks "What's that?" The frequency of this question likely reveals a deeper truth about the valuing of feelings in our society. Websites about empaths offer descriptions—some quite lengthy—that include emotions, behaviors, and psychic abilities attributed to the would-be empath. These sites imply that empaths as a group all have similar qualities that distinguish them from other people possessing "normal" degrees of empathy. The only public figure I know to be deemed an empath with honor appeared on a television show, *Star Trek: The Next Generation*. The character Deanna Troi, portrayed as half-human/half-Betazoid, elevated the role of the empath to meaningful status by helping Captain Jean-Luc Picard navigate the starship, *Enterprise*, through the star systems. She could sense the emotions of many, although not all, beings on their journeys, thus giving her commanding officer invaluable information. She carried herself with confidence and was treated with respect in a world where Klingons and Ferengi were taken equally seriously. What might that mean for we who are fully human on this side of the television screen here on Earth?

Empathy has been defined as "the capacity to sense the inner state of another person"[3]—a necessary ingredient for all close relationships. Yet despite its necessity for bonding, most of us experience the best empathic resonance at a subliminal level, like gossamer threads of web-like connection, ideally carrying heartfelt care, sacred communion, and emotional exchange between two or more people, all communicated in a way that is faster than the spoken word, much

---

[3] Rick Hanson, Ph.D. with Richard Mendius, M.D., *Buddha's Brain: The Practical Neuroscience of Happiness, Love & Wisdom* (Oakland, CA: New Harbinger Publications, Inc., 2009), 125.

less conscious, yet no less powerful. A gentle touch, a warming smile, the loving gaze that greets the soul—these convey in indescribable ways an aspect of relationship for which most of us yearn. It may happen without plan or awareness, or emerge as a directed willingness to engage in the *pathos* of others, and to experience others doing the same for us. Often our awareness of needing this care filters in from beyond the realm of language and logic. Some of us tap into it quickly, others not so much.

Mental health and illness literature, as well as social media, abounds with discussions regarding how lack of empathy has played a role in many recent tragedies. Most of us, having a fair amount of caring capacity, can't understand how someone seemingly feels nothing about or for another human being. Many have begun to wonder if the excessive exposure to violence in the media, both in the news and as so-called entertainment, has dulled the capacity of its viewers for social sensitivity and conscience. Yet violence is nothing new to the human psyche: since the beginning of recorded history, battles between the forces of perceived good and evil have made their mark upon the evolving human story. Many children's fairy tales contain some very grisly incidents, in fact. The popularization of television after World War II has since added a visually compelling element to the mix. This trend of ever more graphic depictions of violence has continued with a progressive blurring of boundaries, and the actions depicted take place right in our living rooms and bedrooms. As a result, the visual and audio effects of current technology more immediately penetrate our bodily senses, not just our imaginations. Our young are indoctrinated early into these experiences. What are we doing to them and to the neurological development of their brains? Are we also affecting the development of their capacity for empathy?

On the opposite end of the empathy spectrum, what of those who feel "too much," who are described as "too sensitive," who suffer the hurts of others—even of animals, insects or plants—in a fairly intense, internal way? How might we better understand the impact and the purpose of so much empathy for them? In the groups I've facilitated for empaths, many participants have spoken about how criticized they felt over the course of their lives for being sensitive. Many were told to "smile" during their childhood years, suggesting of course that this expression of social engagement did not come easily for them. Often they felt alone, that no one in their immediate circle really understood how they felt inside or why. Many even learned to ignore their inner feelings altogether. Consequently, they grew up feeling strange, as if "something was wrong" with them. Socially, they "put on the smile" like one puts on a hat or coat, yet they also acknowledged how they would isolate themselves at times in order to feel safe and at peace. For this, too, they felt defective and criticized.

In contrast, when the care of an empathic person comes our way we tend to really appreciate it. Otherwise, in the busyness of our days, many of us give little attention to the role of empathy in our lives. Most of us would agree that life without it can feel like a sterile wasteland. Infants have suffered from Failure to Thrive when empathic caregiving is denied them for whatever reason. Even adults have died as a direct or indirect result of too little empathy for their story, for their feelings, for their needs. Global events, especially dramatic ones, are significantly driven by this factor. How much do people care? How much do governments care? What and whom do they care about? How do they express this care? With responses that can range from intense passion to complete apathy, from a preoccupation with the welfare of others to the focus on one's own survival needs, from peaceful coexistence and dialogue to violent upheaval and destruction, this issue may well determine whether the human race makes it on Planet Earth. On some level we all know this—and our media deals with that awareness in various ways.

When tragedies occur, in our own country especially, but also across the globe, we quickly try to dissect why. We move "into our heads" as the media typically offers us frequent replays of the event with graphic visual images, yet little recognition for the feelings of the individuals involved beyond their initial shock response. Consequently, the news can fill us with anxiety and foreboding, or perhaps we numb ourselves to the constant onslaught of its painful references. And some of us don't—*can't*—watch the news at all. How might we better appreciate these differences among us?

Mental health standards of normal and abnormal are usually based upon questionnaires given to thousands of people, with tallied results often distributed under a bell curve. The 66.6% of respondents with the most similar responses define what is "normal." Putting empathy under such a bell curve, those with much less empathy would constitute the lower 16.7% of the graph, while an exceptional degree of empathy would be represented by the upper 16.7% of the graph. Like the IQ range, where both the mentally challenged and geniuses are abnormal as represented by the bell curve, those with too little and too much empathy supposedly are as well. Yet all these people have feelings, no matter where they fall on the curve—even sociopaths, whom we will discuss in the next chapter. It comes down to a question of degree, and whatever our place on the graph we all develop ways to deal with how we feel. If we frequently shut down or numb ourselves, we risk losing track of who we are and what purpose we may serve in the world. Ultimately, no matter what our capacity for empathy, it can never manifest if we do not let ourselves *feel*!

Experiences as an Empath

What happens to an empathic young man who loves making music but whose fearful, overly practical father insists he pursue a more lucrative career? Or a sensitive young woman who has tried to please her depressed mother all her life, but who has fallen in love with someone her mother clearly rejects? Conflicts such as these arise when we empathically "tune in" to the needs of another—not just their expressed expectations but to their internal, more deep-rooted distress—and feel compelled to support their fragile inner peace. In such cases, it seems our needs must be subjugated to the maintenance of their tenuous equilibrium. In these examples, the empath's deep longing for beauty or true love can get swept under the proverbial rug. Not without consequences, however: if our budding musician numbs his passion for music or our potential fiancée flees from the relationship with her soulmate, their lives will bear an emptiness that will doggedly pursue them until they direct their conscious attention to the truth held in their hearts. Their inability to ground themselves in the deep rootedness of their own authentic experience will exacerbate the confusion and suffering of their daily lives.

These examples highlight how empathic experiences can influence major life decisions. The consequences of empathy also permeate all the encounters we have in the course of a day. Personally, prior to that summer of realization in 2013, I tried to manage the internal rollercoaster of my emotional life, struggling to understand the many physical and emotional feelings for which I could identify no overt cause. For example, during a social encounter my face felt frozen in place with a friend who, I later realized, was unconsciously masking her feelings.

Professionally, for more than thirty years I could not explain why I get sleepy in sessions when the person I'm with—while talking perhaps with great animation—is not talking about what deeply matters to her in that moment. I have found that asking her simply to tune into her feelings reveals the deeper issue 99% of the time— and I'm fully awake! When some people cry I feel deep sadness, yet with others I feel inexplicable anger. This occurred on one memorable occasion when a sobbing woman begged me for a Valium prescription. While my feelings of anger confused me in the absence of an overt trigger, further questioning revealed that she was trying to manipulate me with her tears. And several times, in the presence of someone struggling with a latent psychosis, I have felt an almost nauseous, seriously ungrounded feeling in my gut.

Why do I feel these things? I would not have thought much about them except for their recurrent patterns. Over time I learned to consider the hidden possibilities in those feeling moments, yet I find they *always* require further exploration. Still, why? How does this happen? And what does one do in response?

Recently, I watched a replay of a televised news interview[4] of a

---

[4] "On The Road with Steve Hartman," CBS Evening News, published August 7, 2015, https://www.youtube.com/watch?v=OCPc2RlMTII.

six-year-old boy, Jaden Hayes, whose father died when Jaden was four and whose mother had died in her sleep just a few months prior to the interview. Jaden's response to these profound losses reflected his beautiful, open heart as he determined to make people who were sad smile. His own grief likely helped him to empathically identify complete strangers on the street who also felt some degree of sadness. When he approached them with his gift of a little toy and expressed his intention, unfailingly they responded to him and his gift with a smile, occasionally with tears, and frequently with hugs of gratitude. In the face of such tragedy, most of us close our hearts for all sorts of reasons. I know when my grandmother died I felt the pain of others around me as well as my own grief, but I had not devised such an ingenious plan as has Jaden. My own attempts, at six years old, to comfort my grieving mother and overwhelmed father met with limited success. Trying to show love in ways others cannot appreciate in that moment can shut down the most giving of hearts, at least to some degree.

When my parents died within 18 months of each other several years ago, the old grief wounds within me surfaced again. Fortunately, I recognized this as an opportunity to heal the past with more conscious intention, and my coincident training in Energy Medicine offered new avenues of exploration and healing. With my life under major reconstruction, I consulted a wise woman in Sedona named Kavitaa and asked, "How will I know what to do next?" In her wisdom she replied, "The signs that will guide you on your path have not yet come into manifestation." In essence, she suggested I follow my heart and be patient. I took some small measure of comfort from her words and did just that. I continued studying Energy Medicine.

WHAT DOES IT MEAN TO BE AN EMPATH?

Books like *The Polyvagal Theory*[5] crossed my path and I read them. I continued to sort out my inner life as well, amazed to recognize so many feeling-based imprints from my childhood still active in my energy systems and emotional life. I experimented with the energy techniques I'd been taught, on myself and increasingly with others. Gradually, I began to feel some measure of renewed centeredness and relief.

In that pivotal moment of 2013 when the group facilitator's fateful question sparked my recognition of being an empath, I felt a spiritual pause and a deep inner knowing to which I responded, "I can do that!" I'd never given such an endeavor any thought, yet my work as a psychiatrist, combined with all the things I'd been doing, reading, thinking about, exploring, and resolving within my own being, had brought me to this moment. The signs had manifested and converged. I designed two classes, one for professionals and one for empaths; both have deepened my insights regarding this work. Because of life's mysteries, my own journey, and the journeys of those who dared this venture with me, this book has now manifested as well.

Having touched upon what an empath can *feel* in any given day, let us now consider who *is* an empath? How does empathy relate to a tender heart? Are we born empathic? Or can this quality be developed, expanded, or shut down during the course of one's life? With the help of metaphor, mythology, and the experiences of real people, we shall explore these questions in Chapter 2.

---

[5] Stephen W. Porges, Ph.D., *The Polyvagal Theory: Neurophysiological Foundations of Emotions, Attachment, Communication, and Self-Regulation* (New York, NY: W.W. Norton & Company, 2011).

CHAPTER 2

Who Is an Empath?

AS THE CONCEPT of "empath" slowly makes its way into the mainstream, it evokes many assumptions. Typically, people expect an empath to be compassionate, sometimes caring to a fault, sensitive, emotional, and introverted. Yet these qualities do not apply to all those capable of experiencing empathy. In fact, the capacity to resonate with the inner state of another person is hardwired into all of us to some degree. Dr. Elaine Aron, a psychotherapist and researcher, began exploring what it means to be a "highly sensitive person"[6] in 1991 and she has since coined that term and reported that between 15–20% of us feel things more deeply than others. This fits with our description of the bell curve in Chapter 1 and reminds us that the other 80–85% of us still feel the world around and within us, just not as intensely.

---

[6] Elaine Aron, Ph.D., "The Highly Sensitive Person," accessed July 13, 2016, http://hsperson.com/.

So, is an empath the same as a highly sensitive person? Our culture certainly has a fascination with labels, but we are each unique. Consequently, we may best concern ourselves with what it means to be sensitive in general, and sensitive to our own inner states, as well as to those of others more specifically. We all know we are sensitive when our hearts are broken. The question becomes, sensitive to what? How do we process and understand our sensitivity? How do we manage it in our response to the outer world? For the most part, our current social expectations dictate that no matter how we feel, we should "buck up and deal." Still, it may be worth teasing these questions apart so as to better understand ourselves and others. Those who do feel the pain of others, who do care about their suffering, and who try to alleviate it (with variable success) can easily become stressed and burned out. In order to identify a more effective, less draining alternative for caring, we first need to appreciate what precedes that compassionate response.

One of my clients, a caring, intelligent, articulate professional woman whom I shall call Lily, initially came to me for combined energy work and psychotherapy to address "a flutter" of anxiety in her gut. It began following a significant relational loss a few months prior to our first appointment and she wanted to explore that flutter, understand it, and help it to move on. During one of our initial sessions, as she focused on this sensation and I held energetic points on her head, she suddenly recalled a relevant experience from her childhood, one that stirred deep and intense feelings of shame. Her experience as a child was not an uncommon one. She had stood on the playground at seven years of age with one of her peers, a physically and mentally challenged young girl who consistently struggled valiantly to do her best. Not far away a group of girls, close in age, taunted her friend cruelly after she fell. Lily's shame came from her inner freeze. She had felt powerless to defend her more vulnerable peer for whom she felt a "soft spot" in her heart. She has lived with that shame and regret—sometimes conscious, sometimes not—for more than forty years.

Our session moved to a beautiful resolution that I will share in the course of this writing. But first let's understand the inner workings of her sensitivity. We all embody the same basic neurology, yet we are uniquely wired and thus respond to situations differently. Many of us perhaps had similar experiences with bullies as children; for some these memories may have "gone underground" and if recalled may stir little emotion in the current day. For Lily, her memory of the incident included her empathic response. What makes her and other empaths different from those who are not as sensitive? Or those who are numbed? And in the context of a continuum, how different is "different"?

What follows will assist the reader to appreciate that the experience of "empathy" does not fit into one neat label. Yet teasing apart the subtle differences of what it means to be human can help all of us honor the complex beings that we are. We can then recognize that whatever our own gifts and leanings, the experience of the "empath" applies to us to some degree. This may also help us better understand those we love and those with whom we interact on a daily basis. Additionally, it will widen the applicability of the information and reflections in the chapters that follow.

I will begin this discussion by addressing three themes. The first involves our receptivity to feeling-state information, as introduced via the metaphor of "ducks and sponges." We will explore the relevant neurology in Chapters 3 and 4 and the energetic aspects in Chapters 5 and 6. The second theme will consider our predilections for how we process the feeling-state information we receive and how we engage with the world. We will explore this aspect by highlighting the concepts of introversion and extraversion. The third theme will address the focus of our care once we have received feeling-state information and processed it. In other words, do we direct our caring behaviors toward self, others, everyone, or no one at all? As we explore the implications of these three themes we will develop an understanding for how they can integrate to create combinations within us which are not only unique, but can shift and evolve. In so doing, we can better understand the flowing nature of empathic resonance and how it can assist us in the process of healing and growth on every level.

Sensitivity to the World around Us

Human feeling responses to every life experience span a host of possibilities that lie on a continuum. From no feeling at all to so much intensity that we cannot bear it, the range of human perceptions and the way we react to them underlie our individual uniqueness. In my work with sensitive children I often try to explain this sensitivity to their parents by describing what I humorously call "the metaphor of ducks and sponges." I find that once parents understand their child's sensitivity, her reactivity and behaviors make more sense. These parents can then replace their judgment, frustration, and helplessness with compassion, patience, and judicious interventions. So, first let's appreciate what this sensitivity is like in a general sense. We will explore more specifically how it affects us physically, emotionally, and energetically in subsequent chapters.

Before I begin my metaphorical explanation, the parents have already agreed that their child seems to be sensitive to the emotional states of others. I then describe how this capacity to sense another's emotions lies on a continuum with ducks at one end and sponges at the other. The metaphor further involves the association of muddy water with the difficult emotions of life. If a duck is waddling along and comes to a muddy puddle, once through it, the duck shakes itself off and waddles away, mostly clean but otherwise unconcerned. If one takes a pristine, lovely sponge and dunks it in the same muddy puddle, what emerges is a muddy sponge. If after this metaphorical experience we ask the duck, "Who are you?" the duck will reply, "I am a duck!" But if we ask the same question of the sponge, the sponge will reply, "I am a muddy sponge." The sponge's sense of personal identity has been muddied, altered by its relationship with the mud. The duck's seeming resilience, however, is based upon being relatively unaffected—perhaps this is not really resilience at all.

In keeping with this metaphor *and* our neurological hardwiring, one cannot change a "sponge" into a "duck" or vice versa. Even though a "sponge" is always a "sponge" the formative years from birth to six may be "muddier" for some than for others, because life unfolds uniquely for each of us. In his book, *The Soul's Code*,[7] James Hillman, a Jungian analyst, describes how in the process of incarnation our souls get muddied by life. This mud includes the learned beliefs that do not match or serve the truth of our soulful

---

[7] James Hillman, *The Soul's Code: In Search of Character and Calling* (New York, NY: Random House, 1996), 43.

essence. For instance, if a child senses her aunt's underlying hostility but her parents insist she respect and obey her aunt, this child may grow up doubting her intuition and believing she must respect hostile people. Sadly, we all experience this to some degree, but for those who intensely sense the pain of others, this mismatch between what they are *taught* and what they *sense* only compounds their confusion and hurt. As sponges they will have unconsciously yet profoundly absorbed distorted lessons about self, personal survival, and relational engagement. If no one in the empath's personal sphere can validate the truth of her perceptions, she will remain trapped in the mismatch, the pain, and self-criticism well beyond her childhood years.

Lily's experience serves as a prime example. On the sensitivity continuum, Lily is and has always been a sponge. In the playground incident, as in other experiences of her childhood and beyond, she deeply felt her friend's vulnerability, fear and helplessness, as well as the anger and arrogance of her peers. Her gut also told her that if she intervened on her friend's behalf, those peers would redirect their aggression toward her. Her prior experiences with authority offered little hope of helpful intervention, and she had been told repeatedly that her emotions were troublemaking. This mismatch between her internal feeling state and her mind's learned expectations created a humiliating paralysis in this otherwise active young girl. The shaming belief that she was worse than inadequate in such situations lasted well past midlife and finally surfaced for attention in our work together.

For Lily and any empathic "sponge" to become resilient, no matter what her age, she will need assistance: someone to see the underlying beauty of her sensitivity; someone to introduce her to a "bucket of clean water"; someone to show her how to squeeze herself out repeatedly until her pristine state has been regained. She will also require successive buckets of clean water so that this process can be repeated every time exposure to mud occurs. In this way, the sensitive person need not criticize herself, nor need she avoid the mud of life. She can learn to name the muddy waters of emotional life, take on some of the mud if she chooses, release it at the proper time, and come to greater consciousness for having had the muddy experience. If others express interest in her newly acquired wisdom, sharing that wisdom becomes an option. None of this is possible, however, if the muddied sponge does not actively learn to appreciate her own intrinsic worth and beauty. Ultimately, the journey of the empathic soul is one of clearer understanding, compassion, self-acceptance, and transformation; when parents support this process for their young empath, they bless their child's journey a thousand-fold.

Processing the World around Us

Now that we have explored what it means to "take in" sensory information, we can consider in general what our bodies, hearts, minds, and energy fields do to process it—to assimilate, digest, and make sense of it—so that in the next section we can better appreciate our instinctive reactions or choices for how to respond. At this point a discussion of introversion and extraversion will prove helpful. I initially became aware of my own introverted nature through the work of Carl Jung, who first introduced these concepts to the field of psychology. He described the introvert as someone who thinks and considers before acting. Consequently, she may present as shy, hesitant, and reluctant to trust what lies before her, yet she also experiences a rich inner life filled with powerful imagery and a capacity for deep reflection. The extravert, on the other hand, feels an attraction to the external world and reacts swiftly, jumping into it with both feet.[8] The extravert processes life events *after* living them, while the introvert will reflect and consider all the aspects of the situation *before* deciding whether to engage.

Jung also noted that while we each have the capacity for both introversion *and* extraversion, in the course of life experience we are typically drawn toward one of these types. We develop and hone the one we favor at the expense of the other, thus establishing for us a primary, *conscious* adaptation to life. In this process, the undeveloped type sinks into the unconscious. In the words of Jung: "…with the introvert, extraversion lies dormant and undeveloped somewhere in the background, and… introversion leads a similar shadowy existence in the extravert."[9] Although our primary conscious adaptation may lean toward one of these poles, the very process of maturation invites us to discover and cultivate the opposite pole within us. Since the psyche naturally seeks wholeness, a dance ensues between the conscious and unconscious realms within: introverts can become more socially engaged as they age, just as extraverts can become more reflective. Consequently, unlike the relatively fixed hardwiring of our sensory receptivity, our capacity to process that information can develop and shift over the course of a lifetime.

To summarize, both the extravert and the introvert respond to feeling-state information taken in through the five senses and beyond. Given the same capacity for receptivity—meaning similar neurology—

---

[8] Carl G. Jung, "On the Psychology of the Unconscious," in *The Essential Jung: Selected and Introduced by Anthony Storr* (Princeton, NJ: Princeton University Press, 1983), 160–161.
[9] Ibid., 161.

the introvert and the extravert receive the same information, yet process and respond to it differently. The extravert will react to the feeling-state information first and then reflect upon its consequences; the introvert will pause to evaluate her inner state and the potential consequences before acting. Let us overlay this continuum with that of the "ducks and sponges" and their empathic sensitivity to the feeling states of others: how do these concepts interrelate with introversion and extraversion?

At first glance, we might readily associate a duck with extraversion and a sponge with introversion—but deeper examination reveals something more complicated. The duck/sponge continuum describes a person's *receptivity*, or *sensitivity*, to the emotional and physical states of others, while the introversion/extraversion continuum relates to how a person *processes* and *responds* to the feeling-state information they receive. Consequently, we might consider that a duck could be an introvert or an extravert and so could a sponge.

To elucidate this point, let's consider a professional's potential response when a family consults with her to make difficult decisions regarding end-of-life care for their loved one. An "extraverted duck" will quickly volunteer for the task, make confident recommendations, and sleep well that night. An "introverted duck" will carefully consider whether to take on this role: having done so, she circumspectly weighs all the options, makes recommendations, and also sleeps well that night. An "extraverted sponge" will quickly volunteer for this helping role and almost as quickly feel overwhelmed by the emotional complexity of such a challenging experience. She will likely have difficulty deciding what to recommend and even more trouble sleeping at night—unless she has developed her introverted capacity for inner reflection. And the "introverted sponge" will pause while she simultaneously perceives the needs and the emotional complexities in the request, as well as the potential consequences of all the decisions to be made. If she agrees to participate, she will likely experience a flood of feelings, images, and dreams that may overwhelm her or, if she has done significant inner work, guide her toward making meaningful recommendations.

Might the spontaneous engagement with potentially overwhelming feelings cause the natural extravert (particularly in the case of the extraverted sponge) to retreat and begin to look like an introvert? If we use Lily's experience as an example, she readily described her child self as active, curious, wanting to explore and experience life to the full; this matches the description of the extravert. Yet in terms of our earlier metaphor she was also a sponge. Her spontaneous ventures into the larger world were often met with criticisms, parental limit-setting to subdue her natural extraversion, and compounding messages that her emotional responses to life were unwarranted. Lily quickly learned to rein herself in before they did it for her. For all intents and purposes she began to look like an introvert, while her more natural extraverted tendencies, now pushed into the unconscious, would present themselves to her consciousness as an unexplainable, anxious flutter in her gut.

In contrast, what might happen to an introverted child who grows up amidst very socially active parents and siblings in a predominantly extraverted culture such as ours? Parental expectations may inhibit the spontaneous expression of the child's natural psychological type—denying her needed quiet, alone time to refuel—to which she may initially respond with emotional outbursts of seeming defiance as she desperately tries to avoid so much stimulation. Eventually this same child may develop her own nature's less "favored" extraversion and grow into adulthood with a deep sense that "something isn't right." She may master the presentation of her less natural tendency by "putting on the smile," but at a price: it takes more energy, more effort to be what feels unnatural to us than it does to be authentic. Energy testing proves this repeatedly. (We will discuss this energetic component further in Chapter 5.)

So how can we tell the difference between an extraverted sponge who feels emotionally paralyzed by the complexities surrounding her and the introvert who naturally pauses to consider options before acting? The discerning factor involves what transpires during the pause. The apparent immobility may be due to a "freeze" reaction—related to the infamous "fight, flight or freeze" response. This can happen to anyone overwhelmed by a threat that cannot be fought, outrun, or changed (we will discuss this further in Chapter 3). During the freeze state, no mental processing occurs; during the introverted, not-frozen pause, mental activity to evaluate the best response predominates. Discerning between the freeze state of no thinking and the introverted state of inner reflection requires fine-tuned awareness which, needless to say, is rarely available in such challenging situations, and is certainly beyond the capabilities of a child's self-awareness. In the midst of this muddle, how do we recognize and nurture the authentic self?!

Responding to the World around Us

To add further complexity, consider the stereotypical "used car salesperson." Unlike the "caring to a fault" image typically assigned to empaths, successful sales representatives must focus on making a sale, yet to do so requires that they "read" their customers well. They do best if they identify what the potential buyer needs and wants while also sensing those vulnerable moments of possible surrender to the sale. Is this empathy? Do they "sense the inner state" of the customer? Does the salesperson feel the customer's inner state in her own body? And/or does she receive the signals visually, by the tone of the customer's voice, by the actual words spoken? A salesperson's agenda is self-serving in many cases—of course! They need to make sales to support themselves—but do empathic abilities assist the transaction? This question highlights our third theme: how we respond to the received information once we've processed it consciously. For example, does the salesperson's response attend to the customer's benefit, or focus on making the sale even if the item does not really serve the customer's needs?

If making the sale becomes the priority, we begin the slide into the world of the narcissist. I am certainly not implying that salespeople are narcissists: this example simply affords us an opportunity to examine where the focus of care lies in a given situation. We all have narcissism—a healthy sense of self and self-worth, one hopes—but some people have too much or too little care for self. At one extreme, the narcissist's agenda is totally focused on care for self with little regard for the other. This clearly opposes the cultural expectation of the empath, who might have too much care for others and not enough for self. Often we describe those who prioritize care for others over care for self as having a good heart. But is that true? Both approaches stem from imbalance, in contrast to the tender heart that serves the good of all. (We will approach these polarities from a healing perspective in Chapter 15.)

The whole topic of narcissism poses quite a challenge in our discussion of empathy. The delicate balance between care for self and care for others often goes awry amidst the complicated agendas and social terms of engagement in our current society. Beyond the middle ground of healthy narcissism lies the conscious torment of the one who has too little care for self and the unconscious torment of the one who has too much. This is poignantly portrayed in the myth of *Echo and Narcissus*[10] as told by the ancient Greeks, who recounted the tale to explain the origin of the narcissus flower.

The Myth of *Echo and Narcissus*

The myth begins as Echo, a beautiful wood nymph who loves the sound of her own voice, engages Hera, wife of Zeus, in conversation. If not distracted, Hera would have proceeded to catch her husband in the midst of his amorous adventures, but as it was, Zeus escaped her detection and fled with another nymph. When Hera realized what had happened she turned her wrath upon Echo, and punished her by denying her the power to initiate speech. Instead, Echo could only utter the last few words of what others said to her. Naturally, Echo was devastated.

Not far away, Narcissus, a beautiful youth, attracted the attention of all the young girls. He scorned them all, however, refusing even to glance in their direction. Initially, both Echo and Narcissus were fairly self-absorbed and unconscious of their impact upon other people. This began to shift for Echo in response to Hera's punishment, as she grieved the loss of her voice and experienced her vulnerability.

---

[10] Edith Hamilton, *Mythology: Timeless Tales of Gods and Heroes* (New York, NY: Mentor Books, 1942), 86–88.

In her desperate, wounded state she cast her eyes upon Narcissus. Echo fell in love with Narcissus, but she could not attract his notice until one day in the wood he became separated from his companions. When he called out "Is anyone here?" Echo could finally respond with words from her heart: "Here!" He asked her to show herself, saying "Come!" She then stepped forward, arms outstretched, from behind the trees and said, "Come!" He turned away in disgusted anger, stating "I will die before I give you power over me." All she could say in response, entreatingly, was "I give you power over me." She withdrew to a lonely cave to hide her shame, as no one could possibly comfort her. Stories tell how she eventually wasted away, with only her voice left as an echo.

Narcissus eventually experienced his own inner turmoil when he first recognized his image in a pool of water and fell in love with it. He suddenly became aware of what others felt as they gazed upon him. He could not tear his eyes away from the sight of his own face, even though he knew he could never possess it. He realized this obsession would kill him, as it interfered with the necessary aspects of living. And so it did. With his last breath he uttered "Farewell" to his image. Echo, hearing him, responded with her own "Farewell." As forgiving nymphs later searched for his body for burial, all they could find was the narcissus flower growing amidst the grasses where he took his last breath.

Reflections on the Myth

This myth offers us perspective regarding the three aspects of empathy. First, along the neurologically hard-wired duck/sponge continuum, Echo seems more duck-like relative to Narcissus's sponge:

she missed the cues of Hera's impatience, while Narcissus might have avoided the maidens to minimize his exposure and consequent sensitivity to their needs. Second, since the introversion/extraversion pendulum can swing toward the opposite pole over a lifetime, we may suspect that Echo was relatively more extraverted in youth than Narcissus, and wonder if retreat to the cave marked for her a shift toward introversion or resulted from shame-based depression. We may also wonder if Narcissus's avoidance of his female peers stemmed from a relative shyness indicating possible introversion. Third, despite the differences between Echo and Narcissus relative to the first two themes, neither one seemed particularly attentive to the care of others at any point in the story.

Thomas Moore, a Jungian analyst, has described Narcissus's eventual healing as a process of dying to himself.[11] Narcissus had to give up his old way of being, as did Echo. But the human story, unlike that of myth, does not end as an echo or a flower: we must learn to listen to others and appreciate their inner beauty *as well as* our own. This sometimes requires a major change in perspective and focus of care. Prior to his death, Narcissus shifted his stance of total disregard for his impact upon others to one of deep suffering, yet he remained unable to actively engage or comfort anyone. His emotions were intense, no doubt, but not channeled through his heart. Even Echo may have experienced her own frustrated desire and grief more than a true compassion for his plight. Thus we see that emotionality does not originate in the heart, nor is it reserved for the traditionally defined empath.

---

[11] Thomas Moore, *Care of the Soul: How to Add Depth and Meaning to Your Everyday Life, The Illustrated Edition* (New York, NY: HarperCollins Publishers, 1998), 53–54.

In reality, many empaths have learned to hide their true emotions—they may even present as unfeeling. In my work with autistic children I have frequently observed their ability to "sense the inner states of others" quite intensely. Unfortunately, they lack the capacity to understand what they sense in a relational context, something we will later discuss as *Theory of Mind*.[12] Their averted gazes, unusual fears and stereotypic behaviors are all attempts to calm an over-stimulated inner world. When they become progressively more overwhelmed, the emotions underlying their flattened facial expressions tend to spill into emotion-laden behavioral outbursts as their own inner state reaches the tipping point. In contrast, when they feel safe with a trusted person in a familiar setting where they have acclimatized to all the stimuli, their sense of humor, eye contact, and conversational exchange become more "relational." I've been privileged to witness these changes in my work with some of these children as they grew into their late adolescent years and early twenties. As a side note, I am convinced they are here to teach us as individuals and as a society how to be more empathic.

As we continue to explore the spectrum of human feeling by way of these themes—sensory receptivity, informational processing, and focus of care—let's also consider the psychopath. Just as with the narcissist and the autistic child, this offers an opportunity to explore the subtleties of the empathic experience. According to an article in the *Psychiatric Times*,[13] psychopaths endure relatively loveless childhoods permeated by deprivation and abuse on multiple levels. They grow up engaging in sensation-seeking, reckless, insensitive

---

[12] Hanson, *Buddha's Brain*, 126.
[13] Willem H. J. Martens, MD, PhD, "The Hidden Suffering of the Psychopath," *Psychiatric Times* (October 7, 2014), http://www.psychiatrictimes.com/psychotic-affective-disorders/hidden-suffering-psychopath#sthash.TW1e3Og0.dpuf, 1.

behaviors, often incurring legal difficulties, while still able to care for family members and pets in their way. "As with anyone else, psychopaths have a deep wish to be loved and cared for"[14] yet for the most part they suffer loss and significant loneliness, the latter especially heightened by their problematic relational limitations. Violent behaviors are often precipitated by times of intense emotional pain. In the extreme, psychopaths do not value life at all, not even their own.[15] While there is still much to discover about the development of psychopathy, its association with devastating childhood experiences leads us to yet another consideration.

We have already identified the impact of *nature*'s neurological hard-wiring upon one's sensitivity as a "duck" or a "sponge" and perhaps to some degree upon one's initial introversion or extraversion. The psychopath's childhood experiences raise the question of *nurture*'s influence upon the development of the empathic child. If a child has heightened empathic sensitivities, how will she grow while in the care of a narcissistic parent, for example? Will she learn to anticipate her parent's and others' needs in advance and "dance on eggshells" so as to minimize their expressions of frustration and anger? If she has a retiring parent, one who retreats quickly, will she learn to keep that parent engaged with whatever works? Irrespective of their intrinsic nature, the former child might look like an introvert while the latter would seem an extravert. In the context of abuse, might an empathic child need to shut down all sensitivity? Will this child dissociate, become psychopathic, or develop some addiction in order to cope? In the context of this wounding, an empathically-wired "sponge" might not seem empathic at all!

---
[14] Ibid., 1.
[15] Ibid., 2.

Putting It All Together

I hope it is becoming apparent that empathic abilities do not mark all those who possess them with similar traits. Extraverts and ducks can still care for others while introverts and sponges may become amazingly self-absorbed. Each person's emotional experience unfolds uniquely, in part a function of inborn sensitivity that develops in the context of family upbringing, social expectations, and challenging life events. Additionally, each person's emotional experience can heal; while we cannot change our innate sensitivity, we can evolve our introverted or extraverted tendencies over the course of a lifetime. More importantly, we can learn to balance the focus of our care in the heart so as to include *both* self *and* others. This process of integration involves unearthing our deep-seated beliefs about safety in the world, the worth of self and others, and intimacy. We must also apply compassion and forgiveness to heal. When we embrace our tender hearts, healing becomes possible, empathy increases, and love abides.

Clearly we humans host a huge range of empathic potential. Figure 2-1 presents a three-dimensional schematic of the three related continuums discussed in this chapter. Here we notice that the intersection of the sponge, the introvert, and the one focused primarily on care for others meets the customary definition of "empath." Rather than encourage readers to determine if they fit this neat label, my hope is that each person will recognize the valuable gradations of this three-dimensional view. By so doing, each of us can come to greater personal understanding and acceptance of our unique sensitivities and gifts, as well as how those sensitivities impact and contribute to our sense of self, our relationships with others, and our ways of being in the world.

WHO IS AN EMPATH?

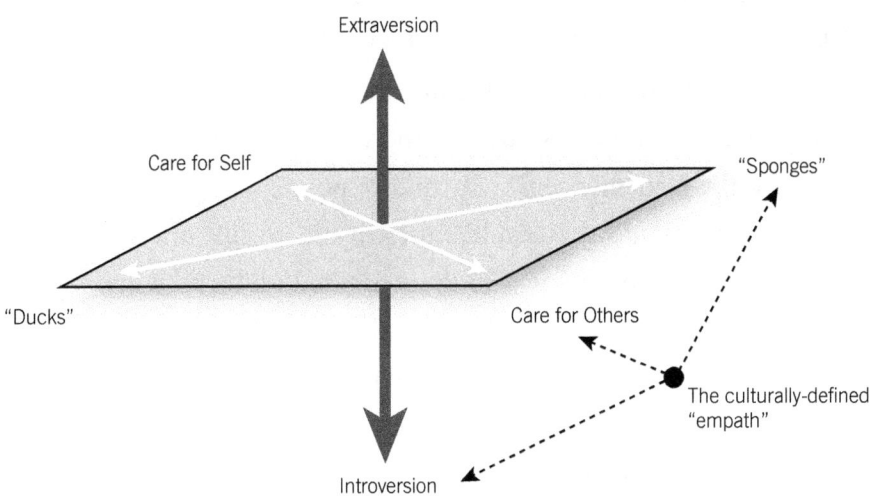

Figure 2-1: A Three-Dimensional Schematic for Empathic Sensitivity, Processing, and Response

Empathy—a form of information-gathering; the capacity to sense the inner state of another via bodily sensation, emotional feeling, and thought/reasoning.

Use of this Schematic:
To better appreciate your own unique capacity for empathy, first identify the point along each continuum that best represents your experience. Where the lines bearing these three points intersect in three-dimensional space depicts your current empathic abilities. Note: points on two of these continuums can shift as you heal and grow. (There is no ideal point on this diagram!)

The Three Continuums:
Sensitivity to Feeling-state Information
- Sponges – very sensitive to feeling states
- Ducks – less sensitive to subtleties

Processing Feeling-state Information
- Introverts – reflect first and then act
- Extraverts – act first and then reflect

Response to Feeling-state Information
- Care for others – others come first, self second or not at all
- Care for self – self comes first, others second or not at all

While I will use the word "empath" throughout this book please know it is only for the purpose of less laborious communication. We all have some capacity for empathy; it is really a matter of degree. While this book focuses on those individuals who possess a greater facility for empathic sensitivity and response, anyone wanting to better understand the complexities of our feeling life will find something meaningful within these pages. With this intention, we will explore the foundation of our feeling states and responses from a neurological perspective in the next two chapters, and from energetic, developmental, psychological, and spiritual perspectives in the chapters that follow. Through these explorations, my hope is to redeem the experience of feeling in our overly intellectualized world.

CHAPTER 3

Our Empathic Brains

FIRST PUBLISHED IN 1637, Descartes' succinct statement, "I think, therefore I am" galvanized a cultural consciousness that placed existential emphasis on the conceptual brain. It comes as no surprise then that today we highly value the brain's cortical capacity to put words to our experiences and to let those words define our very existence. Unfortunately, to this end we have sacrificed our attention to those aspects of our being that take in, process, and express reality without words: our courts of law devalue feelings and impressions; medical practice must be evidence-based; logic, a direct function of language, holds sway over values of the heart. Yet we are so much more than this. Indeed, science has begun to accept that we actually have three brains, none of which relies upon words or the cortex for its functioning. Our ability to put words to our experiences is the last step of an involved process toward a specific form of consciousness. This chapter explores this dance within our psyche, focusing on the empathic experience.

FEELING OUR WAY

In Chapter 2 we noted that during seven-year-old Lily's experience on the playground, when confronted with an intense double-bind—help her friend and bring the aggression of their taunting peers upon herself, or abandon her friend to their bullying and betray her own heart—she froze. A kind of paralysis overtook her body and mind while an emotional equivalent to horror filled her being. Her experience involved no words at the time but, of course, she has since made numerous attempts to explain this experience to herself. None of her explanations has offered a kindness capable of undoing the intense shame she felt that day, however. We have already mentioned that her sponge-like nature, and her nervous system's wiring for sensitivity contributed to the intensity of this situation for her. But what, neurologically, made her a sponge and not a duck? And what set up the freeze response with its consequent shame? The writings of Stephen Porges, Ph.D., offer a deeper understanding of the Vagus Nerve and its relationship to the freeze response. For our purposes, I will summarize aspects of his work and apply his theories in a more expansive context. I refer the reader to a collection of his scientific articles, *The Polyvagal Theory*,[16] for a more detailed description.

In this chapter, after developing a general understanding of the nervous system we will explore our three brains—the Belly Brain, the Heart Brain, and the Cranial Brain—and how they interact or don't to offer conscious and unconscious experiences. Although seemingly obvious, it is still important to note that all experience is the product of transmitted information. Information is impersonal: our sensitivity and response to it makes it personal. In Lily's situation, her memory of the troubling event was filled with conscious attention

---

[16] Porges, *The Polyvagal Theory*, 27-41, 48-51, 125-126, 151-155, 159-162, 263-268.

to the girls in her immediate environment, to the feeling state stirred within her, and to her emotional reactions and judgments, yet she was unaware of how the larger picture and her own neurology contributed to her immobility at the time—her access to information was limited. At seven years of age she blamed herself for something she could not control, and from this experience made long-lasting decisions about her worth, her abilities, and how to deal with such cruel engagements in the future. While as an adult Lily ostensibly often forgot about that decisive moment, it has guided her course throughout her life, for better and for worse.

Empathic Sensitivity and Traumatic Experience

In the mental health literature, trauma is defined as an experience of an external event that threatens one's life or the life of a loved one. As noted by Sandra Bloom, M.D.: "Lenore Terr, a child psychiatrist who did the first longitudinal study of traumatized children writes, '*psychic trauma occurs when a sudden, unexpected, overwhelming intense emotional blow or a series of blows assaults the person from outside. Traumatic events are external, but they quickly become incorporated into the mind*' (Terr, 1990, p. 8). Van der Kolk makes a similar point about the complicated nature of trauma: '*Traumatization occurs when both internal and external resources are inadequate to cope with external threat*' (Van der Kolk, 1989, p. 393). Both clinicians make the point that it is not the trauma itself that does the damage—it is how the individual's mind and body reacts in its own unique way to the traumatic experience in combination with the unique response of the individual's social group."[17]

---

[17] Sandra L. Bloom, M.D., *TRAUMA THEORY ABBREVIATED*, From the Final Action Plan: A Coordinated Community-Based Response to Family Violence, Attorney General of Pennsylvania's Family Violence Task Force (October, 1999), http://sanctuaryweb.com/Portals/0/Bloom%20Pubs/1999%20Bloom%20Trauma%20Theory%20Abbreviated.pdf, accessed April 30, 2016.

Consequently, what may not traumatize one person may be significantly traumatic for another. While Lily's experience of her peer's cruelty would not meet the criteria of a life-threatening situation, she certainly experienced this incident as an emotional blow preceded by other emotional blows, all having long-term psychological impact upon her. Lily's empathic sensitivities also heightened her body's physiologic response to the event: she froze. With regard to the therapeutic setting, numerous reports cite how just listening to the traumatic stories related by clients can trigger physiologic and cognitive stress responses in their professionals. These reports also note that those with a higher level of empathic resonance have a greater risk of suffering these stress-related effects.[18] One of these studies "provides a novel method for examining physiological resonance, and indicates that we can indeed catch another's physiological stress, suggesting a specific health risk for those in the social network of stressed individuals."[19]

The most recent revision of the Diagnostic and Statistical Manual of Mental Health Disorders still defines exposure to trauma as an external event.[20] As supported by the above citations, however, those who resonate with and feel the inner state of others may not require an external "event" to trigger the effects of traumatic stress. And in the face of an actual external traumatic event, they may suffer the stressful effects more deeply than those who are less empathic.

---

[18] *Secondary Traumatic Stress: A Fact Sheet for Child-Serving Professionals,* The National Child Traumatic Stress Network, www.NCTSN.org, 3. http://www.nctsnet.org/resources/topics/secondary-traumatic-stress, accessed April 30, 2016. T.W. Buchanan, S.L. Bagley, R.B. Stansfield, S.D. Preston, *The Empathic, Physiological Resonance of Stress,* Abstract in Soc Neurosci. 2012;7(2):191–201. doi:10.1080/17470919.2011.588723. Epub 2011 Jul 21. http://www.ncbi.nlm.nih.gov/pubmed/21777106, accessed April 30, 2016.
[19] Buchanan, *Empathic, Physiological Resonance,* abstract.
[20] *DSM-5 Diagnostic Criteria for PTSD Released,* PTSD: National Center for PTSD, U.S. Department of Veterans Affairs, http://www.ptsd.va.gov/professional/PTSD-overview/diagnostic_criteria_dsm-5.asp, accessed April 30, 2016.

Under these circumstances, the relatively hidden nature of various triggering traumatic exposures may make it difficult to observe cause and effect in the stress responses of most empathic individuals.

No matter what the trigger, the fight-flight-freeze response is neurologically hard-wired within us to react in the face of perceived danger. Our culture's emphasis on productivity and efficiency does not value the freeze response—one of the many reasons why those who freeze feel shame. It makes intuitive sense that freezing and harsh judgments serve no loving or healing purpose, yet breaking free from what may become habitual, shame-filled freeze experiences can be quite difficult. In order to appreciate how Energy Medicine and Energy Psychology can free those who suffer these seemingly never-ending, self-defeating cycles of freeze-and-shame, we need to first understand what prompts their repetition. And as I will demonstrate throughout this book, the consequences of such painful experiences may not always be considered "bad." This chapter will set the groundwork for our goal to honor the gifts of empathic experience while also learning to transform the stuck, so-called "curses" into blessings. We can then compassionately appreciate our empathic selves and human life as a whole.

The Human Nervous System

As responsive beings we need to receive, process, and exchange information. Other life forms that cannot develop the capacity for word consciousness and expression certainly have other ways to accomplish these tasks—as do we—but evolution added the ability to speak and think abstractly to our armamentarium. As mentioned, word use is the last phase of an extensive neurological process. Other systems within us exchange information, but not with words: most of the nervous system does not use words. Thinking and speaking may make us "normal" by psychological standards, but there's much that goes on below this radar!

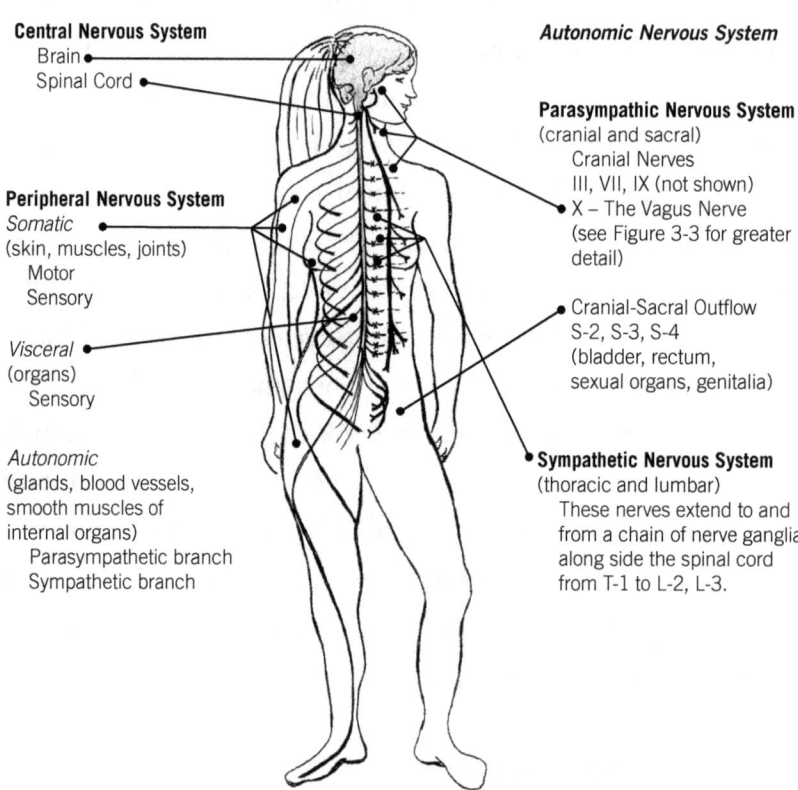

Figure 3-1: The Divisions of the Nervous System

The components of the Central Nervous System, shaded in gray, include the brain and the spinal cord. While the nerves of the Peripheral Nervous System are bilateral, this schematic shows the somatic and visceral nerves on the figure's right side, and the branches of the Autonomic Nervous System on her left.

Neurologists categorize the nervous system in many ways: central vs. peripheral; sensory vs. motor; voluntary vs. involuntary. (Figure 3-1) The Central Nervous System encompasses the brain and spinal cord, while the Peripheral Nervous System involves all the nerves extending beyond the brain and spinal cord to innervate our muscles and organs. The Sensory System receives information about the body's experience of temperature, pressure, and pain in addition to the input of the five senses of sight, hearing, taste, smell, and touch. The Motor System makes things move (both within the body and for the body as a whole) in response to random and focused thoughts, maintenance of basic physiology, and environmental stimulation via reflex. The Voluntary System, as its name implies, responds to our intentions, conscious or unconscious. The Involuntary System works automatically and attends to the organ functions necessary for our survival. A major component of the Involuntary System is the Autonomic Nervous System: this is subdivided into the Sympathetic Nervous System, which responds to perceived danger with "fight or flight," and the Parasympathetic Nervous System, which in times of perceived safety coordinates the "rest and restore" functions of the body. One can see how these categories overlap, creating a vast informational exchange system within the body.

For our purposes, we will focus mostly on the Sensory System, the Autonomic Nervous System, and the brain itself. For an empath, dilemmas arise when the perceived intensity of sensory stimulation and the body's automatic responses to it in the context of safety and danger conflict with what the brain has *learned* regarding appropriate responses to people and situations. We can appreciate this through Lily's experience: she took in information on many levels; recognized the danger of the situation; and experienced conflict between her instinctive response and what she knew would likely happen based on what she'd been taught about life and relationships. The conflict was unbearable and paralyzed her in her tracks. In order to more fully appreciate this process for her and ourselves, let's explore how the nerve cells of the body, working in tandem to convey information, interact in relevant and significant ways to set up the "freeze."

The Belly Brain

As it turns out, scientific exploration has recently revealed that in the lining of the tubular organs of our digestive system we have about 100 million nerve cells similar to those in the cranial brain, and almost equal in number to those in the spinal cord.[21] These cells use the same neurotransmitters as the brain to gather information about what is passing through our guts, both related to food and to energy (more on the energetic aspects in Chapter 5). Serotonin, a well-recognized neurotransmitter in our cranial brain that is often depleted in states of depression, is in fact even more pervasive in our guts. The bowels provide a home for 95% of the body's serotonin, thus explaining why so many of the selective serotonin reuptake inhibitors used to treat depression and anxiety can have gastrointestinal side effects. Serotonin clearly impacts our mood, so no wonder our gut reactions can as well. Additionally, our cranial and belly brains respond to the same hormones, rendering more communication between them than had previously been scientifically realized.

Hormones and neurotransmitters (chemicals circulating in the blood) require time to find their targets—organs and cells with appropriately

---

[21] John E. Hall, Ph.D., *Guyton and Hall Textbook of Medical Physiology, 12th Edition* (Philadelphia, PA: Saunders Elsevier, 2011), 755.

shaped receptors or "docking stations." (Figure 3-2) Once those chemical messengers find their target on the cell membrane they

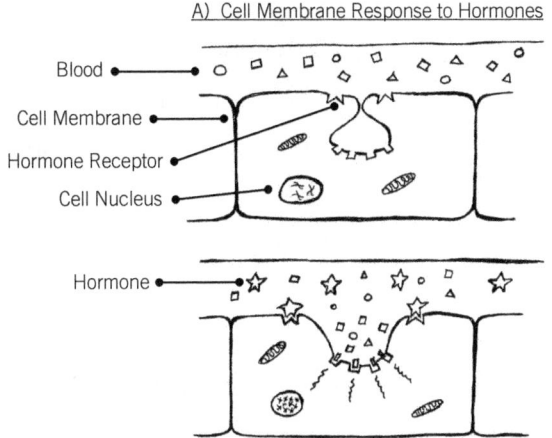

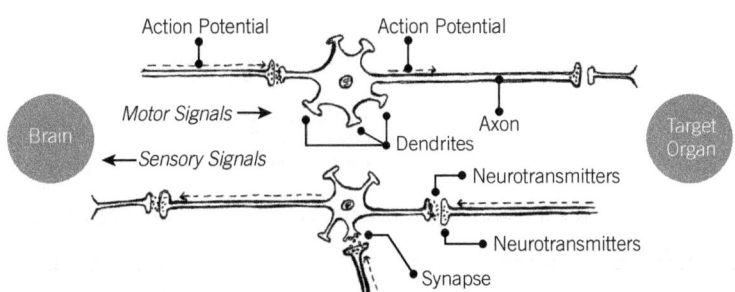

Figure 3-2: Cell Membranes Responding to Hormones and Neurotransmitters

Figure A offers a schematic for how hormones fit into cell membrane receptors like a key in a lock. When the hormone is available to the cell via the blood stream, it affects the cell's overall receptivity to other outside influences and alters its internal function. Figure B expands upon this model by noting that nerve cells use a similar mechanism at the synapse – where the axon delivers neurotransmitters to the dendrite of a neighboring neuron – thus causing the action potential, or polarity, of the receiving neuron's cell membrane to shift. This electrochemical shift spreads along the axon, sending a signal to its bulb at the synapse to release its neurotransmitters. The receiving dendrite can then forward the "message" in a similar fashion along its own neuron's axon to the intended target. In this way, sensory information can proceed rapidly from organ to brain and, just as quickly, motor information can travel from brain to target organ.

behave like a key in a lock: the cell membrane responds by opening or closing its doors to further chemically transmitted information. Nerve signals, which occur both electrically and chemically, move faster than blood-borne hormones. And perhaps it comes as no surprise that we have a major nerve pathway that transmits information from our guts to our brains and back again: the Vagus Nerve. It is important to note that our belly brains know how to digest food even in the absence of any input from the cranial brain.[22] The Vagus Nerve simply creates a neurological connection between the belly brain and the cranial brain so as to coordinate our gut's functioning with the part of us that thinks, and that processes our inner and outer realities.

The Vagus Nerve is part of the Parasympathetic Nervous System, which focuses on the resting and restorative functions of the body. Without it, we would continually burn up energy until we were burnt out. The Parasympathetic Nervous System slows down many of the body's functions in times of safety so that we can replenish our supplies and rebuild what has been damaged. Our guts, of course, are heavily involved in this process as they digest food. In times of stress the Parasympathetic Nervous System goes underground: we are not hungry, digestion slows, and constipation may result. Eighty per cent of the Vagus Nerve functions as a sensory receiver of information coming not only from inside the gut, but from the nerves and energy centers around it. The domain of the Vagus Nerve below the diaphragm includes a portion of the large intestine, and all of the small intestine, spleen, pancreas, stomach, kidneys, gall bladder, and liver. (Figure 3-3) Above the diaphragm this nerve also innervates the heart and lungs before traveling up to its nuclei—its hubs in

---

[22] Ibid.

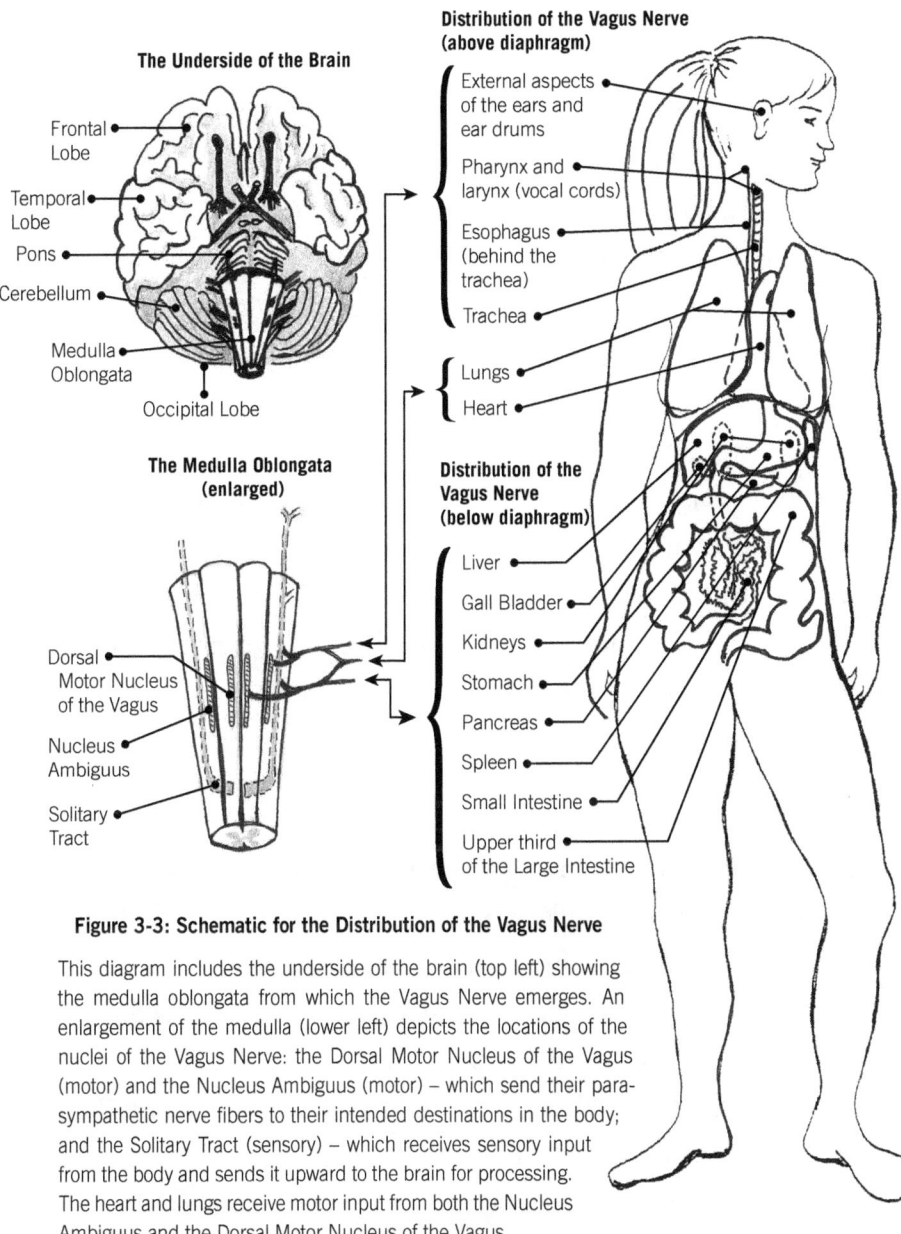

Figure 3-3: Schematic for the Distribution of the Vagus Nerve

This diagram includes the underside of the brain (top left) showing the medulla oblongata from which the Vagus Nerve emerges. An enlargement of the medulla (lower left) depicts the locations of the nuclei of the Vagus Nerve: the Dorsal Motor Nucleus of the Vagus (motor) and the Nucleus Ambiguus (motor) – which send their parasympathetic nerve fibers to their intended destinations in the body; and the Solitary Tract (sensory) – which receives sensory input from the body and sends it upward to the brain for processing. The heart and lungs receive motor input from both the Nucleus Ambiguus and the Dorsal Motor Nucleus of the Vagus.

the brainstem. From there it makes connections with higher brain centers. The Vagus Nerve clearly provides significant input to the cranial brain regarding the state of our internal organs.

Sometimes the belly brain receives information that generates sensations of dread. We've all had those "gut feelings." It makes sense that a hormonal trigger, such as an increase or decrease in the amount of circulating serotonin, would affect our mood as well. We will discuss the impact of energy in Chapter 5 and 6; for now, we can appreciate that not only circulating hormones but our faster Vagus Nerve send these signals of dread to the cranial brain. These signals have no words attached, only sensations, which we may attend to or choose to ignore. Some process this source of information more readily than others (see Sensory Types in Chapter 6). Some people learn to trust their "gut reactions" even when they can't explain them; we will say more about the mechanism of explaining them when we discuss the cranial brain.

The Heart Brain

According to Celtic shamanism, there are three cauldrons within us: the Cauldron of Warming below the navel (does this sound like the belly brain?), the Cauldron of Calling at the heart, and the Cauldron of Wisdom in the head. These cauldrons represent the energy centers for the zest of our lives, the love and yearnings within us, and the deeper knowing that comes with reflection, respectively. The Celts think with their Cauldron of Calling—their hearts. This ancient wisdom has finally been understood and corroborated by scientific discovery: the HeartMath® Institute[23] and others have told

---

[23] Rollin McCraty, Ph.D., Director of Research, *The Science of the Heart: Exploring the Role of the Heart in Human Performance,* HeartMath Research Center (2001), https://www.heartmath.org/assets/uploads/2015/01/science-of-the-heart.pdf, 4.

us for years now that approximately 40,000 or 65% of the cells in our heart are neurons. These nerve cells function with the same neurotransmitters, supportive cells, and transmitting and receiving capacities as the nerve cells in our cranial brain. The French expression, *raison du coeur*—the reason of the heart as guide for our decisions—perhaps makes more sense now as well.

Researchers have also discovered that the heart secretes hormones, endowing it with the function of an endocrine gland. Specifically, its secretion of Atrial Natriuretic Peptide occurs when the upper chambers of the heart distend due to increased blood volume. This hormone utilizes several mechanisms, including inhibition of renin secretion in the kidneys, to reduce sodium and water reabsorption and increase urine output, thus decreasing blood volume and pressure.[24] With less pressure in the arteries and in the cardiovascular system as a whole, the heart has much less work to do. Considering that our hearts beat every second of every hour of every day of every year of our entire life without a break to keep us alive, this kind of efficiency is not only necessary but brilliant! We have just been slower to catch on.

Our heart is not just invested in the efficiency and ease of its own functioning, however. The blood it pumps, equivalent to a gallon and a half of liquid, and the pressure of that pumping action to keep it moving through the closed loop of the cardiovascular system serves the entire body. Our skin is rosy, our toes capable of feeling, our joints fluid, our muscles at the ready for any work required of them, and our bones strong to hold us erect, all because of the pumping action of the heart. Our brain requires an amazing amount of blood

---

[24] Hall, *Textbook of Medical Physiology*, 339.

supply as well—not stagnated blood, but blood flowing past all the cells with a fresh supply of oxygen and glucose minute by minute. Without that ever-ready supply of oxygenated, enriched blood, our cranial brain cannot function properly: thought and mood, perspective and decision-making, sensory perceptions and motor behaviors may be seriously and negatively impacted. While we will discuss these brain functions in the next section, it is important to note here that they can't happen without the heart.

As has been more deeply appreciated in recent years, the heart coordinates the functional processes of all the organs in the body. We will discuss the energetic component of this functioning in subsequent chapters. Here, we can highlight the Vagus Nerve once again. This amazing parasympathetic nerve makes its way from our belly brains and most of the organs in our guts, through the diaphragm to our heart and lungs. In fact, there are two branches of the Vagus Nerve, each providing sensory information from the organs of the body to the Solitary Tract Nucleus in the brainstem. (Figure 3-3) This nucleus acts like a hub or center of activity whose afferent branches bring *sensory* information from the organs of the torso to the nuclei of the cells in the hub. These hub cells then forward the information to higher brain centers, which respond in turn by impacting the two *motor* nuclei of the Vagus Nerve—the Dorsal Motor Nucleus of the Vagus and the Nucleus Ambiguus. These two nuclei, having received directives from the higher brain centers, pass information along their efferent nerve pathways back to the organs to coordinate their action; 80% of Vagal Nerve fibers bring sensory information from the body (afferents) into the Vagal hub. In contrast, only 20% of its fibers return to the body (efferents) with the directives for motor response (muscular or secretory activity) as initiated in higher brain centers.

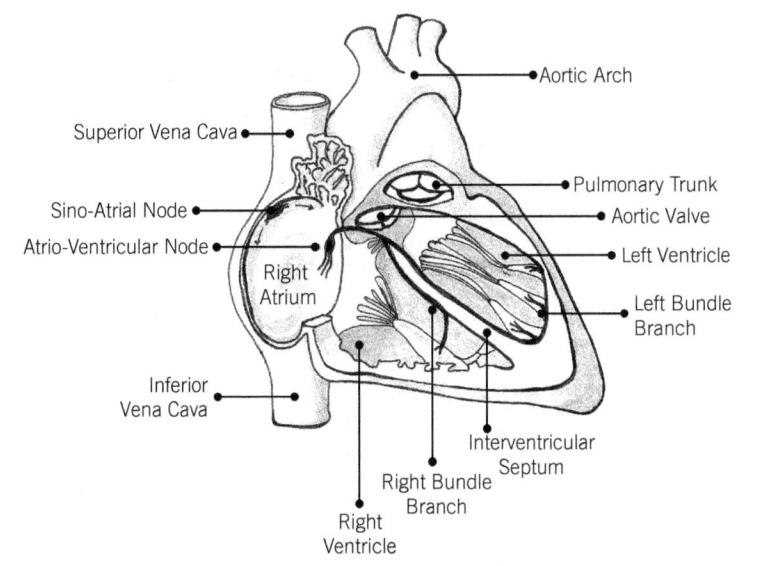

Figure 3-4: The Sino-Atrial Node of the Heart

These efferent Vagal Nerve fibers specifically affect the heart where they interface with the cells of the Sino-Atrial Node (Figure 3-4); these cells beat spontaneously, independent of any other physical source, at approximately 100 beats per minute. As part of the Parasympathetic Nervous System focused on "rest and restore," the Vagus Nerve's connection to the Sino-Atrial Node slows that frequency if the higher brain centers have decided that all is safe and well. In this way, all the organs can shift their functioning to this process of restoration as the heart pumps just the right amount of oxygenated blood to them for their work. Should the environment not seem safe, however, branches from the Sympathetic Nervous System that attend to vigilance and fight or flight will stimulate those cells of the Sino-Atrial Node to beat even faster. With this stimulated pump, the muscles of the arms and legs can engage for an appropriate fight or flight response. Based on this neurology, we assumed that the cranial brain's directives to the heart held supremacy; we are now beginning to realize that this is simply not the case, not only on the energetic level, but at the physical level as well.

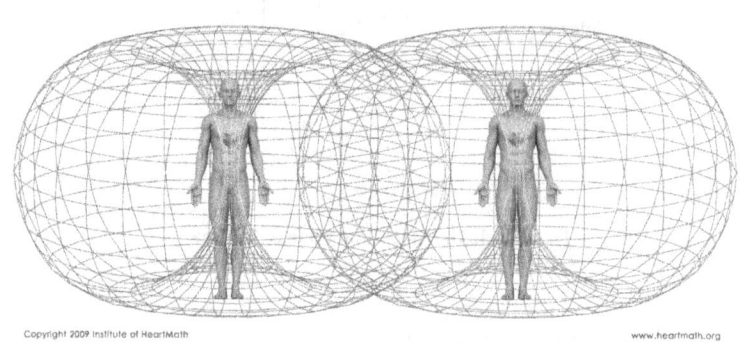

Magnetic Field of the Heart
Our thoughts and emotions affect the heart's magnetic field.

Figure 3-5: The Heart's Electromagnetic Field

Image courtesy of the HeartMath® Institute, www.heartmath.org.

As it turns out, our heart cells beat in unison as they take their lead from the cells of the Sino-Atrial Node, and as a result they generate the largest electromagnetic field in the body: "HeartMath® Institute studies show this powerful electromagnetic field can be detected and measured several feet away from a person's body and between two individuals in close proximity."[25] (Figure 3-5) While we will address

---

[25] "The Energetic Heart Is Unfolding," HeartMath® Institute, Articles of the Heart, October 8, 2012, http://www.heartmath.org/free-services/articles-of-the-heart/energetic-heart-is-unfolding.html, 1.

this in greater detail in Chapter 5, we can note that the heart's energy field has a positive and negative charge like a magnet, and an electron flow like electricity. These powerful electromagnetic properties of the heart invite everything with similar electromagnetic qualities in its proximity (our organs) to engage with it the way people walking in a public setting may synchronize their steps to the prominent rhythm of a drumbeat played in their midst. Given that the heart's electromagnetic field is *sixty* times more powerful than that of the brain,[26] the heart's rhythm can synchronize our brain waves as well. This becomes even more relevant as we now shift our attention to the cranial brain.

The Cranial Brain

Our cranial brain remains a mystery to science in many respects, but what we do know suggests an amazing complexity. Anatomically, the totality of the brain has been divided into four sections: the brainstem, the cerebellum, the limbic system, and the cerebrum. (Figure 3-6)

These divisions provide borders between these different areas, just as state lines distinguish Pennsylvania from Delaware, for example. Functionally, however, we know that to go from Pennsylvania to Washington, D.C., one will likely travel along I-95, a highway that traverses several states (including Delaware) in order to get to that destination in decent time. Our brains have a similar divisional geography or anatomy, but the function operates a bit differently—and, one hopes, without lots of tolls! The limbic system, for example, comprises the thalamus, hypothalamus, amygdala, and hippocampus, while its

---

[26] Ibid.

function also includes the insular cortex. It not only operates as a major coordination center for the entire brain, but serves as the seat of our emotions. So to understand the brain's *functioning* in simpler terms (a risk in terms of accuracy at the least), understanding the anatomy of the brain can guide the understanding of its function, but cannot totally define it. I will first summarize it "simply," then elaborate further to paint a more complete picture.

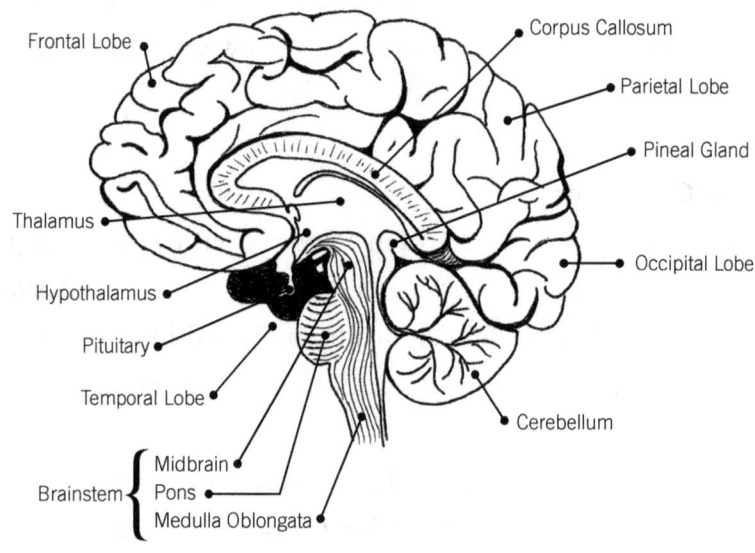

Figure 3-6: The Anatomical Parts of the Brain

Let us first consider each anatomical part in the context of its function. The brainstem, which includes the medulla oblongata, pons and midbrain, receives information from the spinal cord below it, and higher brain levels above it, to coordinate the essentials of our physical existence. The medulla, home to the nuclei of the Vagus Nerve, regulates our breathing, heart rate, and other unconscious survival functions. The pons more specifically connects with the cerebellum to coordinate our voluntary movements, posture and balance, while the midbrain links the neurons of thought with our motor functions. The cerebrum includes the right and left cerebral hemispheres, which encompass the cortex as well as subcortical structures. Much of the cortex is responsible for our thinking: this involves the comprehension and use of words written and spoken; generation and appreciation of images; the ability to think abstractly; and the capacity to plan, self-reflect, and prioritize.

The limbic system responds to the input from three major sources: 1) the brainstem and midbrain, which offer information from the body below; 2) the cranial nerves, which serve our sensations of sight, hearing, taste, smell, and some touch, and that consequently read the environment; and 3) our thoughts, which are generated in the cortex in response to all the input from the rest of the brain. The limbic system accomplishes this feat by attempting to integrate all the information from these various sources in such a way as to stir the emotions and guide us to a behavioral response. Its first priority is survival; socialization only becomes important once survival is assured. These priorities are hard-wired in our brains, and the complexity of all this well exceeds what two paragraphs can describe. It makes sense to elaborate a bit, so as to better understand the experience of the empath.

The Vagus Nerve can serve once again as an anchoring point, as we try to tease apart what goes on in response to any situation. To understand its function in more detail, we need to consider the phylogenetic development of this essential nerve pathway. Stephen Porges, Ph.D. has elucidated the evolution of the Vagus Nerve[27] (also

---

[27] Porges, *The Polyvagal Theory*, 30–42.

known as Cranial Nerve X) by noting that it has two motor nuclei or hubs in the brainstem. (Figure 3-3) The Dorsal Motor Nucleus of the Vagus (also found in a reptile's brain) is dedicated to the "rest and restore" function in times of safety and to "playing dead" in times of danger. Several species rely upon this ability when their protective systems are overwhelmed. The opossum, for example, when threatened by the possibility of a predator, will seem dead for perhaps forty minutes while the Vagus Nerve slows its heart rate and breathing to the point where the predator gives up on it as prey. This mode of survival clearly wouldn't work for us—our brain requires too much oxygen to maintain itself with a "playing-dead-opossum" approach to danger. Our brain cells would die even if our heart continued to pump blood in the short term.

Evolution provided for this contingency by establishing a second vagal nucleus in close proximity to the Dorsal Motor Nucleus of the Vagus. This second nucleus, the Nucleus Ambiguus, developed as species with gills evolved into air-breathing creatures. From these more evolved centers, the vagal branches spreading to the eyes, ears, and facial muscles coordinate with the vagal branches to the larynx, heart and lungs, such that humans can detect safety or danger in facial expressions, tones of voice, and eye movements, and respond with a coordinated heart rate, depth of breathing, and laryngeal capability to speak, swallow, and/or breathe without damaging our lungs, starving our brains, or endangering our bodies. Because the Vagus Nerve is a parasympathetic nerve, its function is dependent upon the perception of safety. As mammals who run in packs and as human beings, that safety also depends upon appropriate social engagement. Here lies the rub for the empath!

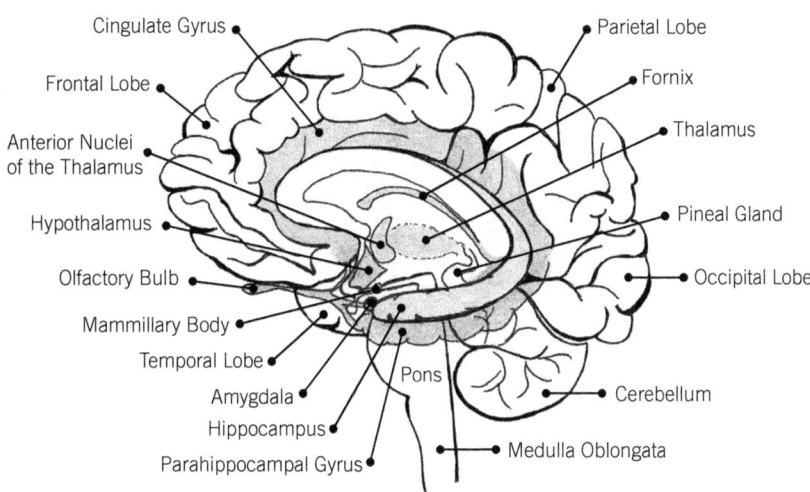

Figure 3-7: The Limbic System

The parts of the Limbic System are shaded in gray.

Picture adapted from Blausen.com staff. "Blausen gallery 2014." Wikiversity Journal of Medicine 1 (2). doi:10.15347/wjm/2014.010. ISSN 20018762.

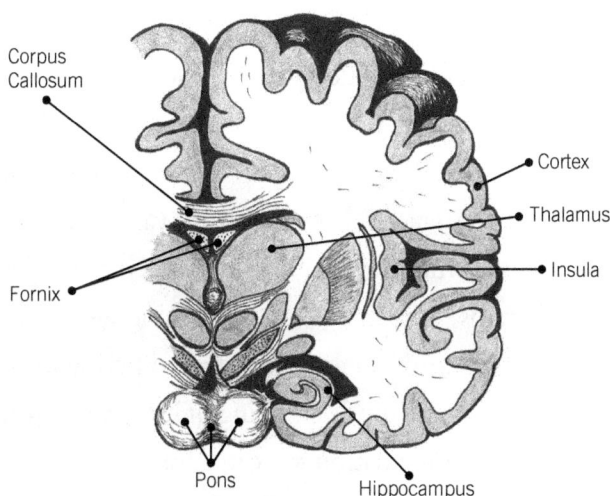

Figure 3-8: The Insula

The Insula is bilateral; note its proximity to the Limbic System and the more peripheral parts of the Cortex.

Before we correlate this neurological understanding with human experience in the next chapter, let's briefly complete the loop of this process. Once the Vagus Nerve has accumulated its sensory information it must relay it to the limbic system (Figure 3-7), where the amygdala evaluates the input for relative dangerousness. The amygdala has the capacity to remember prior encounters with similar dangers and to intensify its response so that danger can be avoided more quickly if it recurs. Consequently, a severe startle response or an intense over-reaction to a minor stimulus may result from the amygdala's split-second reaction to a perceived repetition of frightening circumstances. The hypothalamus then responds to signals from the amygdala by stimulating nerve pathways and hormones that set up the body's readiness for play and engagement if the amygdala is calm, or fight-or-flight if the amygdala initiates the danger response. The insula—a part of the cortex that lies in anatomical proximity to the amygdala, the hypothalamus, and the limbic system (Figure 3-8)—attempts to bridge and coordinate these responses of safety or danger with the rest of the cortex that can think. Here lies the potential difficulty: the language aspects of the cortex know only what they have been taught. If one's family values and/or culture are in conflict with what the body has registered at the level of its three wordless brains—the gut, heart, and limbic system—then the insula serves as a battleground for seriously conflicting information.

Now that we have some understanding of how we neurologically sense and respond to information, we can explore more deeply how this impacts the empath. When what is perceived and what has been learned do not match, we feel stressed! The risk of tension from this kind of mismatch increases for sponges because sponges perceive more than ducks. We will pursue this further in the next chapter as we correlate what happens for the empath on cellular, neurological, and relational levels.

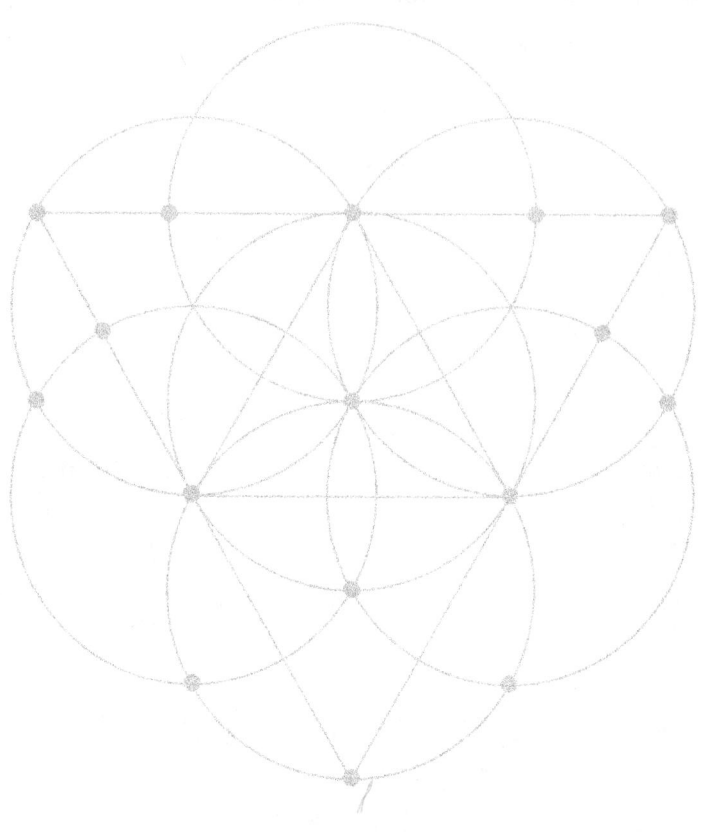

CHAPTER 4

The Empathic Stress Response

EMPATHY AND INTIMACY: how well do they dance together? Empathy supports intimacy, but intimacy challenges the empath. Because a heightened degree of empathy confers upon the bearer subtle and intense feeling-based experiences, many empaths struggle with conflicting desires. They work hard to minimize the emotional pain they sense in proximity to others, often resorting to some degree of isolation. Yet they also long for the companionship that places them in the same vulnerable proximity they desperately try to avoid.

Having experienced this personally while also noting it in my work with clients, I envisioned what I now humorously call the "Porcupine Theory" as a way of defining the optimal distance between two human beings in any relationship. If we place two porcupines side by side, the optimal distance between them is obviously the length of their quills plus a little more for breathing room so as not to get poked. Or if both porcupines show their underbellies to each other at the same time they can comfortably get much closer. Empaths often experience themselves as more belly than quill. The urge to merge belly-to-belly with another porcupine leads many an empath into relationship, only to discover that quills are part of the porcupine package.

Given that most of us have some degree of empathy in addition to our own needs and sensitivities, we can understand why all relationships have their periods of struggle. The Porcupine Theory offers one way to better appreciate these challenges: if one porcupine puts up its quills while the other's belly is exposed, the second porcupine will definitely feel pain. If it retaliates with its own quills just as the first porcupine shows its belly in an attempt to apologize, another hurt will be inflicted, and the cycle will repeat. Relationships can endlessly perpetuate these wounds unless and until someone names the optimal distance or the optimal timing for belly exposure. This requires that we see and accept others for who they truly are—and ourselves as well!

Learning to perceive ourselves and others accurately offers tremendous challenge in a world reliant upon cultural definitions and familial expectations for how to belong in community. Our lessons on "belonging" begin before we even have the words to understand what is expected of us. Our neurological hardwiring brings us into community by supporting conformity so as to keep us safe from jungle predators. Most of us no longer need fear dinosaurs or tigers, however; sadly, our greatest danger comes from other human beings. As empaths who sense the unseen, we know that even having long quills will not keep us safe. Additionally, the challenge to negotiate all this intensifies when what we sense with our three brains does not mesh well with our social education. As discussed in Chapter 3, this battle for supremacy takes place on the bridge of the insula. Which one wins—the educated cortex or the instinctual three lower brains—will determine whether we smile when we are fearful, whether we stay when we want to run, or appease when we want to fight. When both forces oppose each other equally, we freeze.

As an example of this conflict, consider the following: a young girl attends a social function at school where she has been taught to respect authority and obey the rules. Her gut tells her that she doesn't feel safe around a specific teacher, especially having witnessed him corner a boy in her class. Her heart recoils from the way this teacher treats her, especially after he made an off-handed comment that she perceived as hurtful when she asked him for help. Moreover, her limbic system processes his facial expressions and tone of voice as unsafe when he "yells" frequently in the classroom.

The conflict between having to obey his instructions while simultaneously wanting to run away from him or scream plays out in the insula of her brain. If not obeying this teacher's dictates leads to additional stress at home—where she is told she must listen to him and, if she doesn't, she will be punished there as well—the pressure of this conflict mounts. This painfully intensifies if the lack of perceived safety is not only emotionally based, but also physically threatening, as in the case of physical or sexual trauma and/or abuse.

Like Lily, we can expect this girl will likely "freeze." Her thoughts, emotions, and behavior will seemingly come to a halt, while the cellular, nervous, and energetic activity within her intensifies to address her perception of danger. This girl, like Lily, is a sponge, an empath. Why is the sponge more vulnerable to such situations? Let's begin to explore this in more detail.

The Cellular Response

To further appreciate the intensity of this conflict, we need to know what our cells do in response to the information we receive. Certain neurons are more sensitive, and therefore more receptive, to the vibrations of nerve cells in another person. These cells operate like tuning forks of the same frequency. Imagine we have two tuning forks that vibrate at 512 Hertz and both are at rest. We hold them up and stimulate only one of them. Because the other is capable of vibrating at the same frequency, the tuning fork at rest begins to vibrate, because it energetically resonates with its companion. Our nerve cells operate with this same capacity for resonance; if they have been imprinted with a certain vibratory experience, those resting neurons will begin to vibrate in the presence of another's neurons vibrating at that same frequency.

By way of example, consider a person whose history involves exposure to angry people. In the presence of an angry person, she experiences a resonance with those vibrations of anger at the cellular level even if not angry herself. As these vibrations of anger resonate with her past cellular imprints, her cell membranes respond, opening or closing their channels to specific neurotransmitters,[28] thus initiating a cascade of nerve cell functions that parallel those of the person whose anger triggered this chain of events. If we recall the definition of "empathy," we can appreciate how this emotional experience unfolds neurologically and biochemically in the physical body.

---

[28] Bruce H. Lipton, Ph.D., *The Biology of Belief: Unleashing the Power of Consciousness, Matter & Miracles* (New York, NY: Hay House, Inc., 2005), 80–81.

Scientists have identified these resonating cells in specific areas of the brain. Mirror neurons reportedly track the emotional flow, movement and intentions of a person, such that we feel this information in our bodies. For example, if someone picks up a glass of water in my presence, I can feel what picking up that glass of water is like in my own body, as well as sense their emotional tone and intention—are they going to drink it or throw it? My body will know and prepare to respond, especially if I sense the latter will occur. These mirror neurons "transform sensory representations of acts that are heard or seen into motor representations of these acts."[29] For those who like neuroanatomy, these cells are located in the ventral premotor cortex and the inferior parietal cortex. (Figure 4-1)

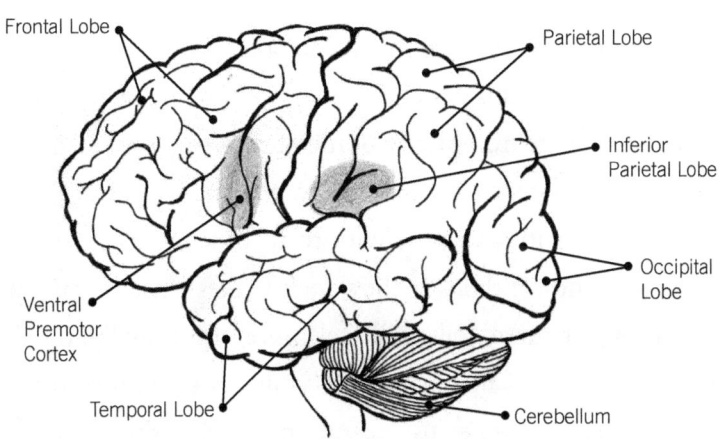

Figure 4-1: Mirror Neurons in the Brain
Mirror neuron locations are shaded in gray.

---

[29] Hall, *Medical Physiology*, 668.

Additionally, we have neurons in the insula (Figure 3-8) and the anterior cingulate gyrus (Figure 3-7) that resonate with the emotional states of others. The more accurately we can interpret our own inner bodily and emotional states, the more accurately we perceive and interpret the inner states of others. The brain centers that provide these mental interpretations of our empathic perceptions reside in the temporal and prefrontal lobes of the cortex. Their activity has been referred to as the *Theory of Mind*[30]—the ability to think about the inner workings of another person. This ability depends upon the myelination of these neurons, a process involving the insulation of the neuron's axons, similar to how rubber insulates the electric cord of a lamp so as to keep the signal moving quickly in its intended direction. Myelination of these cells in the temporal and prefrontal lobes begins at three to four years of age and does not come to full completion until age twenty-five or so.

To complicate this general description further, we are not all exactly the same neurologically. Some of us have more mirror neurons, more cells in the insula to resonate with the emotions of others, and a greater capacity and proclivity to formulate a theory as to why others feel and act the way they do. It makes sense that people who have more of these cells will feel more emotionally: they are the sponges described in Chapter 2, while those with fewer of these cells are the ducks. Let us imagine then what the world feels like for a child/sponge. She picks up on the feelings of others—their anger, sadness, fright, their joy, their excitement. She feels their behavioral intentions in her own body. Because her reasoning skills and perspectives are only beginning to develop, she cannot make

---

[30] Hanson with Mendius, *Buddha's Brain*, 126.

THE EMPATHIC STRESS RESPONSE

sense of these sensations in the context of another person. She can only assume that what is going on within her is of her own doing. If no one has explained to her what her empathic sensitivities can perceive, or acknowledged the source of those empathically-derived feelings, she unwittingly becomes a muddy sponge. We will discuss the consequences of this further here and in Chapter 8.

We can more clearly appreciate that our bodies are exquisitely primed as information receptors—and we haven't even addressed the energetic component of information transfer yet! Even without that component, however, we have a sense of how our brains take in, process, and respond to the emotional states of others in addition to everything else in the environment. Interestingly, "more than 99 percent of all sensory information is discarded by the brain as irrelevant and unimportant."[31] Memory retrieval depends upon the storage of sensory information (the input that has not been discarded) in the hippocampus, a part of the limbic system, and whether or not information can be stored depends in significant part upon how much attention we give it. For example, we often tune out background noise and the sensations produced by most of our clothing (except for those annoying tags). Because these stimuli do not receive our attention, their sensory inputs do not register in the hippocampus. Consequently, our brains do not store the information and it is not available for memory retrieval. In the face of emotional overload, many sensory details—visual, auditory, etc.—may be missed or discarded by the brain as the focus on the specific threat takes precedence. As a result, we do not remember these brain-discarded stimuli. And yet, just because the brain has thrust aside the information, does

---

[31] Hall, *Medical Physiology*, 544.

that mean the remaining cells in our bodies (wordless cells, I might add) have also? Scientists and healers talk about cellular memory in a way that suggests they do not!

As we reflect upon these discoveries and how all this may affect us, our perspective on the reception of sensory information moves beyond the five senses. That "gut feeling" of the belly brain, those "yearnings" of the heart brain, and the inner sense of knowing offered by mirror neurons, insular cells, and *Theory of Mind,* suggest that what we see, hear, taste, smell, and take in regarding temperature, pressure, and pain offers important sensory information. Yet so much more is also available to us. We name that "so much more" as intuition or the sixth sense. We *feel* it wordlessly while it is still making its way to our awareness. Upon arrival in the cortex, if it resonates with something we've already thought we will have those thoughts again. If they are accurate assessments of what is transpiring, we will have a "good intuition." If we haven't sorted it out clearly—we're still angry about what happened in the past, for example—the sensory input will be interpreted through the lens of anger. And if we haven't thought about it at all—because of youth or personal inclination—we will repeatedly feel confused, further entrenching our limited coping response. No wonder low self-esteem so often accompanies the empathic child's developing sense of self!

Responding to Stress

If our thinking cortex cannot make sense of—or downright invalidates—all this cellular and neurological input flooding the brain, the conflict becomes too overwhelming for the insula to manage. It's like two armies battling on a bridge. Because the brain is honed for survival, it will tilt the scale in the direction it perceives as safest. If the situation feels impossible to resolve, the only mechanisms remaining to obtain relief include addiction, dissociation, fainting, and other forms of "freeze." The freeze response only occurs when two conditions are met: the Nucleus Ambiguus, our socialization hub, has gone off-line because social engagement is perceived as too dangerous; and the options of fight or flight, supported by the Sympathetic Nervous System, are assessed to be ineffective or prohibited in response to the perception of serious danger. There is no way out. Only the Dorsal Motor Nucleus of the Vagus remains firing in such a situation, and we know that its only method for survival is to "play dead."

For Lily, caught between the cruelty of a group of girls and the consequent vulnerability of her friend as well as herself, the criteria for "freeze" were met: as a little girl in that situation, she did not feel safe; she could not run without feeling she had betrayed her friend, and she could not fight back without becoming the focus of their cruelty. If she perceived that the adults in her life would not listen and effectively respond to restore safety to her world, her sense of hopelessness would only intensify. She had no choice but to freeze; in fact, there was no choice involved at all. The freeze response was for Lily, as it is for all of us, biologically driven. It always occurs below the cortical brain level of thought, particularly when a thinking solution has failed us. Given that children have had fewer opportunities to develop conscious strategies for managing stressful situations, we can appreciate their special vulnerability to the freeze response.

In our culture of doing, efficiency, and productivity, the freeze response can quickly become associated with feelings of shame. In the same way that death or serious injury is perceived as a potential annihilation of the body, shame is associated with a perceived annihilation of the ego—a death of that sense of self as a separate, worthy entity on the planet. The freeze state, though associated with playing dead, does not threaten actual death of physical form. To save that physical form, however, the sense of self, of agency, of self-empowered choice, is reflexively sacrificed—just as hitting the patellar tendon causes the knee to reflexively jerk because the nerves involved loop in the spinal cord and never travel to the cortex of the brain. No conscious thought occurs during this freezing/shaming process; even so, this reflexive response of freeze causes exquisite pain to the ego. We assume that the opossum does not suffer shame at this level—not having an ego as best we can tell—yet, practically speaking, the opossum does risk that its playing dead state will not fool the predator. We *do* perceive that risk on some level and here lies the painful problem: our egos know they may be annihilated and we feel helpless to protect our sense of self. Shame and the freeze response double-whammy each other: feeling shamed leads to a freeze response, and freezing leads to shame.

From my experience, personal and professional, shame is the most painful emotion we can suffer. It never feels good and often stings in an almost physical way—and the additional embarrassing, tell-tale facial blush of shame certainly manifests a physical component. Most of us will do almost anything to avoid or rid ourselves of the feeling of shame. We can now understand how the insula (the bridge of communication between our three brains and the thinking, culturally impacted cortex) bears the brunt of the conflict, frequently registering its freeze response with a physical and emotional experience/message of shame. And, of course, the insula also does its best to provide a solution.

No surprise then that cravings and addictions to food, drugs, alcohol, shopping, sex, or whatever we find helps to ease the freeze, numb out the seemingly impossible-to-resolve conflict, and subdue the shame, also have their home-base here in the insular part of our brain. As discussed in the following chapters, it therefore makes sense that energetically, as well as psychologically, the insula, the brain's bridge between feeling and thinking, is where our consciousness exits[32] in the form of dissociation or fainting if the conflict is too severe. Needless to say, this log-jam of conflicting information can create potentially severe consequences—habitual patterns of coping not always effective in the long-term, yet unconsciously employed for the rest of our lives—unless we find a way to heal.

The girl dealing with her teacher faced these same issues: freezing and shame. In the course of my work with children I have witnessed several young ones respond to these deep conflicts with physical symptoms, such as an inability to move their legs or to speak. Selective mutism offers a child a means to communicate with trusted others, but not with those she fears may potentially hurt her. In one instance, a twelve-year-old girl's mutism occurred only at school. I can now appreciate that in the context of her sponge-like sensitivity, this educational setting provided the ingredients for her freeze state with all its many expectations and communal activities. On a positive note, she has since grown and become quite accomplished and verbal in all sorts of daunting social and professional circles. Both of these girls benefitted significantly from receiving understanding and

---

[32] Donna Eden, "Advanced Practitioner Class" (presented at The Second International Gathering of Eden Energy Medicine, Orlando, Florida, September 18–22, 2013).

validation of their sensitivity, especially from their family members. Criticism from their loved ones would likely have proved devastating.

I hope Lily's experience as a child on the playground now makes more sense. We can understand how her belly brain registered internally her sense of danger—those girls who made the cruel remarks wanted to emotionally hurt her friend, and Lily by association if she sided with her friend. She may have also felt a sense of disgust regarding their behavior. Her heart brain also recognized the emotional pain of relational hurt and violated love. Her limbic brain more specifically took note of the facial expressions and tones of vocal taunting by these girls, as well as the input from her belly brain and her powerful heart brain. Her natural response at this level may have been an initial shock (such as *how can this be happening?*) experienced both in the external situation and within her own body. She may have felt a strong desire to put a stop to it all, either by verbally fighting back or taking her friend away from the situation, but she would need mobilizing energy for either choice. And complicating the conflict further, her cortex had another set of messages: if she followed the urges of her three lower brains she faced the risk that these popular, socially supported girls would then turn on her. The numbers were not in her favor. And she was seven years old! The social implications were severe and her life experiences had already set up a vulnerable resonance with being on the "outs" with her peers, as well as embarrassment for her intense emotions.

Already a muddy sponge, she could not help but experience this incident as a reinforcement of her inner sense of mud! She felt her friend's fright as well as her own with no ability to discern the difference. We might also consider that she felt the anger of the taunting girls without being able to identify its source as separate from herself. We can now more fully understand how her strong desire and need to protect her friend clashed with her equally strong desire and need to stay safe. At seven, without consciousness of these details, she had no way to resolve this on her own. She froze—and in that freeze she blamed herself for the taunts leveled at her friend. She felt ashamed of her own behavior and developed a cautious approach to social groups of females thereafter. Whenever something triggered the memory, it brought new tears to her eyes and the recurrent sting of shame to her psyche. Her body, heart, and mind had yet to heal from this encounter.

Though the incident receded from her consciousness for extended periods of time, these patterns of coping persisted throughout her life—until she became aware of their root cause, that is. Now she has been able to bring the wisdom and maturity of her adult years and myelinated brain to bear upon this experience and to cleanse it of the mud. A cognitive awareness that there was nothing she could do at that time has helped to some degree. Deeper healing—the restoration of inner peace and an ability to reflect on this past experience with compassion and appreciation for its lessons—came in the context of energy work. Let's now proceed to a more in-depth discussion of what that entails!

CHAPTER 5

Our Responsive Energy Systems

NOT LONG AFTER THE YEAR 2000 made its way into our daily calendars, I developed a neck pain that plagued me for weeks. I tried every pain-relieving strategy I knew—Tylenol, Advil, heat, cold, massage, pillow adjustment, combinations of these, and on and on—but to no avail. For various reasons in the midst of this misery (try backing up a car when you can't turn your head!), I met with a Tarot reader for a consultation. As part of her attunement to the reading she placed her hands on my shoulders. At this point it seemed natural to mention that my shoulders and neck had been quite sore for some time. She lingered and as she did it felt to me like someone had placed a hot water bottle under my skin. She told me to drink plenty of water and that by the evening my neck pain would be gone—and so it was! The healer in me had to investigate further. Over the course of the next two years I learned and practiced the three levels of Reiki. As it turns out, that was just the beginning of my new love affair with energy work.

My path to Donna Eden seemed just as serendipitous, although I prefer to see such occurrences as synchronicities: unrelated events that meaningfully converge and contribute to an enormous internal shift, changing everything. A friend lent me a video of Donna Eden's work, and months later I found an advertisement for a relatively local weekend workshop. I chuckle now as I remember facing the same dilemma every time I had to decide whether to sign up for the first and subsequent early trainings. I'd say to myself, "That's really interesting, but I can't do that." And then I would ask myself the pivotal question, "Why not?" When I realized I had no good answer to that question except that saying "Yes" would take me out of my comfort zone, I signed up each time—with no regrets and an amazingly transformed life as a result. This same pattern repeated itself when I had the opportunity to attend Jonathan Goldman's Transformational Energy Healing workshops, raising the next question, "Why so much initial resistance to what has been so positive?" I now understand that it's part of our energy field AND it's something we can work with. Not everyone wants to do this, however, which I have learned to respect. For those who do, seemingly magical things can happen…

Recently, an acquaintance mentioned that she'd been bothered by a headache for days. Her face looked drawn and weary from trying to live life despite the "throbbing" in her head. Hoping it would be simple, and not wanting her to suffer more than she already had, I asked if she would be open to my doing some energy work with her. She readily agreed. We used me for surrogate testing because we

OUR RESPONSIVE ENERGY SYSTEMS

only had a few minutes and I don't *see* energy the way some energy practitioners can. She placed her hand on my knee to make an energetic circuit between us, enabling me to test her energy systems through my body. I know that pain results from stuck energy, so the goal was to get the energy in and around her head moving again.

I tested the area over her headache and quickly determined that the magnetic polarity of her scalp had reversed itself.[33] To correct this I used my hands—we all have magnetic properties in our hands[34]—and flipped them over the area of pain, back of hand to palm, over and over again to "jiggle" the polarity of her stuck energy.[35] She immediately felt some relief. I then tested to see if she had a vortex[36] of energy spinning over the area of pain (she did), which I corrected by making counter-clockwise circles over that part of her head for a full two minutes, followed by some clockwise circles for balancing. She felt her headache remit completely. All that remained of any tension had gathered in her neck. I suggested she do the Neck Flow exercise, a variation of the Belt Flow:[37] pulling energy with her hands, one after the other, from behind and around the right side of her neck several times; crossing her right hand in front of her throat to her left shoulder; then with her right hand pulling the energy down her left arm and off her left hand. She repeated this whole procedure on the left side of her neck, and again on each side. After

---

[33] Quite similar to the way that the Earth has a North and South Pole, or that a magnet has a north and south side, so do our bodies. In response to significantly disruptive energies, our bodies can experience a reversal or a freezing of their optimal energetic polarities, to be discussed later in this chapter.

[34] Richard Gerber, M.D., *Vibrational Medicine: The #1 Handbook of Subtle Energy Therapies, Third Edition* (Rochester, VT: Bear & Company, 2001), 78, 285–286, 307–308.

[35] Donna Eden (with David Feinstein), *Eden Energy Medicine Certification Program Class 2 Handout* (Ashland, OR: Innersource, Summer 2012).

[36] Donna Eden (with David Feinstein), *Eden Energy Medicine Certification Program Class 3 Handout* (Ashland, OR: Innersource, Fall 2012).

[37] Donna Eden (with David Feinstein), *Eden Energy Medicine Certification Program Class 4 Handout* (Ashland, OR: Innersource, Winter 2013).

doing this, her headache and neck tension were completely gone. The next day she gratefully reported that she had slept well and experienced a lift in her mood. Her headache had not come back!

We're Energy After All!

If someone in the Middle Ages had witnessed me flipping my hands or making counter-clockwise circles above her head, coupled with her report that I took her headache away, they would have burned me at the stake as a witch! What I did with her in literally five minutes worked faster than acetaminophen and lasted longer. To the untrained eye, I am sure it looked weird, if not crazy, yet it worked. The techniques are simple, require no expensive equipment, are easy to teach, easy to learn and to repeat on one's own. Not magic at all, though quite magical in our delight at the results! Donna Eden has made the basics of this energy work readily available to all on her website[38] and in her book, *Energy Medicine: Balancing Your Body's Energies for Optimal Health, Joy, and Vitality*,[39] yet many will opt for a pill rather than try her techniques. Again we notice resistance; change comes slowly until a process reaches the tipping point. We do best when change comes gently, and because we invite it. Otherwise we may experience it as the metaphorical two-by-four whack to the side of the head.

During my grade school years, I learned that energy can be kinetic or potential: I dutifully took notes and got an A in the class. Did I understand it? Not really, certainly not as deeply as I do now. I have since learned that our bodies depend upon the kinetic form

---

[38] Innersource, www.Innersource.net.
[39] Donna Eden with David Feinstein, Ph.D., *Energy Medicine: Balancing Your Body's Energies for Optimal Health, Joy, and Vitality* (New York, NY: Jeremy P. Tarcher/Penguin, 2008).

of energy *moving* in a concerted flow of balance and integration. In its ideal state, it holds us together and provides a template for the physical form we more readily know ourselves to be. An out of balance energy pathway can have too much or too little energy, be congested or depleted. The areas of the body affected by these imbalances may be localized or generalized, in one place or several. We may experience these states of congested energy as pain, or those of depleted energy as exhausted function, and both these states may exist in the body simultaneously. If our energy systems do not communicate with one another, we can feel disconnected from aspects of our life experience. These simplistic statements have significant, deep, and subtle implications, some of which we will explore in this chapter.

Most energy work focuses on supporting kinetic energy. Potential energy, on the other hand, is defined as energy *stored* in an object relative to its position and its relationship with other forces. For example, a rubber band pulled taut holds potential energy while it is not in motion. Once released from that position, its potential energy shifts to kinetic energy and it springs across the room. Similarly, a ball held above an eagerly awaiting puppy bears the potential energy to follow the gravitational pull, and once released its energy becomes kinetic as it drops to earth—unless the puppy catches it, of course! When we walk, our muscles engage by alternating cycles of rest and activity: certain muscles contract and pull us forward while their counterbalancing muscles rest, waiting for their turn to bring the arm or leg back to its starting position. When we consider how our consciousness directs much of our movement, we must now add an additional factor into the mix!

Potential energy offers an amazing mystery if we think about it. It suggests that energy resides within inert objects and us, stored and inactive but ready to move when released from its counter-binding force. We might also wonder if potential energy responds when called forth with intention. This idea specifically relates to the concept of healing, a process that occurs naturally without any thought from us, but that can be enhanced if we "put our minds to it." In the more common approach to healing, if a person sustains a fracture of a leg bone, that leg and other parts of the body will be immobilized or used in different ways to compensate for the broken bone. The leg will swell around the fracture as it provides a natural cast, and energy flow will be diverted to healing instead of walking in the usual way. Muscle spasms may result, and along with the pain of the fracture they reflect energy congested in a certain area or group of muscles. Other muscles may weaken as they fall into disuse during the prolonged rest required for the healing period.

If we apply more consciousness to this process, we can keep some of those stagnant energies moving while allowing the leg bone its needed rest. This shift between potential and kinetic energies can avoid congestion and unnecessary pain, while providing the injured area additional energies to heal and restore. Our emotions operate along these same principles: they are meant to flow so as to provide a steady influx of feeling-state messages from the surrounding environment, from our thoughts, and from the condition of our internal organs. If something prevents our feelings from moving along, they can become "congested" and cause prolonged emotional pain while other feelings fall out of awareness. Consider our example of the fractured leg bone; one might feel frustrated by the consequent immobility. This is natural, but if the feeling overwhelms the person's awareness for six weeks, her capacity for enjoyment will ebb. The ensuing depression, like the pain of a muscle cramp, is stuck energy needing to move.

This same person might become preoccupied with worry—about her leg, her functioning in the world, her future. Or her energies can keep moving through moments of worry while she reflects upon interesting stimuli in her environment, noticed now that other commitments must wait. Spiritually she may get caught in a quagmire of hopelessness, or she can acknowledge those moments with appreciation for the opportunity to reflect upon life's purpose and meaning. In this immobilized state, congested energy is stuck and potential energy is locked away on any or all of these levels, resting, waiting to spring into action once release from immobility arrives. People often register this release of congested energy as relief! It occurs because we harness potential energy to reset the balance. This balancing action facilitates healing.

"Energy Follows Thought"

As physical beings we are surrounded and penetrated by many forces or energy fields. Two such forces that come readily to mind are gravity and consciousness. We experience both when we consciously choose to raise our leg counter to the field of gravity, and then feel gravity pull our leg down when we can no longer maintain the raised position. It is a dictum in the energy world that "matter follows energy"—in other words, our body's functioning will follow the energy flows—and that "energy follows thought." We realize the limitations of this last statement if our leg muscles are not in shape! Thus gravity and its relationship with our body's energy field often dictate much of the functioning of our physical being. Consciousness, on the other hand, extends beyond gravity, just as NASA has been able to design rockets to propel human beings beyond the earth's gravitational field into outer space. To do their job of launching, these rockets must have a source of energy that exceeds the earth's pull, and human consciousness has found a way to provide that thrust. Bruce Lipton, Ph.D., notes in his book, *The Biology of Belief*, that "...the fully conscious mind trumps both nature and nurture."[40] Consciousness seems to possess an amazing power all its own.

We are beginning to realize that our physical bodies, suspended between heaven and earth, between consciousness and gravity, contain receptors for both worlds—our DNA! Since its discovery in 1953, we have attributed our nature to the DNA in our cells and considered that who and what nurtures us also supports that DNA blueprint. How can consciousness trump our DNA? Interestingly, recent discoveries reveal that our very DNA is responsive to energy. An article in the *International Journal of Radiation Biology* reports that "the wide frequency range of interaction with electromagnetic fields is the functional characteristic of a fractal antenna, and DNA appears to possess the two structural characteristics of fractal antennas, electronic conduction and self symmetry [*sic*]. These properties contribute to greater reactivity of DNA with electromagnetic fields in the environment..."[41] It now appears that these energy fields not only affect the cell membrane (its ability to open or close itself to biochemical transmitters in response to vibrational stimuli[42]), but

---

[40] Lipton, *Biology of Belief*, xxvii.
[41] Martin Blank and Reba Goodman, "DNA is a Fractal Antenna in Electromagnetic Fields," *International Journal of Radiation Biology*, Vol. 87, No. 4 (April 2011), 409–415, doi: 10.3109/09553002.2011.538130. http://informahealthcare.com/doi/abs/10.3109/09553002.2011.538130.
[42] Lipton, *Biology of Belief*, 80–81, 86, 95.

that the DNA and its genetic expression can be directly impacted by these energy fields as well.

Consciousness may well extend beyond the electromagnetic fields we can measure. Whether this is so or not, we experience consciousness as an energy that impacts other energies within our bodies and in our world. As Donna Eden states in her Principles of Energy Medicine, "Energy wants to move."[43] And it naturally follows consciousness unless something interferes with that process. When energy does not move, it is held in the stillness. Sometimes that holding serves a perceived need for protection, like the swelling around a broken bone that acts like a cast. Too much protection, however, outlives its usefulness, creates stagnation, and may slide into resistance. In such cases the energy is not moving, nor is it holding in readiness for the next movement. Instead it is stuck. This can happen to us physically, emotionally, mentally and spiritually, thus the state of our consciousness matters. Again to quote Bruce Lipton, with my emphasis, "...the *fully* conscious mind trumps both nature and nurture." I hope we may now consider that with greater consciousness we have the capability to invite that stuck energy to move and to heal (more about this in Chapter 11).

Additionally, not only does "matter *follow* energy." In 1905, Albert Einstein theorized that matter and energy can convert one into the other and back again. More specifically, scientists have come to recognize and accept the inter-convertibility of energy (as photons) and matter (in the form of electrons). This recognition provides a foundation for our understanding that we are basically energy beings who, in part, have condensed into physical form. Given the complexity of the

---

[43] Donna Eden (with David Feinstein), *Eden Energy Medicine Certification Program Class 1 Handout* (Ashland, OR: Innersource, Spring 2012), 8.

human body, the various functions of each organ, and the way our hearts coordinate our larger systems (cardiovascular, endocrine, and nervous systems, for example), it makes sense that, not only do our blood vessels and nerves provide the pathways for this coordination, but energy plays a major role as well. Donna Eden has identified nine energy systems[44] that flow, interweave, and coordinate the functioning of every level of our being. The ancients of various cultures knew many of these systems: Meridians, the Aura, the Five Elements, and the Chakras, for example. By balancing these energies on a regular basis, we support their coordination and resilience as well as our overall health.

This chapter specifically focuses on some of the energy systems relevant to the vulnerability and the well-being of the empath. We have already described how an empath, in response to her neurological "wiring," can sense the intention behind the action, the emotional state, and possible reasoning of another person. We can now deepen that understanding by addressing the energetic components of such sensitivity. Having described the neurological underpinnings of fight, flight, and freeze, we can now layer in an appreciation for the energetic contributors to the empath's reactivity. The underlying principle involves the evolutionary intention of the human body to keep itself safe. We saw this played out with regard to the body's sensitivity to danger via the reactivity of the Vagus Nerve, the amygdala, the hypothalamus, and the Sympathetic Nervous System. Our energy systems have a similar agenda. We will begin by developing a basic understanding of Triple Warmer, our energetic protector, and some of the influences that lie in its domain.

---

[44] Donna Eden (with David Feinstein), *Eden Energy Medicine Certification Program Class 1 Handout* (Ashland, OR: Innersource, Spring 2012).

The Triple Warmer Response

According to Traditional Chinese Medicine, the energetic make-up of the body includes twelve meridians,[45] or energy pathways, that connect to form a flowing, circular system. The Meridian Flow Wheel nicely portrays how each of the twelve meridians flows into the next. (Figure 5-1) To illustrate how the Flow Wheel functions, I like to imagine the beltway around Washington, D.C., being divided into twelve sectors, likening each sector to a meridian. We can readily see that if an accident occurs in one sector the road will be empty ahead of the accident and congested right behind it. If the highway patrol limits access to the highway in an attempt to control the traffic, the sector directly across from the accident on the circle will likely be empty as well.

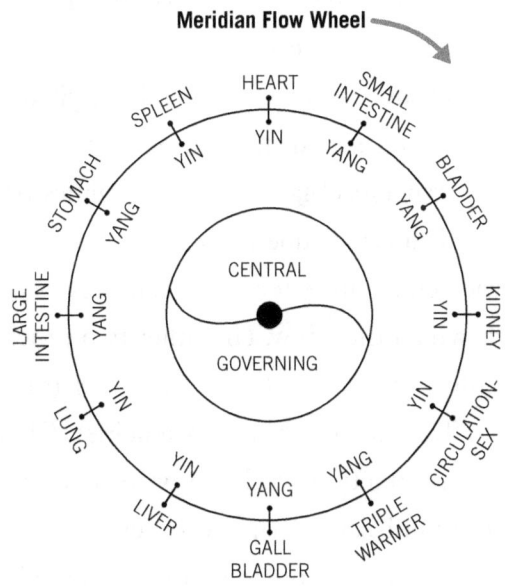

Figure 5-1: The Meridian Flow Wheel

---

[45] John Thie, D.C. and Matthew Thie, M.Ed., *Touch for Health: A Practical Guide to Natural Health With Acupressure Touch, The Complete Edition* (Camarillo, CA: DeVorss Publications, 2004), 30–32.

If we further imagine that each sector of our meridian highway curves in toward the center of the city, taking on the name of the local neighborhood as it does so, we would still have one circle of traffic flow, but each sector would have a different name. So it is with our meridians, which shift to a new direction at the face, fingertips and toes, taking on the name of the organ they pass through as they traverse the length of the body, yet all consecutively connected in one circle. Our meridians, like the traffic around the beltway, do best when there are no accidents! With any sort of imbalance, the whole system is affected: some locations have too much energy, some too little. Fortunately, there's an energetic highway patrol that works to set things straight!

The Meridian Flow Wheel comprises twelve meridians in its circle, with Central and Governing Meridians overseeing their function. These fourteen meridians reflect an equal balance of yin and yang energy. Seven meridians bear archetypal Feminine yin qualities—they are receptive, responsive, inward-directed, deep, and solid—while the other seven carry archetypal Masculine yang qualities, being assertive, activating, outward-directed, superficial, and hollow. Of those twelve meridians in the actual circle, ten are specifically named after the organs through which they flow. The other two provide oversight of systems: Triple Warmer and Circulation-Sex (or Pericardium as designated in Traditional Chinese Medicine). Circulation-Sex Meridian in its yin function works to protect the heart and the internal body from imbalance. Triple Warmer, its yang counterpart, serves to protect the body as a whole from anything it perceives as threatening from the outside world. These perceptions take place on several levels: environmental, physical, emotional, cognitive, and spiritual. Each of these levels in their relationship to the outer world receives Triple Warmer's protection.

Triple Warmer values the familiar and maintains habits on all of these levels. From the neonatal period, once the cord has been cut and the baby must survive as a separate physical entity from her mother, Triple Warmer begins to encode the sensations, encounters, and responses from the environment as "normal" or familiar. In other words, it encodes what it is "taught." These "teachings" come from the present life experiences of the individual, as well as from those lessons accumulated over the course of human evolution. Because Triple Warmer has not evolved for the human species as quickly as our environmental influences have changed, our energetic protector may not recognize food additives, neon lights, nuclear radiation, or microwave ovens, to name just a few modern inventions, as "safe." This reactivity occurs more intensely for some than for others. As these perceived "unsafe" stimuli accumulate in one's energy field, at some critical juncture too much unfamiliarity leads to a protective reaction. In some cases, this may appear to be an over-reaction. We are all too familiar with allergies and auto-immune diseases—these are Triple Warmer responses to a significant degree.[46]

Typically, Triple Warmer speaks to us via physical sensations, such as tight muscles, hot flashes, sweating, or clammy skin. We may also experience hives, panic, hysteria, blushing, an urge to fight back, or an intense desire to run away. On the spiritual level we may feel at odds with ourselves without knowing why, especially if something thought of or experienced runs counter to the wisdom of our Higher Self. When shaming or guilt-inducing experiences happen repeatedly,

---

[46] Eden (with Feinstein), *Energy Medicine*, 246–250.

Triple Warmer expects them and mounts a defense—whichever defense happens to work at the time our need for it develops. This defense then gets encoded as a habit that Triple Warmer works hard to maintain. Unfortunately, a habit encoded when we're three doesn't necessarily work so well when we're thirty, but Triple Warmer doesn't know that. Perhaps it now makes sense how psychodynamic responses—thoughts, emotions, and behavioral reactions—to life

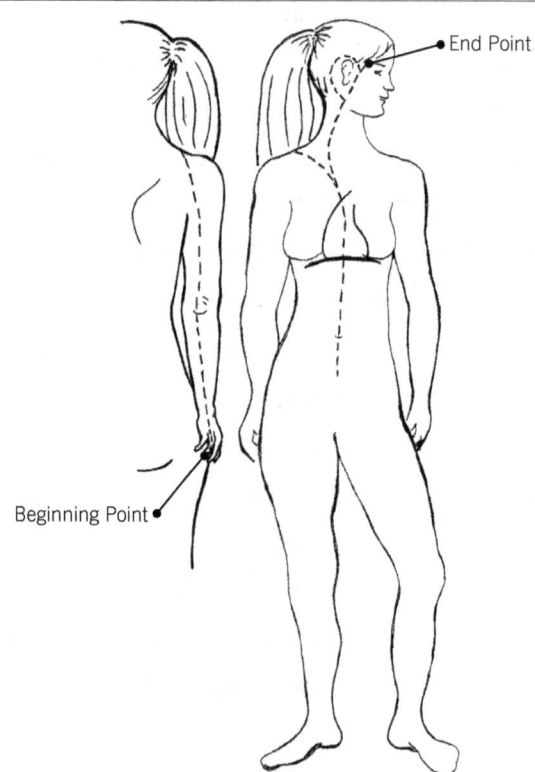

Figure 5-2: Triple Warmer Meridian's Pathway

Triple Warmer Meridian begins at the outside corner of the fourth fingernail (on both sides of the body) and flows up the back of the arm and over the shoulder. The pathway which continues up the side of the head, ending at the eyebrow, is what is traced in Eden Energy Medicine techniques. From the shoulder an interior path runs down the center of the body as well.

Illustration adapted from the work of Depak Muniraj, "Triple Warmer," Wikimedia Commons. June 2012. Accessed May 31, 2016. https://commons.wikimedia.org/wiki/File:Triple_warmer_meridian.jpg.

situations can be energetically encoded as well. We will explore this more fully in Chapter 8. For now, it is important to recognize that an insight that offers cognitive understanding of an old, unwanted habit, coupled with the desire to change it, may not be enough to succeed. Rather than blame oneself for being inadequate to the task, working energetically with Triple Warmer may prove helpful.

One simple exercise to reduce Triple Warmer's grip is simply to trace the meridian's pathway backwards.[47] (Figure 5-2) We often instinctively do something similar when we brush our hair with a gesture extending from the temples to above and behind our ears, with an actual brush or just with our hands. Attentively doing this on both sides of the head, then continuing the brushing motion across the back of both shoulders, down the arms behind the elbows, and off the ring fingers moves excess energy off Triple Warmer's pathway the way a sweep of Godzilla's hand at the scene of a traffic accident would remove many of the cars. Many people feel a wave of relaxation just by doing this once and, of course, repeats aren't a bad idea!

Interestingly, this technique utilizes the path of Triple Warmer's flow on the surface of the body. I was also amazed to discover that this meridian branches deeper into the body, seemingly quite near the path of the Vagus Nerve! Consequently, we may strongly suspect Triple Warmer's role in the process of fainting from a vasovagal response.[48] (The vasovagal response occurs in reaction to a significantly distressing trigger such that the body responds with a drop in heart rate and blood pressure—Vagus Nerve effects.) In this situation we

---

[47] Ibid., 253.
[48] "Vasovagal Syncope," Mayo Clinic, accessed February 9, 2015, http://www.mayoclinic.org/diseases-conditions/vasovagal-syncope/basics/definition/con-20026900.

have Triple Warmer's reactivity to an unfamiliar or dangerous trigger coupled with the response of the Dorsal Motor Nucleus of the Vagus to "play dead" or freeze. Perhaps Triple Warmer's energetic involvement plays a role in preventing oxygen deprivation in the brain during these episodes. In any case, given this apparent interface between neurology and energy we will certainly identify more ways to ease Triple Warmer's tense grip as we explore its many ways of commandeering our energy pathways.

Irregular Energies[49]

Another Triple Warmer response involves "irregular energy,"[50] a term coined by Donna Eden to describe a reversal, freezing, or submergence of energy flow so that its pathway, function, and/or our experience of it become unbalanced. I often like to explain the concept of irregular energies with a visual metaphor: imagine a school of fish led by a single headmaster, followed by two fish, then three, then four and so on, similar to a bowling pin arrangement. The headmaster leads the fish as they swim, floating merrily along, getting where they have to go. Suddenly, the headmaster encounters a large rock in his path. He turns around and faces the two fish following him. They see the rock and perform an about-face as well. The next three fish turn around, so do the next four and five. Somewhere in the middle of this large school, however, the rows of fish in front are now facing the rows of fish in the rear, but all the fish in the middle have no idea why they are now in a stalemate, since

---

[49] Donna Eden (with David Feinstein), *Eden Energy Medicine Certification Program Class 2 Handout* (Ashland, OR: Innersource, Summer 2012).
[50] Stephanie Eldringhoff, M.A., L.M.F.T., and Victoria Matthews, N.D.., "Frozen and Irregular Energies: Hidden Energy Stumbling Blocks," Innersource Handout Bank, accessed March 9, 2016, http://innersource.net/em/73-handout-bank1/hbspecificsituations/228-based-on-the-work-of-donna-eded.html.

the fish in row five and beyond never saw the rock. This immobility describes frozen irregular energy. Energy is now "stuck" and often our physical experience of it is pain.

Should all the fish in the school decide to do an about-face, we would have a reversed energy flow. In this scenario the energy isn't stuck, but it isn't getting where it needs to go either. When the energies of all our meridians flow backwards, every step forward can feel like we're walking uphill. Oddly, we may experience walking backwards to be much easier. This is certainly revealed with energy testing, and the good news is that we have a simple way to correct the directional flow. Eden Energy Medicine's "Four Thumps"[51] include tapping the K-27's (points just under the collar bone where the breastbone, or sternum, ends) for at least twenty seconds to restore a forward flow to the meridian system as a whole.

To continue the analogy, our school of fish might try to go deeper, to swim under the rock. If we were fishermen we would not be able to get at them—good for the fish, not for the catch. When energy submerges itself deep in the body, particularly at acupressure points, it becomes inaccessible to the acupuncture needle or the touch of a finger. Submerged energies are relatively rare in my experience, while frozen and reversed energy flows occur quite often. Triple Warmer has an influence in all three of these examples as it tries to protect us, like the headmaster trying to protect the school. Unfortunately, the effort is not always productive.

Anything energetic can experience irregular energies. A very simple way to restore irregular energies to their forward flow involves using our magnetic hands, as described at the beginning of

---

[51] Eden (with Feinstein), *Energy Medicine,* 59, 74–78, and "Donna Eden's Daily Energy Routine [OFFICIAL VERSION]," Youtube, last modified November 24, 2015, https://www.youtube/Di5Ua44iuXc.

the chapter. Our hands have a gentle magnetic field such that the palm is like the South side of a magnet, putting energy *into* its intended objective, while the back of the hand is like the North side of a magnet, pulling energy *from* the intended objective. When we have an experience of pain—a cramp in a muscle, for example—we can relieve that congested energy by first gently stretching the area around the pain, followed by a single gentle pinch of the skin over the painful area (not to be done over an open wound).[52]

In addition, or instead if we cannot touch the body where it hurts, we can slowly flip our hands back and forth, from palm to back of hand, in the air just above the area to ease the irregular energy pattern. I compare this motion to shaking up a snow globe whose "snow" has landed on one side of its interior. Shaking the snow globe not only makes it look like it's snowing within, but allows the snow to fall evenly over the surface of the interior scene. Similarly, flipping one's hands back and forth can shake up the stuck energy by alternately attracting and repelling the magnetic charges of the cells and energies within the painful area. Once "shaken up" they resettle evenly, the way nature intended, and forward flow is usually restored.[53]

Triple Warmer's Dance with Spleen Meridian

Now that we have discussed Triple Warmer itself and its contribution to irregular energies, we can return to our highway metaphor to explore another aspect of Triple Warmer's protection. If we were to look from a helicopter above the scene of the accident, we would

---

[52] Ibid., 303.
[53] Additional techniques exist should this simple protocol not prove helpful, but they are beyond the scope of this book.

notice that there is likely no traffic on the opposite side of the circular highway. While this metaphor has its limits, it does highlight a relationship between meridians on the Flow Wheel such that, when stressed, they "steal" energy from the meridian directly across from them. In Triple Warmer's case this involves Spleen Meridian, its first target, although Triple Warmer can commandeer energy from any meridian except Heart.[54]

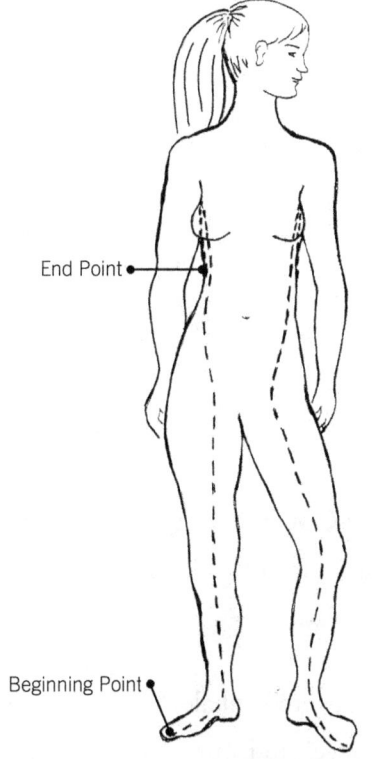

Figure 5-3: Spleen Meridian's Pathway

Spleen Meridian begins at the medial corner of the big toenail (on both sides of the body) and travels up the leg and torso to the underarm where it then turns downward, ending along the side of the ribs.

---

[54] Donna Eden (with David Feinstein), *Eden Energy Medicine Certification Program Class 2 Handout* (Ashland, OR: Innersource, Summer 2012).

Spleen Meridian serves a vital role for us in that it accepts what nurtures us into all the levels of our energetic being and uses it well, metabolizing what we need and releasing what does not serve us. When Spleen Meridian is depleted for any reason, it can feel like attending the most enticing buffet without an appetite: we can't take in a thing—or we eat because it tastes good, but our body can't metabolize it. If we have cravings, they are not satisfied. This energetic dynamic plays a role in many a dieter's frustrated attempts to lose weight. If Triple Warmer is maintaining the habitual higher weight and Spleen Meridian is too tired, or too depleted to notice or use the healthy food being offered, little weight will be lost despite our best efforts.[55]

Helpful remedies for this situation involve calming Triple Warmer and supporting Spleen Meridian. An Eden Energy Medicine exercise called "Cover the Eyes"[56] does this quite well.

Cover the Eyes

Begin by covering your closed eyelids with your middle fingers. Take a full breath.

With your eyes still covered, inhale. As you exhale, drag your fingers across your eyes and out to your temples. (At this point you can open your eyes.)

---

[55] Eden (with Feinstein), *Energy Medicine,* 270–271.
[56] Donna Eden (with David Feinstein), *Eden Energy Medicine Certification Program Class 2 Handout* (Ashland, OR: Innersource, Summer 2012).

Inhale while dragging your fingers just above your ears, then exhale while dragging them down behind your ears, and down the sides of your neck to your shoulders.

Hold your fingers on your shoulders at your neck with pressure. On the next inhale, bring your hands down to cross over your heart, and breathe.

On the next inhale, extend your fingers to the opposite shoulders and exhale as you slide them down the outside of each arm. One hand at a time, slide your fingers from each elbow down and off the back of your ring finger.

Inhale while placing the palms of your hands across your ribs (under the bust); exhale as you slide your hands down the outer sides of your legs and feet, then off the baby toes. Shake the energy off your hands.

Inhale as you trace Spleen Meridian (Figure 5-3), beginning at the big toes and sweeping up the inside of your legs, fanning out at the pelvis to the hips, and up the sides of your ribs, stopping under your arms. Exhale as you sweep the energy back down the sides of the ribs and out into the aura.

Repeat the tracing of Spleen Meridian two more times.

Another exercise, gentler in its effects but simple to do while watching TV, standing in line at the supermarket, or while stopped at a red light, involves a "jumper cable" approach to connecting these two important energy pathways. This exercise channels Triple Warmer's excess energy to Spleen Meridian by holding the outer arm (along Triple Warmer Meridian) with the palm of one hand, while holding the opposite side rib cage (along Spleen Meridian) with the other. One can do this for a few minutes or longer, then switch sides. Donna Eden refers to this as the "Triple Warmer–Spleen Hug."[57]

Both these exercises offer significant benefit in the moment and over time, but it is important to note that Triple Warmer can be tenacious in its hold on habits. Depending on how habitual an energetic imbalance is for an individual, Triple Warmer may quickly restore newly balanced energy to the default imbalance. This certainly happened to me: my Triple Warmer energy was so imbalanced when I began this work that one supervisor told me to do the "Cover the Eyes" exercise ten times a day! I don't think I ever managed that frequency, but I can say my Triple Warmer over-reactivity has changed dramatically over time. From personal experience, I can state with confidence that it is important not to despair. One of Donna Eden's missions is to teach us that Triple Warmer can learn new patterns if we are respectful enough of its intentions to protect us, persistent in our attempts to introduce another way, and thoughtful enough to help it understand that embracing the new, balanced habit is better for all concerned.

---

[57] Donna Eden (with David Feinstein), *Eden Energy Medicine Certification Program Class 2 Handout* (Ashland, OR: Innersource, Summer 2012).

Triple Warmer as a Radiant Circuit

We have not yet discussed Triple Warmer as a Radiant Circuit, another of the energy systems recognized by Donna Eden and first identified by ancient Chinese healers as the Extraordinary Flows. Unlike the defined pathways of the meridians, Radiant Circuits are capable of literally jumping from one place on the body to another, so as to more quickly link whatever energy points or systems need connecting in order to help us survive and to make us more resilient. In our highway accident analogy, Radiant Circuits serve like a helicopter hovering over the scene of the collision, ensuring that medical transport is available to support the injured, even if the traffic-congested roadway prevents access.

Radiant Circuits respond to joy, and Triple Warmer as a Radiant Circuit celebrates life, our own life in particular. Unfortunately, due to our rapidly changing and challenging world, our energy systems emphasize Triple Warmer's protective role as a meridian. We have already noted that when the body's *instinctive* choice is required, survival trumps growth, and protection takes priority over joy; consequently, our energies rarely activate Triple Warmer as a Radiant Circuit. But the Radiant Circuits benefit greatly from our intentional, *conscious* support, and we derive benefit in turn. I refer interested readers to Donna Eden's work for additional information and exercises in this regard.[58] For our purposes here, we must simply recognize the pervasive and powerful effects of Triple Warmer upon every aspect of our being.

Before we leave our discussion of Triple Warmer's protective role, it is important to mention that Triple Warmer is an energy system unto

---

[58] Eden (with Feinstein), *Energy Medicine*, 241–272.

itself. More than a meridian engaging the body along its highway of safety and defense, and even beyond its service as a Radiant Circuit governing our immune reactions with joyful possibilities waiting in the wings, Triple Warmer as a system plays an enormous role in our healing. I often wondered why Donna Eden sees Triple Warmer as its own system, one of the nine energy systems she includes in her work. Yet over the past several years, I have experienced personally and witnessed countless times its impact upon whether a person's energies will reveal their imbalances and vulnerabilities during an energy session. Especially if the client has been chronically ill, or has lived with psychological, energetic armor for an extended period of time, Triple Warmer at this higher level of functioning seems to say: "I will let you, client and practitioner, into my domain when you are truly serious about healing—and then only gradually. Until then, anything you do will disturb the balance I have worked hard to provide, and if you play with this without commitment, you will dabble ineffectively. I am here to protect you. Please honor that and approach me with love, gratitude, and respect."

While we will explore the role of Triple Warmer for the empath later in more detail, it is my hope that the reader can begin to appreciate the power of its protective role and how the intake of unfamiliar or perceived-as-dangerous sensations, stimuli, and energies from the environment can trigger a Triple Warmer response. The more sensitive a person, the more sensory input will enter their sponge, thus triggering Triple Warmer all the more, as certainly occurred on the playground for Lily as a young girl. Triple Warmer works overtime for many of us, but for empaths even more so. And with our energetic armor on, getting to the deeper layers of old traumas and facilitating lasting change for the good can present as a Herculean task. Thanks to Donna Eden's work we now have tools to restore balance to our entire energy field, but we must begin with Triple Warmer, the Guardian of the Threshold. Speaking of "threshold," we can now move on to discuss the aura.

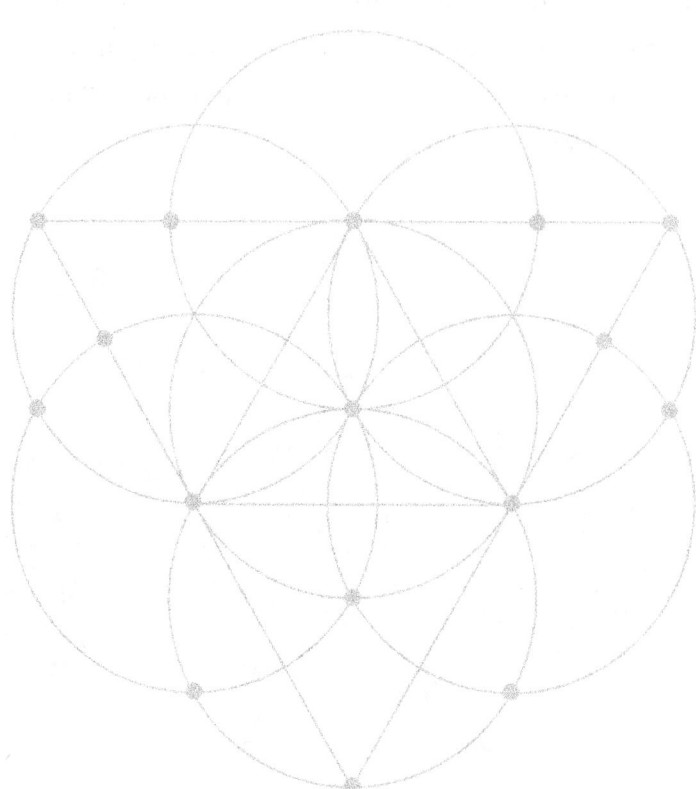

CHAPTER 6

The Empathic Aura

UNLESS WE TRAVEL IN NEW AGE CIRCLES, study Energy Medicine, or follow the scientific discoveries posted by the HeartMath® Institute or quantum physicists, most of us negotiate life without realizing we have an energy field that extends beyond the boundaries of our physical body. Known as the aura, this field holds enormous complexity: vertical and horizontal layers; colors for those who can see them; figures and symbols visible to those with this sensitivity; the energetic thought forms of beliefs and emotions; the energetic template of the physical body; and occasional energetic toxins, holes, and vortexes as well.

We have already discussed how the heart's electromagnetic field can be measured several feet from the body. Stories abound about those with amputations who complain of pain in the missing limb. There are also reports that energy work in the field where the limb used to be can relieve that pain.[59] Many of us respond to leaks or tears in our own auras, as well as to imbalances in the auras of others, without even realizing it. I have come to recognize, for example, that when I feel like crying for no apparent reason I can check for a vortex over my heart and balance it if necessary. I am always amazed that the sad feeling completely resolves in such instances.

So what is a vortex? What is an aura? Does the aura have something to do with gatekeeping? Why does the state of the aura matter so much for an empath? Do we have any control over this energetic entity that most of us can't see, touch, or recognize with *any* of our five senses? Before answering these questions, let's better understand what the aura is and does for us. I like to think of the aura as an energetic space suit providing a level of protection from harmful external influences, while keeping us energetically glued together and simultaneously receptive to the world around us. This closely parallels what we have come to appreciate about semi-permeable membranes on the cellular level: some substances can enter the cell while others cannot.

The aura manages these multiple functions with a fluidity of movement unavailable to the boundaries of the physical body. It can collapse onto the body or extend several feet beyond it, depending upon the needs of the moment. When we struggle with physical illness, for example, the aura may pull in close to the body to help with healing. Or when we feel expanded in a euphoric or mystical way, it can fill the room and beyond. Within its totality it contains layers: the horizontal layers correlate with the major chakras, to be discussed in greater detail in Chapter 10; the vertical layers correlate

---

[59] Eden (with Feinstein), *Energy Medicine,* 36–40.

with energy bodies that surround the physical body like nested dolls. (Figure 6-1) A brief description of these energy bodies will be offered here; interested readers can find more detailed information in *Gift of the Body*[60] by Jonathan Goldman.

The Energy Bodies of the Aura

The vertical layers of the aura include an etheric body residing closest to the physical body that both envelops and penetrates our physical form. We see this energy field in Kirlian photographs as a slight radiance extending perhaps an inch or two beyond the skin, or as rays of light pouring out from the fingertips.[61] According to Jonathan Goldman, the etheric body has well-defined borders, and within its field the meridians make their home. It thrives on constant, calm movement. Health of the physical body depends upon the health of the etheric body and true healing must include attention to the etheric body for the physical body's optimal recovery.[62] Work on phantom limb pain involves this layer of the energy field.

Beyond this layer we have an emotional body that penetrates the physical and etheric bodies, while extending beyond them both. Its fuzzy borders encompass these two denser bodies while overlapping the mental body, binding the mental and spiritual bodies with the others to form our cohesive energy vehicle. The emotional body thrives on freedom and surprise to keep its energies moving. We were designed to feel, and the energy body accomplishes this best when the emotional body's energies flow unencumbered. The "stuck" energies of unhealed wounds can exist in any of the five bodies,

---

[60] Jonathan M. Goldman, M.Ac., *Gift of the Body: A Multi-Dimensional Guide to Energy Anatomy, Grounded Spirituality and Living Through the Heart* (Bend, OR: Essential Light Institute, 2014).
[61] See Google images, Kirlian photography.
[62] Goldman, *Gift of the Body*, 40–46.

but no matter their location, these wounds interfere with this flow. The emotional body draws these unbalanced energies into itself and into our feeling consciousness in order to signal the need for inner healing work.[63]

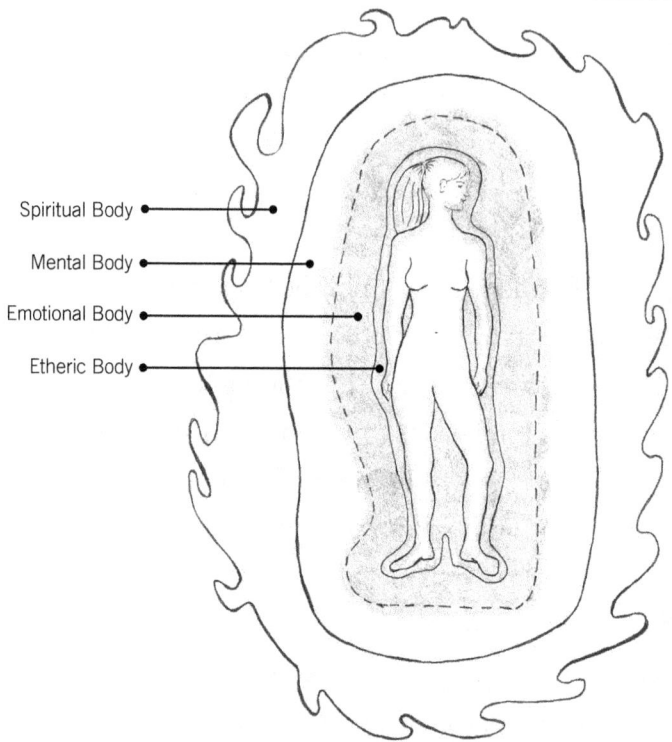

Figure 6-1: Layers of the Aura

The gray shading highlights how the emotional body penetrates the mental, etheric, and physical bodies. This energetic overlap serves as a bridge between the energy bodies of the aura to facilitate the exchange of important information.

The emotional body also makes feeling connections with the outside world. We may sense this body when an angry person, trying to hide their feelings or perhaps unconscious of them, enters a

---

[63] Ibid., 47–74.

room. The mob mentality affects us at this level as well. The size of the emotional body changes in accord with our feeling state: it becomes expansive in the midst of pleasure; or contractive when we are in pain. (Consider the parallels with our nervous system and its experience of safety and danger.) Wounds restrict energy flow; in the absence of freedom, spontaneity and surprise, the energy flow gets clogged. As noted by Jonathan Goldman, clogged energies in the emotional body cause most of our pain; similar clogs in the etheric body, which it penetrates, cause the rest.[64] To ignore our feelings is to invite health problems; attending to them from the heart restores balance and flow. The empath is especially sensitive to the feeling states and the emotional bodies in others, as we shall continue to discover.

The mental body, like the etheric body, has distinct borders that define the aura as a whole. Its field begins within the fuzzy border of the emotional body and extends an inch to two feet beyond it, depending upon how narrow- or open-minded we are, respectively. This body holds our beliefs, and thrives when thoughts and ideas flow freely within it. Jonathan Goldman describes a lower mental body[65] that provides the protective border of the aura, filtering the thoughts coming and going in our energy field. Are they calm? Chaotic? Racing? Slow? Scattered? Fixated? Overloaded? This lower body holds our mental state. The higher mental body,[66] on the other hand, holds our beliefs. These were and are formed in the course of living life. They are meant to serve us for a time then move on. Unfortunately, beliefs developed in childhood before we could consciously

---
[64] Ibid., 47.
[65] Ibid., 78.
[66] Ibid., 81.

evaluate or choose them, often operate from the unconscious, from behind the scenes. We will explore their origins more deeply from the perspective of the empath in the next two chapters.

For now, let's consider this example: if we learn that our emotions are trouble-making, as did Lily, we form beliefs about feelings, about ourselves feeling them, and about our place as a feeling person in the world. Because the mental body penetrates the emotional body and is thus able to impact the etheric and physical bodies, we can see that a belief—that we are defective and trouble-making when we feel, for example—can lead to serious consequences. We may develop excessive self-criticism to rein in feelings whenever they are stirred by life experiences. We may also come to doubt the validity of those feelings, believing that they cannot be trusted to meaningfully decipher or impact the world. These beliefs can cause profound emotional torment and eventually create physical illness. Meanwhile, we lose access to the important information those feelings carry, information meant to protect us from danger and help us engage vitally with the people and the world around us.

Finally, the spiritual body, which some see as having many layers, provides the container for the three lower energy bodies. It holds the vibrational blueprint for our lower energy bodies and the physical body. The spiritual body holds our karmic purpose for this lifetime: what lessons do we need to learn? What challenges do we need to face so as to learn them? What gifts do we bring to accomplish this work? Whom and what do we need to attract, so as to complete this work meaningfully? Not just as theory but in body, heart, mind and soul, we must *feel* these lessons to learn them deeply. We often stumble and make many mistakes, but they are part of learning. Again according to Jonathan Goldman, we fortunately have a receptive space built into the Heart Chakra where we can receive the healing vibration of forgiveness. It is forgiveness that truly allows us to release the past when we are ready.[67] Once we have done sufficient work to clear out the energetically held wounds in the lower bodies, we can experience the fullness of our spiritual body's connection to the Divine in all creation.

Clairvoyants who can see energy name these layers differently, but the essence is the same. For those who see colors in the aura, I suspect we must be gorgeous—unless, as Barbara Brennan depicts in her book, *Hands of Light*,[68] some substance or trauma has darkened the field. Once we remember that colors register in the retina of our eyes (because each color carries an energetic frequency that resonates with the neuron receptors in the optic nerve), we may appreciate that even clairvoyants do not all see these energies in exactly the same way because we are each unique. They have to learn to interpret what they see in a meaningful and useful way relevant to their *own* experience of the physical world. Their abilities to see energy consistently at all correlates with the amazing coherence in our energy field, which science is now beginning to measure. Thanks to their clairvoyance and the growing validation of their vision by science, we can appreciate how these energetic layers overlap and penetrate one another, as well as the layers of another person's field (Figure 3-5), and how we potentially impact one another with or without our awareness.

---

[67] Ibid., 308–313.
[68] Barbara Ann Brennan, *Hands of Light: A Guide to Healing Through the Human Energy Field* (New York, NY: Bantam Books, 1987), Figure 11-2.

Challenges to the Integrity of the Aura

Fortunately, in the face of this complexity we can support our aura to be as balanced and resilient as possible. Considering that its purpose is to facilitate the influx of energies that help us survive, thrive and grow, as well as to resist those energies that interfere with those functions, we need a healthy aura that attracts what it needs and repels what it does not. Via its two-directional flow, it must also release what is toxic to us. Imbalances can occur throughout one's entire energy field when the aura is collapsed, as can happen when we are ill, exhausted, depressed, or terrified. Imbalances may also arise if the aura extends too far beyond the body and detaches from it. This often occurs when we move into a compulsive giving mode and forget to take care of our own needs. In the vacuum created by that detached space, the individual is vulnerable to the accumulation of what I respectfully refer to as "space trash"—the emotions, thoughts, and other discarded energetic baggage of others. Clearly, this kind of intrusion interferes with the aura's ability to provide the protection and healthy flow of energy so essential for life.

A few other imbalances are worthy of note as we consider what can happen for an empath. Holes in the aura offer no protection at all. I once joked to a friend that I might subtitle this book, "My Life as Swiss Cheese!" Just imagine all the energies in the environment, not to mention those of other people's emotions, pouring into auric holes without an effective screening barrier. We may notice this as an energetic "Ouch!" Sometimes holes in the aura are created by vortexes. Vortexes occur in nature when unstable patterns arise. We have likely watched water swirl down an unplugged drain, or viewed films of tornadoes sucking into them anything lying in their path.

The vortexes in our energy field result from similar instabilities.

Energy vortexes propel us toward life experiences or people with "issues," or pull those people or situations into our lives. From my integration of Donna Eden's[69] and Jonathan Goldman's[70] work, I suspect that the spiritual body creates energetic vortexes to attract karmic lessons, or to compulsively draw us toward them for the purpose of deepening our soul's capacity to love or to heal. I also now realize that, no matter how many counter-clockwise circles I do over my heart vortexes to balance them in the moment, I will still have to deal with those feelings and recurrent vortexes until I finally learn the lessons involved. Once we do learn these lessons, however, these same vortexes when balanced may serve as portals to the spiritual realm.

Imbalances in the aura can also be generated by the electromagnetic forces that bombard us daily. While the purpose of the aura involves protecting us from these forces, without resilience and grounding to the earth, the aura's own electromagnetic energies can shift in response to these greater forces in ways that don't always serve us. Jonathan Goldman's description of the Root Chakra includes three columns of energy rooting our body to the energy field of the earth, while also serving as an energetic tripod to provide physical balance. The front two-sided cone[71] connecting the physical body to the earth emanates from the base of the perineum (Figure 10-1), where Central and Governing Meridians also originate, sending their energies up the front and back of the etheric body of the torso, respectively. (Figure 6-2) These two meridians also engage with

---

[69] Donna Eden (with David Feinstein), *Eden Energy Medicine Certification Program Class 7 Handout* (Ashland, OR: Innersource, Fall 2012).
[70] Goldman, *Gift of the Body*, 96.
[71] Ibid., 133.

each other via overlapping ovals, flowing upward from perineum to crown and down the other side, in opposite directions, to support our core. Donna Eden's Daily Energy Routine includes two exercises, the Hook Up and the Zip Up, which specifically balance these two meridians whose function is to protect the aura and "oversee" all the meridians in the Flow Wheel.

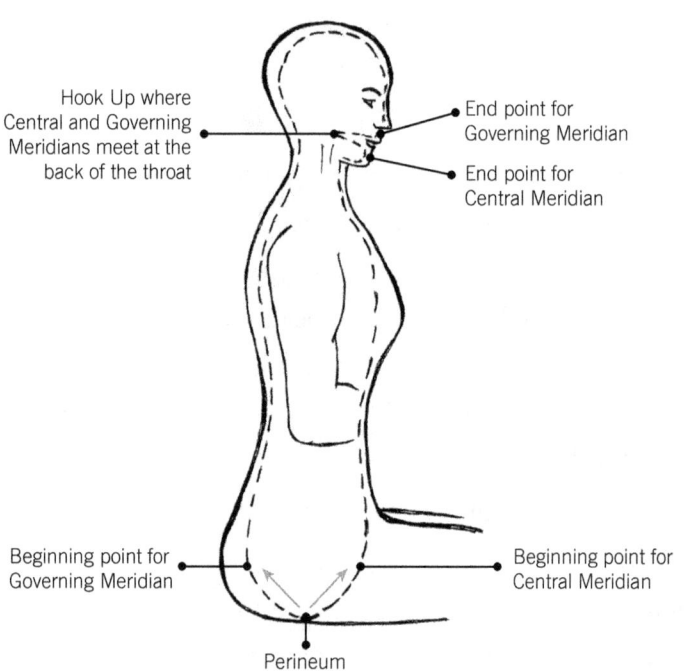

Figure 6-2: Central and Governing Meridians

Both Central and Governing Meridians begin at the perineum where they receive energy from the Root Chakra. From the perineum Central Meridian flows up the front of the body and, after its hook up with Governing Meridian, its less dominant flow continues down the back. From the perineum Governing Meridian flows up the back of the body and, after its hook up with Central Meridian, its less dominant flow continues down the front. The overlap of these two meridians contributes to a strong core. The beginning and end points of each meridian refer to their acupuncture points. These are located where a meridian's pathway contacts the surface of the body.

Central Meridian runs up the front center of the body from the pubic bone to the lower lip, then turns inward to the back of the throat. Governing Meridian begins at the coccyx in the back and runs up the spine, over the top center of the head, and down the middle of the face to the upper lip, where it turns inward and continues to the back of the throat. There it hooks up with Central Meridian. These two meridians need to be balanced, strong, and connected within for us to experience a strong core. In this strengthened state, they can also radiate outward as Radiant Circuits and strengthen the aura. Central Meridian provides support for the front of the aura; Governing Meridian does so for the back. Donna Eden refers to their combined effect as the "microcosmic orbit."[72]

The Zip Up[73] exercise specifically supports Central Meridian whose energy highway travels up the front of the torso. By tracing this meridian forward from the pubic bone to the lower lip three times with the palm of the hand, not only does this exercise strengthen its flow, but also directly "zips up" the front of the aura, the way a jacket's zipper helps keep us protected from the wind. In this way we are less vulnerable to the forces surrounding our energy field that would penetrate our field if we weren't zipped up.

The Hook Up[74] also supports Central Meridian while more specifically strengthening its connection to Governing Meridian at the back of the throat. If we hold the Hook Up points (the navel and the Third Eye) with our middle fingers for a few minutes (by pushing in at those points and pulling up just a tad) while breathing in through the nose and out the mouth, that hooked up energy

---

[72] Donna Eden, "Donna Eden's Daily Energy Routine [OFFICIAL VERSION]," https://www.youtube/Di5Ua44iuXc.
[73] Eden with Feinstein, *Energy Medicine*, 94–98.
[74] Ibid., 98–99.

moves out to the Radiant Circuits of Central and Governing to also support the aura. While these exercises may seem too simple to be effective, I have witnessed and also felt within myself their subtle but perceptible power to support the aura's integrity. Empaths especially benefit from attention to these aspects of our energy field.

Yet even within an intact aura any of its layers can flip electromagnetic fields—their polarities of positive and negative charge—in response to an influx of challenging energies. Solar flares are a great example. Shifts in the earth's electromagnetic field in response to solar flares and other forces also impact *us*. In this context, we must also appreciate the importance of our feet and their energetic placement upon the earth itself. The electromagnetic alignment of our feet with the earth (that is, the South electromagnetic soles of our feet attracted to the North electromagnetic surface of the earth) allows for grounding and the vital connection of our physical and energy bodies to the earth. More specifically, our K-1's—the first acupressure points along the Kidney Meridian located between the balls of each foot—can take in energy from the earth to support our moment-to-moment experience of vitality. If for any reason our feet in general, and our K-1's more specifically, cannot receive the earth's energy, perhaps because these points have become frozen, reversed or submerged with irregular energy, then we may feel tired and disconnected from life. Again we find we must deal with irregular energies to support the health of the physical body and the aura.

The Aura and the Empath

Of special importance for empaths, Donna Eden notes that our emotional sense of feeling supported by life can flounder when

THE EMPATHIC AURA

our electromagnetic fields are not in flow with the energy of the earth. She offers several techniques to correct and maintain the proper alignment of our feet to the magnetic polarity of the earth, including: walking on wet grass; massaging our hands and/or feet; or rubbing a slightly magnetized object like a stainless steel spoon over the soles of our feet to reset their polarity.[75] These methods often prove quite effective and their simplicity makes them easily accessible. I have also found on occasion that these techniques do not work, because a deeper imbalance resides in the auric field. In such cases, Triple Warmer is likely involved and doing its best to protect us with its habitual, but now ineffective response to what it perceives as dangerous. Homolateral or scrambled energies may also be involved in such instances (to be discussed in more detail in Chapter 13). Fortunately, both of these latter issues usually respond to exercises included in Donna Eden's Daily Energy Routine.[76]

Let's now consider the energetic impact upon the aura of a disturbing emotional exchange, or the empathic attunement to the distressed inner state of another. If that exchange or empathic attunement resonates with some misguided—and consequently emotionally painful—belief held in our field, the aura will likely respond by flipping polarities in one or more layers. The entire aura or a layer within it can experience frozen, reversed, or submerged energies, just as the fish of Chapter 5 responded to the rock in their path. The instability of these energies may create holes and/or vortexes as well. As a result, these disturbances compromise the aura's protective function.

---

[75] Donna Eden (with David Feinstein), *Eden Energy Medicine Certification Program Class 1 Handout* (Ashland, OR: Innersource, Spring 2012).
[76] Eden with Feinstein, *Energy Medicine*, 72–100, and Donna Eden, "Donna Eden's Daily Energy Routine [OFFICIAL VERSION]," https://www.youtube/Di5Ua44iuXc.

When a reversal or blockage of electromagnetic flow happens in the aura, that which would normally be attracted into our field is repelled and that which we would better repel is welcomed. Needless to say, this can create more problems than it solves; imagine, for example, what Lily's auric state looked like as she faced her cruel peers and her friend's vulnerability. When the absorption of anger, fear, and other distressing emotional states negatively impacts the aura's optimal electromagnetic alignment, the aura simultaneously becomes more vulnerable to those states in the absence of any healing interventions. Triple Warmer Meridian's protective function then compensates for the aura's vulnerability with fight, flight, or freeze. Consequently, the "duck and sponge" phenomenon relates to the sensitivity of the aura as much as to one's neurological hardwiring, if not more so.

As we have noted, Triple Warmer typically reacts whenever a significant energy field's protective qualities are jeopardized. One can calm Triple Warmer in this situation, but it will likely react again, and repeatedly, until the root of the auric imbalance has been addressed. If this imbalance has an acute onset, the *Cleansing the Aura* exercise below may prove helpful. I have adapted this from Donna Eden's exercise, which she calls "Expelling the Venom,"[77] by including the energy bodies described by Jonathan Goldman and by adding spiritual intention to the movements. This exercise not only makes space inside the physical body for the crucial flow of energy, it serves to remove congested energies from the layers of the aura by combining physical gesture with conscious thought and intention. The goal is to release from our field any energies that rightly belong to others,

---

[77] Eden with Feinstein, *Energy Medicine,* 236–237.

while honoring what remains as belonging to us for our inner work. The final part of this exercise invites a loving spiritual presence to assist us in this process of working on what is ours for the highest and greatest good of all.

Cleansing the Aura

The Physical Movements:
The gesture itself involves some imagination as we gather what stresses us in our hands, making two fists around it. We inhale while bending our arms at the elbows and bringing both fists up to chest level in front of the body. Holding our breath, we swing our arms out to the sides in a big circle, and once our fists are above our heads we simultaneously thrust our arms down and open our fists, releasing the unwanted emotions or energies toward the ground while also exhaling and making a "ssshhhh" sound. This verbalization matters as it carries a vibration to support the release.

The Process:
We repeat this whole cycle four times with the same speed and intensity. Each time we can clear a different layer of the aura, releasing those energies that do not belong to us.

First, we gather any congested energy held in the etheric layer closest to the body and release it.

Second, we gather the desires, disappointments and other emotions not belonging to us that are held in the emotional layer two to eight inches away from the body and release them. Third, we gather thoughts and beliefs not belonging to us that are held in the mental layer eight to eighteen inches away from the body and release them.
Fourth, we gather karmic lessons not belonging to us that are held in the spiritual layer at arm's length in the auric field and release them.

After releasing those energies that do not belong to us in each of these layers, we can focus on what is ours to address in our daily life.

For the final swing, we gather in our hands what congested energy is ours, at whatever distance from the body feels intuitively right, and inhale while we slowly swing our arms upward. We then release what is ours to heaven for cleansing as we exhale. With our arms still raised above our heads, we inhale what is ours in its cleansed state, receiving it into our hands, and slowly and quietly "ssshhhh" it down as our hands descend, placing what is ours back into the aura. We support this exercise with Figure 8's in the aura, especially over the heart, and accept our "work" for the day.

Fortunately, various energy techniques are available to support and balance the aura. More specifically, Donna Eden has offered us the Daily Energy Routine, described in her book, *Energy Medicine*,[78] on her website,[79] and on YouTube.[80] The various exercises in this regimen provide an overall energy system tune-up. A supplemental exercise, the Celtic Weave,[81] helps extend the collapsed aura, attach the detached aura, fix small holes in the auric field, and remove energetic toxins. The reader is referred to her work for more detailed information regarding these exercises. Other techniques will be shared throughout this text with the hope that each person will try them with some consistency to determine which work best over time. We know that empaths naturally absorb energies from others as part of daily living, and that these energies may be perceived as toxic by Triple Warmer. Consequently, attending to the aura, by balancing Triple Warmer in particular and our energy field in general, with the same frequency we give to good dental hygiene supports the cleansing of our auric sponge.

One of the benefits of a daily Energy Medicine practice involves the building of overall resilience. When such a practice does not lead to significant improvement in our ability to respond to life's challenges, or if we've experienced physical ailments over an extended period, the problem may stem from an underlying, more chronic imbalance. In such cases, deeper work will be needed to achieve reliable recovery. We can recognize that this applies to us if we have prolonged physical symptoms. Disturbances usually begin in one's

---

[78] Eden with Feinstein, *Energy Medicine*, 72–100.
[79] Innersource, www.Innersource.net.
[80] Donna Eden, "Donna Eden's Daily Energy Routine [OFFICIAL VERSION]," https://www.youtube /Di5Ua44iuXc.
[81] Eden with Feinstein, *Energy Medicine*, 201.

energy field and gradually move toward the physical; by the time we experience physical symptoms, unless caused by sudden trauma, the difficulty more likely reflects a chronic energetic imbalance. This again highlights how misguided beliefs—usually instilled during our youth then encoded with Triple Warmer protection—may actually perpetuate chronic imbalances by engendering painful emotions that then penetrate the etheric body and affect our physical functioning.

Energy testing[82] can help reveal which of our systems have responded most sensitively to the day-to-day onslaughts of electromagnetic forces, nuclear radiations, environmental pollutants, food additives, and the unresolved thoughts and emotions of ourselves and others. Once we identify these imbalances and recognize their impact, we can utilize additional energy exercises and techniques to regain the auric and energetic resilience we were designed to embody and embrace. This work may involve deep shifts in our energy fields, both within the body and beyond it. Having a stabilizing daily energy practice can allow those shifts to happen more gently and to last. Ultimately, the intention of the work involves living into the uniqueness and authenticity of who we truly are. Now that we have explored several components of our uniquely configured energy systems, we can turn our attention to energetic sensory types and explore how they too may assist us in understanding the experiences of the empath.

---

[82] While a review of energy testing is beyond the scope of this book, the reader is referred to: Eden with Feinstein, *Energy Medicine,* 55–60.

Sensory Types[83]

At some point, usually in later childhood, we begin to appreciate how our five senses facilitate our reception of information from the environment. We have now also correlated these senses with the response of the Vagus Nerve as it impacts our perceptions of safety and danger. From an energy perspective, we also possess a sensory system with four avenues of receptivity: two of these overlie the physical senses of seeing and hearing, while two others correlate better with body/torso awareness and thought. Contained in the aura, these four sensory types affect the way we receive the information encoded in the frequencies and energy waves around us. We can develop all four types over time, but we are born with one as primary. Our primary type was most obvious to everyone around us when we were children; as we grew, we developed some or all of the others. Before we discuss the implications of this for the empath, let's first better understand each one—Kinesthetic, Tonal, Visual, and Digital—and how they play out in everyday life and relationships.

Kinesthetic: In a balanced state, Kinesthetics lovingly take in the world with the whole of their bodily experience. They sense information in the torso of their physical being, as well as through their feelings. Knowing life in this way predisposes these individuals to empathy, intuition, and tremendous compassion. When overwhelmed, however, they lose the capacity to put their experiences into words, feelings become facts, and interpersonal boundaries become blurred if not dissolved. Because boundaries are so distorted,

---

[83] I first learned about this topic in the Eden Energy Medicine Certification Program but the reader can pursue more in-depth information regarding this in their now published work: Donna Eden and David Feinstein, Ph.D., *The Energies of Love: Using Energy Medicine to Keep Your Relationship Thriving* (New York, NY: Jeremy P. Tarcher/Penguin, 2014).

Kinesthetics risk losing an awareness of self and often try to "fix it" for the other person. An underlying, usually unconscious intention involves assisting others so that the Kinesthetic no longer has to feel their pain. Consequently, Kinesthetics may unwittingly prevent others from learning their life lessons. For those with this mode of sensory receptivity, when their energy is imbalanced an energy vortex often develops over the heart and/or sacral chakras (to be discussed in Chapter 10). The challenge for the Kinesthetic is to seek a perspective that resonates with the truth of the heart.

Tonal: People with tonal sensory styles can hear between the lines. They pick up on the nuance of sounds, as well as energy; they appreciate the beauty of music and can sense the subtleties around them. In fact, they can detect untruth and underlying agendas quite accurately when in a balanced state. Tonals constantly try to evaluate their impressions and when stressed can become very judgmental. They tend to be hard on themselves and others, and when overwhelmed will imply meaning from the other's tone of voice rather than from the actual words spoken. The meaning inferred is often perceived as critical of the Tonal and, especially when stressed, they have a difficult time "hearing" any apologies or explanations. In an imbalanced state, energy vortexes can arise on the sides of the ears and over the solar plexus. The Tonal's challenge is to listen with a forgiving ear.

Visual: Those who are primarily visual see the big picture and often have a keen sense of beauty and aesthetics. In a balanced state, they know where things belong: they are the visionaries. When stressed, they do not tolerate well any deviation from the correctness of that vision, becoming critical and quick to point out the faults of the other person, while unable to recognize their own contribution to the difficulty. In an unbalanced state, an energy vortex develops over the chest and head, funneling out the eyes when overwhelmed. The Visual is being invited to learn to see through eyes of love.

Digital: Those with a primarily digital sensory mode have a capacity to organize and integrate a tremendous amount of information and then present it in a coherent, comprehensible fashion to others. When in balance, they can also be very kind. Their keen sense of logic allows them to remain calm under stress, sometimes too cool. They insist that they are right about what they know and they do not compromise unless it is logical to them. When in an unbalanced state, the feelings and emotional expressions of others can disturb them, and in the face of these feelings they can become quite arrogant, cold, and rejecting. When imbalanced, an energy vortex develops over the head along with a major energetic disconnect between the head and heart/rest of the body. The Digital's invitation is to think and categorize with compassion.

While these descriptions offer only a cursory review of sensory types, I hope they provide a sense of how these types affect an individual's experience of life, as well as what matches/mismatches may arise in significant relationships. For example, imagine a female Kinesthetic and a male Digital having an argument. Assuming the argument itself bespeaks an imbalance, the Kinesthetic becomes emotionally overwhelmed and tearful, unable to explain with words her distress. The Digital becomes overwhelmed by the Kinesthetic's inability to understand the beautiful logic being expressed and is repelled by the emotional response. The Digital's tone may become arrogant and the Kinesthetic becomes even more exasperated and non-verbal. This argument clearly needs a time-out. If the argument were between a Tonal and a Visual, the Visual might become critical, the Tonal would hear the criticism, the Visual might try to apologize, but the Tonal might not be able to hear it. Again, these individuals would benefit from taking time to pause and reflect. As human beings in relationship we are constantly challenged because, in truth, any combination of types, even two of the same—such as two Visuals each having a different vision—can increase the potential for conflict when out of balance.

Fortunately, we have more than one sensory type to rely upon in any situation, especially when we have time to recognize an upcoming stressor and can utilize the wisdom of the secondary, tertiary, even quaternary types we've developed over the course of our lives. In such a case, we can reflect upon alternative ways to appreciate the other person's point of view, so that difficult conversations convey more understanding and effective ways to solve the problem. Or we may decide that avoidance of an unnecessary stressor offers the better course of action. If we are overwhelmed by a sudden and/or very traumatic incident, or we've never developed another sensory type, we return to our primary type as the default, and it likely will become unbalanced in the face of significant stress. We will perceive the world and the other person or event through that sensory lens, take the energy in through the developing vortex, and perhaps feel it in our body. If we can appreciate that vortexes develop as part of soul-given lessons for our learning and that our primary sensory type is soul-given as well, perhaps we can shift our perspective regarding the occasional suffering they invite and begin to more deeply appreciate their gifts. Our souls offer these opportunities to all of us.

Before we explore what this means for the empath more specifically, let's first appreciate which types are more likely to present in empaths in general. From the descriptions above, it should be apparent that Kinesthetics and Tonals take general environmental information *into* themselves and experience that information internally—how things feel, how they sound—in specific, sometimes physical, and often emotional ways. They focus more on the internal experience than on the details of the content. On our duck/sponge continuum, these two types are more like the sponges. Visuals and Digitals, on the other hand, focus their perceptions on the world *outside* themselves—how things look, how logical they are—and order their outer world around those perceptions. This outward focus waddles like a duck into, then out of the mud.

Based on the reported experiences of empaths, sensing the internal state of others as they do, in addition to my own observations during personal encounters, most empaths are Kinesthetics or Tonals. No matter what a person's primary sensory type, however, when a person has developed three or four of these sensory types and is in a balanced, relatively unstressed state, she can rely upon her kinesthetic and tonal abilities to relate empathically with another person. Thus we can all be capable of empathy energetically, but some of us experience this more naturally, more consistently, and more intensely.

A Summary Thus Far

To integrate what we have uncovered from this and previous chapters, let us return to the experience of Lily on the playground. Let's say she is a Kinesthetic who, over the course of her life, has attended well to the development of her other sensory types, but who was limited to her kinesthetic sensitivities when she was seven. She certainly heard the anger and aggression in the verbal taunts of the other girls. She obviously saw the distress on her friend's face and the "mean" expressions on the faces of the others. Her mind may have done some quick calculations about how she might survive/handle the painful situation unfolding before her. But as a Kinesthetic, more than anything she *felt* it. The emotional intensity and conflict developing between her peers, and within herself as a witness, held energy, an accumulation of various frequencies that surrounded her and penetrated her aura.

As filtered by her kinesthetic sensory type through the vertical layers of her aura, the energy conveying information of danger flowed into her physical body through her gut and torso. Since energy moves faster than nerve conduction, her Triple Warmer protector engaged. Meanwhile, photons converting to electrons penetrated her body and encountered her Vagus Nerve. This nerve with its 80% afferent fibers received the information in her torso and sent it onward to her brainstem, where additional pathways sent it on to her amygdala and hypothalamus. Her amygdala recognized the complexity of this situation as familiar and dangerous, based upon her past experiences. Her hypothalamus capably conveyed the fight/flight message to her Sympathetic Nervous System: stress surged through her body as she prepared for one of these responses. Emotional correlates from learned parental and societal messages and prohibitions were activated: fighting went against the rules of society and of logic; running away betrayed her care for her friend. Consequently, there was nothing she could effectively do. She froze. She also felt intensely ashamed.

In his book, *Power vs. Force*,[84] David R. Hawkins described shame as having the lowest, densest energetic vibration. This translates experientially into a sensation of heaviness and stinging emotional pain. We associate this emotion with a sense of isolation and "badness," and we all experience it during our early childhood, albeit some more than others. Even as we grow into old age, some event or relational exchange can trigger the recurrence of that dreaded emotion. As an empath writing this, I'd rather do something to "fix" Lily's emotional state than conclude the chapter with her still feeling this way! Yet we have so much to explore and understand about shame and other aspects of our human nature before any genuine healing can occur, for us as we read and for Lily during her healing process. And so I invite the reader to patiently continue as our journeys meaningfully unfold.

Having described the basics of how our energy systems impact our life experiences, we now turn our attention to our inner psychodynamics. These very much relate to what we have learned through perception, word, and deed in the course of life's challenges. While our energy systems encode our responses and maintain them as habits, as human beings we have the additional benefit of consciousness. This frontal lobe capacity for perspective, reflection, and insight can ultimately help us to better understand ourselves and how we came to be the way we perceive ourselves to be. It can also help us

---

[84] David R. Hawkins, M.D., Ph.D., *Power vs. Force: The Hidden Determinants of Human Behavior* (Carlsbad, CA: Hay House, Inc., 2002), 76–77.

explore who we truly are underneath all the cultural and familial messages we've used to define ourselves. If we take the opportunity to unearth a more accurate vision of possibility and authenticity for the person we were born to be, we can use this appreciation of our energy systems to install a more relevant story. First, however, we have to appreciate the current story, how it began and unfolded as we grew. Let us move onward now to the next chapter, which explores the development and dynamics of our inner psyche.

CHAPTER 7

The Holistic Human Being

"PSYCHE," A WORD DERIVED FROM ancient Greece, means soul. Not long into my psychiatric training, I realized I had been seeking its presence in the course of my work. Unfortunately, the educational agenda of my psychiatric residency relied heavily upon psychoanalytic theory, diagnostic categories, and which medications statistically demonstrated the best results for mollifying the psyche's dilemmas and responses to life. I read my archetypal astrology books in secret and tried hard to straddle both worlds. Ten years later, my pirouette on the fence toppled me squarely onto the unconventional side of the established psychiatric perspective.

It so happened that, amidst numerous transitions in my own life, I found a foster care agency in need of a part-time psychiatrist and myself in need of employment. I'd had a year of specialty training in the field of Child, Adolescent and Family Psychiatry during my residency, so I took the position. Not long into the work, I realized that my training had not prepared me for the extreme degree of human suffering delicately hidden behind a child's eyes. When a cocaine-addicted mother gave birth in prison, and thereafter her baby suffered exposure to physical, perhaps sexual, and emotional abuse by unprepared and inconsistent caregivers, her child would arrive in foster care with a trail of trauma far exceeding the scope of interventions I as a psychiatrist might offer. And unfortunately, these children were many. No diagnosis or medication for their aggressive and/or otherwise disturbed cognitions, emotions and behavior, provided in the brief window of time allotted to our appointments was going to "fix" them in the short term. No psychiatric journal or reference book was going to explain to me why these things happen to a human being in the first place. I sought answers in the writings of the mystics.

During my quest for deeper knowing, I came upon the writings of Z'ev ben Shimon Halevi, specifically his book entitled, *Psychology & Kabbalah*.[85] Within its pages I found a model for understanding how psychology fits into the larger schema of the psyche and its true relationship to soul. I have simplified this model for many presentations over the years, trying to capture its essential spirit, although I know I have left out many significant details. I recommend his work to anyone in search of a more comprehensive understanding of Kabbalah, a branch of Jewish mysticism, or the model I offer in this chapter, which was directly inspired by his writing.

I would like to present this model as a way of appreciating our human journey of growth in consciousness and how to recognize the benefits and limitations of our current mental health perspec-

---

[85] Z'ev ben Shimon Halevi, *Psychology & Kabbalah* (York Beach, ME: Samuel Weiser, Inc., 1986).

tives. This relates specifically to empaths, as many experience anxiety, depression, and a host of other difficulties that the mental health system might be quick to label, but slow to understand at the level of deeper cause. Consequently, empaths may walk away from an appointment with a mental health professional feeling diagnosed and disordered without ever appreciating the buried treasure lying beneath the symptom or symptoms with which they struggle. To better recognize the riches hidden in our soulful psyches, we must first explore our humanness from a holistic perspective.

The Human Journey of Consciousness

This holistic model recognizes five levels of human experience: physical body, behavior, emotions, thoughts, and soul. Figure 7-1 depicts these aspects of our consciousness in a vertical hierarchy, in keeping with the energetic or vibrational level associated with each domain. The physical body is the densest and its frequencies reflect that density, while our thoughts in comparison can be quite light when contemplating the beauty of the clouds or a rainbow. We will explore each of these dimensions of human experience in greater detail to more deeply appreciate how we function within the possible limitations of each level. We may also recognize previously unconsidered opportunities to expand our human consciousness, so as to become more integrated and whole.

The Physical Body: We have already discussed in some detail the neurological underpinning of our physical forms. We have also acknowledged the extraordinary amount of information received moment to moment by our five senses. Our physical bodies take up space and have a form that can only exist in one place at one time. If we recognize incarnation as an event of an infinite soul choosing to occupy a finite physical form, we can perhaps appreciate the enormous transition in consciousness required as our souls take up residence in our bodies. Suddenly, time, space, and matter dictate who we experience ourselves to be, where we are, and the reality that we will change, age, and die. The cells of our bodies will grow, divide, die, and be replaced over and over again, unless some illness or trauma alters that process or causes a permanent loss of form. In our human body we experience the sensations of life, comforting and painful, with an expansive continuum in between. Wordless cellular memory operates through neurons, neurotransmitters and hormones, cells, organs and systems, all functioning within the body's domain.

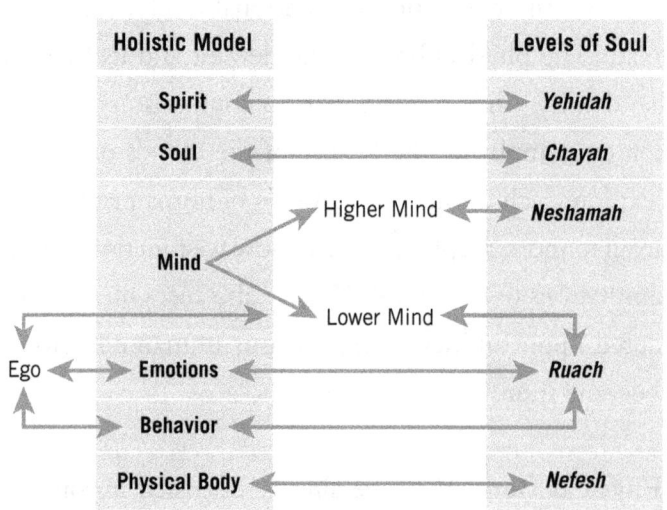

Figure 7-1: A Holistic Model of Human Consciousness and Its Correlation with the Five Levels of the Soul

Behavior (The Body in Action): Because we have motor neurons and muscles, with bones providing structure and support, our physical bodies move. That movement may be something we take for granted until we suffer a broken bone or witness someone bound to a wheelchair. It may seem simplistic to note this, yet because we move we can act in the world. Our bodies can maneuver such that we can be with people, escape from difficult situations, hug a loved one, engage in meaningful work, or play with a child. At this level of consciousness, our bodies experience a great range of opportunities while still struggling with some built-in limitations. Yes, we can move, but only in one direction at a time. We cannot be in two places at once; only in time can we move from one place to another. And if our ability to move is inhibited in any way, the next level of emotional consciousness draws attention to our plight.

Feelings and Emotions: A feeling is generally defined as a response to a stimulus in the moment one experiences it. The amygdala processes each feeling for relative safety or danger, thereby associating our experiences with their accompanying feeling-toned reactions. Ideally, this allows us to respond quickly to any emergent situation then move on to the next moment. In contrast, psychologists define emotions as feeling responses that linger beyond the immediate response to the stimulus. A well-known example involves the feeling of anger, which we may experience if someone momentarily slights us in some way. Generally, it takes ninety seconds for the brain to register and process that slight for a response, thus the accompanying anger naturally lasts ninety seconds before it is released. We tend to feel angry longer, however, because we replay it over and over in our brain: the feeling of anger has now become an emotion. It has shifted from the realm of providing immediate information to that of psychological response.

To elaborate further, we might consider the potential layers of feeling encoded by the word "distress," such as anger, worry, sadness, grief, shock, or fear. In such a distressed state, one might feel some or all of these feelings simultaneously. This kind of layered emotional state had occurred for a woman who called me to request an initial appointment after she'd had a severe reaction to medications. She emphatically described this experience as "horrible" at least 25 times during our brief telephone contact—even though she was physically feeling better at the time we spoke. While I certainly empathized with the upsetting physical and emotional sensations she experienced during the reaction, her ongoing distress about it suggested that her initial feeling responses had become "stuck" in emotional trauma. I also realized that the emotional intensity she expressed through frequent use of the word "horrible" continued to reinforce the horror of that experience for her, thus strengthening its hold on her memory every time she said it. While I trust it was not her intention to prolong her misery, her use of the word "horrible" did convey her desperate need for help.

Returning to our model, we see that as we progress upward on our holistic diagram the energetic density lightens. Emotions have more fluidity and fewer limitations than does our physical body itself or the movement of our body. In this way we can experience several feelings or emotions simultaneously, as noted above. For example, when our teenage children leave for their first semester of college experience, we may feel joy for their burgeoning adulthood, pride for their accomplishments, relief from the many attendant "to-do's" involved in caring for their needs day to day, sadness at their absence from our daily life, and concern, if not worry, for their safety—all at the same time to varying degrees. Interestingly, though our body can only occupy one space at a time or move in one direction at a time, the complexity of this emotional state drives equally complex hormonal and neurological reactions *for each feeling* in the physical body. Ultimately however, all these biochemical exchanges interweave so as to initially offer our cortex an awareness of one overall feeling state. Our physical body is then left with a feeling-toned experience derived from complexity—or "yuck" as I sometimes like to call it. We may feel *something*, but at this level of our holistic model we are not able to describe its many aspects in words.

From an energetic perspective, our feelings and emotions also vibrate and are carried by their frequencies into our auric field. The reader may recall that we spoke of an emotional body within the aura that penetrates the etheric and physical bodies as well. As also previously referenced, David Hawkins has ascribed logarithmic correlates for the power of "specific attractor energy fields"[86] to the various feelings and emotions we often experience, some of these states being denser, or heavier, than others. These feeling-based frequencies not only penetrate the etheric and physical aspects of the body and affect them, they also extend outward, overlapping with the auric fields of others to stimulate resonating energies within the other person.

According to Dr. Hawkins' schema, *shame* carries the heaviest load, weighing us down and dragging much of our consciousness with it.

---

[86] Hawkins, *Power vs. Force*, 75–94.

After shame, *guilt*, *apathy*, *grief*, *fear*, *desire*, *anger* and *pride* successively follow. Progressing up this logarithmic scale, the density of each feeling tone lightens compared to the "heavier" feeling tones below it, yet each is still relatively destructive to the individual and to society as a whole. When resonating with the energy field of these below-200 feeling states, we often instinctively prefer to fight or flee. If instead we are overtaken by "shoulds" demanding we stay present to them, we may emotionally freeze. Fortunately, we also have other options.

Before we consider those options, it is important to note that these relatively destructive feeling states more often earn the psychological description of "emotions" in that we tend to hold on to, or repetitively reinforce them for prolonged periods of time. Not until the logarithmic level of 200 where *courage* first appears can we marshal the energy to support dramatic shifts. Thereafter, we can access states of *willingness*, *acceptance*, *reason*, *love*, *joy*, and *peace* as they, and we in our consciousness, progress along this same logarithmic scale. This progression, or growth, thereby intensifies an individual's and a society's capacity to attract and spark a resonating vibration in others—assuming those others are capable of resonance with that higher vibrational state, or at least are open to the invitation to try.

Just as with the emotions below 200 on the scale, these higher vibrational levels *affect* and *respond* to the state of the body, to stimuli in the environment, and to one's thoughts about one's body and the environment. (We mentioned this from a neurological viewpoint during our discussion of the interactions between the Vagus Nerve, the Limbic System, and the Cortex in Chapter 3.) Unlike the emotions below 200, however, we cannot hold on to these lighter, less dense feeling states above 200 no matter how hard we try. They must be lived moment to moment, cultivated as ongoing experience, and facilitated with consciousness. Perhaps with this model of vibrational resonance we can see more clearly how our feelings primarily serve as pure messengers. Our *attitudes* about our feelings require further exploration in this context.

To summarize, because we are complex beings with complex emotions, we are likely to feel a host of emotions at one time. Hawkins' work suggests that the quality of our attractor energy field, and by implication our overall level of functioning, derives from the combined resonance of these various emotional levels. In the absence of a discerning self-awareness, we may feel the sum total of these emotions in our body, perceiving the experience less as an emotion and more as a kind of weight, be it lightness or heaviness. We recognize the relativity of these experiences with common expressions, such as "light as a feather," "free as a bird," "weight on my shoulders," and "heaviness in my heart." Speaking of the heart, we have yet to discuss its role in the regulation of our entire physical, energetic, and spiritual being. We will expand our understanding of the heart and its role in our life in Chapters 9 and 10. For now, let us consider that to shift emotions requires an additional source of input. Hawkins indicates that to effect such changes for the better, the power of choice plays a major role. This takes us to the next level in our holistic model—Thought.

Thoughts: Pause for a moment and try to rid your mind of the words steadily flowing through it. Those who meditate in this way may not have such a difficult time of it, but the rest of us struggle with the endless mind-chatter and dramas that pervade our waking state. Sometimes our thoughts receive our full attention, such as when we are actively problem-solving or engrossed in interesting or deep conversation. At other times, however, we may be aware of one or two streams of words, songs, or images, not necessarily related to what we are doing in the moment, but filling the day and our minds just as a television offers background noise and the illusion of companionship.

We know that other species are capable of some kind of thinking. My dog, for example, understands some of my words, has the grace to look at me quizzically when I string too many of them together, and can manipulate me to get what he wants if my extra neuron isn't firing in that moment. (I'm joking about the extra neuron—I hope I have a few more than that!) Humans are supposedly capable of much higher level thinking than that of our furry friends, thanks to the gifts of our frontal lobe: the capacity for hindsight, insight, and foresight. In other words, our thinking abilities can self-reflect and handle abstractions such that we can imagine a past, present, and future.

Based on these abilities, it may come as no surprise that the mystics discerned two levels of mind: lower mind and higher mind. They described the function of lower mind as knowing what it takes to survive and even thrive in day-to-day living. With our lower minds we prepare food, pay bills, show up for work, or school, or social occasions on time. We might even get caught up in the local dramas of our loved ones or community. I was once told that the average newspaper addresses its contents to a person with a sixth-grade education: this level of information-seeking accesses our lower mind. This is not to belittle it in the slightest; we all have and need one. In contrast, however, higher mind utilizes those same capacities for hindsight, insight, and foresight—used to some degree by lower mind—and develops them further.

Higher mind accesses the transcendent. When mystics experience oneness with the divine, they have engaged their higher mind. When we make the effort to connect with our Higher Self in the Jungian sense (that part of us that knows our purpose for this existence and holds our purest character) or our souls, we too build a bridge to our higher mind. When philosophers and spiritual teachers attempt to communicate their insights about the intangible realms of existence, they must bridge their higher and lower minds so as to render their experiences and guidance understandable and relevant to their audience, who may not yet have as deep a connection or comprehension of these higher worlds, even though they yearn for them. From this brief description it is hopefully apparent that our thoughts can be complex indeed!

From an energetic perspective, our thoughts carry less density than do our emotions. We also experience the thoughts of our higher mind as lighter and freer than those of our lower mind. Most of us would rather witness and wonder about the mysteries of a sunset and the gradually appearing stars in the vastness of the universe than negotiate the complexity of our taxes, for example. What we don't realize or sometimes forget is that these lighter thoughts and their frequencies have the capacity to penetrate the heavier thoughts of our lower minds. With this awareness and some practice, we can develop some maneuvering room with regard to the denser, lower levels of our human experience.

If our level of consciousness resides primarily at the level of lower mind and we've not yet developed this bridge to higher mind, pain or discomfort in our physical body will trigger our thoughts to naturally gravitate, perhaps literally feel "dragged down," toward the pain and become riveted on what it might mean. We respond similarly if our movements become limited in any significant way, and/or something triggers an emotional response like shame, guilt, or anger. Will it last forever? Did we do something wrong to deserve this? Is another person to blame? These thoughts in turn generate more lower-level thinking and feelings, and will likely also make whatever hurts worse. (We're on the destructive side of Hawkins' bridging "200.") We will relate this dynamic to empaths more specifically later.

If, on the other hand, one has developed higher mind capabilities to some degree, along with a bridge to the lower mind—by applying oneself actively to self-reflection, a process supported by insight-oriented psychotherapy, or meditation—one may be better able to observe that distress on the level or levels involved, doing so with compassion while engaging higher level thoughts of love, memories of joy, and questions regarding the purpose or meaning of the difficulty. Infusing our distress and discomfort with this kind of loving attention and compassion often transforms an illness or stressful situation for the greater good.

While it may seem simple to read this, I realize that putting this approach into practice may prove difficult. I find the reason for this difficulty involves the Inner Critic, an aspect of our subconscious thinking patterns that often runs the show from behind the scenes. We might liken this phenomenon to driving from Point A to Point B in an inner city where traffic is congested, with all traffic lights turning red when we're in a hurry. The timing of our arrival at our destination is completely dependent upon the flow of the lights and traffic. We rarely stop to consider who engineered how the changing lights relate to one another to create or impede traffic flow. That engineer is like the Inner Critic, its presence hidden but real, and its agenda completely different from our own.

We have much to explore in Chapter 9 about the Inner Critic and its relationship to the emotional levels of human experience. At this point, however, it makes sense to note that our thoughts, especially the word components of them, are learned. Parents, siblings, extended family, and the larger community—often in the form of church and school—teach us the words, their meanings, and their relative importance, along with attitudes about those words and the experiences they describe. Consequently, the physical sensations of the body, the trouble we may get into with our actions, the emotions that naturally arise in response to those experiences and other social situations, are given words and value by those who teach us. They interpret our experiences for us, and if those interpretations are not accurate we are left with an internal rift.

Fortunately, as we grow and if we are so inclined, we can learn about the thoughts and values of others, re-evaluate our own, and engage life with newly developed interpretations. Still, the energetic encoding of the original interpretations must be dealt with. We will expand this concept later in this and the next several chapters. Before doing so, however, we need to appreciate the last level of this model, the Soul.

The Soul: In the process of attending to the physical, emotional, energetic, and belief-based challenges of our lives, many of us encounter a sense of Mystery, for some the dreaded Unknown.

Some people deal with the uncertainty of life by trying to make it certain, and they use every avenue at their disposal to maintain and strengthen that illusory certainty. Others sense the uncertain aspects of the Unknown and can only temporarily hang on to an illusory certainty, so that they appear to waffle back and forth in ambivalence. If we choose to face the Unknown squarely, rather than try to define it or avoid it, we may find the inner space and desire to ponder deeper questions, such as: Where do I come from? Why am I here? What is the purpose of my life? What will happen to me when physical life ends?

To wonder about such questions, to explore possibilities with an open mind, and to wait patiently for answers that may never come—at least not to the lower mind—marks a different kind of relationship with the Unknown. These wonderings and how we choose to embrace them, or not, become part of our spirituality, conscious or unconscious. When unconscious, that is, living from the perspective of our lower mind, we may feel mercilessly driven by some unknown Force, or subject to the whimsy of Fate. When conscious and accessing our higher mind, we must still live with Mystery, much as Psyche does in the myth, *Cupid and Psyche*.[87] Cupid, the God of Love, embraces her in the darkness of night, but insists she not gaze upon him in the light. The plot unfolds as a consequence of her need to see, to know who he truly is. As we may recall, *psyche* means "soul." How can we even begin to appreciate the subtleties of Love and Soul when they meet in the darkness, in this mysterious Unknown of our own being?

---

[87] Hamilton, *Mythology*, 92–100.

THE HOLISTIC HUMAN BEING

In his book, *God Is a Verb*,[88] Rabbi David Cooper draws upon the wisdom of Kabbalah to describe five aspects of the soul so as to help us better understand its subtle yet powerful importance in our life. (Figure 7-1) With appreciation for the Kabbalistic perspective that the Divine emanates into our consciousness as *Endless Light*, we must have/be a vessel to receive that Light: that vessel is the soul. At the level of *Yehidah*, our souls receive and merge with the Light. We are wedded as One without the dualistic consciousness required to notice this merger. In other words, there is no "I/Thou."

At the next level, *Chayah*, our souls have begun the incarnating process with some separation. With the emergence of dualistic consciousness, our soul can perceive this sacred merger while still engaging as an active participant in the "wedding." Mystics readily attain this level of consciousness, but the latent mystic in each of us may experience it in those moments when beauty overtakes us with awe. At those times we feel at one with the *All* while still somewhat aware of our separate self. The next aspect of the soul, *Neshama*, holds our purest character. This part of us knows our purpose in this lifetime and serves as the repository for our guiding dreams. Jung spoke of this level as the Higher Self. These upper three levels, *Yehidah*, *Chayah*, and *Neshama* remain forever pure and are never traumatized or wounded. They are never "muddied by life."

In contrast, the next level, *Ruach*, is the aspect of soul that penetrates our personalities, our lower mind thoughts, emotions, and behavior. *Ruach* and the next level, *Nefesh*, which soulfully penetrates our body, can be wounded by life. With or without injury, this understanding helps us appreciate that even the cells of our toes are ensouled, and

---

[88] Rabbi David A. Cooper, *God Is a Verb: Kabbalah and the Practice of Mystical Judaism* (New York, NY: Riverhead Books, 1997), 95–106.

that because of *Nefesh* our bodies serve as "temples of the Holy Spirit" as described in the Christian tradition, or as husks housing "holy sparks"[89] in Kabbalah. When our bodies, temples, or husks are wounded, however (often in conjunction with a wounded *Ruach*), the soulful aspects of both levels—our body and personality—may be forgotten by our everyday consciousness, which becomes consumed with the awareness of pain. In our holistic model, we see that this especially applies if our consciousness remains bound by a lower mind perspective.

Mystics describe the soul as eternal, beautiful, compassionate, merciful, discerning, wise, aware of the purpose of our birth, very loving, gifted with free will, and wedded to the divine. At the highest three levels of our souls, each of us participates in an amazing experience of unity, love and wisdom. *Yehidah*, *Chayah*, and *Neshama* live in perfect bliss. But what of *Ruach* and *Nefesh* which must struggle with the day-to-day challenges of living on a dualistic planet in which misunderstandings abide, even between those we love? In which accidents happen? And worse, when we encounter those who seem to thrill on their separateness and the unloving use of power against us? These questions may bring us back to a more fundamental exploration: why have we incarnated on earth?

If we are here to have an experience that will ultimately imprint on our souls, what kind of experience would we choose? Most of us do not realize we have a choice. Choice requires awareness. In the Kabbalistic tradition, when the five aspects of our soul begin to align and connect consciously within us, healing then becomes available to the wounded aspects of our body and personality. Because our

---

[89] Ibid., 28–29.

soul lives in eternity, it can be forever patient. Because it merges with the Divine, separation does not exist. Because Love resides in the highest levels of the soul, no mistake or crime is unforgivable. Who would not want access to this kind of consciousness? So, why is it so hard to come by?

While I want to be clear that I do not have ultimate answers to these questions, I would like to offer some thoughts for consideration and reflection. The key word that comes to me wherever I search is "consciousness." Mystics have indicated that the soul is the source of higher consciousness within. This concurs with the descriptions of soul offered by Rabbi Cooper. So how do we become more conscious? Again, mystical writers of various traditions agree that to some degree we must expend effort. We must be willing to ask questions, attend to those questions with intention, and wait. The other ingredient is what many refer to as Grace, a gift that comes from somewhere beyond the known realm, in its own time, in its own way. In other words, we can't control, predict, or define it. This brings us back to our relationship with Mystery.

If Grace comes from Mystery, do we dance with it lovingly and with trust, or do we run? In the course of my work I have discovered that part of the answer to this question involves our response to language. Often words carry a power we do not recognize until they "buzz" the psyche with discomfort. Changing the word sometimes changes our response. For example, the words "uncertainty," "unknown," and "mystery" may suggest different associations and feelings for each of us. One person might choose to avoid one of those words and the associated experiences based on their childhood conditioning, whereas another of those words, though similar in meaning, might inspire that same person to respond with openness and wonder. Finding the most comfortable word to make "uncertainty," "the unknown," or "mystery" more accessible also allows for greater openness to moments of Grace.

Additionally, noticing one's own responses to these words from a higher mind perspective invites further exploration and greater self-awareness. The soul's Consciousness includes self-knowledge. Expressed differently, the soul longs to love and connect with all aspects of itself through the totality of our humanness as it penetrates every layer of our human experience. This becomes especially important once we realize that our physical body, how it acts in the world, the feeling-toned messages we receive about the world and our place in it, and how we interpret the whole of it, all serve as vessels for the expression of the soul on this plane. In other words, our soul needs our body and our personality, despite all their imperfections, for this incarnation. In turn, these aspects of our human experience leave imprints upon the soul. If these imprints involve wounds, they need access to the healing love of the soul's three higher levels. Thus, choosing to align *Nefesh* and *Ruach* with our soul's full consciousness marks our path for healing, and impacts the quality of our soul's journey during this lifetime. In this process we learn to recognize the soul's guidance as it speaks to us through the intuition and longing of the heart.

The Holistic Model and Healing

We will expand upon this preliminary description of our beautiful, mysterious soul in later chapters. Meanwhile, I invite us to more specifically consider how our personality gets wounded and how we respond to those wounds. At root cause, wounding comes by virtue of being human and being born into duality, as we shall see. We will also appreciate the good news that healing is available to us on many levels. Perhaps without realizing it, we tend to base our choice of healers and healing methods on the model's level or levels impacted by the wound, as well as on our awareness regarding the source of what hurts us. Use of this holistic model can help us better appreciate which therapeutic approaches to pursue when we find ourselves in need of professional assistance.

Simplistically stated, we know to seek the expertise of chiropractors to align the bones, joints, and nerves of our body; of massage therapists to relax the knots in tense muscles; of physical therapists to assist the body to move with less pain and to restore function when possible; of family doctors to oversee medical care for the body, limitations in its movement, and/or our emotions; of mental health professionals whose diagnoses address dysfunctions of behavior, emotions, and lower mind cognition; of pastoral counselors who work within the realm of mental health, while inviting access to higher mind and soul; and of priests, rabbis, and ministers of religious congregations, who attend to our ego–soul relationship as well as our relationship with the Divine. While this model is holistic and we are whole beings, our healing methods seem to serve us in a piecemeal fashion. Additionally, this model does not specifically name energy as a part of it, simply because energy comprises *all* of it. Working with our energies holistically attends to all the levels at once.

While the contents of this chapter apply to all of us, not just empaths, the particular implications for empaths will be addressed as we proceed. At the conclusion of Part I, we have identified the basics of the empathic experience: the neurology, the energy correlations, and a holistic model for the levels of human consciousness. We have seen how the heart at the center of our energy field is naturally resilient in all these contexts, unless a deep or chronic wound creates a blockage in its healing function. Now that we understand these essentials we can proceed to Part II, where we first explore what wounds us in relationship to other people, and subsequently becomes fixated within the psyche. Having identified what hurts us, we can then address what heals. To mend a broken heart, we must embrace the tender heart, whereby we come to appreciate, draw upon, and cultivate one of its primary healing qualities: compassion.

PART
II

The Compassionate Heart

Healing

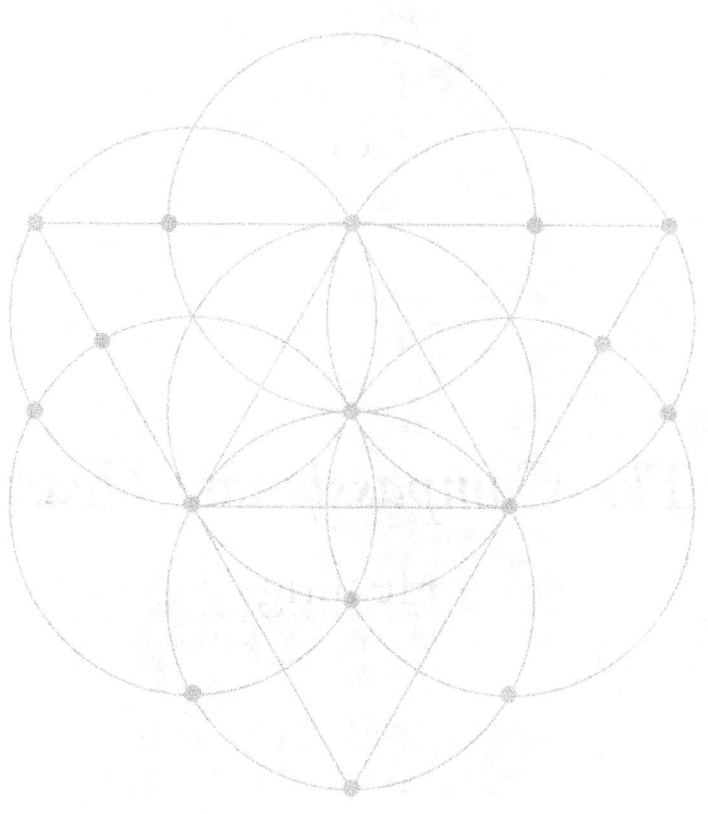

CHAPTER 8

Child Development and Empathy

NOW THAT WE HAVE A BASIC understanding of the neurological, energetic, and holistic building blocks that make us who we are as human beings, we will explore how the human psyche responds to the developmental challenges of life. While this chapter specifically references the work of Erik Erikson and his Stages of Psychosocial Development, it is important to note that energies and events impact us prior to physical birth as separate human beings on Earth. The neurons of our nervous systems are wordlessly proliferating and connecting in the context of sensory experience in the womb. The work of Stanislav Grof[90] has also highlighted the impact of the birth experience itself upon the development of our psyche and the way we later interpret our life experiences. If we dare to layer in factors of our soul's intention, past lives and karma,

---

[90] Stanislav Grof, M.D., *Beyond the Brain: Birth, Death and Transcendence in Psychotherapy* (Albany, NY: State University of New York Press, 1985).

the complexity obviously increases. In any case, the beauty of our human experience incorporates all these layers in consistent themes. A focus on Erikson's work will offer reflections to help us better understand an empath's development, even in the absence of other equally interesting and valuable information.

By exploring Erikson's Stages of Psychosocial Development, we will better appreciate the wonder of our evolving consciousness as we grow. I have given significantly more emphasis to the first three stages, simply because they provide such an important foundation for all the stages that follow. Those aspects specifically impacting an empathic child's development will receive highlighted attention. This review correlates these psychological aspects with the development of the human brain, the energy pathways, and the holistic model already discussed. We will also better understand Lily's struggles in negotiating a response to her peers on the playground. By integrating all this information we will gain deeper insights into the strengths, challenges, struggles, and sometimes ineffective solutions and resolutions that empaths tend to develop in order to cope with life.

Erikson's Stages of Psychosocial Development

Our human journey on Earth as a separate psychosocial entity begins with birth. Prior to this amazing event, mystics tell us that after the soul has decided to incarnate, it penetrates or descends through all the progressive levels of energetic density to enter and guide the formation of the baby's body. During delivery, Triple Warmer surrounds the baby with a Vivaxis,[91] a protective energetic field that assists with the transition between the electromagnetic polarity of the

---

[91] Eden with Feinstein, *Energy Medicine*, 330–333.

mother's body and the child's adaptation to that of Earth. Even after birth the baby's neurological system is still forming, yet is capable of sustaining life through heartbeat, breathing, and sucking on its own (or with the assistance of machinery in the Neonatal Intensive Care Unit). The infant's sensory system takes in information and encodes it as experience, though it is not yet able to discern the difference between inner and outer reality. Later the baby's nerves direct the muscles more intentionally to move and respond. Feelings cry out from the first breath, but words for those feelings come later. Let's now explore this "becoming" in greater detail.

Stage 1 – Trust vs. Mistrust: During this phase, lasting from birth to two years, the baby's brain and nerve cells have yet to be fully myelinated (wrapped in a protective coating, like the rubber surrounding an electrical cord). Without myelin, nerve signals do not get from Point A to Point B quickly or at all, and the neonate cannot sit up or control arm movements. These basic inabilities render the baby totally dependent upon the love and care of a parent or other adult. Still, the lights, sounds, tastes, and comforts of hugs, feedings, swaddling, and diaper changes register somewhere deep in the baby's brain. Triple Warmer's encoding of experiences as "normal," or the way things are, also begins deep in the brainstem: the anatomical territory of the Vagus Nerve nuclei, not far from the energetic Power Point on the surface of the body, just below the base of the skull. (Figure 8-1) The Power Point taps into many energy systems, including Governing Meridian and other Radiant Circuits, all of which support our stability and thriving.

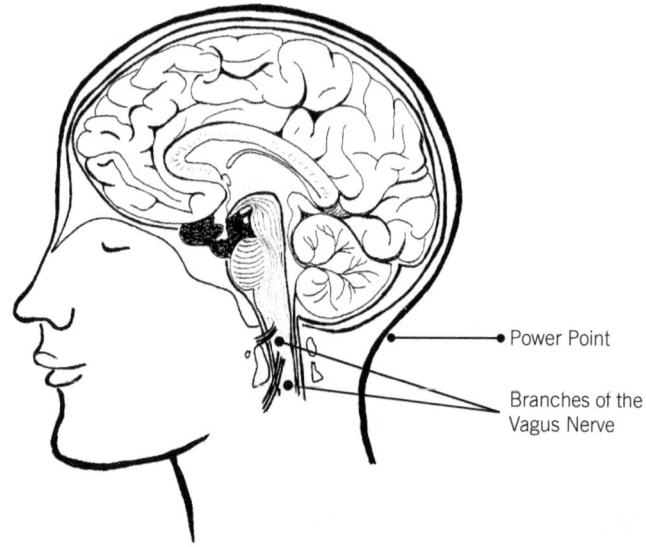

Figure 8-1: The Power Point and Its Proximity to the Vagus Nerve

The Vagus Nerve provides messages about hunger, satiety, bowel and bladder fullness, heart rate, alternating actions of breathing and sucking, and burping, the looks on people's faces, the tones of their voices, and environmental stimuli. Sensory nerves additionally receive information regarding sights, sounds, tastes, temperature, wetness and dryness on the skin, and the pressure of hugs and clothing. Unavoidable moments of stress and discomfort will arise. The real question: will they be followed by soothing and comfort?

Triple Warmer and the baby's nervous system encode the answer to this question as "normal," no matter what it is. From the perspective of the Polyvagal Theory,[92] at this point in a neonate's neurological development the unmyelinated Dorsal Motor Nucleus of the Vagus

---

[92] Stephen Porges, Ph.D., "The Early Development of the Autonomic Nervous System Provides a Neural Platform for Social Behavior," in *The Polyvagal Theory*, 128.

can ingest and process food. The Sympathetic Nervous System has developed well enough to trigger a stress response in the absence of food. Yet the self-soothing and socially engaging capacities of the vagal Nucleus Ambiguus have not developed fully, mostly because the nerve has not yet been fully myelinated. This myelination will continue into the first year of life, so the response of caregivers becomes crucial for what the child's brainstem and energy encodes about the as yet undifferentiated self/world. If caregivers respond to the baby's needs and provide relief, the baby's brain will record this as basic reality. The baby learns to *trust* that the world is safe and that love is reliable—my description, not that of the infant, who at this point has no capability for words.

What if no one responds to the baby's cries, as experienced by some of the foster children with whom I've worked? Or perhaps the response will be anger, yelling, rough handling or physical abuse. Maybe sometimes somebody responds and sometimes no one does. The infant then learns to *trust* that reliable support for their survival or comfort does not exist. The degree of deprivation determines the degree of *mistrust* instilled energetically and neurologically. The Sympathetic Nervous System develops and responds to the natural, as well as extreme levels of stress. The Parasympathetic Nervous System—responsible for our essential "rest and restore" function, and in which the Vagus Nerve plays a significant role with regard to later social engagement—becomes particularly compromised during such *mistrust* experiences.

Those familiar with Attachment Theory will recognize that when an infant is deeply wounded by poor or inconsistent caregiving, the degree of *trust that the world will ignore or hurt her* profoundly affects that infant's ability to bond with any subsequent caring adults. This child's ability to self-soothe is negatively impacted as well. Triple Warmer encodes these now biologically imprinted developments and maintains them as habits. Triple Warmer does not provide global abstract assessments of worthiness at this level: it responds to what is. This individual will expect deprivation no matter how much abundance comes her way so long as the habitual Triple Warmer imprinting holds power. Current theories regarding Attachment Disorder might benefit from exploring the energetic component that holds destructive, albeit unconscious, beliefs and behavioral responses in place. The possibility exists that working with Triple Warmer in these situations may release its grip on destructive coping patterns and make way for a child's more effective, eventually *trusting* response to healing interventions.

For empaths whose sensitivity reacts strongly to environmental stimuli, and whose Vagus Nerve responds to the body's internal reactions to those stimuli, their caregivers may be more than adequate, yet their level of stress and need for soothing may seem excessive in comparison to less empathic siblings. Parents of empaths have to make more effort to soothe their little ones, especially if their life is more chaotic, stimulating, and stressful. This often occurs when older siblings need to draw upon their parents' attention as well, perhaps requiring help with school-related projects or transportation to sports activities, for example. Their empath child may react to these factors with more crying, difficulty sleeping, and increased needs for soothing as compared to other children. Unfortunately, in our world the empath child is often identified, perhaps diagnosed, as the one with the problem. Instead, parents have the option of accepting the invitation to slow down and simplify their lives. They might consider decreasing the amount of stimulation if possible, and more importantly, make efforts to decrease their own stress levels. Their empath children will derive significant benefit from these interventions alone.

Stage 2 – Autonomy vs. Shame and Doubt: During this stage (from two to four years of age), a toddler's nervous system has already accomplished enough myelination along the nerve axons and pathways to allow her to smile socially, hold a bottle or spoon, sit up, and crawl. Most children are walking at this point, which is pivotal for the exploration of their world and the natural experience of separation and reunion with their caregiving adult. At this stage, the toddler begins to appreciate language. They recognize their names, call their parents, and express some of their needs with words. They appreciate the difference between "yes" and "no," and most importantly, begin to recognize themselves as persons distinct from their parents. This recognition marks the onset of ego development, that sense of oneself as a singular entity on the planet. That sense of separateness carries with it the beginnings of exhilarating power—walking, talking, going where one wants, exploring what evokes curiosity—as well as potentially crushing vulnerability. With the budding awareness of separateness comes the painful recognition that one is not always safe. Even the successfully trusting child of Stage 1 must deal with this next hurdle of consciousness.

Besides risking that walking at the top of the stairs can lead to a tumble, or that electric sockets do spark when poked with sharp objects, or that stoves burn, or that scissors cut, a toddler has to deal with her caregiver's reactions to her experience of exhilaration and vulnerability. The socialization aspects of the Vagus Nerve become prominent at this point, as do timely lessons about the relative safety of separation and exploration. The amygdala tracks the child's experiences as safe or dangerous, enhancing its reactivity to dangerous stimuli to avoid the same negative consequence in the future. This response of the amygdala relates to the caregiver's response as well: the interactions between caregiver and child at this time serve as crucial elements for the development of self-worth, revolving around what Attachment theorists refer to as "Separation and Repair."

For example, if a child breaks free of a caregiver's grasp and makes a move to run into a busy street, any caring adult will respond with a panicky, loud, facially expressive, and emphatic "NO!" The toddler, who has no clue that busy traffic could lead to trauma, injury, or death, only records the emotion, tone of voice, and facial expression of the person yelling at her, none of which feels loving or soothing. Now that the toddler realizes she is separate in the world, these caregiver responses portend disaster, because on some biological level the child recognizes that without the care and love of her parental figure all is lost. She cannot fight; she cannot flee. She freezes in the face of this enormous realization. This is the origin of shame.

Shame, as I've mentioned in previous chapters, exquisitely pains us as an emotional experience. In the work of David Hawkins, M.D., Ph.D., it carries the lowest vibrational factor; he describes it as "perilously proximate to death."[93] We have all had the unfortunate experience of someone yelling at us, berating us, criticizing us, mocking us. It stings emotionally and physically, even when, as adults, logic

---

[93] Hawkins, *Power vs. Force*, 76.

tells us we didn't deserve any of it. Shame is to the ego, or sense of self, what the threat of physical harm or death is to the body. This feeling powerfully delivers the message of potential ego annihilation, and the body responds through the amygdala with all its alarms and defenses. Hopefully, most of us have good enough parents who, after the panicked, love-triggered "NO!" quickly respond with a hug, and then explain how dangerous that behavior was, how much they love us, and how important it is for us to listen to them when they hold our hand in the street. This hug and explanation serve as the reunion after the devastating, shameful separation. Repairing the shame serves as a crucial healing factor if the child is ever to develop and maintain a sense of self-worth, especially when challenged later in life.

But what of the child whose caregivers don't appreciate these dynamics? What if a caregiver responds with a spanking, more yelling, or shunning to "teach them a lesson"? That parenting model of the past involved punishment, with some added humiliation, purported to be the great teacher of life's wisdom. Unfortunately, this sets the foundation for a serious problem affecting generations of children who've since grown into adults and are now parenting their own children. If one asks any child who was spanked, for example, what they learned from the experience, the likely response will be "I don't know." They will not remember what led to the spanking. They will more likely remember who spanked them and that it hurt. They may also remember their "badness," or have developed a rebellious stance in life to cope with such hurtful authority. This is the developmental meaning for this stage in Erikson's model. We either learn that it is safe to explore, experiment, fail sometimes, and succeed often, that life forgives us our errors, and that there's always another day, OR we learn that to explore is dangerous, failure is shameful and, consequently, we doubt our abilities and think it is better not to try. For some, these cautions apply only to certain situations; for others, they pertain to life as a whole.

For the empath, the issue may not relate so much to exploration or risky behavior as to one's internal state and the way it gets released—that is, how one ventures to express emotions. Imagine the toddler experiencing an intangible, internal feeling of "yuck," for example. Remembering that this toddler's experience of exploration is colored by what she has come to trust about life's response to her need for soothing, we can appreciate that she may already have developed a coping mechanism of withdrawal and invisibility. If she has been more fortunate, she may cry as an instinctive attempt to relieve inner distress that she cannot put into words. Or she may protest with a series of "No's!"

If her normally loving caregiver doesn't understand the cause of her distress (it may be an accumulation of excitement over great-tasting ice cream, sensing the caregiver's feelings following an upsetting phone call, exposure to tensions from the news on background TV, or her brother's wailing in the next room), she may be told that her tears or tantrums do not befit her age and that she should, in essence, "grow up." If the caregiver delivers this message harshly and frequently, the progression of "feeling yucky leads to shame" will translate into "when I feel bad, I am bad" in the developing mind of the child—and Triple Warmer will encode this as normal. In such an instance, the child at this stage of development cannot disagree with her caregiver (fight) and maintain a healthy self-esteem; separation (flight) holds devastating consequences; thus, freeze is the only option. As a result, shame associates not only with the feeling of "yuck" but also with freeze. Most of us feel ashamed when we freeze, and we freeze when we're shamed. We can see the pervasive and profound danger incurred for the child's newly developing ego (sense of self) in these moments.

If Triple Warmer encodes these experiences with enough frequency, it will mount a defense with non-stop protection. Triple Warmer and the amygdala will recognize feelings of "yuck" and remember that they were quickly accompanied by feeling shamed and the freeze state. Given the unpredictability for when these "yucky" feelings might arise—likely whenever the environment and/or relationships become over-stimulating or complicated—Triple Warmer will drain energy from other meridians to maintain its hypervigilance and tense muscles for fight or flight. It will stand ready to ward off the anticipated shame that may come once again from the impatient, critical caregiver, or from the child's more generalized expectations that past shaming experiences will recur. When words begin to accompany these internal expectations of shaming, the seed of the Inner Critic insidiously makes its way into the psyche (more about the Inner Critic in Chapter 9). At this point, however, let's appreciate that the words used by the Inner Critic are those of a child who has incorporated what he or she has heard from caregivers. Once this has occurred, the danger of ego annihilation can be perpetuated within the child's own mind whenever a disturbing inner state develops.

Due to Triple Warmer's energetic involvement, as well as that of the Sympathetic Nervous System, the growing child may experience the impact of these systems as chronically tense muscles and over-reactivity in the form of startle responses. Additionally, Triple Warmer will encode expectations that life isn't caring or comforting, along with beliefs that relationships with people, no matter how longed for, will threaten one's psychological existence. Even *if* it were true that some people do need something jolting or punishing from which to learn—and *if* this is so, I would propose that these folks have to be ducks—we can see that this "teaching" via punishment is devastating for an empath. Sponges receive instruction best when it is delivered with kindness. In its absence, their entire energetic and neurological systems are poised for protection, defense and survival. If those protective responses have not proven effective in the past, empaths may more habitually freeze as growth proceeds—appearing compliant. In any case, no learning is possible under these survival-threatened circumstances.

With this understanding of an empath's developmental dynamics and needs, parents and caregivers can better appreciate and respond to the emotional expressions of their children. In my experience, at least one parent of an empath often has these sensitivities. Unfortunately, they have also, almost as frequently, learned that their sensitivity serves them poorly, and want their child to avoid the suffering that they have experienced. Without appreciating the gifts of their own empathic natures, they can only pass on their own shame as they try to mold their young sponge into a duck.

No empath ever feels good about trying to become something she is not. If parents are at all successful in shaping their sponge-child into a duck-wannabe, that success is superficial at best. Beneath that socially acceptable mask the invisible sponge has developed an intrinsic self-hatred, with a lifestyle designed to avoid shame as much as possible and, consequently, to perpetuate it. The Inner Critic gains power, all the while hiding in the shadows. The parent's Inner Critic may also be running the show, guiding the parenting interventions from some unseen place. We need to distinguish this dark place from Mystery, home to the soul, and will do so in Chapter 10 when we discuss the Inner Critic. For now, let us return to Erikson's next stage of developing consciousness.

Stage 3 – Initiative vs. Guilt: This stage, from approximately four to five years of age, correlates with increasing language abilities, capacities for creative expression, and deeper bonding as the child becomes more aware of the self as separate, while recognizing the steadiness of caring adults. Awareness of the difference between boys and girls also becomes more grounded. Children at this age look to the adults in their world to model feminine and masculine behaviors, reinforcing or countering their genetic predispositions for future attraction to a potential mate. From Erikson's perspective, this is the stage when we begin to feel guilty—quite different, psychodynamically, from shame. Shame comes from potential annihilation of the ego: one is berated and diminished in one's own eyes, as well as in the eyes of others. Guilt has to do with potential loss of the love bond with a caring other.

Humans experience these psychosocial stages and their problematic emotions as the natural course of development. Our brains are hardwired to store and respond to information that ultimately seeks to have us survive and thrive. In this context, experiences of shame and guilt serve as messengers of danger: something is wrong in our world, inner or outer, and correction is needed. Unfortunately, when swamped by a tide of painful emotions, few of us can think our way to a solution. Paradoxically, our brains are also hardwired to shut down cortical thinking when the limbic system is flooded: in such situations we are primed to react, not to reflect.

This dynamic served an important function when we lived in the jungle and a lion approached from behind a rock. It still serves us when our dear child wanders into the street and a fast-approaching bus could make contact in less than a minute. We need to suspend thought and act in a split second if we are to save the child. Many more tragedies would occur if we paused to think, to consider our options, to reflect on the risks of acting versus not. Survival needs trump reflective cognition in moments such as these. In fact, they do so in general unless we've become practiced at pausing to notice what is transpiring in our inner and outer worlds even while we're upset. Such people have trained their cortex to stay "tuned in" when the limbic system over-fires, and have actively built neuron-to-neuron connections from the cortex to the limbic system where previously there were few neuronal pathways flowing in that direction.

As children we instinctively and even cognitively know, especially by four and five years of age, that we need our loving caregivers in order to survive. Feelings of guilt tell us that something in that bond has gone awry. Because children are ego-centric—a natural state in our unfolding development that initially places our consciousness squarely at the center of the universe—they quickly interpret any emotional disturbance as related to them, and assume it is their fault. So feelings of guilt usually tell a child she has done something wrong. When appropriately felt in a primary relationship, this helps the child monitor and understand the terms of engagement, ideally honoring the child's needs while teaching her about the caregiver's needs as well. This provides an ideal time to strengthen lessons regarding the respectful use of language, listening to instructions, and preparations for life and love in the larger world. The experience of guilt also plays a longer-term role in developing our ability to form social bonds, so that if we steal or lie or murder we clearly have violated a code of behavior needed for groups of humans to live together in peace.

Thus, while feeling guilt is uncomfortable, it does serve a meaningful purpose that supports our human need to live in community. And like shame, it requires repair: re-establishment of the love bond is essential, and experiences of understanding and forgiveness are usually the key. Developmentally, however, this stage does not always go smoothly and some adults continue to be plagued by inordinate amounts of guilt for seemingly minor reasons that make no sense even to them. This takes place because the love bond has not evolved as the child has grown.

For example, let's imagine a five-year-old standing on the curb, holding his mother's hand. She specifically tells him, "Don't cross the street without holding my hand." If he wiggles free and dashes across the street, she will of course be angry (and perhaps frightened). In this instance, it serves him well to feel guilty, enough at least to never ignore that instruction again. Ideally, he and his mother also hug then cross the street together safely, so the child learns the risks of impulsive living and also that love can be restored. If his mother progressively honors his increasing abilities and maturity as he grows, he can become an independent, loved adult who understands and respects the social boundaries of his community.

We all know this scenario may not transpire in that way, however. If this child has been deeply wounded during his earlier stages of development, resolving this stage's issues may not be possible until the earlier wounds have been addressed and healed. Yet even a child fortunate enough to have negotiated a decent resolution of the previous stages may grow into an adult besieged with inappropriate guilt. This will most likely happen if, in the scenario described above, the child's mother does not make efforts to repair their relational disconnect. She may have learned that emotional shunning or angry words will teach the life-saving lesson, for example, but these strategies only exacerbate the child's sense of separation and loss. Without her efforts to repair their relational bond, elements of guilt will remain unresolved for this child and perhaps move into the unconscious, ready to rise up in any situation where the child-grown-adult anticipates the loss of love.

Even if this child's mother does consistently make efforts to reconnect, but does not honor the growing developmental skills of her child and insists that he remain bonded to her as a five-year-old might, then at ten (when he could cross the street by himself), at twelve (when he could ride his bike to other neighborhoods), at seventeen (when he could drive a car), she may still expect him to metaphorically hold her hand while crossing the street. This kind of "love" bond is crippling, and to achieve independence the child-now-adult has to actively, painfully, choose to leave the loved one behind.

From this stark example, we can readily appreciate how the proper resolution of guilty feelings allows a child to grow and develop confidence in her abilities. She can take initiative without risking a loss of love. This is so critical for the successful negotiation of the next stage. Before we go there, however, let's take a moment to acknowledge the risks of this stage for empaths. Children who sense the inner states of others will feel their parents' fears—even if the parents try to hide them—but without understanding their source. Such children may have difficulty separating from the fearful parent, leaving home to go to school, or participating in sleepovers. They may even have dreams or nightmares reflecting their parent's fears and unconscious conflicts, as noted by Frances Wickes[94] and Edward Whitmont.[95] In situations like this, it behooves parents to address their own emotional needs; often their children then amazingly improve without any direct intervention.

We have alluded to the fact that each of Erikson's Stages of Psychosocial Development requires successful resolution for the next stage to unfold at its best. Without it, the wounds of the earlier stage move forward and accumulate more woundedness, resulting in an inaccurate perception of self, poorly adaptive behaviors, and emotional reactions that interfere with enjoyment of life and engagement in fulfilling relationships. I have elaborated quite a bit upon these first three stages for this reason.

Recognizing that "a sponge is always a sponge," we can appreciate that empaths will challenge their caregivers from the very beginning and require significant understanding if they are to flourish in the midst of life's unavoidable difficulties. Caregivers can be the most well-meaning and highly informed individuals, yet life throws curve balls with abounding deviations from the ideal. We will consider the possible deeper purpose of this in Part III, but for now let's consider the immediate impact of these developmental stages upon the empath.

---

[94] Frances G. Wickes, "Chapter 2: Influence of Parental Difficulties upon the Unconscious of the Child," in *The Inner World of Childhood: A Study in Analytical Psychology* (New York, NY: Signet Books, 1966), 42.

[95] Edward C. Whitmont, *The Symbolic Quest: Basic Concepts of Analytical Psychology* (Princeton, NJ: Princeton University Press, 1969), 274.

Sensing the inner experiences of others can weigh heavily upon an empathic child's developing sense of self. Without someone helping empaths to understand themselves and teaching them how to "clean out their sponge," the accumulation of mistrust, shame, and guilt can lead to pervasive experiences of fearfulness, unworthiness, and feeling unlovable and unloving—no matter how caring and compassionate they actually may be. Often empathic children quickly catch on that something is wrong with them, and that the face they need to display for the world is not their own. These experiences and assumptions profoundly affect how the remaining stages will unfold. The good news, however, is that healing can occur at any moment over the course of a lifetime.

I describe the remaining stages in less detail, simply because the variations expand exponentially. My intention is to provide enough information to demonstrate the complexities of an empath's possible journey through life.

Stage 4 – Industry vs. Inferiority: This stage, which occurs during the elementary school years, ages five to twelve, invites the child to work on her own behalf so as to promote learning and the satisfaction of social success. The ego has more fully developed, and a clearer sense of self has been established. Children at this age begin to appreciate the concept of death and that they too may die someday. They also realize that, while family remains central in their life, they live in a larger world where friends become progressively more important. Activities such as sports, music, and art may tap into natural talents that can be developed during this time, facilitating a more solid sense of self as they recognize their ability to master a challenge and contribute meaningfully to a larger community.

Unfortunately, our culture supports academics and sports more than the creative arts. Consequently, those children whose gifts lie in these creative fields may not have opportunities to recognize and appreciate their talents. Even if empaths have had difficulty negotiating the earlier stages and learned to become invisible to some degree, they can blossom in narrow ways by discovering abilities that support their mask while also giving them personal satisfaction. Creative arts in particular may allow expression of the authenticity hidden beneath the mask. When witnessed by someone who understands and does not judge, empaths may learn how to better appreciate their sponge-like nature, clean out what does not belong, and heal.

Stage 5 – Identity vs. Role Confusion: This stage incorporates the teen years, during which the child transitions to adulthood with all the confusion this process entails. Somehow the naive freshman in high school grows into the nineteen-year-old who might go to college, be drafted for war, get pregnant, or already have one or more children to parent. This is also a time of questioning what was taught in religion classes, if the child was exposed to spirituality at all, and coming to terms with oneself as not only separate from others, but responsible for how one's life will unfold. Relationships with parents and caregivers change; relationships with peers take priority. If one has been negotiating life from behind a mask, feeling intrinsically invisible, and hiding deep feelings of fear, shame, guilt, and inadequacy, this will prove to be a very difficult time indeed. On a positive note, if empathic teenagers are able to courageously thrust themselves into the difficulties of living life, they may meet an adult who validates their uniqueness and introduces them to possibilities beyond the scope of their familial dynamics. Again, healing may happen.

Stage 6 – Intimacy vs. Isolation: During this stage, lasting through the twenties and thirties, making one's way in the world becomes the priority. This not only involves finding financially sustainable work, but sharing intimately with others as friend, lover, or spouse. To be negotiated well, this level of intimacy requires a willingness to take off the mask and let another soul see one's deepest core. If doing so is too daunting, some choose never to marry; others do marry, only to discover the ineffectiveness of the mask. If the partner can love deeply what is revealed, healing may happen. If the partner reacts with critical surprise to what is discovered, divorce and/or separation may follow. These painful experiences further justify, for some, their unworthiness and inability to be loved. For others, they trigger and fuel the process of self-discovery and growth. If this latter path is chosen, it becomes an opportunity once again to identify and appreciate one's sponge-like nature, clean out the mud, remove the mask, and learn how to shine as one's authentic, sensitive self into one's remaining years.

Stage 7 – Generativity vs. Stagnation: This stage begins at mid-life and extends to sixty-five, what used to be considered the traditional age of retirement. At this point, we recognize that the peak of life is behind us, and the years now count more than ever if we are to figure out why we were born and live that purpose to the full. Often the talents and skills developed earlier serve us well in this quest, while new ones—those dreams unlived or gifts unexplored—may take center stage. This is a time for considering how we will age, if we dare consider that directly. Some put on more masks and gear their lives toward the pursuit of eternal youth. Others recognize that they have been accumulating wisdom and that now is an ideal time to share that wisdom with those who have an interest and will take it to heart.

Stage 8 – Ego Integrity vs. Despair: My mother-in-law used to joke, "Old age is not for wimps!" She often coupled this with the advice, "Don't get old!" as if she or I had some choice in the matter. She marched forward gracefully and passionately despite her advice, and continued to play a meaningful role in the lives of her loved ones as well as in her community. Seeing her and my parents successfully negotiate this final stage of life has taught me that this process truly requires courage, patience, endurance, trust, and deep love. With those gifts, the rewards of reflecting upon a life lived fully can bring peace to one's eventual transition. Without those gifts, life becomes drudgery, with death both feared and longed for. Some measure of healing can still happen at this final stage, although how much better for it to have been happening all along.

A Step toward Integration

We now turn our attention back to Lily, both as a seven-year-old and as an adult. At seven she had already learned many things, mostly unconscious, about how the world, and the caregivers and authority figures in her life, respond to physical and emotional needs and behaviors. While her parents attended to her basic needs and more, as an empath she also felt their unresolved emotional and psychological issues weigh upon her. She sensed that she had to take care of them in some way, though to a young child that kind of task proved daunting and impossible most of the time. She knew that her urge to explore and experience independence often led to trouble, especially with her mother, as her adventures were usually followed by the constriction of time-outs. She knew that as she sought escape from the internal pressure of all this, without understanding its source, she risked her mother's disapproval and the perceived loss of her love. Consequently, Lily learned to live in an emotional box. At seven, these lessons and coping patterns were firmly entrenched: when the scene unfolded with her peers, she had already been primed to freeze.

By the time Lily became a professionally and relationally successful adult, at least in the world's eyes, she had learned to divert her body's signals of disruption into sports. She had also learned to ignore the more sensitive side of her nature, the side that could appreciate her own needs. She actively engaged in life with an unconscious mission to avoid shaming experiences. She declined most offers for female friendship and struggled with ongoing loyalty issues, as these related to her bond with her mother, which, notably, had been forged on her mother's terms. This bond dictated that, even as a grown woman, Lily could not trust that her instincts, her desire for freedom and exploration, and her sensitivity to the unresolved emotional needs of others held validity and that the terms of relationship could be renegotiated on her own behalf. Something within her held these childhood loyalties and beliefs about herself and the others in her world with a lion's grip. What was that "something"? We now turn our attention to the Inner Critic.

CHAPTER 9

The Inner Critic and the Broken Heart

WE CONCLUDED THE LAST CHAPTER by asking how Lily might renegotiate the terms of relating to others as an adult. Before addressing her situation, I would like to digress with some reflections based upon my own experience. Having struggled with my own intensely critical inner voice for years while depression loomed large in my psyche, I have given this seemingly powerful character much attention, both negative and positive, in the course of my life.

When I finally came to recognize this elusive aspect of myself, it had a masculine voice. I have since discovered that for some the voice is feminine, whereas others associate no gender with their Inner Critic. The gender associated with our Inner Critic comes from many possible sources and, ultimately, doesn't matter. What does matter is that we recognize our critical inner voice for what it is, what it does, and why it does it.

First, let's consider these questions from a broader perspective. When does analysis slide into criticism? When does discernment slip into judgment? What criteria define the midpoints of these slippery slopes? One ingredient involves valuing: is one thing or person better or worse than another? Whose agenda distinguishes the good from the bad? Analysis assesses what *is* by sorting out the details, while discernment identifies the path to which these details may lead. Criticism in the arts may take a respectful or derogatory tone. Judgment in a court of law is supposed to serve justice. In the practical world of the day-to-day, however, we more frequently experience criticism in its devaluing mode. When we describe someone as "judgmental," we imply that they place high value on certain ideals related to a person, situation or thing and find that person, situation or thing lacking—thus justifying their disapproval.

These qualities differ significantly from humility, a quality of the heart, which also acknowledges what *is*, but with love. Humble people accept themselves as they are, embracing all their strengths and weaknesses, gifts and vulnerabilities. Humble people discern well, but do not judge others with hostility or condescension. According to these descriptions, the critical inner voice seems quite divergent from humility and the heart.

Additionally, the critical inner voice can aim its fire in two directions. For some people, the Inner Critic habitually directs critical judgements outward, blaming and sometimes decimating others as the cause of their internal discomfort. In the extreme, this tendency combines fear of humiliation with pride so as to protect the bearer from the distress caused by *any* criticism, including the self-generated kind.

Jonathan Goldman has described pride as an imbalanced sixth chakra energy[96] that isolates the prideful person from others to ensure their protection. Unfortunately, it also deprives the prideful person of the opportunity to look within and identify what needs healing attention—one's broken heart. Pride compensates for shame by shaming others. It, and the people who rely upon it, spark wars, aggression, and violations of every kind. Tragically, people who primarily direct the activities of their Inner Critic outward do not consciously hurt within and, therefore, do not feel any compelling need to heal, nor any sensitivity to their disparaging impact on others.

In contrast, those who have suffered their Inner Critic's harshness toward the self are primed to heal once they no longer believe that they deserve these criticisms. They are also more sensitive to the impact of their own critical judgments toward others. With this in mind, I address this chapter to those individuals whose Inner Critics turn inward. While I refer to my own Inner Critic as "he" in this section, the reader may feel free to substitute the most appropriate pronoun for personal use and healing. Howsoever we perceive it, we must give appropriate attention to the critical voice within because, when not recognized, it directs the unconscious assumptions and conscious decisions we make every day, every minute, of our life. Because its interventions become ineffective as well as destructive over time, empaths—all of us really—need to recognize the Inner Critic and its energetically encoded, habitual, and misguided attempts to help us so that we may redeem the soulful treasures within.

---

[96] Goldman, *Gift of the Body,* 433–435.

The Inner Critic

Having never met a person who denied they have an Inner Critic, I am left with the question: Where does the Inner Critic come from? Why would an inner voice agree to so much self-criticism? To so much self-loathing? To decisions that ignore one's basic needs? For what purpose would this Critic accuse one of cruelty toward others for acts as simple as saying "no" to an off-the-wall request? Why would that inner voice reproach one for being fat, or ugly, or selfish, or heartless, when none of that is really true? Anorexics think they are obese and eat less to keep the Critic at bay. Beautiful models struggle with not feeling pretty and have one more surgery or facial to cover their self-perceived flaws. Kind-hearted souls give away their resources on a regular basis even though they need them, all to avoid the Inner Critic's comments about being self-centered. Parents give in to their child's extreme requests lest they have to listen to their child's screams, matched by their own inner voice telling them how mean and insensitive they are. How does this come about?

The Development of the Inner Critic

I do not think we are born with this Critic, but I do think we have neurological receptors and energetic pathways that encode our experiences with criticism. We have discussed the Vagus Nerve and its ability to perceive safety and danger: no matter what the intention behind it, criticism always feels dangerous to some degree. The amygdala recognizes the repetition of this experience and intensifies its response with each reactivation. The hypothalamus sets off the hormonal and nervous system alarms to prime the body for fight, flight, or freeze. The insula's bridge succumbs to the weight of the conflict between what the body and limbic system perceive as necessary for survival, and what the cortex (lower mind) has learned to think about those needs. In the midst of such harshness, where, oh where, is the "voice of reason"?

As noted, the insula is perfectly positioned on each side of the brain to transfer information between our limbic emotions as messengers and our cortical thinking response. A meaningful exchange can occur, as in the following example: if during my childhood an experience feels overwhelming and equates to a synthesized "yuck" physically and emotionally, my brain has to make some sense of it. If my mother explains she is having a bad day or a difficult time (without burdening me with serving as her confidante), that her feelings are not mine, nor are they my fault, that she will be okay, and the best thing I can do is go out and play, and let her have some space, I may still feel for her, but I can also feel I am helping her by following her request. At the very least my cortex learns that my feeling of "yuck" came from somewhere outside me and is not my fault.

If, on the other hand, my mother does not explain any of this, but instead berates me for crying or not wanting to go outside (maybe because I sense that she needs me on some level), my cortex deduces that I am now in trouble for the yucky feeling AND I must have deserved this criticism. If I am to avoid future repetitions of this experience, I had better stay on top of the "yuck" when it arises. I had better find a way to release it if I can, or bury it if I can't. The disengagement of the insula—the collapse of the bridge—helps with the latter option.

The insula shuts down and I ignore my body. I lose track of what it wants or needs and how it feels. This is the brain's last ditch effort to keep the tension within me manageable, the equivalent of putting the enemy out of commission so one no longer needs to engage in conflict. It gives supremacy to what the world expects of me, so as to maintain a compromised harmony. This form of dissociation often goes unnoticed unless it becomes severe. Needless to say, depression follows, since one's essential physical and emotional nature has gone down under.

The Inner Critic develops in the midst of situations such as this; it sides with the outer world to help us fit in. It takes on the injunctions of our caregivers, perhaps affecting whether the Critic's voice is predominantly male or female. In my own case, I think the voice reflected my mother's inner masculine critic, derived from her father. I suspect that when his own mother died suddenly when he was twelve, he learned quickly that some measure of control matters. My mother, in her love for her father, unconsciously absorbed his insistence on the rightness and wrongness of things. The Critic's gender then can vary, and perhaps reflects how this voice has an ancestral quality that transcends actual connection with individuals in space and time. In any case, its power, whatever its roots, grows with each perceived criticism.

Personal Reflections

For an empath, these criticisms need not come exclusively through another's verbal or facial expression. They may be felt as the inner experience of the "other," not caused by or even related to the empath herself. Admittedly, this scenario is especially difficult to identify and address. Fortunately, life also offers some buffers, and many empaths can identify at least one person who helped them greatly during their formative years.

THE INNER CRITIC AND THE BROKEN HEART

I know my maternal grandmother served as that buffer for me, such that I felt "seen" by her with all my sensitivities, and understood for my reactions and needs. I remember that when peers teased me for being overweight she said I was "pleasingly plump." I didn't know what that meant really: I only knew that she smiled and loved me while she said it, making it and me "okay." After she died when I was six, I lost her kind transformation of the Critic's voice; after her death, he became progressively more severe and powerful…

Every time someone scowled at, criticized, or corrected me, my Inner Critic gained power. He somehow knew these things were going to happen and became more righteous with each instance. I began to trust him as my solid ground, my inner strength, my "go-to" to avoid disaster. And if I weren't so lucky, he would just get stronger for having been right when I didn't listen. I felt kicked from behind to produce, to study, to achieve, to please, so I decided to work even harder to avoid the kick. I got straight A's and won scholarships, all of which pleased my dad. In social situations, I smiled the way my mom had taught me. I imagined myself to be smaller, minimized my accomplishments, and made myself less attractive, so as not to awaken any jealousy or notice.

If I stayed invisible, the Inner Critic would not be fueled by outside forces—or so I thought. He had already taught me that life is unpredictable and disaster looms at every corner: if hardship struck, it was my fault; if Dad yelled, I hadn't anticipated well enough how to ward off his anger; if Mom withdrew, I hadn't done enough to make her happy. I once described myself to friends as "an anxiety-ridden goodie-two-shoes" who could never relax or surrender to the moment. I didn't sleep well, especially when academic pressures mounted during my sophomore years of high school, college, and medical school. I couldn't keep up—my Inner Critic was not amused!

No wonder I wanted to die. I am still amazed at how I kept going and am oh-so-glad that I did. The toll it took was enormous at the time, and yet no one knew. I hid it carefully behind my smiling mask—Mom had taught me well. So how did I heal? Falling in love more than once, studying astrology, participating in insight-oriented psychotherapies, reading the works of Carl Jung, and exploring spirituality, each in their way helped me see myself more clearly.

Following my heart allowed for the entrance of a balancing, valued Feminine into my consciousness. Suddenly, the Inner Critic was accountable to another emerging Force—and She was a force to be reckoned with! When my Jungian analyst pointed out how cruelly I treated myself, I decided then and there to change that. It took years of observation and gentle redirection, but all the perverse self-wounding has stopped. It may steal its way in for brief periods of time as I resonate with the Inner Critic in others, but my pausing to notice the ensuing heaviness and the message it contains shifts the energy within me immediately.

I now appreciate myself as a woman, a fallible human, a wounded individual who also has developed considerable self-discipline, endurance, self-acceptance, and compassion. I extend the latter two graces to others as I can, and deal with inner criticism as it arises—not so often these days. The years of peace have given me many opportunities to reflect upon "his" intentions and to invite clients to deal with their own version of the Critic as well.

Through these reflections, I have come to realize that the Critic's power originally came unannounced and uninvited, with no official mandate from me. From behind the scenes of my lower mind, he intensified my painful feelings and voided those that were pleasurable, telling me I didn't deserve to be happy, besides which it wasn't safe because it wouldn't last. I suspect he was trying to prevent me from getting hurt… but did so by hurting me all the time! Once my adult, higher mind consciousness engaged with him, it became surprisingly clear that I had more power than he did. I found him willing to maintain his focus on my protection, yet able to shift his interventions to include my inner peace. My clients have engaged with their own Inner Critics and have come to appreciate this willingness as well.

Consequently, my Inner Critic (whom I now see as an inner, wordy, Triple Warmer-protected phenomenon) has learned to redirect his cannons, sometimes pointing them outward to spare me the gunfire. He has also learned to put his cannons to rest most of the time, although I do catch him internally criticizing people in my world on occasion. I wonder, what is he trying to tell me? Not that they are bad, because they are not. Not that they intend me harm, because they do not. Not that I am better than they are, because I am not. He is telling me perhaps that some basic need of mine is going unmet, that I am looking to the outer world for its satisfaction when true resolution must come from me or from something I must initiate with others. He may even be telling me that an aspect of sacredness in a relationship is not being honored.

When I make the effort to understand what he wants me to know, I often feel I have traversed the darkness of my unconscious to discover treasures hidden in the Mystery. One of the deepest lessons I have discovered in the midst of this is that I must become my own best friend—my Inner Critic turned inside out; his strength marshalled for self-defense when needed; his ground recognized as a loving place to land; his stamina acknowledged and his vision advanced to include my need for love. I am not invisible. I am not invincible. I am sensitive. I am vulnerable. I need protection. I need to be seen and valued for who I am. I need to give and receive love. I need to love myself, as we all must—unconditionally—without expectation that others will make up for our lack in this regard. This kind of interior focus and love promotes inner peace. Can we imagine a world in which human beings live into this premise?!

The fruits of these personal reflections are the result of inner work spanning several decades. Some might say I've been fortunate, while others might think me a bit slow! In my experience the timing of these revelations has little to do with our merit or lack of it, our abilities or seeming inabilities, our stated intentions or limited focus. Rather, it seems to me the process is guided by the wisdom of the soul's unfolding, and because each of us is unique and called to share and trigger different aspects of life experience for one another, we come to know things in our own way, in our own time.

Lily's Inner Critic has been distinctly her own, guarding her own truths, awaiting the right time and place for liberation and transformation. Prior to that transition, her Inner Critic held on for dear life, literally and figuratively. For the Inner Critic to let go, something had to assure it that letting go would be safe. That "something" lies in the heart…

The Broken Heart

When we talk about love we automatically "think" of the heart. I have already mentioned how the Celts also think *with* their hearts, their Cauldron of Calling or Yearning. We discussed how as an organ the heart keeps us alive, coordinates our organ functions, and feeds our brain precious oxygen so we can think those amazing thoughts. The heart's Sino-Atrial Node also contains its own pulsing generator that beats every second, every minute, every hour, every day, and every year of our life. This generator derives its source from somewhere beyond us and sends out an electromagnetic field extending at least eight to ten feet beyond the confines of the physical body. The electromagnetic field of the heart is sixty times more powerful than that of the limbic brain so, like a mother drum entraining less powerful djembes, our word-filled brain can truly think what the heart dictates—if we let it!

Yet so often we are not at peace because our thoughts run counter to the heart's intentions. We see from our discussion of the Inner Critic how this can come about: familial and cultural beliefs determine what we do, how we think, and what we feel. If our natural instincts or the messages we receive from the environment oppose those learned beliefs and expectations, essential feeling-state information clashes with cortical thought at the insula.

The rift in our brain and our consciousness reflects the brokenness of our hearts.

The Wounded Heart and the Brain

We have noted how the insula on each side of the brain serves as a bridge between the Vagus-informed, emotional, survival-focused limbic system, and the more reflective cerebral cortex. The Inner Critic stands guard at the door, as if in the receiving room of the cortical castle, quietly filtering and criticizing what might otherwise wish to make itself known to the more evaluative cortex. Consequently, the brain learns to completely or partially ignore physical sensations like hunger or pain in an attempt to minimize the criticism. Desires that threaten the status quo may stir inexplicable anxiety, rather than enthusiasm. Grief may register in consciousness as dull apathy.

In a figurative and not just diagnostic sense, dissociation may assume many such guises. These masks present on a continuum, unique to each of us and dependent on the severity of the clash between the limbic messages and the cortical refusal to accept them. Such protections as excessive fantasizing, feeling invisible, freezing, fainting, addictions, cravings, and the severity of Multiple Personality Disorder lie on this continuum. They reflect a broken heart.

As noted in the previous chapter, Triple Warmer encodes what we learn in a process that parallels our brain's development. Our brain's development parallels our psychosocial development so, no surprise, Triple Warmer accepts those childhood experiences as truth, all encoded and repeated by way of habitual responses to life's situations, all for the purpose of survival. These energetically protected habits include whichever personal avenues of dissociation work best for us. Additionally, those self-criticisms that seem to help us avoid impending disaster receive Triple Warmer's committed support.

We also know that, during times of stress, the evaluating cortex naturally shuts down unless we have trained it to do otherwise with a meditation practice or psychotherapy, for example. The hippocampus also shrinks in response to the floods of cortisol sent forth by the unchecked cascade of limbic reactivity in response to perceived danger: neural transmissions from the amygdala to the hypothalamus send hormonal messengers to the adrenals, which then release high levels of cortisol throughout the body. New healing experiences have difficulty finding a place to land within the memory center of a shrunken hippocampus. We may feel forever doomed to domination by the Inner Critic and its repetitive messages of misery.

Love and the Wounded Heart

These self-critical messages and the deep wounds that engendered them maintain our broken hearts, and the Inner Critic takes on the mandate to protect the wounded part. But the heart has a natural inclination to heal; beyond its anatomy and physiology, beyond its powerful electromagnetic field, the heart has a capacity for a phenomenon we call love. When we speak of the love we feel, we touch our chests, under which the physical heart resides. Yet we speak it from the consciousness of the brain.

This experience of love as a vibration registers differently in specific parts of the brain. In the limbic system, love and lust become easily confused as limbic receptors respond to the safety or danger of physical attraction. In the left hemisphere of the cortex, love stimulates the logical guidance that ensures the needs of relationship are met. In the right hemisphere, love fuels our recognition of the less tangible qualities of compassion, mystical union, and joy.

Whatever way we experience love—and it isn't always a feeling—its purpose involves meaningful, mutually beneficial connection between two or more beings on one or more of the levels described in our holistic model. Love serves as the vibrational and metaphorical link holding us together, both internally, within ourselves, and externally, among those with whom we gather. Its meaning extends well beyond emotion, although we certainly often feel emotional when we express love. The heart as the center of its own powerful energy field seems to provide a home base for this intangible, yet essential and multi-level experience. It even entrains those parts of the brain that interpret our experience of love to our word-dominated consciousness.

The need for love predates our development of language, however. Studies of infant survival clearly demonstrate that without love we die. Even as adults, we cannot thrive or survive for long without love, especially love of self—we cannot receive love from others if we do not deem ourselves worthy of it. Infants and young children remain dependent upon love from others to learn love of self. Triple Warmer encodes the belief about whether or not this love is deserved. Thus, the strength of the Inner Critic directly and inversely relates to our ability to love ourselves!

While Lily continued to experience persistent and unloving inner criticisms about how she handled that situation on the playground so many years previously, the major cause for her immediate and prolonged distress involved the fact that she cared for her friend, that she froze, and consequently that she could not act in accord with her care. Her heart had engaged her body for a loving response: to protect her friend. Yet understandable fear, stirred by learned injunctions about her emotional reactivity over the seven years of her life, blocked the expression of her love, not only for her friend but for herself.

The power of her heart could neither align with, nor entrain her body or her mind. Given how easily and naturally less powerful entities entrain with those of greater power, that *lack* of alignment between her heart, body, and mind required considerable energy to maintain. We have no reason to think anything happened to her physical heart or its ability to transmit its powerful electromagnetic field. So how might we understand what happened to her love?

The Mind and the Heart

In the review of the Holistic Model of Human Consciousness in Chapter 7, we noted that our mental capabilities include a lower mind and a higher mind. The lower mind developmentally gathers words to it—as we discern the separateness of concrete objects—long before its higher mind counterpart acquires words for its experience at the level of abstract thought. This challenges us to consider: what *is* our consciousness in the absence of words? And what role do these aspects of mind play in our development and understanding of self?

We have noted how the brain and Triple Warmer incorporate life's imprints prior to the development of language. Then the lower mind learns how to interpret what transpires in its midst via the language of parents, extended family, childcare workers, and culture. In our day-to-day functioning, lower mind grasps the importance of love at the level of physical and psychological survival. It knows when love is threatened (via shame and guilt) and it recognizes safety and care. Our four-legged friends teach us that one does not need a full vocabulary to experience the dynamics and feelings of shame and guilt, or safety and care. With the capacity for words, however, the Inner Critic takes its cues from this lower mind discernment to help us avoid these threats and dangers—its primary mission. And when its mission is not threatened, perhaps we may enjoy some pleasure along the way.

Higher mind, on the other hand, experiences love as an eternal phenomenon available to us in every moment, on every level, whether we live or die. There is no need for an Inner Critic at this level of consciousness. Existing in eternity, higher mind recognizes love as forever patient, discerning, merciful, and compassionate, even as we experience it in time and space here on Earth. The key word here is "experience." Factors related to intelligence and maturity may make it easier to appreciate the abstract nature of higher mind as a theoretical construct, but that understanding is not a substitute for living it. To embody the love higher mind can appreciate does not require intelligence or maturity; in fact, sometimes these qualities fuel the Inner Critic and get in the way. A compelling story entitled *Flowers for Algernon*[97] serves to illustrate this point.

Flowers for Algernon

In the novel, the main character, Charlie Gordon, is a mentally challenged adult with an IQ of 68. He works in a bakery where his natural joy and blissful ignorance buoy the moods of his co-workers (who also take advantage of him, but he doesn't know that). Charlie is exceptionally motivated to learn and has a teacher, whom he has quietly grown to love in his way. Meanwhile, two scientists discover a surgical procedure which, when performed on Algernon, a laboratory mouse, makes him amazingly intelligent, such that he can run a maze in record time. These scientists want to test this procedure on a human being, and Charlie becomes their first human subject. Just as with Algernon, after the procedure Charlie is no longer mentally challenged. Instead, his amazing IQ of 185 earns him an advanced education, prestigious positions, compensatory wealth, and opportunities for intimate relationships.

---

[97] Daniel Keyes, *Flowers for Algernon* (Orlando, FL: Harcourt Brace & Company, 1966).

THE INNER CRITIC AND THE BROKEN HEART

Unfortunately, as Charlie's intelligence and success increase his stress level mounts, his relationships deteriorate, and his mood plummets. Using his intellectual brilliance, he continues the research begun by the scientists and discovers a flaw in their theory. Not long after, as Charlie predicts, Algernon's intelligence reverts to a state below that of his pre-surgical level, quickly followed by his premature death. As his own intelligence begins to fade, Charlie finally becomes capable of engaging in a loving relationship with his teacher. As his intellect becomes progressively more compromised, however, he retreats from all those who have known him, lest they see him in this diminished state. He departs, making a final request to the woman he loves to place flowers on Algernon's grave.

In this story, Charlie's advanced intellect serves many aspects of his lower mind: use of personal power, pursuit of desire, and assurance of survival on a daily basis. In contrast, his mental limitations, initially and during his slow decompensation, lessen the restrictive impact of his Inner Critic and quicken access to the higher mind experiences of love and joy. This story highlights how intelligence serves a different purpose than do our lower and higher minds. Intelligence can support or interfere with lower mind's access to higher mind's wisdom. We can use our intelligence to fuel the Inner Critic or to undo him. Lower mind's access to higher mind and its capacity to appreciate a soulful level of consciousness makes all the difference.

The *experiential* consciousness of higher mind penetrates the cells of our bodies, directs our behaviors if we let it, fills our emotional lives with joy and meaning, and connects us to a greater presence in our social community. On reflection, it would seem that higher mind has much in common with healing heart consciousness. Still, faced with important decisions, we often struggle with the divergence of our higher and lower mind. For example, how often have we heard or said, "I have two minds about it"?

Consciousness and the Brain

This period in our history and in our evolution as a species places significant emphasis on the functioning of our mind. We recognize the risk of "living in our heads" and know how sterile and futile it can feel. This "talking heads" phenomenon really applies predominantly to our left cerebral hemisphere and its ability to name things, yet we become acutely aware of its limitations when we have a problem and what we "know to name" can't fix it. Interestingly, our right cerebral hemisphere has easier access to the less defined, gestalt, symbolic and impression-based dimensions of our human experience.[98] The right side of our cortex can tap into wordless dimensions quite unfamiliar to its left brain counterpart. Thus, when confronted with the limits of our left-brain knowledge-base, we must consult the Unknown for a solution. We must admit that we do not know.

Not knowing greatly disturbs the lower mind. In essence, it excels at retelling the stories it hears, but it was never meant to lead. Our lower mind originally took instruction from the teachings of caregivers and the outside world. Ideally, with increasing maturity we learn to shift our lower mind's allegiance from others and society to our own higher mind and heart. When our relational heart has been broken, especially during childhood, the lower mind unfortunately never has the opportunity to experience the fullness of love offered by the heart and the higher mind. Having been betrayed by

---

[98] Jill Bolte Taylor, Ph.D.'s book, *My Stroke of Insight: A Brain Scientist's Personal Journey* (New York, NY: VIKING, Penguin Group, 2006), 29–31, describes this right brain experience beautifully.

others, the lower mind metaphorically realizes that it alone must take charge of a sinking ship. As the wounded heart submerges into the unconscious, the Inner Critic emerges from lower mind to assume its unnatural, but protection-intended command.

In desperation, the Inner Critic and lower mind manage life without access to higher mind's inspiration and trust in a loving Beyond. The Inner Critic and lower mind cannot appreciate that higher mind engages freely and easily with the Unknown. In the course of living a complex life, the Inner Critic has not considered the possibility of, or even the necessity for developing a bridge between itself as lower mind and its higher mind superior. This divide plays out in the communication between the left and right hemispheres of the brain as well.

Within the anatomical confines of our brain, the corpus callosum serves to connect these two cerebral hemispheres. (Figures 3-6 and 3-8) Yet here, too, we may experience a selective barrier inhibiting important communications between them. The messages and logic of the Inner Critic, for example, seem to be more language-and left-brain-bound, while the acceptance, patience, love, and broader perspective of the right brain seem inaccessible when the Inner Critic rules our inner world. No physical, structural barrier has been identified to explain the impact of the Inner Critic in this regard. Might we consider an energetic component?

Despite more traditional perspectives, which view the brain as the *source* of our thinking, new paradigms sparked by quantum physics and the experiences of noted individuals such as Eben Alexander, M.D.,[99] suggest that our consciousness is really an energy field. This field surrounds and penetrates our physical awareness, making itself

---

[99] Alexander, Eben, M.D., *Proof of Heaven: A Neurosurgeon's Journey into the Afterlife* (New York, NY: Simon & Schuster Paperbacks, 2012).

known to us via processing *through* the brain. This view is further supported by Richard Gerber, M.D., who describes how information from the Higher Self is energetically received through the crystalline structure of the pineal gland,[100] after which it travels to the right brain. If the as yet unconscious higher mind needs to share this information with the conscious lower mind, the right brain can speak to our lower mind consciousness via dreams—or physical symptoms if we cannot work with, or choose to ignore our dreams.

If the left and right hemispheres have learned to communicate well with each other, the left brain can meaningfully interpret the symbolic message of the right brain's dream, or the physical symptoms, with words. For this energetic informational exchange to occur at all, it logically follows that right brain and left brain—and by extension higher mind and lower mind—must achieve a state of resonance, or entrainment, with one another. Specifically, when both hemispheres of the brain enter the theta state of four to seven cycles per second, conscious and unconscious processes interface.[101] "Insight quickens and creative intuition flourishes, giving one the ability to visualize and bring into manifestation ideas more readily."[102] What makes this possible? In addition to the healing power of rhythmic drumming and other trance-inducing activities, might we also consider the tender, powerful, vibrational heart?

Without the healing power of entrainment, Lily's love as filtered through her broken heart unfortunately had to deal with relational heartache and a sense of personal inadequacy on the one hand, and the simultaneous awareness that a greater love exists that would

---

[100] Gerber, *Vibrational Medicine,* 255–258.
[101] Robert Lawrence Friedman, *The Healing Power of the Drum: A Psychotherapist Explores the Healing Power of Rhythm* (Reno, NV: White Cliffs Media, 2000), 43–46.
[102] Ibid., 45.

never support such cruelty on the other. The break in her heart was also reflected in the split between her "minds." The Inner Critic dominated her lower mind and rendered her higher mind more difficult to access and trust. We all have endured the same struggles: we confront this issue and the divisions within us whenever fear and the urge to retaliate or defend override the call to honor life with respect and dignity. It seems a skillful negotiator is needed to heal these splits in the heart and between the two levels of mind.

Fortunately, the heart is well suited to fulfill this need: despite having been wounded it is capable of healing. While we have already identified many of the heart's qualities, there are many more to consider. The next chapter explores ways to bridge the heart's *knowing* intuition and its capacity for compassion, humility, trust and forgiveness, with the power of the Inner Critic and its relationship to the ego and the mind. In this way, the strength and the protective agendas of the Inner Critic can be redeemed and redirected to serve the intentions of the heart.

CHAPTER 10

The Healing Heart

AS WE WITNESS, experience, and influence the consequences of the new paradigm struggling to emerge, we notice the tumultuous aggression surrounding us and the rising voices of men and women all over the globe clamoring for a more compassionate, socially responsible, and inclusive path toward healing. The politics of the world reflect the brokenness of our hearts: some focus on power and use criticism, divisiveness, guilt and shame to feed their agendas; while others acknowledge we are all one and that compassion and forgiveness will help us live into that truth. On the global scale, we can see how we are teetering on disaster. Within our psyches the challenge feels no less frightening. Will we submit like victims? Use power badly? Risk everything based on our faith in goodness and the power of love?

Feelings carry information; information is power. We have the power to choose—a function of our divinely given free will. At specific points in our life we all know the anguish of having to make important choices without sufficient information. Often we have nothing to rely on except our gut feeling or the heart's wisdom. That gut feeling will likely tell us what will work for us and our survival. The heart's voice, our true intuition, values the wellbeing of all beings, including us. To appreciate the heart's capacity to "know," we now turn our attention to the heart as a chakra, an energy center, in more detail. In this way we can truly appreciate its amazing ability to heal what feels broken and, perhaps more importantly, live into the experience of our heart as the center of our lives.

The Heart as a Chakra

As a dominant energy center amidst other energy centers, the heart is perfectly poised to serve as a bridge between the various levels of our consciousness and existence. The best way to explore this further involves an understanding of the chakras. "Chakra" is a Sanskrit word meaning "wheel of light." The seven major chakras[103] present as vortexes of colorful swirling light to those who reportedly can see them. Minor and lessor chakras exist throughout the body as well. Seen or unseen, they wield their power over localized areas of the body, such that each is associated with nearby organs, blood vessels, muscles and bones, specific endocrine organs and nerve plexi, and aspects of our emotional, mental, and spiritual lives as well. Taking some time to appreciate those correlations will deepen our understanding of the heart's significant role as bridge on almost every level of our human experience. This review of the chakras

---

[103] Many authors describe more than seven chakras, both below the torso and above the head, but for our purposes I am limiting this discussion to the traditional seven major chakras extending from perineum to crown.

also highlights those themes relevant to our understanding of the empathic experience. The reader is referred to the work of Jonathan Goldman[104] and Donna Eden[105] for more detailed descriptions of their amazing beauty and function.

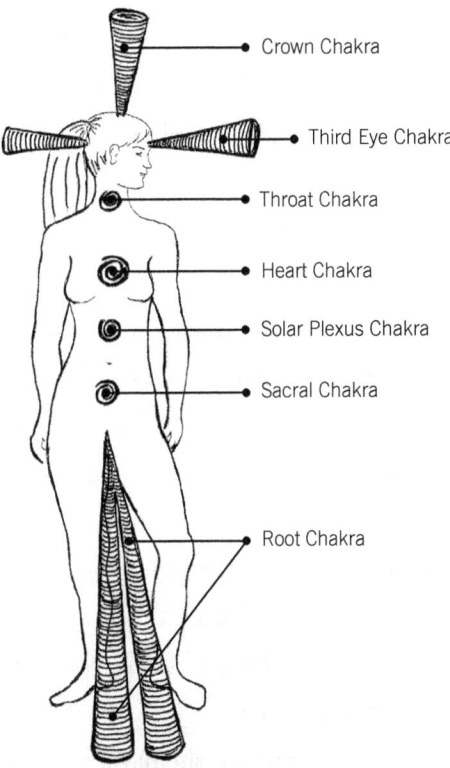

Figure 10-1: The Seven Major Chakras

The Root Chakra extends downward from the perineum (two cones) and from the coccyx (one cone, not shown) to root us to the earth. The Sacral, Solar Plexus, Heart, Throat, and Third Eye Chakras extend frontward and backward, as depicted in this illustration at the Third Eye. The Crown Chakra extends upward, connecting us to divine energies beyond our auric field.

---

[104] Goldman, *Gift of the Body*, 121–472.
[105] Eden with Feinstein, *Energy Medicine*, 147–186.

The Root Chakra sits at the perineum (Figure 10-1) and governs the bones, legs and pelvic area. It sends down three cones of energetic connection to the earth and receives the earth's raw energy into our being.[106] In keeping with the holistic model, the Root Chakra grounds us in the physical body and roots us to the earth. How we feel about incarnation resides here. Do we feel safe in our body? Do we wish we weren't living in a body, in part or at all?

According to Jonathan Goldman, when we are not deeply rooted in the earth's energy we experience "a feeling of constant insecurity"[107] and tension. The experience of dissociation to any degree can contribute to a vicious cycle: not wanting to be here makes us more anxious; constant anxiety makes us not want to be here. In this context, those systems that associate the Root Chakra with the adrenals make the most sense to me; others correlate this chakra with the sexual organs. Either attribution acknowledges the Root Chakra's relevance to our survival as a species. Themes related to survival, our ancestors and their karma, and sexuality as a means to ensure the perpetuation of the human race are all implicated with this chakra. In this chakra, relationships become important to the degree that they ensure survival.

The Sacral Chakra sits just below the navel and governs the uterus, as well as the ovaries and testes if one hasn't assigned their governance to the first chakra. This chakra relates to "sweetness" (the meaning of its Sanskrit name), which we experience through our need for rest and restoration, the comforts we desire, the joy and nurturing we need and long for. It holds the urge to merge and thus positions us in proximity to others so as to receive empathically derived information.

---

[106] Goldman, *Gift of the Body*, 133.
[107] Ibid., 137.

The Parasympathetic Nervous System's development via completed myelination of the Vagus Nerve allows us to take in this sweetness socially, via smiles and softly spoken tones; emotionally, through repair of whatever emotional rifts may occur; and physically, with nurturing food, hugs, and other pleasures.

Learning how to self-soothe plays a critical role in the process of socialization: without it, we are at the mercy of others who cannot read our minds nor anticipate perfectly our inner needs. Self-soothing extends into the realm of sexuality for pleasure, not just procreation, and the creative act of making babies. In our holistic model, at this second chakra level of consciousness the physical body mobilizes to explore and to gratify in the context of this chakra's pursuit of freedom. Relationships are sought to provide soothing connection and enjoyment. When they don't, and especially when we feel violated in any way, the inner protector associated with this chakra reacts with tantrums and rage.

The third chakra, also called the Solar Plexus Chakra, resides in the area just below the center of the rib cage and above the navel. Many organs of the abdomen come under its energetic domain, including its associated endocrine gland, the pancreas. At this level of development we become aware of ourselves as individuals; we hold beliefs about what it means to be alone; and we wield power for the manifestation of our desires, hence competition and dominance find a home in this chakra. Here resides the seat of lower mind and ego as well. The lower will of the third chakra also governs the two chakras below it. Feelings stirred in relationship to these three chakras inform the lower will's response when survival is assured (safety) or threatened (fear and paranoia), when sweetness is gratified (pleasure and contentment) or denied (rage), when the ego perceives itself to be in control (confidence) or challenged (angry, anxious, overwhelmed).

Jonathan Goldman describes how the front emotional body of this chakra not only receives all these feelings from our other chakras, but also receives and carries the feelings of other people.[108] Ideally, the third chakra's mental body accurately discerns which feelings belong to us and which do not—so necessary for an empath. Unfortunately, impaired discernment breeds judgment, usually the critical kind. It is here that the Inner Critic energetically takes hold and distorts our capacity to value ourselves accurately in the context of what we feel.

The Inner Critic takes its directions from the back of the mental body of this chakra where, again according to Jonathan Goldman, we hold beliefs about whether we are supported or not in our aloneness.[109] Especially when we learn that "no one has our back," the Inner Critic may shut down the second chakra's justified rage so as not to make things worse: this typically leads to depression. Consequently, relationships at this level respond to the accuracy of our discernment and thus serve to support or challenge our valuing of individual self.

The Heart Chakra, in the middle of these seven major centers, resides at the midpoint of the chest under the sternum, just to the right of the physical heart. As a powerful vibrational force, the heart coordinates the energies of all the organs and bodily systems so that they flow and integrate into a smoothly operating whole. We have already mentioned how 65% of the heart's cells are neurons and how it also functions as an endocrine gland. The thymus as an endocrine gland and an immune center also resides in the fourth chakra's domain.

---

[108] Ibid., 239.
[109] Ibid., 244.

From an energetic perspective, the heart's influence doesn't just synchronize the rhythms of the physical organs and brain. The heart's vibrational bandwidth, wider than that of the other chakras, resonates in such a way as to connect the three chakras below it with the three chakras above it.[110] The heart's frequency also extends out into the community. Thus, in the Heart Chakra the horizontal and the vertical aspects of our energetic existence meet and cross.

We now know that the heart's electromagnetic field has been measured at least ten feet beyond the body. When individuals meet, their Heart Chakra's radiance makes the first energetic connection between them through this powerful extension within their aura. (Figure 3-5) Thus, the degree to which individuals are consciously attuned to the energies of their Heart Chakra can significantly impact how the connection between them unfolds.

Relevant to that process, the Heart Chakra's energy resonates with truth and speaks to us through the intuition born of that resonance. Lack of harmony, or dissonance, causes the heart's energy field to contract, just as love and harmonic resonance lead to its expansion. The Heart Chakra also holds our capacity for humility, compassion, forgiveness, and faith.[111] Compassion in particular can have a feeling tone sometimes felt as love, but emotion does not define it because compassion is a vibration. Currently, we are slowly transitioning from a third chakra consciousness of individuality, competition and achievement toward a more heart-centered appreciation of oneness, cooperation and compassion. We will explore this development and its relevance to the empath further in this and succeeding chapters.

The Throat Chakra, the fifth of the seven, resides where we would

---

[110] Ibid., 265.
[111] Ibid., 264–326.

imagine: in the home of our vocal cords, airway, and neck, which connects torso to head. The thyroid and parathyroid glands come under its influence, as do all the chakras: their energy streams course up and down the body in channels that most closely connect with one another in the throat.[112] Consciousness at this level includes the value of opposites as contributors toward potential balance. Reasoning and diplomacy become the fruits of this chakra when it operates in an open and activated flow.

Feelings stirred in lower chakras, specifically shame and guilt, find a home in this chakra if the person's consciousness has not found a path of healing and release for these emotions. Shame resides in the front emotional body of this chakra,[113] while guilt wields its power from the mental body in the back.[114] Clearly these feelings can shut down, or at least negatively impact our capacity to express our truth and creativity. They can also make it difficult to receive the abundant good that comes our way.

At its best, the Throat Chakra supports gratitude and higher level creativity. Unlike the lower mind's and ego's perspective that opposites cause trouble (necessitating that one of them must dominate in order to survive), the awareness of opposites at the level of the Throat Chakra conveys an appreciation of Yin and Yang, black and white, night and day, receiving and giving—all as separate, but essential aspects of a greater whole. In the tension between these opposites, the Throat Chakra recognizes creativity of a more abstract order than making babies. The fifth chakra's creative efforts make possible music, art, poetry, and speaking one's personal truth while

---

[112] Eden with Feinstein, *Energy Medicine*, 172.
[113] Goldman, *Gift of the Body*, 366–368.
[114] Ibid., 345–348.

recognizing that other truths exist. The fifth chakra begins to journey into higher mind. Relationships at the level of the Throat Chakra respect "the other" as different, and acknowledge that an unknown third energy may come from cooperation.

The sixth chakra, also known as the Third Eye, resides at the center of the brain behind the eyebrows. The pituitary gland and the hypothalamus come under its governance, as does the Limbic System. Its name supports the understanding that it can "see" beyond the tangible, thus offering perspective regarding one's interior world, the outer domain of relationships, and the spiritual realm of the Divine. At this level of consciousness, ideally opposites can wed, not just co-exist, and peace reigns. The implication here includes reliable communication between the right and left hemispheres of our brain.

Those for whom the Third Eye is active see potential where others may not. They may be able to organize aspects of the known world to produce a new, previously unknown outcome. Some esoteric traditions refer to this level of consciousness as the highest level our unique integrated personality as an incarnated human being can achieve. From this place, the mystics of old and the mystic in each of us have our visions. Relationships at this level recognize the oneness within which we all reside.

Unfortunately, our visions can lose touch with all levels of reality when this chakra's filter is clouded with opinion and other distortions. Manifesting sixth chakra distortions with third chakra power in the absence of Heart Chakra consciousness can lead to considerable destruction. Pride often resides at the root of such dynamics and makes its home in the back mental body of the sixth chakra.[115] It

---

[115] Ibid., 433–435.

FEELING OUR WAY

serves to spare the bearer painful feelings of shame. It carries an "I know better than you" or "you should have known better" attitude that distances the prideful person from the recipient of that admonition by shaming that person as well.

A different kind of distortion involves those who have experienced traumatic consequences as a result of what they have "seen." They may shut down their Third Eye in an attempt to prevent any similar visions in the future. This tragically limits a person's access to the support available in the intangible realms.

The Crown Chakra, the seventh and last of the traditional major chakras, resides at the top of our head, extending into the brain and beyond into our energy field. The pineal gland (Figure 3-7), which maintains our circadian rhythms by secreting serotonin in the light of day and melatonin in the darkness of night, comes under the governance of this chakra. In his book, *Vibrational Medicine*,[116] Dr. Richard Gerber describes the pineal gland as made up of a crystalloid substance capable of acting as a transmitter and receiver of energetic information originating beyond the body.

Physical, scientific and spiritual worlds converge as we realize how this chakra supports our physical well-being through access to higher realms of consciousness. Consequently, through this chakra we access the joy of our essence. We can receive Light and be open to enlightenment. Healing traditions that honor chakra work note how the soul enters the body at birth through the Crown Chakra and leaves through this portal when we die. Writers of more esoteric traditions also describe the hurdle challenging us as consciousness shifts from the sixth to seventh chakra levels. Here the individuated

---

[116] Gerber, *Vibrational Medicine*, 257–259.

personality must ultimately choose if it will surrender to, experience, and serve the Divine.

As already suggested, one can view the chakras on many levels. Physically, each includes specific endocrine, nervous system, and organ functions. Emotionally, they reflect our responses to the thematic issues associated with each chakra. Psychologically, we can correlate the chakras with the psychodynamics of development, as well as states of consciousness, while recognizing that a person's primary way of viewing the world—her predominant 'seat' of consciousness—lies in one of these chakras and can shift. Culturally, we can expand upon this to appreciate at what chakra level we, as a species and society, approach most life dilemmas.

With an understanding of these chakra themes, we can also better understand how individuals, whose chakra level of consciousness differs from that of the prevailing societal level, experience themselves in relationship to their community: as belonging or isolated. Spiritually, with an understanding of the chakras we can better attend to the related chakra themes within our being for the purpose of aligning our energies into greater harmony, not only internally, but as part of a cosmic web and with the Divine.

We may also recognize that we're well developed at the level of certain chakras, but not so balanced when it comes to others. Some people, for example, live consciously in the lower three chakras and see the world as a competitive place, where the life goal is survival and/or the pursuit of pleasure and power. Others spend most of their conscious time in the upper chakras. They develop an advanced understanding of opposites, thus philosophizing and balancing the tensions of life, but they have difficulty grounding in and appreciating their own body, or dealing with the practical necessities of living in the physical world. Some individuals know well the compassion in their hearts and are quick to share that care with others, yet neglect their own lower chakra needs for safety, comfort, and responsible functioning in their daily life.

I hope we can each appreciate that balance among all the chakras offers the best support physically, emotionally, psychologically, socially, and spiritually. In the context of that balance, the Heart Chakra literally and figuratively plays a pivotal role.

Heart Chakra Challenges

We began this discourse on the chakras to better understand what made it so difficult for Lily to recognize or experience the effectiveness of her love. We have already alluded to the concept that Heart Chakra consciousness must evolve both within each individual and as a culture. If we consider the theme of each chakra, we begin to appreciate how stages in human history have successively reflected each chakra theme, beginning with the Root Chakra and advancing upward. Having developed the consciousness of Solar Plexus individuality to its frightening extremes, we are now transitioning into the era of Heart Chakra Consciousness. That progression moves slowly, however.

When Lily was seven, societal norms emphasized Solar Plexus values like getting ahead, achieving, competing, and coming out on top. These values, transmitted to her through her parents, became part of her own unconscious view of the world. Given these factors, at seven years of age she could barely have consciously recognized this amazing energy center, her Heart Chakra and all its values, as an essential part of her being. Cultural injunctions regarding how one should deal with the needs of another, what risks one might take in the face of peer criticism, and how adults respond to one's hurt feelings, had already broken her heart in two. Triple Warmer's energy pathways registered and stored all this information about her energetic heart's division in the cells of her body and brain. These life experiences had also informed her then predominant lower mind. The Inner Critic, being an aspect of the *should*-driven Solar Plexus and lower mind, held sway in that moment on the playground. Her heart cried out for love of her friend—but silently, only to her own inner ears. She had learned that no one else would listen.

Consequently, the wounded aspect of her Heart Chakra went underground, while other chakras developed. Lily's sixth and fifth chakras can now readily recognize and describe the tensions and issues played out on that fateful day. Yet this recognition did not offer enough to heal the stinging shame for her freeze behavior or the hurt in her heart. This inadequacy developed because, as her heart broke in two and went underground in certain respects—she is still a very caring individual—she lost the *fullness* and the harmonizing capacity of her heart's sensitivities and expression. Caring people often bury their second chakra rage and their third chakra power for fear that their fifth chakra expression of those emotions will hurt others. But their rage arises to protect them from violation and injustice, and an appropriate use of their power can actually do something about it. Without the gifts of protection and power we are left vulnerable to the dictates of other less conscious beings. Yet in the absence of a mending heart, we know that rage and power can wield incredible destruction. Thus, the Inner Critic fulfills its mission to keep those forces in tow.

The quotes of two sages when read together shed an interesting light on this dilemma. "The word hatred means the desire to destroy the other."[117] None of us likes to admit we are capable of hate but we are—all of us. Furthermore, "Unless you can hate you cannot possibly love. And vice-versa."[118] These quotes imply that love and hate know each other very well. Where hate is divisive, love is inclusive; they inform each other. Hate offers love a challenge, and love responds by including hate in its loving embrace. From these quotes we can appreciate the tensions bombarding the Heart Chakra from the chakras below and above it. In the heart, intense emotions of personal need and survival meet and potentially conflict with the recognition that we are all in this challenging life together and that somewhere, somehow, sharing love is possible—and necessary! An intact, mending heart can bear the tensions of these opposites in its broad bandwidth. This likely explains why a heart bursting with love sometimes feels the same to us as a heart near to breaking.

We can especially relate to this if we have the good fortune to find someone to love intensely, passionately, and in full complementarity. If one's heart is truly open to this experience, the intensity of all the complicated emotions clambering for attention can challenge one to the core. Those who have truly loved another know that, if they can find a way to honor their own needs while caring for the needs of their beloved as if they were one's own, the possibility for a life greater than the sum of their two parts opens wide. In the words of the oft quoted Kabbalist, the Ba'al Shem Tov: "From every human being there rises a light that reaches straight to heaven, and

---

[117] Osho, "Discourses," in *The Quotable Spirit: A Treasury of Religious and Spiritual Quotations, from Ancient Times to the 20th Century,* compiled and edited by Peter Lorie and Manuela Dunn Mascetti (New York, NY: Macmillan, 1996), 157.
[118] Wei Wu Wei, "Open Secret," in *The Quotable Spirit,* 157.

when two souls that are destined to be together find each other, the streams of light flow together and a single brighter light goes forth from that united being."[119]

This approaches what many refer to as 'unitive consciousness,' so distinctly different from our everyday perceptions of duality. What happens when we fall from this conscious state of oneness with the beloved as offered at the level of the Crown Chakra? This fall from graced unitive consciousness can occur countless times in the course of a committed relationship and perhaps for the last time when a loved one dies. How does one deal with the grief of loss when duality consciousness returns? "When one has once had the good luck to love intensely, life is spent in trying to recapture that ardor and that illumination."[120] Loving fully from the heart requires an enormous capacity for bearing the pain and the joy of it all. "Great loves too must be endured."[121] Needless to say, this depth of experience requires a whole heart and far exceeds what a seven-year-old with a broken heart might manage.

What happened to Lily's love as ideally experienced in Heart Chakra fullness? It split in two and the frozen part went underground into the unconscious for safekeeping, until one day it might be resurrected and rediscovered like buried treasure—except that the map to find it had been lost. Meanwhile, her Inner Critic operating as lower mind in a third chakra/lower mind-dominated world gained power. The Inner Critic came into existence in the "civilized" parts of a world without love, secretly trying to protect her wounded heart. He knew well how to live in such a world, so he never questioned these circumstances.

---

[119] Ba'al Shem Tov, "Prayer," in *The Quotable Spirit,* 150–151.
[120] Albert Camus, "Return to Tipasa," in *The Quotable Spirit,* 157.
[121] Marcel Haedrich, "Coco Chanel, Her Life, Her Secrets," in *The Quotable Spirit,* 155.

The Inner Critic had learned to mistrust love due to love's inadequate delivery over the course of many developmental years. The Inner Critic learned to ignore the healing aspects of the heart, to devalue its offerings as weak and ineffective. Consequently, the Inner Critic barricaded itself on the lower chakra side of the heart's bridge to higher mind consciousness. The heart's conduit of direct communication between lower and higher chakras shut down. The Inner Critic acted like a tyrant accountable to no one, and crowned itself ruler of the lower chakras, wearing blinders regarding all else.

Lower mind dominance and its emphasis on the lower three chakras predisposes us to experience those emotions below the 200 mark as described in the work of David Hawkins, M.D., Ph.D., *Power vs. Force*.[122] We have seen how shame equates to a physical- and feeling-toned message of potential ego annihilation, making it the lowest and densest on Hawkins' logarithmic scale of energies associated with our emotional states. With regard to our discussion, shame, guilt, apathy, grief, fear, and anger emerge when the Inner Critic offers its judgmental response to our dealings with life's challenges, while desire and pride stir when we feel safe and have met the Inner Critic's agenda. None of these below-200 emotions helps us heal, however, and often they painfully deepen our psychological wounds. Oddly, in their density, they offer us something to hold onto when the Inner Critic obscures a healthy sense of groundedness through the Root Chakra. As a result, giving up these painful states may prove challenging.

In contrast, healing requires the perspective of higher mind and its attendant emotional states: courage, neutrality, willingness, accep-

---

[122] Hawkins, *Power vs. Force*, 75–93.

tance, reason, and love. These range between 200 and 500 on Dr. Hawkins' scale. In their relative lightness, however, these qualities are more difficult to grasp and maintain; we have to consciously work to experience them over and over again. Thus Dr. Hawkins recognized courage, at the 200 level, as pivotal in the transition from the pseudo-ground of destructive emotions to those which heal and bring meaning to life. Since ancient times, our ancestors have associated courage with the heart. To turn from the status quo, to set out on a quest, and to seek something unseen and unknown requires nothing less. Thus, whether it be experienced cognitively or simply perceived and lived, access to higher mind consciousness must be bridged through the heart. Once that bridge has been sturdily built, joy, peace and enlightenment—levels above 500 on Dr. Hawkins' scale—become possible.

Lily's Inner Critic, in its dedicated commitment to maintaining the habits of survival developed during the painful moments of her childhood, had not discovered that her healing heart offered a less strenuous, safer, and more comprehensive way to survive and thrive. In fact, her life experiences so far had taught her to doubt her ability to love effectively. After all, she certainly felt she wasn't taking care of her mother well enough. She consequently judged herself most critically, on all levels, through the eyes of her lower mind, even though her healing heart and her higher mind operated according to completely different criteria. Because her Inner Critic governed access to these aspects of her being, it denied her admittance to what it did not trust. It could not recognize that her heart's and higher mind's terms of judgment were infinitely more discerning, gracious, and forgiving than its own. Even more perilous, to do so might spell its demise.

Healing the Inner Critic through the Heart

In my personal and professional experience, just because the Inner Critic doesn't trust the heart's capacity to love doesn't mean it cannot grow to do so. Several factors require attention before this can happen, however. Using Lily's journey as an example of this healing possibility, first she had to recognize the existence of her Inner Critic and acknowledge its power over her when it runs her life from behind the scenes. This step in itself offers significant challenge, as most of us initially accept the criticisms of this inner figure as true and unquestionable, as natural as hunger and thirst. This process requires that we give up our identification with this figure and acknowledge that, while it may command some of our energy at the moment, the Inner Critic is *not* us.

The Inner Critic hides in the shadowy darkness, rendering the darkness scary. This can affect us on a literal level if we fear being alone in the dark of night. More abstractly, we may find ourselves trying to control the uncontrollable, with pseudo-solutions like obsessions and compulsions, or by resigning ourselves to the control of an external critic in a demanding or manipulative relationship. This fear of the shadows can also negatively impact our relationship with the sacredness of Mystery: how can we possibly tell the difference between the Inner Critic and the Sacred Darkness? And given the natural tendency for hasty retreat from this shadowy, painful criticism, how might we even muster the courage to look?

As noted earlier, the Inner Critic develops in conjunction with the lower mind, which attends to the needs of the three lower chakras. In its efforts to negotiate issues of safety and danger, comfort and rage, power and inadequacy, the lower mind has unknowingly adopted the voice of the Inner Critic and received Triple Warmer protection to maintain its grip. To the lower mind, darkness and Mystery can hold threats of danger. Demons may reside there—better to know, define, and control. Higher mind, on the other hand, accepts darkness as a balance to light in the Throat Chakra, recognizes the essential oneness from which they emerged in the Third Eye, and embraces Mystery as home for the soul at the Crown Chakra.

Higher mind welcomes the darkness as it welcomes the light—in peace. There are no demons there, instead we find complementarity and unity. When balanced, the upper three chakras (particularly the sixth) allow the witness within us—that unbiased capacity to see clearly—to emerge into consciousness. Higher mind can subsequently view the Inner Critic with an appreciative, yet discerning eye. Typically, this capacity to witness evolves in response to time, attention, and effort. Many of us who have engaged in psychotherapy or meditation can speak knowingly to the work required and the benefits derived. Needless to say, this witnessing ability does not come readily to a child.

After recognizing its presence, Lily had to encounter her Inner Critic from the perspective of her own developed, witnessing adult, rather than as a controlled, blind-sided, and victimized child. Next she had to engage with her Inner Critic by inviting it into dialogue, asking direct questions about its intentions, methods, and beliefs. (Jungian analysis often utilizes this type of encounter, referred to as "active imagination," which entails taking seriously the thoughts and feelings arising from the unconscious during this process, even if they can't be known or proven as factually correct.) For many this step requires considerable courage but, if successfully negotiated, a deeper understanding and more respectful relationship with the Inner Critic develops.

From this higher mind perspective, Lily could then express appreciation for her Inner Critic's efforts to keep her safe and to keep her wounded heart from being shattered, while also stating her own recognition that living with shame and guilt, with feelings of inadequacy and sadness, have not served her best interests. With courage and commitment to her own well-being, she needed to clearly state that these critical, hurtful responses to her past experiences and to her present-day decisions, feelings, and actions not only no longer contribute to her survival, they jeopardize her current emotional and functional integrity as well.

No matter how many times this dialogue has to happen, the outcome must eventually be a partnership between the individual and her Inner Critic, even if tentative, for any healing to occur. That partnership becomes an important preliminary entrance to the realm of the heart. Together they need to explore the possibilities of love viewed from the eyes and heart of an adult, who is no longer vulnerable to the psychological limitations of her parents, nor to the imposition of circumstances from which she can now walk away. In this process, the Inner Critic's capacity for discernment evolves.

Lily's journey became one of disentangling her sense of self and of love from the expectations of her mother. As an empath, she had taken these on as if they were aspects of her own being. Letting them go initially felt disloyal to her mother, for whom she still felt love despite the confusing and painful messages received from this significant person over her lifetime. Loyalty to our loved ones endures beyond death. This highlights how disentangling ourselves and freeing our hearts requires inner work: it may never manifest directly in the outer world relationship, but its effect extends well beyond us. It may even free the other, whether still in a physical body or not, to do their own inner work to heal.

Lily's capacity to love had grown enormously over the years in response to all her experienced heartache and confusion. Her healing simply required a change of direction. She had to learn to direct her healing heart's love toward herself, to the wounded part of her heart and, just as significantly, to her Inner Critic so that it might come to trust that love is safe. In this process, the experience of compassion and forgiveness is essential.

Jonathan Goldman describes compassion[123] as built in to the emotional body of our Heart Chakra waiting for us to awaken to its presence and stimulate its use. The healing heart can do this readily and Lily, for example, had already well developed her heart's capacity by extending this gift to others. Her work now involved redirection of compassion: toward her own wounded heart; toward a misguided Inner Critic who had been doing all it could for her even though ineffective in the long term; and toward the part of her that had accepted the cruel dictates of the Inner Critic without question.

In addition to compassion, forgiveness is necessary. Again, Jonathan Goldman describes forgiveness[124] as a built-in space in the Heart Chakra's energy field but, unlike compassion, this space is empty, waiting for us to call upon the spiritual force of this gift to enter its place. When we are ready, we need to forgive those who hurt us, as well as ourselves for being hurt. We must also forgive ourselves for perpetuating the cruelty of our own self-criticism. We need the healing heart's capacity for both compassion and forgiveness to heal.

---

[123] Goldman, *Gift of the Body,* 299–304.
[124] Ibid., 308–313.

Love: Sustenance for the Journey

We have much more to say about love, but let us acknowledge here its relationship to the soul and to the Source of Love, as depicted in the holistic model of human experience on Earth. We are clearly not the source of love, yet when all the levels of our holistic human experience align, healing from that Source beyond us can flow through us and fill our entire being with love, even the soul-filled cells of our toes. Our hearts not only transmit powerful energies, they attract and receive them as well, with love serving as the primary energy and avenue for the integration of all aspects of our being.

Words on a page make this process seem simple and direct, yet the truth lies in the venture, which entails considerable hard work. Here lies the paradox of our modern-day emphasis on language. Even putting this into a book supports the priority of words, but the great sages and chefs have always known better: "The proof is in the pudding." After we have read the map we have to travel the road. We now recognize the importance of the heart, but that recognition alone does not quell the fears and defenses long established by the Inner Critic's focus on keeping us safe. Its efforts are held in our energies, and to the degree that our hearts and our heads are not energetically connected we still have a problem. Here lies the value of Energy Medicine.

We now realize that Triple Warmer and the Inner Critic have a tightly bound relationship. In response to the dictum that "energy follows thought," a shift in our consciousness can also lead to a shift in our energies. Dialogue with the Inner Critic can thus impact Triple Warmer, but we must also acknowledge that Triple Warmer, in its efforts to maintain habits, will slow our progress with the

Inner Critic. Consequently, the task at this level can take quite a long time, to which my years of twice-a-week sessions in Jungian analysis attest. Despite the apparent lack of connection between the Inner Critic and the healing heart, Triple Warmer's primary mandate involves diligent efforts to protect the heart—especially when it is broken or divided. It commits to keeping the wounded heart safe from further wounding.

While Triple Warmer can commandeer energy from any other meridian, it cannot trump the heart—that would defeat its primary mission, which is to help us survive. Strengthening the heart, physically and energetically, as well as psychologically with a new consciousness, offers a path toward healing. Simultaneously calming Triple Warmer renders efforts to mend and strengthen the heart and to transform the Inner Critic even more effective. As Triple Warmer relaxes, it releases its grip on old, outworn habit patterns and makes room for more effective coping pathways, not just in our mind but throughout our energy field. Effort of a different nature can now serve the whole with less struggle, greater speed, and more effectiveness.

Here lies the importance of Energy Medicine, with its understanding of how our energy systems support the heart and our overall well-being, how these energy systems can get blocked or imbalanced in response to stress, shock, or trauma, and how they attempt to protect us and do their best to restore resilience. Working with our energy field offers a way to balance our imbalanced physical, emotional, belief-based, and spiritual energy pathways, so that those neurological and psychological patterns that seemed "written in stone" can begin to shift and flow like water. Oddly, these transitions from "stuck" to "flow" then facilitate a more accurate experience of the body's physical sensations, a more authentic emotional response to life's situations, more realistic beliefs about who we are at core, greater clarity regarding what meaning we ascribe to our life circumstances, and more spontaneous access to a sense of spiritual connection. Life from a balanced energetic state looks and feels very different indeed!

Lily initially approached our time together with the intention of working through what she experienced as an unnamed unease or "flutter" in her Solar Plexus. She had already acquired considerable skill in self-exploration, yet the troubling sensation in her gut would not remit. Her willingness to journey into new territory by combining energy work, with which she was unfamiliar, with her capacity for self-exploration opened doors of discovery for both of us.

During the course of our work, which relied heavily upon Eden Energy Medicine, Lily began to identify the details of that initially nebulous flutter in her gut. Her empathic abilities clearly contributed to the many component physical sensations, emotions, images, and memories unearthed during the process of our work together. These emerged, often to her surprise, as I held energy points on her head. With this and other Eden Energy Medicine techniques, we were also able to energetically support the insights and redeemed emotions at the conclusion of each session. She, other clients, and I myself have experienced profound shifts and surprising discoveries in the process of energy work. In the next chapter we explore the interweaving of consciousness, energy medicine and healing in more detail.

CHAPTER 11

The Role of Consciousness in Healing

WHEN A CLIENT LIES FACE UP on a table, often with eyes closed, and an energy medicine practitioner holds specific points on her head, is the practitioner performing a Vulcan mind-meld? Does the client have an opportunity to download communications from the Pleiades? Will she arise from the table healed? Or worse, will the client have experienced nothing at all? Depending on whether one has received energy work in the past, some of these questions may provoke a twisted smile. For those who have never felt their own energy flowing through their bodies in a recognized and specific way, some of these questions may have crossed their mind at least once. In the Middle Ages, witches were burned at the stake or drowned when healing happened and the common folk couldn't explain it. Clearly, fear presided over the decisions of those times.

Our insistence upon evidence-based medicine in part responds to that fear of being hoodwinked. Unfortunately, research designs limit their focus to the physical realm for the most part. To explore the effects of energy medicine, studies can only hold value if researchers are willing to stretch their parameters of evidence. Energy Medicine is not magic: explanations exist for why and how it works, especially now that quantum theories can explain life beyond the third and fourth dimensions. Special equipment and research designs were necessary to elaborate these new paradigm theories, however, and the same is true for Energy Medicine. The context of this research involves what can be measured and what effect it has upon the recipient: we find ourselves in the infancy stages for identifying the former; recipients of energy work can speak for themselves.

What clients report about their energy sessions depends to a significant degree upon the awareness they have developed regarding their own energy field. People who make a commitment to this work often grow in their ability to recognize which energy systems need attention, even in the absence of energy testing that later often confirms their suspicions. As we have already discussed via the holistic model in Chapter 7, consciousness can manifest on several levels—the physical, behavioral, emotional, mental, and/or soulful—even as it simultaneously impacts all of our energy systems, with or without our recognition. Inversely, through energy work we become more aware of physical sensations, our underlying emotions, our thoughts about them, and our psychodynamics—how those aspects of our past and present experiences interrelate and affect the way we think, feel, and act. Energy carries consciousness as information, and consciousness impacts energy flow. Consequently, combining energy work with psychotherapy offers an exciting new avenue for healing.

When we left Lily as an adult, she still painfully remembered her childhood playground experience with feelings of humiliation. This experience, among others, had a significant impact upon her sense of self and the relationships she chose to nurture or dismiss throughout her life. Her Inner Critic loomed large in her psyche, often inciting periods of inner distress, anxiety, and occasional shame. Lily addressed this inner tumult over the years by using and mastering several psychotherapeutic tools. Its roar had toned down significantly, yet it persisted to her dismay, with each episode quickly followed by further self-criticism. Despite years of deep inner work, aspects of this painful cycle remained a mystery to her. She had not yet experienced the impact of energy work in her healing process.

To summarize the information in previous chapters, we now have some understanding about the way her three brains, her Vagus Nerve, limbic system, insula, and cortex received and processed the sensory information of that humiliating experience, contributing to her freeze reaction. We appreciate how her kinesthetic sensory type and her auric field energetically vibrated in reaction to the frequencies of the individuals, their emotions, and the situation as a whole, and how Triple Warmer responded with irregular/frozen energy patterns, tense muscles, and an overall state of alarm. We now also realize how the repetitive messages of her caregivers and social environment throughout her developmental stages contributed to the increasing power of her Inner Critic. That judgmental inner voice consistently engendered feelings of shame about this experience and so many others. It strengthened the unconscious expectation that her love would be inadequate to change similar situations and that somehow, no matter what happened, she would deserve the blame. We now come to the part of her journey where we explore what might heal these deep hurts.

These inner wounds naturally arise for many of us in the course of living an empathic life. Understanding why we are sensitive and vulnerable to relational encounters, how our emotional injuries have occurred, and what strategies we have unconsciously incorporated to deal with these hurts affords us the recognition that we are not to blame for what lies in our past. We can also derive support from knowing we are not alone as we suffer the consequences in the present.

Realizing this often brings some relief, but the story does not end here. If it did, we would remain caught in the snare of a victim mentality, endlessly suffering the disturbing frequencies of discordant energies in our field. We recognize that acting, feeling, and thinking like a victim serves no one. To heal, we must acknowledge what hurts, recognize what we have done and continue to do to maintain the suffering, and be willing to change our perspectives about ourselves, others, and life in general, sometimes at a very deep level. Some commit to this path and spend years in psychotherapy, making progress but never really wrestling free of the pain. Is this all there is?!

Based on our discussions of Energy Medicine thus far, we recognize that much of what we try to change has been encoded in our energy field as a habit. Suffering accompanied by the expectation of more suffering becomes a habit we'd like to break! It may seem odd, but our energies will resist changing that painful habit because our energies do not think. To change an energetic habit pattern requires an additional source of energy.

THE ROLE OF CONSCIOUSNESS IN HEALING

An oft-quoted saying in the world of energy healing—*energy follows thought*—suggests that thought should be enough to make a difference: affirmations should provide the extra energy needed to make a positive change. Yet what if our thoughts have no established access to the ingrained energy patterns? What if the energy patterns have thoughts of their own, associated with past experiences long forgotten? What role does unearthing those thoughts play in the healing process? Let us explore this further—Lily certainly did!

The Role of Consciousness in the Healing Process

At this point it strikes me as superbly fitting to quote Albert Einstein, not only a brilliant man but also wise, who stated: "No problem can be solved from the same level of consciousness that created it."[125] The application of this principle extends well beyond quantum physics: our inner psyches and how we approach life's dilemmas reap benefit from this wisdom as well. If we return briefly to the Holistic Model of Human Consciousness described in Chapter 7, we can discern different states of experience. Physical consciousness notes our awareness of overall energy level, aches, pains, comforts, and pleasures. This differs from consciousness related to our body's movement in time and space, which may now trigger some physical awareness of aches and pains or pleasures in the context of movement, but also registers how it feels to run or walk or swim, for example.

The awareness associated with emotions has its physical correlates, heart pounding or stomach burning when we're upset, for example, but emotional upset possesses a quality of its own. Emotional distress often responds to and sometimes generates specific thoughts, but

---

[125] "Albert Einstein," BrainyQuote.com, Xplore Inc, 2015, accessed March 11, 2015, http://www.brainyquote.com/quotes/quotes/a/alberteins130982.html.

these differ from the feelings connected with them in the context of how we experience thought, being lighter in quality, less dense. Soul consciousness at even higher levels offers the most ethereal, peaceful, awe-filled feelings.

We have also discussed how each level of consciousness in our holistic model is ensouled, and how specific levels of soulful awareness can merge with or become isolated from others in the context of life's wounding. Factors such as our innate proclivities for sensory receptivity, our early childhood experiences, our capacity for processing life attentively on each of these levels, what we've been taught, and how wounded we've become all affect how conscious we are of our soul's presence in our life.

Further reflection on Einstein's quote reveals that therapeutic recommendations that address an injured aspect of our human experience often involve an application of some remedy from another level of the model. For example, we may ease physical aches and pains with rest or movement of the body. Muscular tension may respond to emotional release of stress. Changing our thoughts often changes how we feel. Becoming more soulfully attuned to our place in a loving universe can shift what and how we think.

In contrast, trying to correct a problem on the same plane of the wound turns into a battle, the winner ultimately determined by which is stronger. Are the antibiotics stronger than the infection? Does the surgical removal of an organ or replacement of a joint eliminate the source of pain in the body? Do affirmations really win the war against the Inner Critic's endless commentary?

On the emotional level, we may try to manage this struggle with a counter-emotion and idea. For example, "A friend just made me angry" turns into "I am NOT angry with my friend. I really do care about her. I must have done something to deserve this. (I don't know what I did, so my mind will make up a believable story, at least to me, to explain this.)" Fortunately, the body remembers the anger and what stirred it: the hormones and neurotransmitters continue to flood the cells; and the issue resurfaces in some form such as skin rashes, painfully moving muscles or joints, repetitive, unwanted thoughts, or an intense emotional explosion when we least expect it.

Sometimes positive affirmations have a similar effect. Trying to stamp out a negative thought without understanding its origin may find us mumbling the same mantra hundreds of times each day in a battle for dominance of the positive. Many of today's "quick fixes" unfortunately rely upon the application of Band-Aids to a deep, sometimes festering wound. Only another level of attention can truly relieve the pain, bring the cause to light, and allow for the recognition that living from the wound no longer serves us. Once we accomplish this we can make the choice to really let it go.

Carl Jung, a psychiatrist whose therapeutic focus embraced a more spiritual perspective than Freud's, described a *transcendent function*: a numinous "third" residing above the plane of conflict on which the "two" opponents (whatever they may be) battle. From the transcended perspective, resolution for the dilemma occurs by integrating the previously separated opponents into the whole. Unlike the Borg (in the *Star Trek: The Next Generation* series), who frequently stated, "Resistance is futile," the transcendent function does not co-opt the opposing forces into unity against their wills. Instead, the transcendent function welcomes the opposing forces into the common bond they share on a higher plane. It makes peace without sacrificing the essence and integrity of each entity; the complementarity of their previous differences now serves a common goal.

It perhaps comes as no surprise that Jung and Einstein were contemporaries. Their reflections offer a framework within which to appreciate that healing comes from somewhere beyond the plane of the wound and that to resolve a dilemma in this dualistic universe we must seek a higher frame of reference. In other words, we must stretch, grow, learn, apply some effort, muster some courage, and sometimes step into the unknown. What do we fear when we do so? Perhaps that the past will endlessly repeat itself in the way a closed circle has no beginning and no end? The 1993 film, *Groundhog's Day*, portrayed this nicely. What do we seek? Dare we hope that the closed circle of wounding will open into a spiral that can access another realm and offer a fresh solution to our problem? By stretching, will our awareness more closely approach and perhaps better comprehend the Source of Healing? Will we experience a greater sense of conscious, soulful unity as a result? Or might the experience of these shifts frighten us in some way? These questions are for pondering: there is no cookbook approach, there are no guarantees…

During my years of providing a more traditional medical/psychiatric practice, I often experienced frustration as those in my care relied solely upon medication to help them feel better and thus make their lives more manageable. Yet this approach clearly proved helpful for some. With deep respect for the role of ego functioning in our lives, I learned that medications prove necessary for those needing that level of support if their stage of development, or their soul's intention for the current state of their mission, requires it.

There were others for whom the prescribed medication no longer seemed to work after a time, at which point higher amounts were required to achieve the same effect. With higher doses, side effects might also arise or intensify, further reducing the person's quality of life. Intuitively I sensed that a deeper healing might be possible—which might include medication or not—but that without a shift in the person's consciousness, that "depth" would elude us. Not being omniscient, I couldn't know the timing for each soul's unfolding. In essence, I was feeling my way.

Consequently, I often offered a more insight-oriented approach for healing, and many continued to want only medications. Respecting their decision, for a time I tried changing the antidepressant or adding a little of this or that—which often felt like applying the pointillist technique in a Seurat painting—and sometimes it would work. Inevitably some further adjustments would be required and in the meantime, while we did achieve maintenance often, something deeper called to me. An inner restlessness burned within me that I could only counter for brief periods. Eventually I decided I would listen to it: that call and the convergence of specific life experiences allowed my current path to unfold.

Reiki and Spirituality

As mentioned in Chapter 5, my introduction to Reiki came unannounced in the course of my search for insights regarding more emotionally related concerns. My body registered these emotions in my neck and shoulders—the bearers of our *shoulds*—and the alleviation of that pain followed a brief exposure to Reiki coupled with a Tarot reading. I no longer remember the specific emotional issues or what the cards revealed, but I will never forget the Reiki.

It felt like someone had placed a hot water bottle under my skin. Hours later the pain was gone! I was so impressed I decided then and there to learn it.

Practicing Reiki has changed my life, not because of its *to-do's* but because of its essence. It accessed that Higher Source of healing referenced above and initiated my conscious awareness of and connection with energy. Reiki became a way of life for me in all its subtlety and beauty. It has impacted my experience of Eden Energy Medicine in particular and Energy Medicine in general, and deserves some attention here to understand more deeply the process of healing.

Reiki, a Japanese word, means "Universal Life Force Energy." Its origins remain obscure, but its modern day *re*discovery by Mikao Usui in Japan during the early 1900's led to its spread across the Pacific to Hawaii and the US mainland during World War II, despite its association with Japanese roots. In fact, myths about Mr. Usui's link to Christianity and American institutions of higher learning emerged to justify its use in the United States. While these tales held no truth, the healings associated with the practice of Reiki captured the attention of many people, even though medical science could not explain them. The use of Reiki, in its simplicity, defies our Western expectation that healing interventions necessarily entail equipment, discomfort, and expense. Studies have supported its use to relieve anxiety, as well as some physical aches and pains. Nurses, always on the forefront of what is truly healing in my experience, were quick to learn Reiki. To the credit of many hospitals, they have permitted the practice of Reiki within their walls.

One of the first things taught about Reiki involves its primary purpose: the spiritual growth and enlightenment of the practitioner.

THE ROLE OF CONSCIOUSNESS IN HEALING

All other healing ensues from that directive. A person becomes attuned to the Universal Life Force Energy by a Reiki III level practitioner, whom many call a Reiki Master. I personally appreciate Mr. Usui's take on this, the word "Master" being given to practitioners by their students, not by their own choosing. Once students become attuned, Reiki energy flows through their field. Additional attunements can deepen the Reiki energy within one's field, and advancement through the levels of Reiki does indeed involve more attunements.

Traditionally, the training protocol involves waiting specified periods of time (ninety days between levels I and II; one year between levels II and III) before the next level attunements are offered. In the US some practitioners offer all three levels in one weekend. The traditional approach obviously encourages student practitioners to more deeply integrate Reiki into their consciousness and way of life before receiving the attunements to the next level. Non-traditional practice cares more for the rapid promulgation of Reiki within the culture. I honestly didn't realize the impact of this choice when I received my attunements more than ten years ago, but I appreciate having pursued the traditional approach.

Initially after my Reiki level I attunements I experienced some frustration as I couldn't feel any energy at all. I persisted, however, and before the ninety-day period came to its conclusion I could feel energy in my hands. It had different qualities, seemingly influenced by how long I held my hands in one place, with whom I worked, and what concerns required attention. As with all the energy interventions I have learned, then and since, I always practice on myself first. I will never forget one occasion when I fell forward on cement, landing *hard* on my knees: I felt sure I'd have black and blue marks at the very least. I immediately placed my hands on my kneecaps, hoping I hadn't cracked them, and centered into the flow of Reiki energy from beyond me. I felt the pain leaving my knees and minutes later I felt no pain at all. I never did bruise from that experience and I know that Reiki energy made all the difference.

I have really come to appreciate these physical healings through Reiki, but what has amazed me most is the deepening spiritual connection, not only in my mind and heart, but in my body. Feeling energy flow through my hands as a direct result of placing my attention and intention upon healing love and wholeness as it enters my Crown Chakra from a Healing Source beyond my comprehension continues to engender awe within me. Trusting the wisdom of Reiki energy entails a true spiritual surrender to Mystery which, in conjunction with its physical and emotional healing, highlights the transcendent nature of this process while facilitating a deep sense of centeredness in one's core.

Practicing Reiki has helped me appreciate how simple needs offer a doorway into the transcendent. For example, during the winter months, I place my freezing, red, white and blue Reynaud's fingers on my thighs and channel Reiki to them—which includes my attention to the love in the universe—and experience the one quick solution to that otherwise painful, prolonged misery, and simultaneously come to peace.

I once overheard one of my Eden Energy Medicine supervisors telling a fellow student that Reiki energy has its own intelligence.[126] "Reiki never harms."[127] It knows where to go no matter where

---

[126] My thanks to Amy McDowell, EEM-AP, for this insight.
[127] John Tompkins, Jr., *Mastering Reiki: A Practicing and Teaching Primer* (St. Paul, MN: Llewellyn Publications, 2002), 1.

one's hands are placed. Reiki energy knows what needs healing so the practitioner must surrender any expectation of specific results. For example, if a man requests an energy session to help with his painful knee, and he also struggles with pervasive issues related to flexibility in his life, Reiki energy may subtly attend to the flexibility issue and leave the knee painful until his psyche can more deeply integrate the lesson of flexibility.

A friend of mine tells a contrasting story about someone seeking healing for similar concerns from a non-Reiki practitioner. This client left the session having experienced relief from the pain in his knee then promptly fell down the steps, breaking another bone in his leg. I have no way of knowing for sure what caused what, but as a result of practicing Reiki I have learned to trust the wisdom of the body and of the healing energy we access to ease our distress.

Reiki and Eden Energy Medicine

Eden Energy Medicine, unlike Reiki, offers specific exercises suggested by assessing the client's energy flows and imbalances through energy testing. Once the practitioner determines what is imbalanced she can employ cognitively learned techniques that work for explainable reasons—in an energetic frame of reference, that is. Rather than the simple placement of hands on the person or in their energy field as with Reiki, Eden Energy Medicine offers specific exercises, protocols, and techniques the practitioner can use and the client can learn. Intuition matters as the practitioner and client follow the energy. Their heartfelt attention deepens the work and its effects. Re-testing confirms a positive response to the exercise or technique used and this suggests what "homework" will support the positive shift once the session ends. If a stronger energy test does not result from the intervention used, further exploration may lead to the root of the imbalance. Test—provide Eden Energy Medicine intervention—retest. Whatever brings balance to the prior imbalance is repeated at home to support a new pattern, and the recipient is empowered as an agent of her own healing.

An Eden Energy Medicine session differs from a Reiki session in several ways. The latter relies solely upon the Reiki practitioner to facilitate the flow of Reiki energy. Once the client leaves the session, unless she practices Reiki as well, the newly balanced energies will last only as long as the impact of life circumstances—and the client's beliefs about her experience of those circumstances—does not override the depth of healing achieved. Once that balance gets tipped into imbalance, another Reiki session is needed.

Eden Energy Medicine sessions also provide the greatest benefit when scheduled as a series. What the client can do between sessions on her own behalf differs significantly, however. With Reiki, the understanding of what needs healing and how that is energetically accomplished is held by the Universal Life Force Energy. In Eden Energy Medicine, the practitioner and client learn about the client's energy systems through energy testing; the client does homework to build resilience and help newly balanced energies hold the positive shifts; and successive sessions can then delve more deeply into the client's energy systems to consciously promote healing and greater resilience.

While Eden Energy Medicine does offer its clients greater awareness of their energy systems, along with their habitual energetic patterns and responses to daily living, consciousness of psychological or emotional issues is not required. With both Reiki and Eden Energy Medicine, consciousness need not be stimulated or pursued on the part of the recipient for the energy flow to have a positive effect. To support this claim, cynics who are at least open to the possibility that something *might* happen often leave energy sessions amazed by what they have experienced. Those committed to refusing an energetic shift will likely not feel one, however. In my experience, the energy of a consciously or unconsciously refusing will, if stronger than the balancing energies offered, can counter a healing effect: this applies to Energy Medicine approaches as well as to medication effects.

In contrast, a willing consciousness does enhance the flow and effects of energy healing (which many downplay as the placebo effect). I strongly suspect that greater awareness of what has hurt us and how we have coped with that hurt in the past allows for better choices in the present. The pursuit of better options can lead to fewer repetitive assaults on our energy systems and more resilience for the present and the future. Thus the dictum, "Energy follows thought," supports the development and use of intention and insight to promote energetic healing effects more rapidly, especially because we provide our energies with new thoughts to follow.

In summary, even in the absence of conscious intention and developing insight, energy healing can provide balance to our energy systems. How long that balance lasts may directly correlate, at least in part, with the depth of inner awareness we have dared to discover. Lily courageously journeyed into the depths of her psyche to explore confusing emotions. During this process, surprising, long-forgotten memories of past events emerged to reveal how they have deeply colored her present life. They surfaced in the course of our energy work together and, often for the first time, she experienced those memories through adult eyes. Through the energy work we were then also able to balance her energies around her new insights. We will explore this journey in greater detail in Chapter 14.

For the record, I need only add that I am grateful for both Reiki and Eden Energy Medicine. I continue to appreciate Reiki energy and its spiritual connection, trusting that it will always flow through my heart and hands, thus providing what is needed. I also enjoy the cognitive understanding of my clients' energies and the creative ways we partner to balance and restore their flow for their highest and greatest good.

Energy Psychology

In addition to my deep appreciation for Reiki and Eden Energy Medicine, I must add my profound gratitude for the impact of Energy Psychology[128] upon my life. Just as with Reiki, I had no idea it existed before the experience of it opened doors in ways I'd never imagined possible. I still smile remembering my first encounter with this phenomenal protocol.

My first exposure to Donna Eden's work came through a video lent by a friend, and months later I saw an announcement for her weekend workshop at the Omega Institute. After managing inner reservations about something so out of my comfort zone—the transportation—I decided I would find a way to deal with it and registered to attend. I have never enjoyed driving, and merging onto highways at high speeds always stirred enormous anxiety within me. I would literally "say my Hail Mary's and prepare to die." Travel to

---

[128] David Feinstein, Donna Eden, and Gary Craig, *The Promise of Energy Psychology: Revolutionary Tools for Dramatic Personal Change* (New York, NY: Jeremy P. Tarcher/Penguin, 2005).

THE ROLE OF CONSCIOUSNESS IN HEALING

the Omega Institute by car required merging onto several highways unless I chose "to go the chicken route" (which I did, of course). I had dubbed myself "Queen of the Back Roads" in joking with friends, but my queenly attitude sometimes added hours to my travel time. This case proved no exception.

The night before my departure I slept fitfully, all the while giving myself pep-talks. The next day I found several circuitous routes to circumvent three of the mergers, but two were unavoidable. I arrived safely, but drained and weary, after several hours of driving with white knuckles. That first evening I sat amidst at least two hundred other attendees, totally amazed by Donna Eden's radiance and energy. During the break, many gathered around her. I spied David Feinstein, Ph.D., her husband and a well-known psychologist, talking with a person who soon left his side. I engaged him in conversation, during which I mentioned my psychiatric background. He graciously thanked me for coming, to which I replied, "I wouldn't have missed this for anything, driving phobia and all." He raised an eyebrow quizzically and said, "Driving phobia?" He needed a volunteer for his Energy Psychology demonstration the following evening and asked if I might consider it. Without any idea of what might follow I enthusiastically said yes.

The next night I sat on a stage with fifty participants in attendance, all of us hoping to explore and experience the Energy Psychology protocol. David began by asking me about the development of my phobia. I explained that it likely took root during my childhood while sitting in the back seat of the car driven by my father, who every Sunday negotiated the merger on to the Schuylkill Expressway on our way to visit my paternal grandparents. In those days, before engineers re-worked the entrance and exit ramps, that merging proved enormously challenging as cars raced by without letting another vehicle onto the highway. After this merger we had to quickly cross three lanes of high-speed traffic in order to take the next exit, not too many feet away.

My father handled it the best way he knew how, unintentionally hurling all his tension, aggression, and anger back in my direction. When I became an adult, my friends dubbed that expressway "the Sure Kill," which didn't help my anxieties in the least! David listened to all this then explained the protocol. I and members of the audience were to repeat what he said while tapping specific points on our own bodies as he modeled the process. The audience joined in, having identified their own fears and phobias and rated them on a one-to-ten scale as I had done. We did several rounds; at their conclusion, I and the audience discovered that these ratings had dropped dramatically when we brought to mind our phobic stressors. Mine reached the therapeutic goal of two or less—it had dropped from ten to one!

While thrilled at the shift in my stress level when thinking about the drive home, I had no idea if this protocol had done anything of practical significance. The drive home would test it, of course, but I'd be on my own with five highway mergers to face. David suggested that I tap the protocol again before beginning my journey, which I did. Then the miraculous occurred! I began the merger onto the first highway, aware that in the past I would have been anticipating the possibility of disaster, but on this occasion I did not feel one blip of anxiety! Not one. I then proceeded to merge onto the next four highways, repeating the same peaceful experience. I could not believe it. For the first time in my life I experienced freedom from this imprisoning fear. Would it last? If Energy Psychology could work for this, what else might it do?

Before too long, I discovered the answers to these questions. Less than six months after my release from this life-long fear, my mother's first visit to the Emergency Room required me to make an hour's drive via—yes!—several expressways, during rush hour on the Friday after Thanksgiving. I felt stress, not knowing how serious her condition might be, but the drive itself proved quite negotiable. Gratitude doesn't express the half of what I felt for that gift.

Since then I have continued to study and use the protocol with great benefit to my clients, and I rely upon its unfailing assistance myself when the need arises. In instances when I have some idea of what is bothering me, or at least can *begin* to put words to my emotional confusion, I name the feelings that come to mind and tap the meridian beginning and end points. The message travels along the meridian pathways and enters the deep recesses of my brain, where the spoken word, or thoughts unspoken, might never penetrate on their own. With the resonance of word and energy images arise, as do additional memories and greater clarity about the problem. As I tap and talk, I know I've really unearthed the root of the issue when deeper, previously hidden emotions flow forth. I then acknowledge these feelings with compassion and appreciate Triple Warmer's efforts to maintain outmoded habits to deal with the issue. I install a new message of more optimal functioning while acknowledging, with respect, my adult capabilities and, with gratitude, my spiritual resources. These new truths replace the previous wound-derived messages deep within.

Thus unlike Reiki or Eden Energy Medicine, where consciousness need not be accessed, in Energy Psychology some degree of awareness plays an important role in selecting the best words to coordinate with the tapping locations so as to facilitate the shift. Consciousness can deepen and expand in the process of tapping as well. While the protocol can address a variety of issues, I have found Energy Psychology to be especially helpful in my work when a distressing emotion or belief is cognitively recognized as inappropriate or unwanted, but that recognition alone proves powerless to shift the experience of distress or alter the power of the belief. Energy Psychology harnesses the power of consciousness to the energy highways that hold old beliefs and traumatic patterns hostage in their blind alleys. When consciousness and energy pathways work together, profound, deep, and lasting healing can happen.

...And More!

As science begins to validate what the ancients knew, it becomes increasingly clear to me that I will always have something new to learn about Energy Medicine. Most recently—after Lily and I concluded our work together—a friend introduced me to the work of Jonathan Goldman, who respects and honors Light and our ability to call upon Its Presence for healing.[129] His attention to Light's healing power reminds me of Kabbalah's *Endless Light*, the Source of the Radiances (*Sefirot*) of the Tree of Life. His approach invites us to become more heart-centered and conscious of the heart's tremendous capacity for compassion, forgiveness, and faith, so that when we call upon Light we experience its gifts and extend them to others through our heart.

---

[129] Goldman, *Gift of the Body*, 125, 129, 450–451, 470, 482.

THE ROLE OF CONSCIOUSNESS IN HEALING

Jonathan Goldman acknowledges that our hearts have been wounded and need to heal, but also that we have everything we need in our energy fields to effect that healing. Becoming aware of these gifts and the endless presence of Light, and learning to trust our hearts as resonant with the truth of our existence and all that extends beyond us, constitute important aspects of his teaching. Again we see the value of consciousness on our human journey.

As I explore Jonathan Goldman's perspective with regard to healing work more deeply, it strikes me that his approach integrates the spirituality of Reiki and Universal Life Force Energy with Eden Energy Medicine's respect for the chakras, alongside Energy Psychology's recognition of our psychological/emotional struggles and how they respond to energetic interventions for healing. In Jonathan Goldman's work, however, chakras serve as the primary energy system, in contrast to the meridians of Energy Psychology. This highlights the fact that the beauty of energy work—and the challenge of proving its merit—lies in the ubiquitous nature of energy and its many doorways of access. Various schools and methodologies of Energy Medicine exist currently and I trust that more will emerge in the future. We need only follow our heart to discover the approach/es best suited to us.

Now that we have a deeper understanding of energy as a significant avenue of healing, and a greater appreciation for the importance of our heart, whole and involved in the process, we can turn our attention to changing the self-sabotaging beliefs that have perpetuated our suffering, but which also respond to these healing interventions. We have all the tools needed to begin to mend our broken hearts. The healing heart loving the wounded heart translates into learning to love ourselves. We will explore this further in the next chapter.

CHAPTER 12

Learning to Love Oneself

"EVERYBODY IS A GENIUS. But if you judge a fish by its ability to climb a tree, it will live its whole life believing that it is stupid."[130] This quote, often attributed to Albert Einstein, serves well to describe the experience of empaths. Sponges do not make good ducks. Still, none of us *deserves* to believe we are stupid. None of us *wants* to hate ourselves. It just happens in significant relationships as we respond to the expectations and feedback we perceive from others, especially while we are young.

We've described in detail how the Inner Critic develops and how, in the context of this quote, it insists we continue to measure ourselves by our ability to climb trees even though we can outswim any monkey or squirrel! If no one ever tells us we're exceptional swimmers, we won't value our capacity for depth or speed. We won't

---

[130] Matthew Kelly, "Everybody is a Genius," in *The Rhythm of Life: Living Every Day with Passion and Purpose* (New York, NY: Simon & Schuster, 2004), 80; or *Quote Investigator: Exploring the Origins of Quotations.* http://quoteinvestigator.com/2013/04/page/2/.

see the benefits of breathing under water; we will only focus on our inadequacy for not breathing air. The beliefs instilled about our *in*abilities will deeply etch themselves into our consciousness. After a time, no surplus of compliments will change the ingrained belief that we are terrible tree climbers—or muddy sponges. Something else, something profound, must occur within us before any change in our self-perception can emerge.

Partnering with the Inner Critic to Find Love

The wisdom endlessly echoed in most spiritual and healing circles suggests that we need to love ourselves as much as we love others. Even if it makes logical sense in the moment, this Herculean feat remains truly impossible while the Inner Critic reigns within. We have come to recognize how the Inner Critic controls the script of the shadowy unconscious, as well as its eruptions into consciousness when life experiences challenge us. We now also understand how that script has become a habit, maintained by Triple Warmer energy so that positive affirmations do little to temper the Critic's insensitive rule.

If these critical habits are to change, consciousness matters here. The first step in learning to love ourselves requires that we notice the consequences of *not* loving ourselves and acknowledge that we are just plain sick of it. We're tired of it. We're done! Without that first reactive feeling/recognition, all else becomes theory without power. When we've exceeded our tolerance for being bullied by an elusive inner force, we marshal the energy of protest. We need this! Now we're ready and more empowered to do the work of freeing ourselves from the Inner Critic's grip.

Because the Inner Critic's voice has seemed so much like our own, we likely have accepted its criticisms as absolute truth originating from a shadowy, deep place within. The next step in loosening its grasp on our sense of self involves seeing it as the separate entity that it is. The Critic sprang from experiences in which we felt painfully alone; its intention was to help us survive them by being strong and in alignment with prevailing opinions around us. That we might feel even more lonely in response to its methods has never mattered: at least we would not be taken by surprise and humiliated or abandoned by others.

The Inner Critic speaks to us in self-definitions that always find us lacking in some way—the very situations that spawned its existence. During its term of dictatorship, it couples these definitions with a critical push for us to make up for that lack or to hide our inadequacy. While its voice directs our inner life, it is difficult to discern what is true regarding our essential nature and what is not. We need to develop that discernment, as it provides a crucial step toward freedom and self-love.

Thus we must recognize that we *have* an Inner Critic, but that we *are not* the Inner Critic. When it comes out of the shadows and reveals itself in a metaphorical face-to-face encounter, we can finally engage in a real dialogue. By surrendering our role as puppets yanked about by the Inner Critic's commentary, we realize we can maneuver on our own: we can ask questions, try to understand its intentions and methods, tell it how its efforts affect us, and state our needs. Notably, it is not uncommon for fears to arise during this engagement. Because this work seriously upends the status quo, Triple Warmer will likely make its presence felt with symptoms of anxiety, tense muscles, facial flushing, and other related discomforts, all to spark inner resistance to this process. At this point we need a conscious reason to persist in our efforts.

If we take responsibility for our inner state (not that we caused it necessarily, but that it is ours to address), we then have the painful task of recognizing how cruelly we have treated ourselves. This humbling practice strips the Inner Critic of some power while re-allocating that energy to the healing heart's compassion and observing Witness within. That Witness sees things as they are—without judgment. A dialogue between one's heart-informed Inner Witness and the Inner Critic can help us understand why those harsh self-assessments took root in the first place. What past experiences stirred fears or other emotions too difficult to bear? What misguided beliefs were adopted to render the situation more tolerable? What vital aspect of self was sacrificed in the process?

Dialogue with intention—and most importantly, without judgment—allows information to pour forth from the hidden recesses of the unconscious. Energy Medicine facilitates that dialogue as it provides access to long-forgotten memories from childhood. Once the flow of energy has helped those memories surface into the consciousness of the cortex, they can be examined through the eyes of the now-grown adult. Professional guidance may be helpful here; at the least we need another pair of eyes that can witness from a vantage point free of the old, self-punishing beliefs.

Sometimes the source of the struggle lies deeply buried and encased by Triple Warmer protection, rendering the issue inaccessible to energy work until consciousness opens a doorway. By way of example, another of my clients, George, struggled with a particularly painful dilemma that took months to uncover. Even his energy systems reacted strongly to any attempt to touch the points on his head that might bring greater awareness and resolution to his suffering. His Triple Warmer energy would not let us get close energetically to what bothered him. Even though George had suffered deep anxiety and depression most of his life—a consequence of living with pervasive feelings of shame and guilt—and even though he felt more than sick of it all, he also felt trapped for reasons that eluded us.

As we explored his feelings and associations in depth over the ensuing weeks, we finally realized that as a child empath he had grown up perceiving and believing that if he asserted his own needs, his mother's emotional stability would collapse. He felt deeply responsible for maintaining his mother's precarious emotional balance, and deep guilt should he threaten it in any way. His mother unwittingly reinforced this belief by shaming him with labels like "self-centered" and "greedy" if he denied her the expected response or expressed his own emotional needs. With the receptivity of an empath and the loyalty of a child to his parent, George received this information of self-centeredness and greediness as ultimate, shameful truth.

We can pause to appreciate that George's mother likely did her best to teach her son how to care about others and how to negotiate social situations. She also likely tried to provide better parenting than she herself received. Yet she did not realize that her son is an empath, that her own unattended and unresolved emotional state had such an impact upon him, and that her child really needed more guidance about how to care for his own needs than for those of others. Not having received any of this, George worked hard to understand his hidden heartaches throughout most of his adult life.

Unfortunately, despite his ability to recognize some of the issues, his Inner Critic and Triple Warmer proved to be enormously powerful and protective of this core belief: his responsibility for protecting his mother's fragility necessitated that he unconsciously sacrifice his own path to healing.

Consequently, any attempts to heal, to care for himself, would inevitably earn him Inner Critic labels of self-centeredness and greediness; worse, these labels were unconsciously paired with his belief that his mother's emotional stability would crumble. Once this inner situation made its way to the light of consciousness, we could reassure his Triple Warmer and Inner Critic that we would make every effort to respect his aging mother's legitimate needs. George could finally begin to explore what healing might offer him in other aspects of his life without risking life-threatening disaster. Our energy sessions reflected this shift as Triple Warmer became more welcoming of our interventions.

Mustering the Courage to Love

As we explore this process of learning to love oneself, we must realize that once some consciousness emerges regarding old, entrenched beliefs, an individual working to free herself from the strictures of the Inner Critic needs even more courage as she ventures into new relationships to explore healing alternatives. Fears that the past will repeat itself are natural here. The use of Eden Energy Medicine techniques can help Triple Warmer, however, by balancing its protective excess so that it will relax and welcome new experiences. With hope and intention, these new experiences eventually constitute a "new normal."

Assisting Triple Warmer and Spleen energies to embrace new habit patterns makes these profound shifts less energetically daunting and more successful. Supporting Kidney Meridian, whose correlated balanced emotion is courage, facilitates this venturing into a new way of experiencing life with less fear and consequent resistance. Working with Water Rhythm, which includes both Kidney and Bladder Meridians, adds a dollop of hope into the mix. We discuss these energy systems in more detail in the next chapter. For now, the point remains that with the assistance of Energy Medicine and Energy Psychology, this heroine's and hero's journey toward self-love becomes a viable option and an attainable goal.

So what does the experience of love for oneself look and feel like? For some, this may seem foreign and impossible to even conceive. Without a model, an image, or some prior experience, leaving the Inner Critic's ground behind to venture toward love can feel like stepping off a cliff into a void. Fortunately, most of us have had at least one special person or one profound experience of love to draw upon in this work of learning to love oneself. Caring empaths have high standards for what is required to love others. The task is to hold that remembered loving experience and those standards of care and apply them to oneself.

For this process, as with any relationship, it is easy to love a person who is funny, pleasant, engaging without being oppressive, and authentic without making demands. When a loved one is sick, moody, angry or despairing, unable to do or provide what has become expected—then challenges to love arise. Caring empaths may be quick to sacrifice themselves under these circumstances, even when the other is critical, ungrateful, and sometimes frankly abusive. They may not understand why they are not loved in return to the same degree and depth. Without devaluing the empath's capacity to love others, let us recognize that the heart is a *both/and* energy center. The empath must learn to include herself and her wounded heart in her loving equation.

When the healing heart receives an invitation to approach the wounded heart, coupled with the Inner Critic's cooperation, the empath's amazing capacity to love can begin to satisfy the wounded heart's deep longing to be seen, heard, felt, known, and appreciated. As we extend compassion to ourselves for all the wounds suffered in the name of relationship, remembering to include all the vulnerabilities that led to those wounds, we begin to embrace our heart-centered humanness.

Over time we can learn to love ourselves unconditionally despite all our blemishes, perceived defects, our emotional outbursts and failures to act. We can compassionately accept how we were doing our best when we felt invisible, inadequate, or unable to fix people, situations, or things. We can gently reassure ourselves when we fear we haven't loved well enough, or that we will become engulfed by the needs of others. We can lovingly soothe ourselves for all those moments of feeling humiliated in the past and the present, in our imaginings of the future, and for our misguided belief that we deserve that humiliation. We can forgive ourselves for all the guilt we feel when we sense that we have failed others, disappointed them, or hurt them in some way.

We can also learn to love ourselves for our desire to be loved and appreciate ourselves for our strengths, our talents, our joy and our passions. Oddly, our gifts may have threatened significant others in the past and consequently we learned to regard them as dangerous, rather than worthy of love. Allowing love to penetrate what once lived in lonely isolation offers a completely new experience of life.

This brings us to the important aspect of choice. Learning to love oneself does not just happen: one does not wake up from a dream one morning and decide suddenly that self-love is one's new normal. Years of beliefs, habits, reactions to triggers, and inner condemnation cannot be magically swept away by a moment of magnanimity toward oneself. The choice to love oneself must become a way of life. It must be chosen and practiced moment to moment, day by day.

This "prescription" can feel like the burden of eating one's vegetables, brushing one's teeth, or doing one's homework. We may recognize it as important, but not *feel* like doing it. Unlike these wisdom-driven routines, loving oneself also requires courage as one says "no" to previous behaviors and ways of being in relationship. It becomes necessary to stretch one's "bravery" muscles in order to face Triple Warmer anxieties and calm them, rather than give in to them. Choosing to love oneself requires a new relationship with guilt and shame—and with self-competence and strength. On the plus side, the practice of self-love stirs the fires of creativity as one considers how different life can be. Additionally, unlike the significantly delayed feedback derived from the benefits of tedious self-care, the blessings of loving oneself provide immediate, deep gratification and centeredness.

One of the odd fears stirred by this process of self-love involves the risk of becoming narcissistic. Empaths often experience the needs of others as encroaching on their inner space, especially when others do not monitor how their need-gratification affects those around them. Empaths worry that caring for their own needs will affect those in their personal world in the same way that they themselves have been affected: being intruded upon or engulfed. While this is often not the case, it doesn't change the immediate perception or fear.

The broader question to be addressed involves the fact that we humans live in community. Where is the boundary between one person and the next? From the perspective of energy, we have already seen that their auric fields overlap! So how does one take responsibility for one's energy field and its impact upon others? Ducks may not even recognize this as a problem, while sponges may take on the burden of everyone's field! In the midst of this confusion, an empath must somehow find peace. This brings us to our next topic and its impact upon our beliefs about deserving and sharing love…

The Empath Contract

Most empaths do not realize that at some point in their childhood an Empath Contract began to dictate how they live their lives. It developed in the context of a family culture, specific to the needs of the caregivers and their expectations of how the family should function. The line-by-line items on the Contract differ for each empath based on each unique family system, but the following themes often present, singly or in combination:

When those who care for me feel a distressing emotion, I have unconsciously agreed to:
- fix it for them
- protect them from painful emotions by feeling their feelings for them
- feel responsible for what they feel and consequently guilty, as if I caused it

- make excuses for them, so they don't have to take responsibility
- try to anticipate their needs and behavior so they don't suffer, or explode, or hurt me or others in some way
- do what they seem to want me to do, so we maintain a seemingly peaceful relationship
- act on what they feel so they don't have to, thereby taking the blame for problematic behaviors, such as expressing their anger or other feelings (without letting anyone identify the real source, of course)
- pretend the pain I *do* sense isn't there, especially if they don't want to acknowledge their own feelings
- accept their vision and definition of the world and of me in order to maintain a relationship with them, even if it means losing my sense of self
- make it easier for them to bear their feelings by doing whatever it takes, including sacrificing my own needs

From this list emerge the familiar roles of the scapegoat, the "identified patient" in a family system, the perpetual victim, "the helping hand that strikes again,"[131] the numbed one, the "bad boy" or "bad girl" in the family, the long-sufferer, and many variations on these themes. The labels stick, the behaviors engender attitudes, and the script seems defined for a lifetime. Yet contrary to the requirement for a formal legal contract, one of the parties engaging in this arrangement was not of mature age and mental capacity. The child in this instance can never be legally recognized as able to sign on the dotted line.

---

[131] Adam Grant, "Helicopter Managers: The Helping Hand Strikes Again," accessed March 13, 2015, https://www.linkedin.com/pulse/20130421122648-69244073-helicopter-managers-the-helping-hand-strikes-again.

We have already alluded to Lily's unconscious agreement as a young child to stabilize her mother's emotional life with whatever might work in the moment. This often required that she dissociate from her own needs, expect feminine weakness, anticipate an undercurrent of criticism, and keep quiet about what was really going on beneath the superficial presentation her family offered to their larger social circle. As a child, she did not understand the long-term implications of the terms to which she had unconsciously agreed. Her Inner Critic enforced them, however, with all the power of a police state. Whenever she violated the Contract, she felt shamefully punished, guilty of some unnamed crime, and emotionally imprisoned, with her Inner Critic serving as the guard at the door. Her story may hold a unique combination of details, but its theme will likely resonate with most, if not all empaths.

The above-mentioned themes of the Empath Contract reflect an empath's tendency to feel the emotions of another person, along with the emotional consequences of the coping strategies the other employs. George's mother, for example, experienced frequent periods of emotional overwhelm, which George felt and interpreted as "crumbling," and her coping style relied upon George to stabilize her. If his own needs interfered with this "contract," he (like Lily) had to negate his needs or his mother would do so for him by telling him he was selfish.

His mother's unconscious coping strategy demanded that George either sacrifice his own needs or suffer humiliation for being a selfish—bad—person in her eyes. Given the choice between his mother's crumbling psyche and his own emotional decimation he chose the latter, without ever pausing to acknowledge that his inner world could bear what his mother's psyche could not. Instead his Inner Critic told him he was weak, inadequate, incapable, and selfish. His lower chakra drives for safety and security, personal worth and freedom, power and identity, met with piercing criticism in the context of "mother love." It appears that his mother's coping strategy proved even more destructive for George than did her unresolved emotional limitations.

When situations like this occur repeatedly, the child empath absorbs these feelings and strategies as habit patterns into her energy field and brain pathways. Consequently, her reactions to similar triggers become automatic. The Empath Contract arranged in childhood with a significant caregiver can become an unconscious agreement for all close relationships for the rest of one's life. By way of example, let's say an empath's father has difficulty expressing and dealing with intense emotions. When overwhelmed by anyone's anger, especially his own, he withdraws emotionally, perhaps even physically. During these many incidents, the empath child senses her father's anger without recognizing its source: his face doesn't register much emotion and he never speaks of it. Consequently, the empath feels her own internal upheaval in response to her father's hidden anger, coupled with relational abandonment by her father who may have also physically retreated from the room. In the midst of this muddle, what Contract terms is our empath being asked to accept?

The empath child naturally feels sad at the loss of her father's availability; perhaps also ashamed, thinking she might have caused it; afraid of her own inner turmoil in response to feeling abandoned; confused about what may be going on in the family; and angry that she has to hurt this way while unknowingly feeling her father's anger as well. How can a child possibly comprehend all aspects of what is happening within her? This scenario offers a prime set-up for an interior sense of "yuck!" That feeling becomes paired with unspoken anger, emotional abandonment, the need to keep the peace, to make the other happy or at least not angry, and to retreat if her efforts do not work. If this Contract is never examined as she grows, she will behave like her father in relationships without ever realizing that she is dutifully honoring her Empath Contract. But does this Contract truly reflect her own natural ability to express anger and her desire to be with others in relationship?

This empath child may have no one with whom to confide, no one to help her sort out the complexity of her internal distress, no one to acknowledge these as natural feelings, no one to soothe her. If the family agenda requires peace above all else—as her father's behavior would seem to imply—this child may become quite gifted as a peacemaker, but at tremendous personal cost. This may take the form of social isolation and/or dissociation from her feelings in general, eventually contributing to an internal sense of numbness or deadness, if not active thoughts of dying or wishing to be dead. As this empath child grows, whenever she encounters those who deny their anger she will likely fulfill the Empath Contract originally handed to her by her family of origin. She will remain quiet, keep the peace, and retreat. Such behavior may contribute to recurrent internal numbing and depression, not to mention loneliness. Without conscious inner work, she may never realize why.

A Time for Renegotiation

Fortunately, an adult empath can explore the terms of the Contract to which she unconsciously agreed during her childhood. While these terms may escape her notice upon first examination, she can recognize them in the way she deals with her current relationships. What happens to her needs in the face of another's seemingly more pressing agenda? When people are upset, what is her knee-jerk response toward them? How does she relate to herself in the midst of that response? What inner tapes run non-stop when the boundaries of self and other blur?

The ability to evaluate this Contract through adult eyes offers good news: it was never legally binding and can definitely be re-negotiated. Renegotiation requires consciousness, however: an empath cannot begin to establish a new Contract without awareness of the old Contract's detailed expectations, an equitable evaluation of those terms, and acknowledgment that they no longer serve one's best interests (and likely no one else's for that matter). Once those conditions are met, the empath must then recognize her own authority to define the new terms of her life. She must give herself permission to write an Empath Contract that honors the principles most supportive of her nature and her soul's intention. By loving herself, she can better define how to pursue her highest and greatest good, thus naturally serving the highest good of others as well.

A New Empath Contract

What might better serve as new terms for an Empath Contract? This depends upon the principles that guide one's life. We might ask ourselves the following questions:
- What do I believe about the role of suffering in life? When is it meaningful? When is it meaningless? What criteria determine those categorizations?

- Does service require suffering? If I'm enjoying the process of giving and receiving, for example, is what I am doing still service?
- Does sensitivity have a meaningful purpose? Does that purpose obligate me toward others in some way?
- Do I assess the conditions of a new Contract according to the criteria of soul-growth or ego-satisfaction? Or simply put, do I provide what I/they *need* in order to heal or grow? Or do I provide what I/they *want* in order to *feel good*?
- How does the Contract address situations where the needs of self and others seem to conflict?
- Can I live a joy-filled, creative, and meaningful life and still provide a service to humankind?

We can perhaps acknowledge that these questions and some potential answers lead us into the realm of spirituality. We will address this aspect of the empath's life and decision-making more specifically in Part III; for now, let's simply explore possibilities. If we consider the option that an empath deserves to experience happiness and joy in life often, what would the new Contract entail?

Given that an empath will always sense the pain of others, she must decide how much exposure to these painful emotions serves the Contract. Does she still want to be available to others in their hurting moments? Her Contract then has to define the balance between the other's needs and her own: will the Contract weight one greater than the other, or will the needs of both self *and* other apply? In addition, she must decide for how long she will endure those painful emotions and for what purpose.

Will this new Contract require her to make others happy because they want it, expect it, or think they can't make themselves happy on their own? Or will the new Contract enable her, by recognizing the hurt in others, to invite them to shift those painful emotions to something more authentic and balanced? If others do not make that choice toward growth, how long will she stay in their company?

And what about situations in which others do not say what they feel: will the new Empath Contract require the empath to honor the person's unspoken feelings? If so, the empath will need to accurately monitor her own inner state and use that information to surmise what the other person really wants or needs. Or will the empath honor only a person's spoken words even if her sensory perception tells her that the other really wants something else? What criteria will help her decide how best to engage with this person?

If she bases her decision on the feelings she perceives, she risks that the other will not consciously or verbally agree with her. If she makes her decision based on the words spoken, she will *feel* the discrepancy as well as the inadequacy of her response. Such a situation forces the empath to clearly define the terms of her new Contract: must she please others? In this situation that may be impossible; will she choose personal authenticity? She risks disturbing the relational peace; does she care about personal growth (for both parties) even if the other doesn't? What are her values? What is she willing to risk? What will she decide?

Please notice I have not once suggested that the empath *not* feel what the other feels. Neither have I stated that the feelings perceived through association with others make anyone "bad" or abnormal. Given the empath's neurological and energetic wiring, she cannot stop sensing these feelings, as we know. We know that others cannot stop feeling, either. Empaths have come into this incarnation to experience emotions, their own certainly, as well as those triggered by the internal state of others.

If we choose to accept this as a reality with a purpose, not a disorder needing a treatment, then we must learn to work with these emotional, sometimes physical inner states: accept them, understand them, allow them to deliver their message—then help them to move on! In this way we cleanse the sponge on a regular basis without criticizing the mud, the sponge, or the need for frequent bucket baths. Energy Medicine and Energy Psychology provide some of the best tools I have learned to date to help an empath/sponge restore, maintain, and restore again her pristine, beautiful state.

We now turn our attention to some wonderful and very effective Energy Medicine techniques to balance our energies, build resilience, and heal the deeper wounds that continue to scream at us when they resonate with the shared pains and heartaches of others. In this process of personal healing we discover that caring for others and sensing their emotional wounds provides the information we need to be truly and authentically present, without having to re-experience our own deep, personal traumas over and over again.

As we develop energetic resilience through the practice of these exercises and techniques, we also promote greater emotional strength and capacity to be with others. We may frequently and more meaningfully redefine the terms of our Empath Contract as we heal and grow. In so doing, we can experience more fully and courageously the life we were born to live. So now let's turn our attention to these interventions, how they assisted Lily in her healing process, and how they can help each of us become more fully who we are.

CHAPTER 13

Energetic Coping Techniques for the Empath

MY OWN JOURNEY into the world of energy work has offered me many jaw-dropping moments. I love watching the shift in my clients' facial expressions as a gentle look of surprise and awe emerges in response to their first experience of their own energies. I appreciate the feedback that energy testing affords, offering validation or correction as we follow an intuition and engage in mutual "play" while exploring those hunches to see if they hold some value. As my clients become more accustomed to their own energy balances and imbalances, their intuitions often prove amazingly accurate.

While energy testing is easy to learn, it is difficult to teach from the printed page. It involves developing a "feel" for energy flows and is best learned in person with an experienced instructor. Testing offers those of us who can't see energy the opportunity to trust another aspect of our knowing. Like children learning to balance on a two-wheeler, after some practice we "get it" and the new ability becomes a part of who we are and what we know. Life is never the same!

While Energy Medicine offers benefits to everyone, empaths can experience significant shifts in their energy systems especially because they are sensitive. That sensitivity to energy may seem foreign at first, but I have found that our awareness of it quickly develops with some attention and practice. I have personally and professionally experienced the fruits of this work in addressing three aspects of daily living: 1) building overall resilience; 2) restoring resilience when something knocks us into an imbalanced state; and 3) healing the deep wounds whose energy patterns underlie and often impact the energy systems of daily coping.

Lily and I employed various Energy Medicine interventions particularly directed toward the third aspect during our work together. Attending to the first and second aspects of this practice has enormous value, however, especially for empaths wanting to connect with others from a place of internal grounding and heartfelt care.

A disciplined attempt to build energetic resilience, and knowing what to do when imbalances arise, not only facilitates easier integration of the new patterns that emerge from attending to deeper inner work. They also make daily exchanges with others less problematic and more effective for everyone involved. So as to encourage empaths to consider these energetic interventions, I shall discuss these three aspects in more detail.

Examples of the applicability of Energy Medicine and descriptions of some of these exercises are provided in this chapter. For more detailed discussion of Eden Energy Medicine techniques, the reader is referred to Donna Eden's book,[132] her website,[133] and/or her workshops and trainings. In this chapter, I offer what energy exercises I know to be beneficial as an introduction to Energy Medicine with the hope that readers will pursue whichever energy techniques feel most meaningful for them.

Building Energetic Resilience

The first benefit of a daily energy practice is to build general resilience in our energy field, as discussed in Chapters 5 and 6. We considered how this practice supports all our energy systems and how we can stabilize our aura, the first receiver of energetic information.

When our aura functions well in sorting out what belongs in our field and what doesn't, we become less vulnerable to the intrusion of energies around us: our energies do not so quickly reverse or freeze, and Triple Warmer does not excessively engage. Our energy systems also come to trust that we will consciously take them seriously. Once energetic balance becomes a habit, these energies of daily living know how to find their way back home when pushed into an imbalanced state. They seem to have their own inner wisdom *as well as* a willingness to learn. It just takes our own belief system a little while to catch on!

A participant in one of my classes for empaths made the commitment to do Donna Eden's Daily Energy Routine for periods of time, interspersed with periods of distraction and forgetting. This on-again, off-again approach to the exercises gave her a direct experience of their benefit. She noticed significant differences in how she felt when she did the Daily Energy Routine every day and when she

---

[132] Eden with Feinstein, *Energy Medicine*.
[133] Innersource, www.Innersource.net.

didn't. Her sense of inner resilience directly correlated with her daily energy practice, and periods of emotional vulnerability coincided with those days when she did not do the exercises, supporting her awareness of what an Energy Medicine practice can do for her. The following example illustrates this subtlety in greater detail.

Each of us has an aura which, every minute of every day, actively tries to screen and deflect forces such as radiation, pollution, electromagnetic flares from the sun, and the frequencies associated with overhead fluorescent lights, food additives and dyes, and wireless communications, to name just a few energies foreign to the balanced state of our energy field. For an empath whose aura is naturally sensitive, Triple Warmer runs on hyper-drive; her muscles are usually tense if not sore; she maintains a hyper-vigilant view of her surroundings; she may even unconsciously anticipate disaster at every turn.

Her auric energies have likely moved into a reversed or frozen imbalance, doing their best to protect her from further energetic assault. Unfortunately, with a flipped magnetic field the "wrong" things are welcomed into the aura, while the "right" things are electromagnetically repelled and left at the proverbial door. Life is just plain challenging. Our empath finds that solitude provides the greatest sense of safety and peace. With daily repetition of these challenges, these imbalanced energy patterns become entrenched and "normal" for her. Continuing this not-so-hypothetical story (I have lived this one!), our empath lovingly agrees to meet a friend for lunch to offer her support for a recent heartbreak.

Let's say our empath has not yet engaged in a daily energy practice. Like most of us she perceives herself as coping as best she can, perhaps with a pervasive "uninspired" mood and a drain on her energy that she assumes is the normal consequence of living. She likely manages well enough, even with holes in her aura and frozen energies abounding, but at this meeting with her heartbroken friend she absorbs her friend's pain and quickly feels undone. Her energetic field has tipped beyond overwhelm; her Triple Warmer has engaged with even more excess.

Her body soaks up her friend's inner state and mounts its own reaction, neurologically, energetically, and psychologically. This encounter dramatically drains her. In addition to the grief and possible anxieties she perceives, she may even feel angry or guilty, adding confusion to the mix. Which feelings belong to whom? Will this overall "yuck" of a feeling tone color the rest of her day, drain her energy, and deplete her capacity to feel joy in response to the encounters and experiences yet to unfold?

If, on the other hand, she has committed to a daily energy practice, these effects will likely be less pronounced. Her energy routine will have reset irregular energies in her energy field, just as sleeping eight hours each night and eating well also help. Her aura can now engage with her friend during the luncheon encounter from a more balanced state, better able to flow with her friend's many emotions without having them penetrate so intensely. Without a flipped auric field she can attract her friend's caring energies, recognizing but not deeply absorbing the energies of anxiety, guilt, or anger that her friend never intended to pass on. With an intact aura, Triple Warmer does not need to so readily engage and our empath can remain more physically relaxed and emotionally present for her friend. She may even enjoy the encounter, glad for the opportunity to cry, laugh, and share other stories together!

If our empath has suffered losses in the past, the degree to which she has processed and healed her own heartaches will affect how deeply she resonates with her friend's distress. Her own depth of healing also impacts how much clarity and perspective she can bring to help her friend shift into a more healing mode herself. If our empath is savvy to her own energy needs, she will know to do the *Cleansing the Aura* exercise (Chapter 6), utilize some grounding techniques, and pursue whatever else she feels is needed to reset her own energetic balance once the encounter has ended. Should any residual emotions remain, these may be her own to address, and she can then pursue the inner work required to understand what still needs healing within her own psyche. Given the enormous stressors of daily living, we can all derive significant benefit from this practice of communing with our energies, thereby supporting our awareness that balanced energies feel good and that the path back to balance is familiar and easy.

The Restoration of Energetic Balance

It is important to realize that the forces bombarding us daily can negatively affect our energy systems even if we faithfully engage in a daily energy practice. As described above, knowing how to recognize the consequent imbalance and rebalance it can make a world of difference. Fortunately, Eden Energy Medicine offers many techniques to address various concerns specific to the empath, but that also benefit everyone.

For example, due to the Earth's electromagnetic shifts we often can feel ungrounded. I have already mentioned how rubbing our feet with the curved side of a stainless steel spoon can energetically reconnect us to the ground and support the electromagnetic field of the aura. Personally, I sometimes begin to feel tired while I'm driving and find that my head polarity has flipped. At a red light, I reach into my glove compartment, pull out a stainless steel spoon, and spoon my feet. The polarity corrects, the tiredness passes, and I am good to go! In Chapter 5 we also discussed the importance of calming Triple Warmer and supporting Spleen Meridian with the "Cover the Eyes" exercise. Most of us need this often!

Occasionally, we need specific reinforcement for the crossover of our energies. Neurologically, the right brain governs the left side of the body while the left brain governs the right side. Our energies need to cross as a general rule, and Donna Eden has offered two helpful energy exercises for this purpose.[134] A simple homolateral correcting exercise, known as the Crossover Shoulder Pull, involves placing one hand on the opposite shoulder, pressing the fingers deeply into the back of that shoulder, then dragging them firmly across the top of the shoulder and diagonally down the front of the torso to the opposite hip. After repeating this several times from the same shoulder, one then switches hands to do the same movement on the other side of the body. This quickly restores energies to their optimal crossover pattern.

While homolateral energy patterns initially invite us to slow down and rest when needed, sometimes they outlive their usefulness and become habitual. Pervasive homolateral patterns can occur during chronic illness, for example, and their persistence may prolong our feeling tired, judgmental, and/or depressed. Activities such as walking, swimming, dancing, and jogging (if not contraindicated) can

---

[134] Donna Eden (with David Feinstein), *Energy Medicine EM101: Introducing Energy Medicine Class Handouts* (Ashland, OR: Innersource, 2015).

return energies to their crossover patterns, promote more effective healing, lift a mildly depressed mood, and facilitate a greater sense of relaxation and calm. Difficulty initiating these activities, however, may be due to homolateral energies (feeling tired and sluggish is a great indicator): beginning an exercise program with Homolateral Repatterning and the Cross Crawl may override that initial inertia. The practice or simple visualization of these energy balancing exercises also provides benefit to those with limited mobility.

The Homolateral Repatterning exercise begins by moving the right arm and right leg together, then the left arm and left leg, in a marching mode, thus engaging the homolateral patterns of energy running through the same side of the body. After doing this twelve times, take a deep breath. Next, to support energies crossing from one side of the body to the other, simultaneously move the right arm and left leg, then the left arm and right leg, marching in place for another twelve rounds. If anyone feels tired after completing this series, it needs to be repeated in its entirety, sometimes several times. Whether done lying in bed, seated or standing, the goal is to restore the sense of energized relaxation and appropriate receptivity so natural to our body's energy flows. As an aside, I find this exercise offers an insight that extends well beyond energy work: the principle of meeting an imbalance where it lives. Engage with it on its own terms, like a gear, *then* shift. Unlike warfare's approach to conflict resolution, this method invites gentle, cooperative change.

The Lessons of Irregular Energies

When our energies become irregular, testing a specific energy system can sometimes give a false result. A dramatic illustration of this came my way during a session with a friend,[135] also an empath, whose treatment for breast cancer involved several rounds of chemotherapy. For one of our sessions, she presented as energetic and capable, having engaged in numerous activities that day despite having received a chemo infusion just a few days before. When we tested her thymus, an indicator of the immune system, a strong energy test raised our suspicions. With that much chemo still being processed by her system, we expected her thymus and immune system to be struggling. We explored further and discovered that her thymus energies had electromagnetically flipped in a seeming attempt to protect her. As soon as we corrected that irregularity, she became instantaneously exhausted and could no longer stand. Her thymus then tested weak—no surprise!

While she certainly wanted to feel capable despite the chemotherapy treatments, in truth her body needed to rest. She astutely described her chemo-induced irregular energies as supporting her "appearance management." Recognizing this strategy in her energy systems allowed us to pursue and correct the deeper imbalances. In this case she tapped on her thymus to give it more support, strength, and resilience, something we would likely not have done if we had contentedly accepted the initially strong energy test result. She received the clear message to rest and did so. We both learned to respect irregular energies as the body's attempt to maintain a semblance of function.

I still find it fascinating that our energies support "appearance management." This correlates with Carl Jung's concept of the "persona"—the mask we wear or the face we present in social settings

---

[135] My thanks to Patricia J. Morrison, L.M.T., L.L.C.C., for this insight and for her willingness to share our discoveries with a larger audience.

to hide our more vulnerable, authentic self. I simply had not appreciated the degree of energy imbalance required to maintain it. When we pretend all is well while internally working hard to subdue a seething roar or overwhelming feelings of vulnerability, we too engage in "appearance management." To maintain this in the long term we must draw upon the body's energy reserves, sometimes to the point of depletion.

Over time this can lead to chronic illness. Recognizing this possibility and re-balancing the deeper energy systems needing attention resets the auric field and restores our ability to utilize the energy resources of earth, sky and beyond. It therefore makes sense that the practice of Energy Medicine and daily energy exercises preserves the body's reservoir of energy and can refill it if depleted. In this way we can live a healthier life and possibly extend our lifespan.

Emotional Overload and the Empath

In addition to the general benefits of a daily energy practice, empaths especially appreciate those energy exercises that help them better manage emotional overload. We have already discussed how use of the *Cleansing the Aura* exercise can release toxins in the aura, as well as accumulated tension or emotions at any point in the day. Before or after visits to a shopping mall or other crowded event, before anticipated challenging encounters and certainly afterwards, performing this exercise can clear toxic or simply excessive energies from one's energy field. I once had a very angry client who, having done this whole exercise, still struggled with residual anger. We did it again in its entirety and at its conclusion she felt free of the anger and able to process her situation more meaningfully. Additionally,

ENERGETIC COPING TECHNIQUES FOR THE EMPATH

doing this before getting into bed often helps release the emotional residue of the day and thus facilitates more restful sleep.

The Main Neurovascular Reflex Points

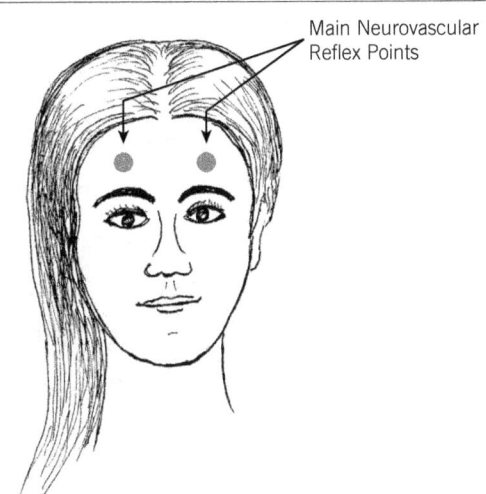

Figure 13-1: The Main Neurovascular Reflex Points

Holding the Main Neurovascular Reflex Points offers a less strenuous and more socially discreet way of bringing balance and perspective to emotional overwhelm. (Figure 13-1) These points, located on the forehead above the pupils of the eyes and midway between the eyebrows and the hairline, help connect the energies of our emotions and the blood supply of the frontal lobe so that we can think! The reader may recall that in Chapter 3 we discussed how our brains funnel their resources into the Limbic System for emergency response and simultaneously shut down the frontal lobe. This exercise provides an energetic solution to that problem, but it is best to practice it in advance. Counting on the frontal lobe to think of this intervention during a period of overwhelming emotion won't work, obviously: we need to have already incorporated it as a habit, so that the Limbic System has ready access to its use.

Donna Eden often refers to these Neurovascular Reflex Points as the "Oh my God!" points[136] because for centuries humans have been slapping their forehead when overwhelmed! It is important to hold these points for perhaps three to five minutes in order to experience a positive effect. I use these points often during my sessions. I especially remember one woman's experience as I held these points for her, felt the energy synchronize in my fingertips, and simultaneously witnessed her shoulders relax. She reported feeling all her stress simply leave her, moving out through her fingertips, so that she could breathe deeply again. We were then able to more effectively process her concerns.

The Five Rhythms

We can address emotional overwhelm even more specifically with the Five Rhythm Neurovascular Reflex Points.[137] In Chinese Medicine, the Five Elements derive from the interrelating Yin and Yang, which in turn emerged from the Tao, or One. These Five Elements, or Five Rhythms[138] as Donna Eden refers to them, readily manifest as aspects of nature, specifically Water, Wood, Fire, Earth, and Metal. (Figure 13-2) Their qualities influence the many dimensions of life, including our energy fields.

Water most naturally resonates with winter, Wood with spring, Fire with summer, Metal with autumn, and Earth with the equinoxes

---

[136] Eden with Feinstein, *Energy Medicine,* 103, 234.
[137] Ibid., 232–235.
[138] Ibid., 213–240.

and solstices. Each Rhythm also has a special affinity with two—or in the case of Fire Rhythm, four—meridians. One meridian (two in the case of Fire) maintains the Yin quality of the Rhythm, while the other (again two meridians for Fire) manifests the Yang quality of that Rhythm. Energetically, these Rhythms interweave to promote flow and balance.

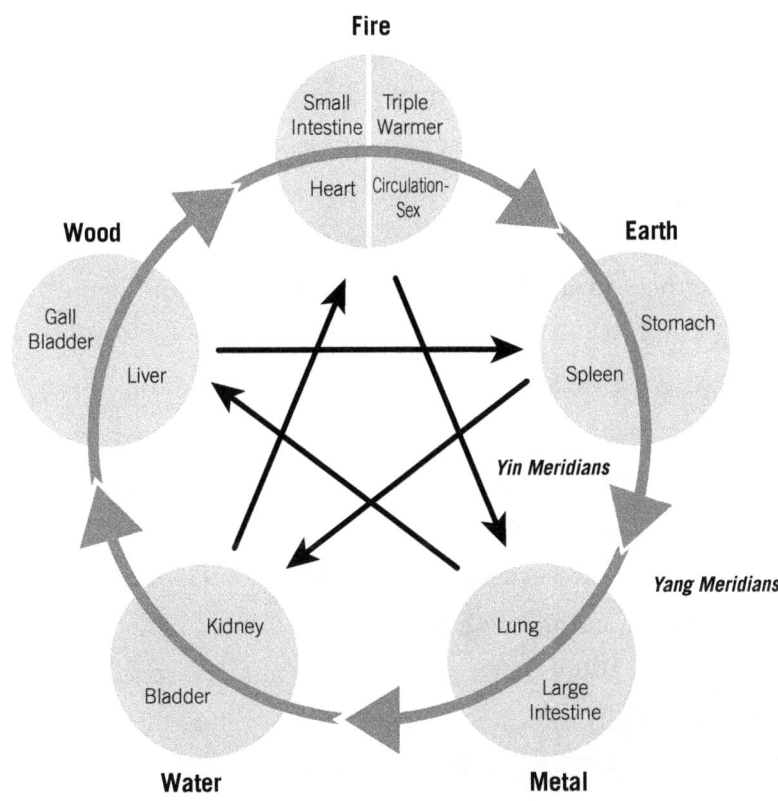

Figure 13-2: The Five Rhythms Model

In the Five Rhythms Model, the meridians are grouped according to their element (Water, Wood, Fire, Earth, and Metal), with Yin meridians interior to the circle, and Yang meridians exterior to it. The Flow Cycle moves energy around the perimeter of the circle in the direction indicated by the arrows. Meridians balance one another according to the Control Cycle as indicated by the arrows in the center of the circle.

We have already identified meridians as similar to a highway marking a specific path of traffic flow through the body's terrain, and the Radiant Circuits to be like helicopters that can airlift needed energies from point to point without getting stuck in traffic jams. I often like to imagine the Five Rhythms as the weather over the highway, affecting the flow of meridian traffic according to its conditions, and even how the helicopter Radiant Circuits do their job. Water Rhythm may impact all the highways with snow or rain, for example, while Fire Rhythm may deliver scorching heat. The Five Rhythms, like the weather, affect every aspect of the highway, but parts of the highway have perhaps been better constructed to support safe traffic through snow vs. desert, for example. Thus, specific meridians affiliate their qualities with their associated Rhythm (Figure 13-2): Kidney and Bladder Meridians with Water; Liver and Gall Bladder Meridians with Wood; Heart, Small Intestine, Circulation-Sex, and Triple Warmer Meridians with Fire; Spleen and Stomach Meridians with Earth; and Lung and Large Intestine Meridians with Metal.

Each meridian, with the Yin or Yang qualities of its particular Rhythm, correlates with a particular emotion (Figure 13-3). Consequently, we can address emotional issues through the doorway of our energies. While a detailed description of this work lies beyond the scope of this book, it is important we recognize that work at this level is possible. Those techniques that we can do on our own will follow; the rest require additional resources. The reader is referred to trained practitioners and/or Eden Energy Medicine training for greater depth regarding this topic.

Emotions and the Meridians[1]

MERIDIAN	BALANCED EMOTION	IMBALANCED EMOTION
Kidney (Water/Yin)	Courage for new beginnings, Gentleness with self	Internal fear, Shame
Bladder (Water/Yang)	Hope and Trust in the world	Despair, Fear of the world
Liver (Wood/Yin)	Kindness toward self	Inward-directed anger, Guilt
Gall Bladder (Wood/Yang)	Assertiveness, Tolerance, Kindness toward others	Anger directed toward others
Heart (Fire/Yin)	Joy, Peace, Love for self and others	Hysteria, Heartache
Small Intestine (Fire/Yang)	Discernment	Indecisiveness
Circulation-Sex (Fire/Yin)	Prioritizing the needs of one's heart to love self as well as others	Difficulty with commitment to the needs of one's heart to love self as well as others
Triple Warmer (Fire/Yang)	Feeling safe	Survival-level anxiety, Fight, Flight, or Freeze
Spleen (Earth/Yin)	Compassion toward self	Limited compassion for self, Unable to take in the good
Stomach (Earth/Yang)	Trust in the bigger picture	Over-involvement, Worry
Lung (Metal/Yin)	Inspiration, Surrender in faith	Deeply experienced grief, Detachment
Large Intestine (Metal/Yang)	Releasing, Letting go	Controlling, Holding on
Central (Yin)	Feeling centered and secure	Feeling vulnerable
Governing (Yang)	Sense of Inner Strength	Lack of inner strength or "backbone"

Figure 13-3: Chart of Correlation between Meridians, Yin/Yang Qualities and Emotions

[1] Adapted from Donna Eden (with David Feinstein), *Eden Energy Medicine Certification Program Class 5 Handout* (Ashland, OR: Innersource, Spring, 2012).

Returning to those exercises we can do ourselves, the use of Five Rhythm techniques best suits our intention to address and balance our emotional responses to life. Located at various spots on the head (Figure 13-4), the Five Rhythm Neurovascular Reflex Points provide easy access to the energy systems involved with particular imbalanced emotions: fear and hopelessness for Water, anger and aggression for Wood, panic and hysteria for Fire, worry and imbalanced compassion (usually lack of compassion for oneself, too much for others) for Earth, grief and fear of losing control for Metal. These imbalances occur in response to life's complexities.

We have already discussed how our evolution has prioritized survival via established pathways of neurological and energetic response, such that when we are overwhelmed the limbic system shuts down the cortex. Thus we react spontaneously based on the

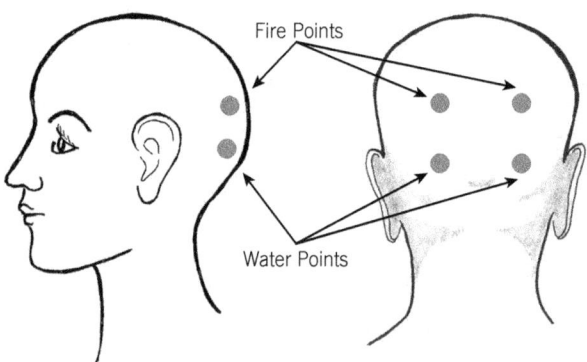

Figure 13-4: The Five Rhythm Neurovascular Reflex Points

Each rhythm's set of points is held along with the Main Neurovascular Reflex Points to bring balance to the associated emotions.

Fire Points (on the back of the head at the level of the eyebrows)
Hold these points to balance feelings of panic, hysteria, anxiety, and burnout.

Water Points (on the back of the head at the level of the eyes)
Hold these points to balance feelings of fear and hopelessness.

ENERGETIC COPING TECHNIQUES FOR THE EMPATH

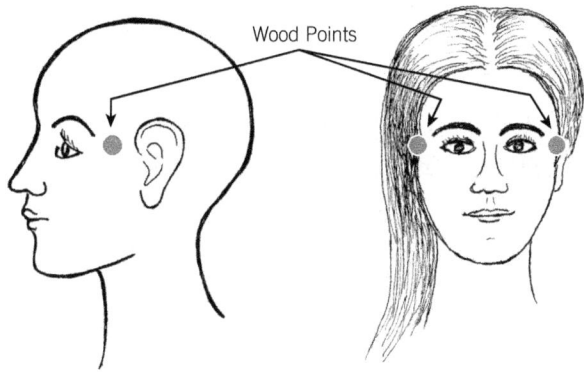

Wood Points (at the temples)
  Hold these points to balance feelings of anger, frustration, and self-criticism.

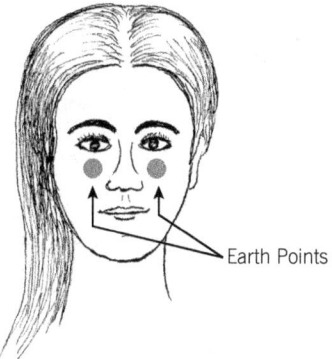

Earth Points (on the cheekbones below the pupils of the eyes)
  Hold these points for worry and/or too much concern for others at the expense of compassion for oneself.

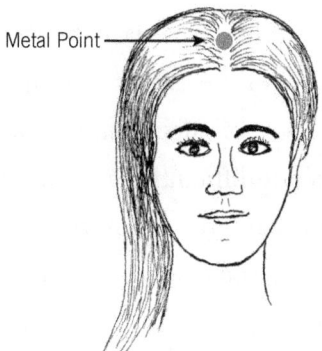

Metal Point (on the top of the head at the crown)
  Hold this point for grief, feeling stuck, or difficulty with control issues.

apparent immediate need, without the luxury of time to think and problem-solve. However, we now have an alternative. By holding these specific Five Rhythm Neurovascular Points (described below) together with the Main Neurovascular Reflex Points (Figure 13-1) for several minutes, we can connect those specific, disconnected limbic emotions with the frontal lobe's capacity to reflect and consider. We can bring perspective to the feelings flooding through us and process our options. We can solve the problem from a more relaxed state and create better consequences for ourselves.

The Five Rhythm Neurovascular Reflex Points[139]

We can readily apply these simple interventions in almost any setting for ourselves and others (with their permission, of course). For three of the Rhythms and their associated emotions, it is easiest to hold the forehead (the Main Neurovascular Reflex Points) with the palm of one hand and the associated Rhythm points with the other—it doesn't matter which hand. So for fear and/or hopelessness, with the second hand we hold the back of the head at the level behind the eyes—the Water points—to bring balanced courage and hope to the situation. For anxiety, panic or hysteria, place the second hand on the back of the head at the level of the eyebrows—the Fire points—to bring joy, discernment, a sense of safety, and personal commitment back into balance. For grief or difficulty surrendering control, place the second hand on the crown—the Metal point—to restore faith in inspiration and appropriate surrender to a Higher Power.

For the remaining two Rhythms, a slightly different approach to the hand positions makes it easier to hold both sides at the same

---
[139] Ibid., 232–235.

time. Place three fingers of each hand on the same-hand side of the forehead at the Main Neurovascular Reflex Points; place the thumbs on the relevant points described in the next few sentences. For anger or frustration, place three fingers of each hand on the forehead and with the thumbs hold the temples—the Wood points—to bring balanced assertiveness to one's concern and circumstances. For worry, over-investment in the needs of others, or loss of compassion for self, place three fingers on the forehead and the thumbs on the cheekbones below the pupils of the eyes—the Earth points—to restore a sense of trust in a larger, loving universe and a sense of compassion for one's vulnerability and efforts in the midst of life's challenges.

Because our energy systems interweave with one another, working with the Five Rhythms balances the Rhythm itself as well as the specific meridians and other energy systems associated with it. Another beauty of these techniques is that we need not make ourselves feel anything other than what we feel. We can bring our upset to the held hand positions and simply breathe. If we engage our emotional overwhelm with these points long enough, our energies as well as our thoughts and feelings *naturally* shift. We need only hold these points for perhaps three minutes—or until we sigh, yawn, or notice a shift in our emotional state—to ensure an optimal effect.

The Insula and Dissociation

Finally, if the empath feels a real disconnect from her bodily experience, she can place the palm of each hand on the same-hand side of each temple and let her fingers point backward, caressing her head just above her ears.[140] This brings energy to the overwhelmed,

---

[140] Donna Eden, "Advanced Practitioner Class" (presented at The Second International Gathering of Eden Energy Medicine, Orlando, Florida, September 18–22, 2013).

momentarily challenged insula and connects it to Triple Warmer's Neurovascular Reflex Points and Alarm Points. The insula learns it is safe for its energy and consciousness to stay in the body, thus restoring its service as bridge to the cortex for reflection and balance to body and mind. This technique often serves best when we feel dissociated or in the process of dissociating in response to a significantly overwhelming event. It may be necessary to hold these hand positions for several minutes to allow the Triple Warmer system and the insula time to reconnect in a balanced and integrated way. Grounding techniques, such as massaging the hands and feet and sweeping energy down the body with one's hands, may also prove helpful.

We can see from these simple techniques (which I have witnessed as helpful to myself and others time and again) that it is possible to consciously reclaim one's center in the midst of overwhelming stress. These interventions take only minutes to relieve the energetic log-jam that disconnects our thoughts and emotions. With this relief we can experience an ease from the intensity of our emotions and pursue a perspective of resolution previously hidden in the cortex, inaccessible until the bridge of the insula could be restored. Only after the overwhelming intensity of our emotions subsides and the consciousness to reflect via the frontal lobe's hindsight, foresight, and insight returns, can we do the deeper work of discovery. What caused these problems in the first place? Does the origin of those problems still require attention? What can heal these deeper wounds so we can move on, free of their power over us at last? It is time to address these questions in more meaningful detail.

CHAPTER 14

Deep Healing and the Empathic Experience

NOW THAT WE HAVE ADDRESSED ways to build resilience in our energy systems, and to reset the balance when unbalancing forces overwhelm us, we can discuss what Energy Medicine and Energy Psychology have to offer for deeper healing. Once the energy systems of daily coping find balance and we move out of emotional overwhelm, Triple Warmer usually allows respectful, delving explorations into our energy field. Often in this depth we discover the root cause of our seemingly stubborn, trying-to-cope imbalances. This deeper work is not for everyone, and those who undertake it must commit to the work, both consciously and energetically.

The insights that emerge from the deeper, unconscious levels within us can be humbling in their intensity and simplicity. Previously confined energy becomes available for a new use, but the client must support the shift that occurs in a session if she hopes to establish a "new normal." As soon as she steps onto the sidewalk at the end of the session, life will offer the old triggers. Her life circumstances will likely change over time, but not immediately. It sometimes seems to me that these recurring triggers challenge us to notice that we have in fact changed, and that the shift is something we wish to honor and maintain. A daily energy practice provides the necessary support to negotiate these challenges while standing in our balanced and newly healed truth. The path to healing is ongoing!

Deep Healing via Eden Energy Medicine and Energy Psychology

As mentioned previously, Lily came for energy work to address an uncomfortable "flutter" of unknown cause in her solar plexus. Her ability to attend to sensations in her body frequently offered doorways for us to consciously enter and explore her inner terrain. We often began our sessions with calming Triple Warmer and ensuring that Lily's energies were crossing and hooked up. We also made sure that her head and torso communicated with each other energetically via the Neck Flow exercise described in Chapter 5. We then began with Donna Eden's energy balancing protocol[141] as together we held the question or issue for that day's session as our intention. As I facilitated the balancing of her energies, she focused on her physical sensations and what images, thoughts, and feelings emerged as her energies began to shift.

Moving through each step of the process, I remained silent for the most part unless she brought her inner experience to my attention. Sometimes I would simply acknowledge it and encourage her to

---

[141] Donna Eden (with David Feinstein), *Eden Energy Medicine Certification Program Class 1 Handout* (Ashland, OR: Innersource, Spring 2012).

stay with it; sometimes I asked questions to direct her exploration. There was no cookbook. We journeyed together into unknown territory. Rarely did a session feel incomplete; this did occur at least twice, only to reveal its deeper meaning to Lily a few days later. It became important for both of us to trust the process and to surrender attachment to results. We remained open to wonder as amazing images, experiences, and insights emerged. She has felt herself changing in ways she sometimes struggled to describe. The flutter, when it reappeared, always took us somewhere meaningful. We had learned to listen!

One might wonder how we managed to accomplish all this. For those new to Eden Energy Medicine, the following at least offers a sense of possibility. For those who have studied it, the protocols will resonate but the detailed content of our sessions may never be repeated, because it emerged from the uniqueness of Lily's energy systems and from her energies dovetailing with mine. What I love about energy work is its constant invitation into Mystery. It requires honoring It and surrendering to It, trusting that what comes to light will serve the greater good. This taps into the spiritual aspect of the work, which we shall explore further in Part III. For now, let me describe in more detail the Eden Energy Medicine interventions we employed. I can only encourage those new to this to realize that these protocols exist and that they can render deep inner work more effective and easier to integrate into one's new sense of self.

Early on in our work together, Lily and I tuned into the "flutter" with intention and followed the energy, images and feelings that emerged. This "flutter" has since revealed itself as a significant communicator for various issues and feelings spanning lifetimes. When it became difficult to determine the deeper feelings underlying this sensation, we used the Advanced Star Diagnostics protocol[142] to uncover which meridians became imbalanced when she focused on her inner experience and the question at hand. By identifying which meridians tested weak in a Five Rhythm context, we were able to name the associated imbalanced emotions related to the "flutter." Then, while I held the correlating Neurovascular Reflex Points on her head and she processed these emotions in relationship to the flutter, amazing memories and images emerged.

The memory of her playground shame emerged in the course of one of these sessions. She hadn't thought about it in years. As we explored this memory, in conjunction with releasing the stuck energy patterns associated with it, we also employed the Energy Psychology protocol to lessen shame's sting. We came to realize as our work together progressed that her playground memory revealed a developing theme that later surfaced in other memories and images, although less intensely. We have attended to healing these memories one by one, with their associated physical and emotional components. Each time, the tangled snare of shame has loosened its hold over her psyche and energy field.

This became especially obvious in the midst of an energy session during which we were exploring her difficulty with speaking her truth. An even earlier childhood memory of shaming in the context of her larger community emerged. As a little girl she had responded by clapping with enthusiasm and joy to a beautiful experience in a church setting where she was expected to be quiet and self-controlled. She had no idea of these expectations, but the congregation's quick, almost

---

[142] Donna Eden (with David Feinstein), *Eden Energy Medicine Certification Program Class 5 Handout* (Ashland, OR: Innersource, Spring 2012).

shunning reaction cut deep into her emotional core and taught her to check her joy and enthusiasm at the door of any future gathering.

As we followed her energies and the images that energy balancing seemed to unveil, a past-life memory spontaneously surfaced. Interestingly, this memory held a similar theme and shunning experience though her gender, social position, and age were much different: she lived then as an older man, a leader in his community. We worked with this past-life incident of shame and betrayal by correcting the energy imbalances arising in association with the memory. We also consciously addressed its deeper meaning and the gifts imparted by this past experience in the midst of its stress.

We then invited the energetic balance and healing consciousness developed during this past life experience to come forward into her early childhood memory. I did not direct this content other than to say, "Invite him forward in time if you like so that he can meet your inner little girl…" along with a few "…and then what happened?" inquiries. In response, the following images spontaneously arose from the depths of her psyche and were carried into her consciousness through her energy. She reported that the older man of her past life, now free of the former betrayal and shame, knelt before her child-self in the midst of that shaming current-life memory. He gazed deeply and lovingly into her eyes and offered her his healing hand. An enormous and beautiful release occurred, such that she felt "seen" in an entirely new way. She later reported that she could now also see the world with new eyes. She described this as a major shift; it was just one of the amazing sessions we experienced together.

Other sessions have addressed similar themes that were activated by her current life circumstances and which sometimes triggered unusual sensations in her body. Psychological splits in her consciousness related to Yin and Yang dynamics took on various expressions, often revealing themselves in her experiences and relationships as conflicts between receptivity and assertiveness, passivity and achievement, and other feminine and masculine ways of being. Also in this context her relationship with her mother and father often called for our attention. Through her energy systems we specifically addressed her experiences with them and how these were unknowingly intensified by her empathic abilities at the time. We worked to reconcile her parents' humanity with the difficulties they set before her, along with the consequences of those difficulties. Her Empath Contract required attention at this point.

We used a Chakra Clearing[143] technique to consciously address the embedded residues of interactions, memories, coping strategies, and beliefs that no longer served her. As she released these older, outmoded energies, new perspectives related to the themes of each Chakra replaced them in her energy field. Similarly we provided attention to her Inner Critic, and when no loving image or memory came forth to serve as a more positive replacement we invited spiritual assistance. She has since gone on to experience life from a more grounded, self-aware, and awe-filled perspective, open to the adventures life offers. She has come to trust in the guidance her energies hold as they connect with what lies beyond.

Even from this cursory description, the reader may observe that while our work relied heavily on the techniques and protocols of Eden Energy Medicine and Energy Psychology, psychotherapeutic interventions and spiritual invitations have offered Lily's consciousness

---

[143] Donna Eden (with David Feinstein), *Eden Energy Medicine Certification Program Class 6 Handout* (Ashland, OR: Innersource, Summer 2012).

a deeper ground in which to incorporate a new experience of self. Via Energy Medicine techniques, such as chakra clearings, holding Neurovascular Reflex Points, and attention to Triple Warmer, we were able to access deeper memories and previously unconscious contributors to her current dilemmas. We also occasionally used very helpful Energy Psychology interventions to clear any residual, outmoded beliefs if they still held her energy patterns captive after the work of deeper balancing was completed. Energy has served as vehicle for the amazing shifts in Lily's consciousness. Psychotherapeutic insights have enjoyed the ride in that energy vehicle as welcome passengers, and spiritual awakening has provided the fuel, the path, and the destination.

Fortunately, as our human consciousness becomes more attuned to the effectiveness of Energy Medicine, the rediscovery of ancient methods and the inspiration of new techniques become available for the purpose of our healing. Having spent decades witnessing the slow progression of psychotherapy's emphasis on the spoken word, I have been amazed and excited to realize that combining those insights with Energy Medicine offers significant promise for deeper and quicker healing when the client is truly ready for such work.

Protocols that release emotions locked in the body prove especially helpful when insight-oriented work either stalls, or has fulfilled its mission in the cortex of the brain yet residual energies remain stuck in the body's cells and tissues. Advanced protocols provide amazing levels of energetic repair and insight when the client is ready for these deeper interventions and has committed to a daily energy practice of whatever contributes to an ongoing healing process. Because these deeper interventions benefit from the support of consciousness, we will address this aspect of the work from psychotherapeutic and spiritual perspectives in greater detail in Part III.

The Empath as Practitioner

To be complete, this chapter must include what happens for the empath as an Energy Medicine practitioner during healing sessions. Here I can only speak to my own experience with any certainty and even that certainty continues to evolve. Truth be told, I am still learning to understand and interpret my responses to energy. Some Eden Energy Medicine faculty members have addressed this issue on occasion, and there seems to be no universal "right" or "typical" response. I recognize that we each process our experiences in a unique way, and that how we perceive and react to them can change as we heal and grow. Therefore, I offer the following reflections so that we can respect our individual differences while entertaining possibilities we might not have previously considered.

As mentioned in Chapter 1, my first unrecognized responses to another person's energy came via falling asleep, feeling my face stiffen, experiencing the hairs on the back of my neck rise like those of a raging dog, or noticing a vague emptiness in my solar plexus. This says nothing about the constant state of muscle tension I experienced day to day. For the record, I did not enjoy any of these experiences. That lack of enjoyment bordered on distress before I realized I was reacting to someone else, and that my reactions could provide information regarding the other person. Until then, I had judged myself as "over-reacting" to situations and people and often hid myself away to recover as best I could.

Once I realized that I respond to certain people and situations this way, I began at least to feel less critical of my reactions. Yet I still judged myself inadequate when I couldn't get rid of the residue. This struggle likely supported my spiritual questing, since nothing earthly could help me resolve it. Discovering Reiki, Eden Energy Medicine, and Energy Psychology opened new doors for me, not only to release these emotional "messengers" from my body, but to explore my inner energetic terrain, which has stored all sorts of information either never recognized or long forgotten by my conscious mind.

Cleaning One's Own Sponge

I will certainly describe some of what happens for me during sessions with others, but first I must stress that as an empath doing this kind of work I have to constantly attend to my own energy field. An empath working with others in any kind of daily exposure must regularly clean her sponge. This not only offers clients the best energy flow possible, it prevents an unwanted, unhelpful build-up of imbalanced energies *within* the empath practitioner. I have had to work diligently to monitor my energy balances and imbalances.

I honestly admit I enjoy this part of the work. I don't like feeling "yucked up," yet I appreciate the adventure of discovering what in me resonates with whatever is "yucky" in any given situation. I enjoy questing on the inner terrain—for myself and as a guide for others. To be a worthy guide, however, I have to map out the territory first. As the Universe conspires for our good, I find that as I work through my own emotional baggage clients often come to me needing help with those very same issues. This kind of occurrence only deepens my sense of the web that unites us all.

My tools for self-discovery include years of personal psychotherapy and Jungian analysis, and even more years of delving into the archetypal symbolism of astrological charts. Combining the wisdom derived from years of self-exploration with access to my energy systems has offered a golden opportunity to unearth long-buried treasures. Often I begin with a sense of unease, locate it in my body, check out associated emotions, thoughts, lyrics of songs that won't leave me alone, recent dreams, or any other intuited correlation with the sensation or emotion. Sometimes I test my energies while making a positive statement about my suspicions. If my field maintains an energy flow and tests strong, I take the statement seriously. If the energy test loses strength, I know the statement does not apply to me in that moment. By consulting my body's energies, I discover what truth may be known to them, even though that information escapes my consciousness.

For example, if I recognize that in a certain situation I have a "yucky" feeling, I make statements such as "I feel anger," or "I feel sadness," or "such-and-such bothered me," and energy test. By turning my questions into statements, I discern more details concerning my energies' response to the situation. It is important to note that this kind of energy testing can lead one down the wrong path if one holds an agenda, or specific expectations, conscious or unconscious. I tend to trust it most when the answers surprise me. This guidance, I find, must be viewed as *suggestions* regarding paths for exploration, not as directives for decision-making, and certainly not as predictions for the future. The body's energies register our reactions *in the present*—that is, our *current desires or emotional responses* to events in the past, present, or the anticipated future. Our energies may also hold what has remained unresolved from the distant and ancestral past. Since the future offers so many possible paths of unfolding, in my experience our energies can co-create the future, but they cannot predict it.

Once I've gathered enough information to put a name to the issue or situation related to my current reaction, I may do an Advanced Star Diagnostics protocol on myself to identify more specifically the emotions involved. By personal preference, I then turn to Energy Psychology to tap my way to the deeper core of the matter. This protocol evolved from the Emotional Freedom Technique, which draws upon the wisdom of Chinese Medicine and the associated meridians/emotions by tapping on specific meridian beginning or end points. The reader is again referred to the work of David Feinstein, Ph.D.,[144] for a more detailed explanation of its uses and method.

Since I first experienced this protocol with regard to my former driving phobia (described in Chapter 11), I have found that it not only disengages old triggers from their habitual responses—so that I can now merge onto a highway without the panic—but offers us one more path for bringing deeper issues to consciousness. When I use this protocol for myself, I know I've gotten somewhere when a deep emotional release rises to the surface. I then continue to tap, relying on the Divine to bring healing and new perspectives to the issue at hand. I can retest my energies to see if the healing is complete for the moment. Usually I know it is, just because I feel so much better.

Not everyone can access all these tools for their own personal healing work, nor does everyone need them all. Given the uniqueness of each of us, we may find ourselves drawn to the particular healing modalities that work best for us. In any case, the skills we need can be developed one by one, and in the meantime we can tap into the

---

[144] Feinstein, Eden, and Craig, *The Promise of Energy Psychology*.

"web" and ask to access someone, human or spiritual, who can help us should we choose to follow this path. I have developed the skills I describe because I sought help from many, many others over many, many years. When I found something helpful, I studied it and made it my own. Each step along the way has changed me to a greater or lesser degree: I now realize that this often marks the progression of healing.

We have already acknowledged how human nature, through our energy systems, fronts a resistance to this healing process via Triple Warmer activation, so awareness of this potential stumbling block can help. The reader may recall that in an earlier chapter I mentioned how this impacted my own decision-making process about learning Eden Energy Medicine. Once my interest was piqued, I went through the first three stages of learning—a weekend workshop, a Five-Day Intensive, and the two-year Certification Program—saying each time, "But I can't do that." Unbeknownst to me, Triple Warmer was making every effort to maintain my old habits and ways of being. When I realized I didn't feel peace about "I can't," I asked myself, "Why not?" I didn't have a good answer! The rest is history… With gratitude, I smile.

Working with Others

As for doing this work with others, once an empath has made a commitment to care for her own energy systems she still has to engage with everyone else's energies. Contact with those energies gets "up close and personal," especially during sessions. The energies of the client literally run through one's body during some protocols. Thus it is imperative to know how to stay grounded and resilient, as well as how to utilize methods for releasing what doesn't need to stay once the message has been received and understood.

On a positive note, often the healing process for the client brings that same healing energy to the practitioner. Nor are all the sensations experienced during energy work unpleasant: I often yawn when the client's energy shifts, for example, and more rarely I may feel a gentle surge and subsiding of heat. I have heard that other practitioners have their own characteristic physical responses. For those of us who do not see energy, these sensations guide us in knowing how long to provide a balancing correction. We also receive validating feedback from the client directly, and/or when energy testing the client confirms that the shift has indeed occurred.

In addition to yawning when energies move into balance, I have experienced other reactions. I have on occasion felt sleepy, which I've come to understand for me means that the person's issue remains lodged in the unconscious as they attentively wait for its release to awareness. At other times I have felt sensations in my body and through asking general, non-directive questions I learn that my client is having the same experience, which she didn't think to mention. Its pursuit often takes us someplace meaningful. Then there are those times when I suddenly feel profoundly scared or sad. Again, asking my client to check in with her emotional state often reveals that she too is having this experience. We can then consciously address the feeling with all its associations and let it move on.

My own sensations sometimes guide the work in meaningful ways, but I must *feel* them first. Consequently, I have had to learn not to be afraid of my physical and emotional experiences. Knowing I can move the energies associated with them along if the healing work with the client hasn't already done so—and it often does—provides an avenue of enormous relief and opportunity. Because of it, deeper work becomes possible, both within me and with others. This journey has been rich, to say the least!

Tying It All Together

Healing can happen at various levels, at different times, in different ways for each of us. Consciousness need not always accompany a healing session, but the joy of healing comes from the recognition that *something* has happened! Some of us are called to delve more deeply into our psyches than others. I suspect empaths receive such a call by virtue of the emotional burdens they carry. These can become quite weighty before consciousness helps relieve an empath of their load. Consciousness must embrace and surpass the Inner Critic for healing to occur. This does not happen by accident—empaths have to *choose* this path.

To quote Einstein again: "No problem can be solved from the same level of consciousness that created it." In the context of the Holistic Model of Human Consciousness from Chapter 7, we see that physical healing receives its source from a higher plane, but that some higher planes need not entail consciousness. Physical healing can simply come from appropriate rest or exercise, or from a restoration of emotional balance. Emotional imbalance, however, must resort to the even higher plane of the intellect. We have to think our way through the pain, examine old outworn beliefs, get a new perspective, choose to maintain it, and develop it further to promote greater healing and functioning. This not only facilitates the healing of old wounds, but provides tools for managing the daily onslaught of internal states to which we are exposed every time we encounter a fellow human being or pet. The intellect of lower mind only repeats what it knows for day-to-day survival; the wisdom of higher mind offers new inspiration with its sense of purpose and meaning.

We now turn our attention to higher mind and its access to soul and Spirit. Empaths are particularly called to explore this realm if they ever want to know that their experience offers value, not only to themselves, but to those whose inner states they feel so deeply. This understanding invites all of us to release the victim role and to embrace an empowered consciousness of purpose. This recognition now informs all the work I do as it extends beyond psychotherapy.

With respect for the importance of the psychotherapeutic process, I no longer simply help people to develop stronger egos so they can survive our difficult world more easily. My work now offers a spiritual perspective encapsulated in a quote by Carl Jung: "The goal is to make the ego as strong and as small as possible."[145] In this way we can courageously journey into mysterious realms with humility, gentleness and respect, yet without fear or judgment. We can then receive the rich gifts offered us, and bring them back to our four-dimensional world for healing. Let us now explore some of the realms of possibility for empaths that lie in the intangible, mysterious All!

---

[145] Carl G. Jung, Chapter 4, title page, in *The Way of the Small: Why Less Is Truly More*, by Michael Gellert (Lake Worth, FL: Nicolas-Hays, Inc., 2008).

PART
III

The Spiritual Heart
Purpose

CHAPTER 15

The Longings of the Soul

AS HURRICANE IRENE MADE HER WAY up the coast in late August 2011, my practical sister cautioned me to remove any potential "fly-away" objects from my premises. Recognizing the wisdom of her advice I did so. During a last scan of my small yard, my glance rested upon two angel statues, one positioned in the east, the other in the south. I hesitated, wondering if I should bring them indoors. My fear that the statues would be damaged in some way struggled against the thought that they represent a spiritual force stronger than any wind. I opted to pray to that spiritual force, asking for protection of the yard and house, all the people in the neighborhood, and those affected by the approaching storm. I left the angels standing in their places.

Hours later, Irene hit hard with fiercely howling winds. In the midst of it, I heard a loud crack followed by a thud. Gazing out my back window, I realized that my treasured flowering pear tree had split in two. Half still stood while the other half had fallen away from the house into the yard. I went outdoors when the storm had cleared to discover that the tree had landed between the two angels, limbs touching stone on both sides, yet neither statue was damaged. Of course, I paused, felt gratitude, and wondered...

What makes the miraculous happen? Healing can seem like a miracle, so this question applies to the therapeutic process as well. Despite all the "how-to" books, courses and degrees available to guide the many paths of healing and healer, the experience of healing itself still holds a magical, mysterious quality. We struggle with words to explain its effects yet those who have reaped its fruits or who have witnessed others doing so stand firm in their "knowing" of its power.

These rewards often come in response to a deep longing for something difficult to name, though the associated feeling in the heart is unmistakable. We usually do not content ourselves with pure feeling, however: we want to know with our ego minds, and we need words to communicate what we know to others to share or prove our knowing. If what we long for, what we feel in the heart, what we "know" in our core, conflicts with what our minds and the minds of others define as acceptable, we may opt to sacrifice our longing. If we do this, unfortunately, the heart-feeling accompanying our longing turns into heartache and grief.

If we choose not to forfeit what we long for, we risk another complication that arises when we name our longing incorrectly. In so doing we may set out on a quest for the wrong thing and, as a result, never find what truly satisfies our yearning. If we ask the wrong question, we will go in search with narrowly focused binoculars, missing what we truly need even if it presents itself right in front of our eyes. Thus, the struggle to identify properly what we long for holds considerable merit.

This task falls to the domain of our ego mind, which serves as our communicator with the outside world and other egos. The challenge emerges when the ego, preferring as it does the known world, must somehow form a relationship with our longing, which lives in Mystery and speaks to us through our heart. The first question then becomes: is our potentially frightened, wounded, defensive ego willing and able to search, to boldly venture into the unknown terrain of heart and soul?

Healing poses a tremendous unknown to that part of us that has habituated to pain. Our ego and our protective Triple Warmer and Inner Critic paradoxically prefer that we avoid the journey. In our ambivalent attempts to override them we may ask the wrong questions, and not until we are truly ready are we able to coordinate asking the right question when opportunity strikes. A measure of endurance, persistence, and patience is required. As we have seen, conscious intention plays an important role as well. A Celtic myth, often referred to as the Grail legend or the story of *The Fisher King*,[146] aptly depicts the nature of this dilemma.

The many versions of this tale commonly involve a fisher king whose duty is to protect the Holy Grail, the sacred cup from which Jesus drank at the Last Supper and which, in some tales, also held some of his blood as he suffered and died on the Cross. The fisher king sustains a wound and cannot fulfill his mission; his kingdom turns into a wasteland, and the Grail goes into hiding. Meanwhile, a vision of the Grail appears to the knights of Arthur's Round Table

---

[146] Edward C. Whitmont, *Return of the Goddess* (New York, NY: The Crossroad Publishing Company, 1984), 153–156.

who choose to go in search of it. They each journey far and wide and one of them, while lost in the woods, stumbles upon the kingdom and the king. Unfortunately, because the knight fails to ask the proper questions of the king, the ruler and his kingdom fade back into obscurity.

The knight wanders for five more years before he finds the king once more. To procure the Holy Grail, for the kingdom to thrive, and for the king to heal from his interminable wound, the knight must ask the king these questions: "What ails thee?" and "Whom does the Grail serve?"[147] When the knight finally asks the necessary questions, he learns to correctly name and therefore appreciate the nature of the king's wound and the truth and purpose of the Grail. The Grail and its healing issue forth.

In various mystical traditions our souls are depicted as vessels, sacred cups serving as receivers of Spirit and keepers of the Divine Spark within each of us. We discussed in Chapter 7 how the soul and its sacred contents penetrate every aspect of our being. John O'Donohue, an Irish poet, author and mystic, often refers to the soul as the source of our longing,[148] reverberating its message through the feeling tones of the heart to remind our incarnated consciousness of its presence. Yet, not unlike the fisher king's struggle, the longing within us can easily feel like a wound. Similarly, we cannot seem to protect the Grail, nor connect consciously with the soul in the midst of this pain. The Grail—the soul—seems to disappear, yet the health of our inner kingdom depends upon its return.

If we attend to our longing, we can consciously wonder our way

---

[147] Ibid., 154.
[148] John O'Donohue, *Eternal Echoes: Celtic Reflections on Our Yearning to Belong* (New York, NY: Perennial, HarperCollins Publishers Inc., 1999), xxiii-xxvi.

back into the soul's mysterious territory. Our wondering must ask the right questions, however, if we are to succeed in our mission: to heal our wounds and discover the purpose of our sacred vessel. Our efforts to attend to this challenge mark the quest of those who truly want to heal, to become "whole" in body, heart, mind, and soul.

"What Ails Thee?"

We know that empaths feel within their own skins the joys, excitement, fears, heartaches, and anger of others. We also know that at times these feelings can be quite difficult to bear. An eight-year-old accurately described this to me, along with her uncomfortable "disconnect" from people, while telling me she didn't like to be around others. She recognized that she felt their pain and didn't know how to let that pain go. In fact, when it came to her loved ones she didn't want to let the distressing feelings dissipate at all: she perceived her painful resonance as offering a means of feeling close and "connected" to them. Already at that young age she felt swamped in the quagmire of her empathic resonance with the suffering of others, her protective "disconnect" from them, and a desire to feel close to loved ones in the only way she knew—by hurting with or for them. She was slowly beginning to name what "ails" her.

She didn't want something to be "wrong" with her yet she knew things weren't "right." The discomfort of her "disconnect" had already sparked her longing, though she is too young to name it as such. Fortunately, her mother recognized her daughter's challenges and continues to learn about her daughter's gifts so as to effectively guide her as she grows. Questions such as why she has come into this incarnation with so much sensitivity are just beginning to form in this young girl's consciousness. As she matures she may wonder why her sensitivities have such impact upon her relationships with others as well. We can hope that if this young girl pursues her questions effectively, she will become a wise woman in time.

As she wonders, so may we. For what reason might a soul choose to incarnate as an empath? Why would our essence choose to flood our egoic sense of separateness with the feelings and sensations of others? As discussed from many perspectives thus far, connectedness between an empath and another person or being happens spontaneously, on many levels simultaneously. Auric receptivity connects us to the energy fields of others while also penetrating the other energy systems of our own energy field. The interplay between our chakras, endocrine glands, and the nervous system coordinates with mirror neurons and other aspects of our neurological wiring, as well as with the heart and our other two brains to provide physical sensations, feelings, and other wordless information to our thinking cortex. The five levels of our soul's perfusion into every aspect of our life simultaneously connect us to others in our world. All these aspects of human being-ness on earth connect us intimately to one another in a fine web of interchange and energy flow. While this is true for all of us, our consciousness regarding it varies.

For the empath, this multi-leveled attunement to the web happens more deeply, and life experiences impact more profoundly. As mentioned in Chapter 6, our emotional bodies gather dissonant energies from other energy bodies in our aura to signal us to pay attention. Consequently, the intensity of emotional life looms large in the consciousness of the empath. Life makes no requirement that we find meaning in this experience, yet if we care to float or swim in these sometimes tumultuous waters, perspective offers us a buoy and meaning guides us to shore. When we ask ourselves "what ails thee?" we need words to answer the question, and those words need to be accurate. How does "what ails us" reflect our longing? What incompleteness needs completing? What purpose might it serve to live as an empath?

"Whom Does the Grail Serve?"

If the Grail serves as a symbol of our soul, whom does our soul serve? And as our soul penetrates every aspect of our being, who or what might be served by our sensitivities? We have already acknowledged that there lurks within the empath a drive—perhaps a longing—to attend to the needs of others. What internal passion cares so much about how others feel? Is it simply a self-absorbed preoccupation with trying to feel better oneself? It does logically follow that if the empath helps others come to greater peace, the empath will feel it and do so as well. Yet might some deeper purpose underlie all the emotional and physical sensitivities innately wired into the empath's neurological and energetic pathways? Might those sensitivities, more quickly and deeply stirred for the empath, touch upon "something" common to all human beings? If so, might the wisdom gained prove valuable? Perhaps that "something" may have profound implications for providing a true service for others and for healing the self.

During yet another weather prediction of disastrous winds, Superstorm Sandy in late October 2012, I performed the same scan of my backyard, left the angels where they stood, and made the same prayer. I also noticed a beautiful pink rose in full bloom swaying gently on its stem as the winds began to blow. That storm wreaked even more havoc than Irene. As I took inventory afterwards in the quiet of the power outage that would last days for many, I noticed siding blown off buildings, rooftops with dangling shingles, downspouts strewn significant distances from their home turf. Tree branches and in some cases whole trees blocked many roads and sidewalks. But that rose still bloomed beautifully, attached to its mother bush, a living testimony of endurance and durability through the worst of storms.

We all recognize that roses in their exquisiteness often lose their petals early. Especially on Valentine's Day, we pay large sums of money for their short-lived bloom, preferring them over carnations that last weeks longer and cost much less. How amazing then that despite its tender vulnerability, that rose not only survived but continued to thrive!

Of course, again I wondered… That exquisite rose held a message for all of us. Beauty has its own strength; sensitivity can stand up to hurricane winds and survive intact. Something within us makes that possible. I strongly suspect that something is soul, but our ego needs to figure that out, determine that the soul is trustworthy, and relate to it as one would a best friend. That challenges us when the Inner Critic looms large, the heart is broken, and our longing feels like a wound.

Anyone who has dared to love has known minor or major heartaches as the upheavals of life have their way with us. Loss, grief, worry, anger, frustration, helplessness, the frozen overwhelmed state of fear or anxiety, depression—all significantly impact the ease or difficulty with which we relate to our heart experience. Desires, long buried in the process of putting others first, may slowly rise to the surface and deeply challenge the Empath Contract. To connect with soul through a heart laden with such burdens requires significant healing attention indeed.

When one finally acknowledges that help is needed, how does one proceed? Traditional approaches to healing, including psychotherapy and sometimes medication, have their place when one's focus and attention become scattered or riveted by internal distress. For example, problems with insomnia, frequent panic attacks, or thoughts of suicide that find no relief from encounters with love or creativity may require professional assistance. These approaches may then free one's consciousness of painful distractions so as to engage in the deeper questions.

Developing a humble sense of ego—that sense of individuality and the right to exist on this planet, to take up space, breathe, create, impact others, and to love—must find a way into one's consciousness and be greeted with some degree of acceptance in order to do the deeper work. Over time, the deeper work will likely better inform these issues, but some preliminary access to these rights of existence by virtue of birth on earth must first be embraced. Without them, it's like going on a quest as a stowaway with no map, no intention, no equipment, and no question for exploration. Once we acknowledge our needs, our rights, and our access to these essentials, however, the deeper, more intangible work can begin.

Can the poetic, the magical, and the mystical aspects of life guide an empath as she explores the wonders and wounds of her inner world, struggles to balance the needs and realities of the outer world, and works to define a purpose for her life during this incarnation? Can there be more to life than neurology, energy systems and psychodynamics? What sparks the soul and fills the heart with love and longing for an intangible "more"? Can one take these yearnings seriously and pursue them as a life path? How and where to begin such a quest?

These questions have no tangible, easily prescribed answer. Each of us has our own path, our own soul, our own mission in this lifetime. We even have our own energy patterns and ways of sensing and bringing balance to our internal and external worlds. So how to describe what may assist us in our search for healing at this deeper level? What process can help us access our experience of soul: our own soul first and perhaps also the cosmic soul that resides in the "web" and beyond?

We can turn to myths and fairy tales as repositories of archetypal patterns, intangible blueprints for ways of being in the world, dramatized by the human fondness for story, and stored in our collective unconscious over the centuries. Because these stories have been gradually altered in response to cultural differences and the course of our evolving consciousness, many versions exist. Consequently, there is no definitive right or wrong way to tell or interpret any of these myths or fairy tales. Instead they offer a springboard of possibility, flowing within the energetic rivers of life, carrying with them opportunities for expansion and ongoing contribution to the evolution of human consciousness. Thus, to the degree that we are willing to explore their depths and live into their resonating truths, we ourselves can contribute to the evolution of human consciousness. We might consider this contribution one aspect of an empath's *raison d'être*.

I have selected one of my favorite fairy tales to better elucidate the journey of an empath trying to rediscover her soul's voice and mission in the midst of ego wounds and the plethora of sensitivities around and within her. Of course, I had no idea why, as a child, I resonated so deeply with this story. *Beauty and the Beast* has found its way into the Disney archives as well as television shows and other films. To quote the Disney film's theme song, it offers "a tale as old as time"[149] within which to explore what transpires internally when we seek to comfort others at our own expense.

I have approximated an older version of the plot[150] because it works well for my intentions here. After telling the tale, we will explore the deeper meanings for each important character and then relate them to our inner and outer worlds. Finally, we will consider ways to bring healing to our own dilemmas as suggested by this plot's unfolding. Given that our souls live in the realms of time and timelessness, I offer this as a magical doorway through which to journey to soul…

Beauty and the Beast

As all good fairy tales begin, "once upon a time" there lived a wealthy prince. As a young man he experienced life in the invincible way that many young people do. He had many servants and a large castle to protect him from most of life's adversities. Life went along in its usual mode until one evening an enchantress, disguised as an old beggar, knocked upon his castle door and petitioned him for shelter from the rain and the cold. She offered him an exquisite rose to repay him for his trouble. The prince, in his ignorance and arrogance, refused her. In response to his refusal, she transformed him

---

[149] Howard Ashman, lyricist, Alan Menken, composer, "Beauty and the Beast" song, in *Beauty and the Beast* (Walt Disney Pictures, 1991), accessed March 8, 2016, http://www.disneyclips.com/lyrics/lyrics74.html.

[150] "Beauty and the Beast," Wikipedia, plot summary adapted from Jeanne-Marie Leprince de Beaumont, "La Belle et la Bete," in *Magasin des enfants*, 1757, accessed January 24, 2016, https://en.wikipedia.org/wiki/Beauty_and_the_Beast.

into a beast and all his servants into household items. She also left him with gifts, including a magic mirror that would enable him to view faraway events, and the enchanted rose she had initially offered. She told him that this curse could only be reversed if he could learn to love another and earn her love in return, all before the rose's last petal fell. If he failed, he would remain a beast forever.

Meanwhile, in a not so far away village in France, Belle lived her not so ordinary life as the sixth child born to her father, Maurice, a wealthy merchant. (No mention is ever made of her mother.) The story describes Belle and her older brothers as "pure of heart," and her two older sisters as wicked and selfish. Belle's beauty, intelligence, and love for reading marked her as unusual in the village. In fact, many of the young men were intimidated by her intelligence and her tendency to resist their advances—all but Gaston, a weightlifter of sorts, who found her differences very attractive. He remained undaunted by her lack of interest while she experienced their dissimilarities as significantly boring. He repeatedly made advances toward her and she repeatedly retreated.

As the action of the tale begins, Maurice has come upon difficult times and consequently has to move his family to lesser quarters. When he receives news that one of his cargo ships survived the recent storms at sea and has returned to port, he prepares to go to town to settle his financial affairs. He asks his children what they might like as gifts. His two older daughters ask for fancy dresses and jewels; Belle asks for a rose. Once in town, Maurice learns that his goods from the ship have been confiscated to pay his debts. Consequently, he does not have the means to buy the requested gifts for his older daughters. Maurice makes his way home, weary and dejected, until he finds himself lost in the woods. As night quickly approaches, he unknowingly spies the Beast's castle and makes his way there. Upon his arrival, doors magically open and a lavishly spread table of food awaits him. He spends the night in a cozy bedroom without ever meeting his host. The servants/household items are most gracious, however, thrilled to have appreciative company!

As Maurice prepares to depart the next morning, his gaze falls upon a beautiful rose in the garden. He plucks the rose from the bush, only to be confronted by the growling Beast who condemns Maurice to death for trying to take his most valued possession. Maurice begs for mercy, explaining that he only picked the rose for his beautiful, youngest daughter. The Beast, not being stupid, agrees to allow Maurice to return to her and give her the rose, on condition that Maurice then return to the castle as the Beast's prisoner. The Beast also provides jewels and fine dresses for the other daughters and insists that Belle must never know about their agreement. Maurice gives his word.

Belle, being sensitive to her father's emotional states, pries the secret from Maurice and insists upon returning to the castle in his stead. For some reason, Maurice allows this. Once she arrives, the Beast provides her with lavish meals and fine clothes. He also proclaims her mistress of the castle. She dines with him every evening and they talk at length. He describes himself as her servant and every night asks her to marry him. While Belle feels enamored with their discussions, every night she refuses him. Confusing her further, after each refusal she dreams of a handsome prince who pleads with her to answer why she keeps refusing to marry him. In her dream she replies that she cannot marry him because she loves him only as a friend. She never makes the connection that the prince of her dreams and the Beast of her castle experience are the same. Instead, she strongly suspects that the Beast is holding the prince captive somewhere in the fortress. She decides to search the entire castle only to discover multiple enchanted rooms, but never the prince of her dreams.

During one of her searches she wanders into the forbidden West Wing, where the Beast comes upon her and frightens her with his sudden outburst of anger. To escape him she runs into the forest in a blind panic, only to encounter a pack of hungry wolves. The Beast, having chased after her, fends off the wolves to protect her, but by doing so he sustains numerous cuts and bites. Together they return to the castle where Belle, feeling a mixture of forgiveness and gratitude, nurses his wounds. In response to her tenderness, the Beast finally begins to experience genuine care for her. He invites her into his private quarters and shares with her his extensive library. They begin to truly bond.

During one of their more romantic evenings, Belle mentions to the Beast how much she misses her father. He shows her the magic mirror and together they observe how her father is grieving her loss. The Beast agrees that she may visit her father for one week, and that for her journey she may take the magic mirror so as to know what is happening at the castle. He also gives her a magic ring which, if she turns it three times, will return her to the castle instantly.

After Belle returns home, her jealous sisters immediately plot to jeopardize Belle's relationship with the Beast. They use onions to make themselves appear to be crying while begging her to stay one more day. Belle reluctantly agrees though this breaks her promise to the Beast. She feels guilty and so uses the magic mirror to see how he is faring back at the castle. In horror she discovers him to be lying half-dead from heartbreak near the very bush where her father had initially picked a rose for her. Unbeknownst to Belle, the last petal of the enchantress's rose is about to fall. Fortunately, Belle turns the ring three times to return to the Beast immediately. She weeps over him, telling him how much she loves him. As her tears fall upon him, he turns into the handsome prince of her dreams and reveals his true past to her. Then, as most fairy tales end, they marry and live happily ever after.

Understanding the Symbols of the Story

On the level of its telling, this fairy tale carries its own intrinsic merit and enjoyment. We can delve further into its symbolism, however, and use the story to better understand the dilemmas, struggles, gifts and opportunities for growth available to all those who "feel their way" in relationships. We may recognize people we know in each of the characters described and may even strongly identify with one or more of them. The real challenge and growth lies in our willingness to see every significant character as playing a role in our own inner world. Not only do we have our Beauty, we also have our Beast. Fortunately, in this tale the Beast is released from his curse, the beautiful and the redeemed-beastly marry, and they find a way to live happily together. This kind of integration marks the path of healing.

As the story begins, Belle represents a youthful aspect of life experience in a family where the nurture of the mother is absent, the father is engrossed in his own losses and grief, the brothers are respected individuals but likely off on their own, and the two older sisters preoccupy themselves with fantasies of wealth and demands for their own gratification. In this setting, opportunities for authentic connection, validation, and sensitive reciprocity seem scarce.

Belle, as an empath, finds a solution to the emotional distress and disconnectedness in her family of origin by retreating into her intellect. This offers further protection from the desires of the young men in her world—except Gaston who seems clueless about her lack of interest. His endless advances fuel her capacity to say "no," yet we can see she refuses her father very little. This capacity to retreat from Gaston and the other young men of her village serves her well as she also refuses the self-invested advances of the Beast. Her capacity for genuine concern, her curiosity, and her dreams—her longing—ultimately guide her toward healing.

The qualities and behaviors of the Beast offer significant contrast to Belle's empathic sensitivities and her tendency for self-sacrifice. He grumbles and roars when his wants are violated. He threatens, punishes, barters, and manipulates without regard for the impact of his actions on their recipient. He expresses no concern that his servants have been turned into things, likely having treated them that way even before the curse of the enchantress descended upon them. The Beast behaves like the classic narcissist: charming, engaging, polite when it serves him, but should anyone cross him his bellows will roar.

Eventually, his self-invested interests propel him to protect Belle from the wolves. These may in fact reflect an angry, devouring aspect of himself. In taking on the wounds *she* would have experienced, he perhaps feels the effects of his own past behavior for the first time.

As he begins to take some responsibility for his own actions and intentions, Belle's kindness is released from empathic compulsion and defense, and freed for authentic sharing. Together they begin to engage in a different relational dance.

Maurice, Belle's father, also plays a significant role in this tale. As a parent living his own challenging life, he resorts to his own well-established ways of coping. In his self-absorbed misery, he tries to attend to his beautiful, sensitive daughter and to please her in moments. Yet when it comes to what really matters, he defers to Belle's willingness to sacrifice herself for him. She senses her father's distress, uncovers its source (the secret promise he made to the Beast) and chooses to take on her father's pain and its consequences by surrendering to the unknown agenda of the Beast. Maurice, who knows what she will face while she yet does not, lets her go.

Her father's limited self-care and lack of personal responsibility for his own emotional needs have their beastly equivalent, which Belle will have to live out with the actual Beast. No longer having his youngest daughter to carry his feelings for him, Maurice must live with his own grief. When Belle becomes aware of this, she sacrifices herself once again by leaving behind the Beast she is growing to love, and then again by breaking her promise to return to him. When she sees her Beast dying of heartbreak without her, she makes the choice to honor her own heart despite the tears of her sisters, the grief of her father, and pressure from Gaston. Clearly, something in her has shifted.

In addition to the characters of this story, some of the magical objects symbolize qualities of transformative power. The magic mirror, for example, offers the perspective so needed for an empath to rise above the emotional intensity of any given moment and to explore what is really happening beyond one's immediate vision or internal experience. The ring serves as an agent of reunion for those who truly love one another and wish to reconnect. It requires intentional use however (turning it three times), and needs to be safeguarded when not in use. The rose presents as a prominent symbol to further this plot in all its transformative moments. Its beauty, vulnerability, unfolding, and eventual death mark, respectively, the Beast's initial refusal to care about another person; the enchantress's gift to him with time-limited opportunity for redemption; the facilitation of Belle's arrival at the castle; and the Beast's surrender to love and potential loss. Likely there were roses at their wedding as well!

Telling the Inner Tale

If we reconsider this fairy tale from the magic mirror perspective of the interior world, deeper reflection may lead us to greater healing and integration within. As empaths, our inner world may feel like an interior swirling chaos at times, but if we dare to attend to a deeper story, to ride out the swirl and seek the ground beneath, we may find truths we can trust to carry us through future experiences of confusion and doubt. Empaths live in a constant inundation of emotion: input from every person, every situation floods in, especially if we are not grounded energetically and are taken off guard emotionally and cognitively. In addition to the energy exercises already discussed, a practice that includes journeying into the inner world can help us sort out the components of the swirl. We can then more easily deal with those components from a deepening, more authentic inner ground.

In the first two chapters we explored what an empath is and is not; this fairy tale helps us to better discern those differences. Belle sets a shining example of one who serves another by sensing the Beast's inner state and attending to his needs, often at the expense of her own. Her ability to say "no" to Gaston and to the Beast's proposal of marriage may seem evolved—and I don't want to diminish that—but we need to appreciate the self-protective effect of that "no" as well. It keeps uncomfortable intrusions at bay to some degree, and serves her emotional survival, but it doesn't put an end to their incursions upon her inner peace.

Her "no" has limited power while she compulsively continues to relate, to feel, and to serve. She never plans to run away from the castle. She never makes demands of the Beast or her father. She seems to operate in a numbed survival mode, enduring her circumstances, saved only by her curiosity as she explores the castle the way she used to read her books. When confronted by the Beast's rage she finally runs, but this happens from her Limbic System. There is no cortical planning involved, no consideration for consequences, no strategy for how to proceed upon her escape. She gives no cognitive consideration to her own needs. Most empaths readily identify with Belle's sensitivities and behaviors toward others, and less so with her apparent lack of regard for herself.

Maurice, her father, appears caring on the surface. He means well, but his grief and preoccupation with his inner turmoil distract him from noticing the needs of his daughter. He does not fully appreciate what she sacrifices to make his interior world less painful. Consequently, he sets up a difficult dynamic for Belle: she loves him because he is lovable in many ways—he did try to bring her a rose after all. Yet he abandons her when she really needs him. She has her own grief over the loss of her mother. Her father has not attended well to that and also lets Belle sacrifice herself in an outstanding manner when he confides the secret promise he made to the Beast and permits her to go in his place.

Did Maurice name his daughter's gift as sacrifice? Did he validate any meaning for her or express gratitude for her offering? Probably not. At least, the tale does not indicate this. Instead, she goes forth fulfilling her Empath Contract, wordlessly, selflessly, unknowingly. For an empath, such sacrifice occurs regularly—and often without recognition when the inner Maurice turns a blind eye to the consequences of that self-sacrifice.

The Beast, in marked contrast to Belle, cares only for his own needs. Any violation of his selfishness and self-absorption quickly leads to an irritable, angry, or worse, violent response. Any show of civility serves his own agenda—to be rid of the curse—and Belle's goodness completely eludes him. Most people, especially those who are not narcissists, assess his beastly behavior as bad, undesirable, important to curb and to keep to oneself. The few acceptable places for such behavior in our culture can be found in courts of law, film, and more recently, the political stage.

Those who have learned to keep their bellowing behaviors in hiding, either consciously by choice or unconsciously by habit, often feel intimidated by the roaring and grumbling of others. Empaths certainly do. Not only does inner *resonance* with the grumbling Beast feel disturbing, his outer *behavior* feels assaultive. Belle, however, with her practiced capacity for numbed endurance, bears his presence—his disturbances, his assaults—well. She is no stranger to such undercurrents. Her forbearance fulfils part of her Empath Contract, and keeps her from noticing her own beast within.

While these descriptions may echo an empath's life experience, they don't necessarily feel good. Empaths rarely recognize how the Empath Contract has defined the plot of their interior life and left them feeling stuck in a quagmire of caring for others while struggling to avoid the Beast. Yes, empaths generally do try to avoid the beastly behavior of strangers, but that same intrusively self-serving behavior seems welcome if the beastly "other" touches the empath's heart in any way. So often empaths "see the good" in those they love, just as Belle dreamt of the prince.

Consequently, the empath does not run away, and self-invested others receive few prompts from her to examine and take responsibility for the impact of their beastly behavior. Instead the empath keeps hoping and expecting that the Beast will live into his best self. That vision and longing galvanizes the empath's search for redemption. Yet initially, like Belle, she searches for it and the "prince" in all the wrong places. The beauty she seeks is not readily accessible within the outer Beast, but her quest at least mobilizes her energies on her own behalf.

Something needs to happen for the inner shift to occur. Sometimes the bellowing of a Beast out of control is enough to propel the empath's escape and her first feelings of righteous indignation. Working to gain *insight* into these dynamics can offer less dangerous, less violent options, however. This discernment becomes especially helpful when the loyalty bonds of the Empath Contract loom large.

If we can appreciate that this fairy tale, as well as the drama of our outer life relationships, play out on an inner stage, we can develop new ways of relating to them and experience a happier ending. Attention to these dynamics in the inner terrain holds the greatest power for self-change. No one likes to acknowledge it, but the Beast, the abandoning father, and Belle live within each of us. The challenge and beauty of this awareness put each of us in the director's chair. We can stay stuck in the castle before the shift; get caught in "Groundhog Day" repeats of escape and wolf-attack; prolong the love affair without a deeper commitment; feel desolate in the separation; or work toward the wedding. We now turn our attention to this last option.

The Empath as Beauty and Beast Redeemed

Drawing upon our understanding of the Inner Critic and the chakras in Chapters 9 and 10, we can now explore the healing possibilities for the Beauty and the Beast within us. If we correlate Belle with the Heart Chakra, we recognize that she loves deeply; she cares for others. But she is wounded and consequently imbalanced. Her heart has been broken by the loss of her mother, the selfishness of her sisters, the needs and emotional abandonment of her father, and the insensitive expectations of her peers. She has learned to abandon herself.

Being a good student of life, she no longer considers her own needs when making decisions about the care of others. Belle tolerates her own self-criticism and the excessive demands of others because she intuits something is wrong: her heart has been split in two. Her beastly Inner Critic keeps any negative response she might feel toward others in check by heaping on the guilt. She anticipates shame should her own Inner Critic or others not value what she does, feels or thinks. Her wounded Heart Chakra cannot integrate her higher and lower chakras, nor her inner and outer life, to help her heal this painful divide.

The Beast, on the other hand, correlates with the third chakra, the energy center for self-empowerment. Unfortunately, he uses his power for self-serving agendas. He has all the resources he needs for a comfortable life—second chakra themes. Survival is not a concern for him—first chakra satisfied. His identity, as governed by the third chakra, has been challenged by the enchantress, however. Once a prince, he must now experience himself as the beast that all along lay not far beneath the surface of his persona.

In this context, we might distinguish the narcissist from the sociopath, as referenced in Chapter 2. The narcissist has likely experienced a measure of comfort and indulgence in life and simply expects more of the same: violation of that expectation elicits an angry response. The sociopath, in contrast, has likely been deprived of those comforts. Shame and torment have become "the familiar," and witnessing those feelings in others while also feeling them himself may satisfy a highly pathological need for bonding—except that now he is in control. Both the narcissist and the sociopath may sense the inner experiences of others, but that appreciation remains unconscious and self-serving. The narcissist, the sociopath, the Inner Critic, the Beast—none has access to Heart Chakra consciousness. The wounded part has gone into hiding; the healing part is unwelcomed.

We have already described the powerful role of the Inner Critic in the empath's inner world. It requires little stretch of the imagination to see the Inner Critic as the Beast. All those interior grumbles, the unspoken criticisms of self and others, the "depressed" moods as we struggle to shove those irritations and grumbles "down under," offer an opportunity to recognize our Beast up close and personal. The redeeming aspect of this lies in the realization that he is grumbling on our behalf.

Every time something violates one of our basic needs, the Beast makes an interior audible sound. The loudness of the sound, ranging from grumble to roar, probably reflects the degree of deprivation and/or the frequency of our attempts to ignore it. While our inner Belle is out in the world sacrificing herself for everyone else's needs, demands or perceived expectations, the Beast is desperately trying to get her/our attention. When we ignore him, he just criticizes more intensely. He uses words that don't actually reflect the nature of the issue because we aren't really listening to him anyway: he simply tries to get our attention. When we give it, he tentatively invites us, as caring Belles, into the castle.

Belle, on the other hand, has heard his roar so often she has found a way to tune him out. She continues on her path of service to others, deaf to her own needs, until his bellow becomes so intense, her guilt so pervasive, her attempts to submerge all of it so ineffective, that she has to stop and listen. If she finally realizes that her inner Beast is trying to save her from ravenous wolves, if she notices how hurt he—she—has been in the process of taking care of everyone else, and if they find common ground upon which to base future mutual decisions (such as the Beast allowing her to go to her father with the "right equipment" so that she may return when she promises/chooses), then they begin to define a new way of relating in the world.

Her inner Beast informs her when danger approaches, or the selfishness of others makes inappropriate demands upon her sensitivity and care. He protects her with his roar, turned outward when necessary, to keep devouring wolves/demands at bay. She agrees to consult with him before committing to the care of anyone and appreciates the power and presence he brings to her life. The inner Beast transforms into the Prince.

For an empath to imagine that within her own heart resides an inner lover—a prince who values her needs as important and essential in rendering any decision—often proves quite challenging. Yet this is the love and the lover she has longed for and sought all along. Not until this lover within—a version of her healing heart—is acknowledged, chosen, and embraced by the empath can her broken heart truly heal. To imagine an inner presence/prince that loves the empath *and* their relational "other" simultaneously offers a significant step toward integration, toward wholeness. The Heart Chakra can now function as an integrating unit amongst the other chakras, amidst other people, and within the empath. The third chakra's identity now serves the love of the Heart Chakra, rendering the empath's gifts more effective in the world. In essence, the power of the empath's love becomes more profound.

Summary

Throughout the centuries, in the midst of life's challenges and the suffering that often accompanies major transitions, we have frequently resorted to the telling of story both to escape the difficulty, and yet manage it at the same time. Myth and fairy tale have offered humankind powerful ways to make sense of life in cultural, social, interpersonal and intra-psychic contexts. These insights offer poetic doorways to exploration and growth so we may more fully develop our human potential.

We began this chapter with two important questions from the Grail legend—not to escape, not just to manage, but to learn and grow. We explored the longing in the empath's heart and soul, and the wound engendered by living this longing amidst life's muddy waters, so as to address these questions more meaningfully. What ails the empath? Might it be an unsatisfied longing to feel connected to others in harmonious, joyful ways? This becomes particularly challenging when empaths so easily feel what is dissonant, painful, and disconnected. What purpose do the soul-given sensitivities of the empath serve? Might they guide us toward what needs healing, for ourselves and others, so that our longing may be satisfied? This suggests that the empath must find a way to complete the uncompleted, to wed darkness with light, to heal and to find peace.

We have delved into the fairy tale of *Beauty and the Beast* to uncover its many layers of meaning, and its applicability to these questions and the journey of the empath. The magic mirror of the tale serves as a reminder that perspective matters, especially for the empath, whose emotions and sensitivities are so readily impacted by life. Holding the magic mirror up to the situation at hand and learning to accurately interpret the sensations of our inner terrain offer useful and practical tools with which to honor our place in the world, and to grow in every circumstance confronting us in daily life.

The rose so beautifully reminds us that this journey has vulnerable aspects, yet remains intensely wonderful, even miraculous. The work of integration brings us to wholeness and the tale itself reminds us to take excellent care of our heart. We realize that a balanced, mending heart allows for deeper, more authentic soul connection. Thus the path to wholeness is sacred.

As we continue to appreciate the empath's role and purpose in the world, we must include our experience of the sacred. We will again utilize the power of myth as we explore the mysterious terrain of the holy in our midst. Honoring the sacred as we are "feeling our way" offers an even deeper dimension of healing. When we embrace the tender heart, we discover soul-filled Mystery and the next dimension of the empath's sacred journey.

CHAPTER 16

The Empath and Spirituality

WHEN I INITIALLY ENVISIONED this manuscript and how writing it would unfold, I imagined this chapter would be my favorite. Yet I feel a daunting sense of smallness in the face of the enormity of the topic. Not only is the breadth of what is meant by "spirituality" indescribable, but our culture often deems it suspicious, lacking an evidence-base, or potentially evangelistic. Nonetheless, I have had the privilege of meeting many empaths over the past few years, and now realize that amidst all our sensitivities, challenges, joys and heartaches, one thing shines forth as a common path: we share a quest for meaning, a need for purpose, and a sense of the "spiritual"—described by whatever name each person feels most called to use.

This common bond notwithstanding, we may find ourselves at different stages of inquiry and discovery. For many of us, the fruits of this quest have developed over the span of a lifetime and continue to do so in the face of ongoing challenges. Yet at times we may feel we haven't progressed one bit. I am reminded of a quote from *The Book of Runes* by Ralph Blum: "In the life of the Spirit, you are always at the beginning."[151]

This sense of "beginning" challenges me more specifically as I introduce this topic of spirituality for the empath. I have been blessed to read many, many authors as I have searched and struggled to make sense of my own interior journey. Those writings have afforded me enormous guidance, yet in this moment I am acutely aware of the intellectual nature of the reading and writing process. We have already noted how our minds communicate with one another and within our own consciousness in an attempt to explain things. But what can we do with a topic that defies explanation? Our feelings capture the depth and height of the spiritual experience; our feelings also inform our minds. My task, my challenge, is to communicate through the mind how our feelings correlate with spirituality and why this is so relevant for the empath.

Personal experiences of a challenging kind come to mind. During the two weeks preceding the first anniversary of 9/11, I felt an emotional heaviness, a "funk" that seemed unrelated to the circumstances of my life. I mentioned this to my Reiki teacher, who suggested I might be feeling the mood of the country related to the anniversary of this tragedy. As soon as she said it, I felt a knowing resonance within me. I also felt my heart embracing all those grieving the loss of a loved one, and the mood lifted almost immediately.

Since then I've become more aware of times when my internal feeling-state reminds me of an ocean retreating from the shore, like

---

[151] Ralph H. Blum, *The Book of Runes. A Handbook for the Use of an Ancient Oracle: The Viking Runes*, Tenth Anniversary Edition (New York, NY: St. Martin's Press, 1993), 94.

there's a vacuum, an emptiness, inside me. I have learned not to label myself as defective when I feel this, but to see it as a process of preparation for the next wave to eventually form and reach land. These times arrive unpredictably. I find myself wondering if I'm sensing something larger, although I don't know what. I have taken to putting a prayer into that empty feeling with hopes it might matter somehow, somewhere. At the least, it eases the vacancy within.

At times like these we may ask ourselves, "What ails thee?" If larger fields of sadness, anger, fear, or joy float like clouds across the face of the earth, it may be that they cause those occasional uncomfortable feelings. If so, we must recognize that our inner tuning forks are resonating with those fields. The next questions become: Why do we have those tuning forks? For what purpose have we incarnated to feel so much? Do these feelings relate to our longing? And what do our souls long to receive? We bring these questions out of the shadows in an attempt to free ourselves of the sometimes consuming pain we experience with others, while also trying to love ourselves and others as best we can. This challenge marks our search for meaning. All that we have discussed so far brings this point front and center.

Our understanding of the neurological, energetic, psychodynamic, and mythological elements of being an empath has not released any one of us from the capacity to feel the inner state of another. But we now have tools to shift our affected inner state and to rebalance ourselves after receiving the input. Why must we do this dance at all? Are we victims of neurology and psychology, doomed to endless repetition? Or is there a meaning in this that we can pursue and live into, so as to facilitate our own redemption as well as that of others in our personal and larger circles? Whom does the Grail serve? Is there a greater intention to the forces surrounding us, offering us a chance to rebalance the planet through steadfast commitment to rebalancing ourselves? If so, what is that intention? What is our relationship to it? How shall we proceed?

The Secret Gift of Confusion

Empaths approaching any avenue of healing bring the traumas, big and small, of the recent and distant past, along with shame, guilt, grief, fear, anxiety and other emotions experienced in response to those traumas. The memories of those experiences likely include the intertwined emotions of others, absorbed during the original event. Whenever we recalled those memories or experienced their awakened resonance through later life occurrences, they accumulated additional layering: the feeling-states of those involved in the more current experience, as well as our judgments about those feelings. As a result of all this "mud in our sponge," no wonder so many of us really struggle to know and appreciate who we truly are at core.

My own experience as a six-year-old, seeing each of my grandparents quite sick before they died, filled me with a host of feelings—anxiety that something "bad" was happening; helplessness since I could do nothing to "fix" them, or prevent what might occur; and grief at the loss of their usual contact with me. I also unconsciously sensed my mother's confusion, fear, sadness, and unspoken anger as she cared for her bedridden parents, along with three young children. She didn't understand what was happening to her father, then her mother, especially during the beginning stage of their illnesses. Helplessness became a trigger point for me thereafter, and I did whatever I could to avoid that feeling.

Consciously and naively, I chose medicine as a career so that I would never feel that loss of control regarding illness. Instead, of course, I felt bombarded by the steady repetition of helpless moments, for myself, my colleagues, my patients, and their family members. I suspect my soul's deeper wisdom hoped I would come to respect helplessness as a doorway to something profoundly meaningful, while also learning to appreciate myself more authentically. But first I had to learn that the hidden inner rage I experienced whenever I felt helpless was not a reflection of my basic nature or essence, nor that of anyone else. Rather, that deep-seated seething protest arose from intensely activated wounds and their need and longing for healing.

The hope and longing that something "out there" will fulfill or complete us in a way that *doesn't hurt* lurks not far beneath our "spongey" surface. This fuels our quest for an experience of wholeness. When human relationships do not satisfy this longing—and if we do not resign ourselves to failure, be it ours or the other's—we inevitably turn our attention to the Divine, who seems to live in the mysterious Unknown. From the perspective of ego consciousness and its sense of separateness, we experience the world of Spirit as "Other" and, therefore, as potentially relational, though perhaps also foreign. In fact, the very essence of relationship suggests the involvement of two or more distinct entities. Unfortunately, issues of trust and faith arise when human relationships have not satisfied, or worse, have confounded this deeper quest. The ego's sense of hurt and its need for protection from further hurt, struggle with the soul's longing to heal that hurt and become whole. Will boundaries blur, or will ego armor prevail?

Some of us may begin a therapeutic process filled with confusion about who we are—I certainly did. Others may start with what feels like a solid sense of self only to experience some unsteadiness as the course of healing work strips away illusions. Difficulty defining oneself feels uncomfortable, but if we have enough ego strength to endure it without becoming psychotic or destructive, we also become more receptive to the Mystery that lies beneath the ego's unstable—or perhaps more accurately stated, porous—surface.

It is in the healing and reconstruction of a more authentic sense of self that we comprehend what the spiritual world "is" and what "it" may both offer us and seek from us. This may sound a bit intimidating or perplexing, yet the truth is we have been dancing with this Mystery all along. Every time an empath senses the inner state of another person, boundaries blur and Mystery beckons. We *feel* this. We feel the intangible aspects of relationships, and the more we explore that unseen world, the more we grow in awareness of our relationship with the Divine.

As vessels perfectly poised to receive the radiance of Spirit, our souls straddle the borderlands between Mystery and our human consciousness. In Chapter 7 we discussed the five levels of soul and how the two "lower" levels penetrate our personality[152] and body. We also came to understand that we experience soul at these lower levels through our separateness, our relationships, and often through our wounds. As our lower mind learns to better tolerate confusion, blurred boundaries, and intense feelings, healing opportunities teach us to appreciate these lower levels of soul, and to recognize that

---

[152] Personality describes a human sense of self—likes and dislikes, talents, vulnerabilities, and idiosyncrasies. Ego technically describes a psychological structure designed to keep a person's sense of individual self and identity intact by utilizing defense mechanisms such as projection, rationalization, and humor, to name just a few. Both words—ego and personality—imply a distinct, separate sense of self and in that sense I use these words interchangeably.

every cell of our body is ensouled no matter what its health status, as are our joys and heartaches.

The three "higher" levels of soul remain conscious of our communion with the Divine and with other souls, so that Unity, Essence, and Presence forever dwell within the realm of our higher mind awareness. Our higher mind consciousness already embraces us. The challenge we must address involves our lower mind's readiness to recognize and return that embrace. This soulful higher mind/lower mind re-connection not only impacts our relationship with the Divine, but also helps us appreciate our empathic role in relationships with other humans.

Often we begin to *live* this process of re-connection before we *understand* it. Even as we grope in the dark and feel our way, empaths experience less separateness than others who do not sense relational inner states so readily. The feeling of sadness offers an excellent example. When an empath unconsciously agrees to carry another's sadness, perhaps as part of her original Empath Contract, she may feel sad much of the time. Her "sadness tuning forks" receive much stimulation over the course of her life. From that familiar feeling-place, she can instinctively tune in to the sadness of others and know well how to *be* with them.

Those who prefer or can manage to keep their "sadness tuning forks" inactivated don't share this empathic resonance. Instead of feeling sad, those less empathic may struggle with a sense of inadequacy as they try to bridge the chasm between their own emotional state and the other's sadness, so as to offer comfort. In contrast, when facing someone who has experienced a loss the empath will *feel* that loss; she will *know* it inside her skin. In that moment, to a significant extent, the "other" lives within her. Oddly, it is the empath's capacity to love and *be* with the "other" that eventually teaches her how to love and *be* with herself.

Even the psychological defenses and unspoken barriers raised by another person in relationship offer the empath important information regarding that individual in the context of a larger web. When we as empaths come to appreciate how our empathic resonance informs our lower levels of soul, another kind of communion can take place, even if in its extremity it doesn't *feel* very pleasant or sacred. So while one might philosophically argue about the unity versus the duality of human consciousness in relationship with the spiritual world, this discussion borders on irrelevant for the empath, who feels *all* of it at every level of soul. As an empath comes to appreciate her gift, complete separateness, and duality, becomes an illusion.

Guidance for the Journey

Thus, in the midst of these pseudo-boundaries that blend and overlap we may consider Spirit, at least in part, as the Essence holding the Universe together. Some refer to this Essence as Love. In this context, Love may seem impersonal in higher dimensions—functioning like cosmic glue, ethereal elastic, or metaphorical Velcro—while we also experience love as very personal in the four dimensions of space and time in which we live and breathe. Whatever we choose to call it, the fact remains that *everything* is held together by *something*, even if to varying degrees.

The Big Bang Theory hypothesizes that the Universe expands steadily in a cohesive, unified process. Might we also consider the Earth's gravitational field as one form of this impersonal, cohesive attraction, even while it bonds us individually to our planet in the most fundamental and intimate of ways? From this perspective a poet might eloquently describe how the Earth "loves" and holds us in her gravitational embrace.

The mysticism of Kabbalah approaches this question differently, yet offers a similar awareness. "According to some rabbis, God wished to behold God,"[153] so the Divine as Absolute-All-and-Nothingness allowed the Nothingness aspect of Itself to create a space of non-existence, the *Tzimtzum*—the receiving Void. The Absolute All then surrounded this Void with Itself as *Endless Light*, pouring Itself as radiance into the Void to create the ten *Sefirot*[154] of the Tree of Life. (Figure 16-1) "Those *Sefirot*, as they were called, unfolded in an instantaneous sequence to set out a configuration that was to be the paradigm for everything that would be called, created, formed and made in Existence. Composed of pure consciousness this realm of light was the reflection of the Holy One. As such, it both revealed and concealed the Absolute in an image of Divinity."[155] The *Sefirot*, or Radiances, are frequently referred to as Divine Attributes. Interestingly, we find Lovingkindness flows forth from Wisdom and Understanding, in turn pouring Itself into the Radiances that follow, with Compassion and Beauty at the very center, the heart of the Tree of Life.

In their mythology, the Greeks also described the origins of creation as a great yawning void, an abyss of chaos and darkness,[156] out of which emerged Eros, the god of Love. He in turn created Light and was later served by Himeros, or Longing.[157] Myths regarding

---

[153] Halevi, *Psychology & Kabbalah*, 10.
[154] Ibid.
[155] Ibid.
[156] Hamilton, *Mythology*, 63–64.
[157] Ibid., 36.

Eros have evolved over time, such that his name is now associated with a host of attracting forces: psychic relatedness, platonic love, intimate love, and Cupid, to name a few. Again we might wonder if the Eros of the Universe reveals itself through our personal experience of gravitational fields.

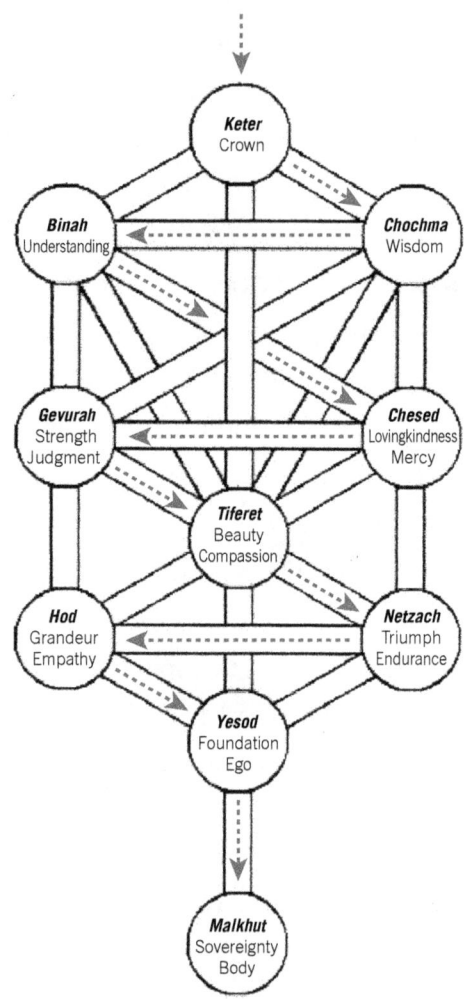

Figure 16-1: The Ten *Sefirot* of the Tree of Life

This is a derivative work of Morgan Leigh's "File: Tree of life wk 02.jpg" by Regina Bogle. M.D., 2016.

In any case, the human psyche has struggled to understand the nature of the intangible and the Divine in the context of relationship from the beginning of consciousness. As our earliest ancestors looked up into the night sky and perceived "the deep," they began to tell stories about where we came from and why. Shamans, priests, mystics, gnostics, philosophers, hermeticists, and many others have continued these explorations, sharing their wisdom with whoever might find it of value. I dare say many empaths have read some of these writings.

Reading wisdom shared by others can expand the mind, as well as offer swirling, uncomfortable emotions a conceptual place to land; understanding offers a place of refuge and grounding. This is easier said than done, however. When overcome by painful emotions, it requires Herculean effort to raise one's eyes and heart from the depths of turmoil, to continue past the perceived insanities of one's current situation, and to courageously wonder and wander into an upper realm of greater perspective—what some call higher knowledge, or the wisdom of higher mind. Instead, in an attempt to cope, many of us get caught in addictions that cloud our vision and dull our senses, so we can numbly muddle through the misery of our days. Those who dare to explore beyond this option often discover an even stranger world, where true peace surrounds one, creativity reigns, and love abides.

Because the experience of such peace and love can feel strange and unfamiliar, some turn away in fear or disbelief. Some tell themselves their perceptions are delusional, and question how they can trust them. Others try desperately and possessively to hold on to this new state but, having stumbled upon it by accident, can't seem to retrace their steps if they lose their grip. In conjunction with these potential reactions, Triple Warmer's maintenance of the habit of suffering rises to the forefront. Engaging Triple Warmer through appropriate attention to its current agenda, extending gratitude for its helpful though misguided intentions, and inviting it to help us change for the better, offer healing and new vision. These efforts can facilitate the search, discovery, and development of a *new habit* that allows us to eventually appreciate and live into this new awareness of peace, creativity, and love.

Sacrifice as Part of Healing Work

So to begin the healing process energetically and psychologically, we must first realize that old habits of suffering usually involve long-standing beliefs about who we are, why we're here on Earth, and what life is about. I have no desire to persuade anyone to change their beliefs: not only might it sound evangelistic, but our energy habits simply won't readily incorporate such strangeness. Instead, I invite the reader to take a few moments to breathe deeply while centering conscious attention in the heart, and from that place, to consider these questions:

- By what standards do you choose to live your life? What makes a decision or action right? Good? Acceptable? Required? Expected?
- From whom did you learn these standards? Do they accurately reflect who *you* are at core?
- What guides you as you consider your own worth? The worth of others?
- What beliefs do you hold about your responsibility to attend to your own needs? To the needs of others?

- Where in your body and/or your energy field do you feel those standards or beliefs held? How does this place in your body and/or energy field feel? For example, is it heavy? Light? Burdened? Joyful? Something else?
- How would you describe the current overall condition of the world? Of your community?
- How would you describe the current overall condition of your life in the context of your community and the larger world?
- What do you sense or believe about the purpose of your birth? How does the experience of pain and suffering factor into this purpose?
- Were you born with an innate capacity for joy? If so, how naturally and easily can you access this experience? If you feel that you were not born to experience joy, what belief do you hold about why not?
- Have pathways of release and relief presented themselves to you? If so, how have you responded to those opportunities?
- Is something calling you from deep within, beckoning you toward further learning and development?
- Are you willing to learn and engage with whatever presents itself as the next phase of your own human evolution?

As we reflect upon these personal questions, broader, more socially oriented queries arise. For example, what impact can the development of one person have upon the larger web connecting us all? According to the Talmud, "whoever saves a life, it is considered as if he saved an entire world."[158] If this is so, can there be value in learning to transform pain into joy, even if those efforts attend only to oneself? It occurs to me here that this question concerning transformation parallels the quest of the alchemists of old who tried to change lead into gold. Despite dubious success on the physical plane, their work has been referenced as valuable in the psychological and spiritual realms ever since.

Might empaths, like the alchemists of the past, come into the world to discover the tools and techniques to transform their sensitivity-engendered pain into joy? This concept offers empaths an amazing healing experience and the opportunity to model a capacity for deeper, joy-filled relationships. They might also feel called to guide others along this meaningful path.

The answers to these wonderings dwell in Mystery, as do the tools and teachings regarding their use. As these questions rise from the depths to our consciousness, we each ultimately decide whether to explore them in the realm of the Unknown. If we do so, we then choose our response. In the absence of any defined "right way" or "wrong way," we have no guarantees for how our personal story or the story of the planet will unfold. Yet our responses to these questions do influence the plot: we set the course of our life in one direction or another in four-dimensional spacetime. We get to choose and must realize that even making "no choice" still has an impact. Those who appreciate the process of co-creation will welcome active choosing as an option.

Obviously, whenever we select one option we reject others. Similarly, when we choose to heal or grow, we must leave behind the old habits and beliefs we employed to cope with our wounded or

---

[158] Mishnah Sanhedrin 4:9; *Yerushalmi Talmud,* Tractate Sanhedrin 37a, in "Talmud," Wikiquote, last modified February 28, 2016, https://en.wikiquote.org/wiki/Talmud.

less mature state. Relationships sometimes change as the intensity or focus of one's inner life shifts. These changes give us pause, even as we approach a deepening sense of the spiritual within us. We feel the risk of loss. Sometimes we use the word "sacrifice," which comes from the Latin word *sacrificium* (*sacer* = sacred; *facere* = to make), to describe our experience of these shifts. Most simply, the word "sacrifice" means "to make holy or sacred." In our common parlance, however, we usually use the word to suggest "the destruction or surrender of something for the sake of something else."[159]

Empaths who so readily sacrifice their own needs for others may benefit from questioning whether that form of sacrifice truly promotes something sacred for themselves *and* the other. While choice on the earth plane requires that we accept the experience of separateness in duality—selecting one *or* the other—sacrifice on the spiritual plane promotes unity and harmony—becoming one *with and for* the other. Thus the question now before us involves the nature of what is left behind. Has what we sacrificed been abandoned, or integrated? Did we ignore our essence, our soul in the "sacrifice" we made? Or have we left behind the old habits and destructive patterns so that the energy that fueled them can be used for better ways of being? This question constitutes the next aspect of our exploration.

The Horizontal and the Vertical Paths[160]

We live our lives on the earth plane moving about in the horizontal dimension, tending our affairs across the surface of the earth, subject to the cycles of the sun and the moon which mark time for

---

[159] "Sacrifice," Merriam-Webster, accessed March 8, 2016, http://www.merriam-webster.com/dictionary/sacrifice.
[160] Anonymous, *Meditations on the Tarot*, 44–45.

us—unless we only look at digital clocks! A tree, on the other hand, stands tall and goes deep. It cannot move so it stands in place all its life, witnessing the movement around it and offering various gifts to anyone who cares to approach it.

We may find ourselves drawn to trees as we contemplate their strength through all kinds of weather, their graceful beauty as their leaves change color and their branches bend gently in the breeze, and their provision of a home to birds, squirrels, and other forms of life. Their wide trunks may shield us from the wind or offer support as we lean against them. Their roots penetrate deeply into the earth to establish well-grounded stability, and their limbs stretch high to provide refreshing shade or shelter from the rain. Here we discover two paths: one a horizontal plane of existence, the other vertical. Human beings are capable of both.

Many of us become so caught up in the busy-ness of life on the horizontal plane that we hardly notice this vertical option. I do not suggest we are meant to climb trees like monkeys, or fly like birds. Rather, that our consciousness has access to these two paths. More simply put, the horizontal experiences of our life occur predominantly in a world external to our physical body: our body moves toward or away from them; we choose directions, we venture out; we have experiences, we return to home base.

The Vertical Path, in contrast, takes us up and down the invisible ladders of our interior world. What resides in the heights and depths? Here we find less "evidence" unless we rely upon our own experiences, or the writings and journeys of mystics and shamans, as well as those who have suffered deep torment or enjoyed blissful ecstasy. As with the Horizontal Path, we move in one of these two directions: we have an experience, we return to center. At the center, these paths cross. What can this mean for an empath?

In the process of attending to the physical, emotional, energetic, and belief-based challenges of our life, many of us encounter uncertainty, a sense of Mystery—for some, the dreaded Unknown. In the midst of this confusion, we may not recognize the mysterious Vertical Path beckoning us from its crossroad with the Horizontal. To the degree that it stirs uncomfortable feelings, we may work very hard to avoid it. If we choose to face it rather than run away, however, we may sense an interior space and a desire to wonder about deeper questions, such as: Where do I come from? Why am I here? What sustains me? What is the purpose of my life? What will happen to me and to us when physical life ends? The information available along the Horizontal Path cannot answer these questions. These wonderings lead us to the Vertical Path.

Personally, I have come to appreciate spirituality as a loving dance with Mystery. In this context, I particularly appreciate the Kabbalistic understanding of one of the 72 names of the Divine: *Ehyeh-Asher-Ehyeh*, as noted in Exodus 3:14. This name is commonly interpreted as "I AM THAT I AM." [161] However, a more accurate interpretation of the Hebrew is "I SHALL BE WHO I SHALL BE,"[162] or paraphrased, "I AM BECOMING WHO I AM BECOMING,"[163] an *Endless Light* in motion.

From this understanding we can appreciate that Mystery is constantly present *and* dynamic. We can never understand all of it, in

---

[161] Everett Fox, *The Five Books of Moses: Genesis, Exodus, Leviticus, Numbers, and Deuteronomy*, The Schocken Bible: Volume I (New York, NY: Schocken Books, 1995), 273.
[162] The Hebrew verb is in the first person singular imperfect, reflecting an action yet to be completed. See Gerardo Sachs, "Ehyeh-Asher-Ehyeh," in *The Jewish Bible Quarterly* (Vol. 38, No. 4, 2010), 152.
[163] My thanks to Barbara Sussman for this insight.

significant part because our mind is too limited, but also because It is Itself in the process of Divine Becoming and Self-discovery. Created by this Mystery, we are consequently just as mysterious as the Source that gives us life. Mystics across the centuries have suggested that we can tap into this Mysterious Unknown of Becoming along the Vertical Path within us.

Should we opt to avoid the Vertical Path, we may feel mercilessly driven by some unknown force, or subject to the Horizontal Path's seeming whimsies of fate. Alternately, if we consider that we, too, might wish to access the depth/height awareness of life, we need to consciously turn our attention from Horizontal external preoccupations to the still center within, so as to be present to, and conscious of a Vertical flow. The lessons offered by *Beauty and the Beast* show us how living from a mending, fully flowing, and open heart can help us access soul consciousness, a Vertical Path experience: we become more receptive to what lies above and below our everyday awareness of life.

To journey into Vertical Path territory requires trust, and we must first develop a conscious relationship with Mystery and its ongoing revelations. Most of us are afraid of the Unknown. This fear is driven by an ego consciousness that actively defends itself against anything which might threaten its existence. Shame signals potential ego annihilation, while love's embrace might well dissolve the ego's separateness—or so it fears. The potential for both shame and love lives in the Unknown, and the ego is frightened of all of it.

Consequently, the development of a conscious relationship between ego and Mystery happens slowly. People often become religious in their initial efforts to embrace this mysterious dance with spirituality. When individuals band together to share mutual responses to the deeper questions cited above, when they choose to worship an agreed-upon aspect of Mystery together, a religion comes into being. Religions become part of the culture and, for many of us, serve as a bridge between psychology and spirituality. Even without this bridge of religion, however, psychology and spirituality remain fundamental, even if unconscious aspects of our humanity. They serve as interface between the Horizontal and Vertical Paths.

The Empath's Approach to the Vertical Path

While religion can offer a sense of community and serve as a bridge to spirituality, our core relationship to Mystery remains personal and individual. Additionally, our level of consciousness significantly impacts the quality of that uniqueness. While the human experience does not require perspective-taking or the effort to witness ourselves, our brains contain the capacity for these developments. This fact makes us distinctly human. Yet as discussed in previous chapters, this potential, while present at birth, cannot function for many years and must mature along with our nervous system and energy systems before we can actively engage in self-reflection and self-definition. Thus, the installation of beliefs about who we are takes place in the deeper recesses of the brain, below our conscious awareness, while we are young and incapable of accepting or rejecting the information that comes our way.

This information gets encoded along well-worn neurological pathways and in habitual energy patterns in the context of familial and social expectations. As children, without the capacity for self-reflection and perspective, we take in what parents, life circumstances, and others in our extended community offer in a fashion similar to a computer download, incorporating viruses and all else if we don't have caregivers able to sensitively monitor our security system. When this happens to a "sponge"—before self-awareness has developed enough to allow objective assessment—she will incorporate the mud into her sense of personal identity. The unconscious logic of the child sponge becomes: "I am what I feel. I feel bad. I am bad."

The incorporated "mud," being essentially foreign to the essence of the "sponge," feels uncomfortable at best and otherwise hurts. It also impacts ego development, the selection of its needed defenses, and their effectiveness. No mystery here—these feelings and their defenses are all too familiar. Yet they significantly affect how we approach Mystery and the Vertical Path as we grow.

These kinds of "muddy sponge" experiences mark the early Horizontal Path of most empaths. Typically, one's path to the center becomes so laden with "muddy yuck" that avoiding the mud and, thus, the center becomes the unconscious life goal. Later in life we may even consciously attempt to "wall off" the fragments of our broken heart that reside in the center as well. Here lies the function of the Inner Critic: to make the misery of the known (the Horizontal Path) seem safer than the Mystery of the Unknown (the Vertical Path). This avoidance of the center, and our broken heart, receives reinforcement when we approach this crossroad only to feel an invisible wall of resistance; a more tangible image would have "caution tape" barring the entrance. The energy may feel like coiling ropes of old negative thought patterns and self-doubt—again, meet the Inner Critic—that entangle the would-be entrant, making further progress impossible.

This invisible resistance might include psychological defenses that unconsciously divert the real issue onto someone or something else. Phobias or projections, for example, ensnare us in fear or blame, respectively, while hiding the real cause of our distress. From an energetic perspective, this resistance is likely encoded with Triple Warmer energy, thus forcing us to exert significant effort if we are to bypass its protection and the anxieties resulting from something as unfamiliar as healing. Spiritual literature offers many references to the "Guardian of the Threshold."[164] If we imagine this field of resistance to be like a bubble around the "cross" of the Vertical and Horizontal Paths, we might understand this "Guardian" as the protector of a sacred space, an image differing significantly from the others mentioned. Taken together, they speak to different levels of consciousness.

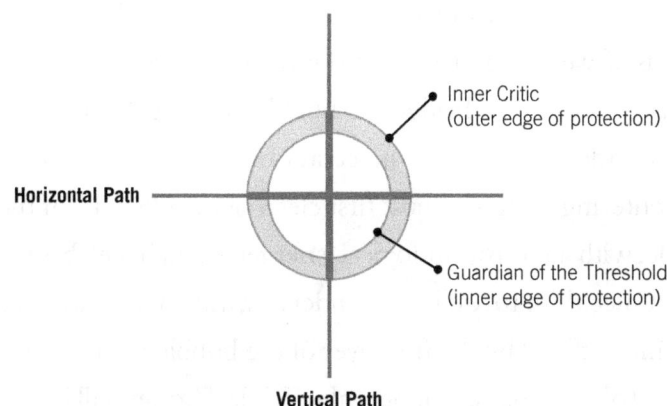

Figure 16-2: The Crossroad of the Horizontal and Vertical Paths and Its Protection

---

[164] Rudolf Steiner, *How to Know Higher Worlds: A Path of Modern Initiation,* trans. by Christopher Bamford (Hudson, NY: Anthroposophic Press, 1994), 184–194.

We may imagine our center's protective "bubble" as having two layers. (Figure 16-2) The outer layer takes on all the mud and wounding of the Horizontally-lived life: the Inner Critic and the lower mind live here. The inner layer, in contrast, serves as protector of the sacred Vertical Path, and here resides the Guardian of the Threshold and higher mind.

From an energetic perspective, Triple Warmer serves both purposes. As a meridian, it provides body-armor and defense while maintaining habits to protect the outer muddied bubble from the challenges of Horizontal Path living. As discussed in Chapter 5, Triple Warmer's role as a joy-filled Radiant Circuit more aptly serves as Guardian for the inner sacred bubble. As human beings with an ego, we quickly learn the importance of survival on the Horizontal Path. Consequently, we naturally give priority to this path and to the outer layer's energetic protection of ego, rather than consciously activate Triple Warmer's Radiant Circuit function.

Thus, if we choose to access the Vertical Path, we need to make a conscious effort to bridge the bubble's double-layered protective field in order to approach the center of these two pathways. To do this centering work we must first clean out the "yuck" of the outer bubble, with all its psychological, energetic, and belief-based distortions. Once this process is well underway, usually with assistance, the resistance offered by the first layer of the bubble gradually dissolves. From a balanced place of inner calm, Triple Warmer will have learned a new way to protect us. It does so because in the process of healing, which can only come via the Vertical Path, our consciousness has already begun to recognize the connection between the Horizontal and the Vertical. Moreover, when we approach our healing with love, respect and gratitude, we activate Triple Warmer as a Radiant Circuit. Given the beauty and flow of this mending, we may wonder if our wounds serve a higher purpose.

Our personality may wish to avoid our wounds at all costs, and our ego may defend us as best it can from having any consciousness of them, both preferring to honor the caution tape plastered across these painful areas. But our soul and its healing energy patiently wait while we find the courage to take down the tape and let the healing wonder pour forth. Our soul appreciates our wounds as doorways and loves them for the access they provide between the Vertical and Horizontal Paths. I have had the privilege to witness this repeatedly in my sessions. I will never forget the first time I became aware of this aspect of the soul. During a session in which a client focused attentively upon her wounded experience, I asked how her soul perceived her wound. Her answer surprised me and simultaneously opened my eyes. She said, "My soul loves my wound" with amazement in her voice, and in that moment I understood something profound.

An important aspect of our journey along the Vertical Path is the development of a relationship between our soul—its upper three levels—on the Vertical Path, and our ego/personality as they dwell in physical form—the lower two levels of soul—on the Horizontal Path. In the midst of this partnership, the five levels of soul can begin the process of conscious reunion. This involves a dialogue between ego/personality and all the levels of soul; we appreciate this budding relationship as our wounds provide the doorway and our longing acts as guide. In this process, we befriend and transform the Inner Critic, and begin a dialogue with the Guardian of the Threshold. If we approach the inner "bubble" with an attitude of honoring the sacred, we find ready access to the center where our mending heart lives, wounded and healing, and which our soul calls "home."

For the reader wanting to explore and develop this soul/personality relationship in greater depth, I would suggest a book that found me at a local bookstore. *Soul Love*[165] by Sanaya Roman offers a path of soul/personality connection that I cannot hope to duplicate; I recommend it to anyone who feels called to this pursuit.

Given the many challenges we face every day of our life, I dare say most of us understand the Horizontal Path all too well. Let us now turn our attention to the Vertical Path more particularly. Does the Vertical Path welcome our sadness, our anger, our fear? Is there a place for these more challenging feelings within this spiritual trajectory? We will explore the depths and heights of the Vertical Path to discover a deeper sense of purpose and meaning through the wisdom of an ancient myth. This myth will also more deeply inform our sense of the spiritual, with respect for the Mystery that we are and in which we live, and for the process of our own "becoming."

---

[165] Sanaya Roman, *Soul Love: Awakening Your Heart Centers* (Tiburon, CA: H J Kramer, Inc., 1997).

CHAPTER 17

Appreciating Ancient Wisdom

WHEN ASKED TO VENTURE into the darkness, we pause. Will we run away from it? Will we leap into it? Will we discover a new ground as we step forward? Our lower mind initially approaches the domain of Mystery with trepidation as it both beckons and disturbs us. If, however, we loosen our identification with the lower mind's need for the known and shift to higher mind awareness, we can center our consciousness in the resonating truth and love of our heart, trust its access to what lies in the mysterious beyond, and experience the process of mending it. By reuniting the heart's wounded and healing aspects, we can embrace our mending heart, our feelings, and the whole of ourselves as valuable and lovable. Through heart awareness and healing, our personality can then consciously engage in more deeply connecting and communing with our soul. Mystery becomes a welcome friend that now reveals Itself as we are ready to receive It: "only that which is loved can be known."[166] From this loving, mending place within we can explore the Vertical Path of spirituality more meaningfully.

Because the mind's words originate in Horizontal Path consciousness, their ability to convey Vertical Path truths proves limited. Consequently, to better appreciate Vertical Path wisdom necessitates some facility with the realm of symbols. To quote Carl Jung, symbols serve as images that provide "expressions of a content not yet consciously recognized or conceptually formulated."[167] They offer "an unknown quantity, hard to recognize, and, in the last resort, never quite determinable."[168] These symbols gently facilitate connection between the conscious and unconscious aspects of our being, offering a safe and meaningful transition into the realm of Mystery. This connection between conscious and unconscious, known and unknown, facilitates a reconciliation of opposites, as discussed in the context of *Beauty and the Beast*. Transcending and integrating opposites also promotes healing.

For most empaths, the Beast moves into the shadows of the unconscious during childhood, when they experience wounding in relationships, freezing in response to those wounds, and paralysis due to consequent shame. The tale of *Beauty and the Beast* offers a path to re-discover and integrate the Beast's power and necessity into our conscious life: the symbol facilitates the emergence of the mysterious beast from our personal shadows into the light of awareness. Through the expression of the transcendent function—"'a third' which can reconcile or unify the apparently irremediable conflict"[169]—love,

---

[166] John P. Dourley, *The Psyche as Sacrament: A Comparative Study of C.G. Jung and Paul Tillich* (Toronto, Canada: Inner City Books, 1981), 36.
[167] Carl G. Jung, "The Practical Use of Dream-Analysis," in *The Essential Jung*, 184.
[168] Ibid., 185.
[169] Dourley, *The Psyche as Sacrament*, 45.

symbolized by the rose in this tale, invites the integration of these opposites (care for self *and* other) into our conscious experience. In this way the Beast finds meaning and redemption within us; the Prince can now emerge. This story and the symbols within it guide us toward wholeness and healing. We again appeal to symbol through the myth of Inanna to help us better appreciate the Vertical Path within.

Inanna

Eight thousand years ago in the land of the Tigris and Euphrates rivers, a culture arose among humankind now known as Ancient Sumer. In that land the people worshipped a Mother Goddess whom they called Inanna, Queen of Heaven, Earth and Underworld.[170] In that time, her heavenly domain consisted of the "waters of the deep" (their reference to outer space[171]) and she was revered as Goddess of the Moon and of the Morning and Evening Star, now recognized as Venus. She wore blue garments and lapis jewels to reflect her Queendom of the Heavens. Her necklace of the rainbow and girdle of the zodiac also adorned her with their beauty and power. Additionally, her representations included lunar crescent horns and the eight-pointed star. The people beheld her as a Goddess of Justice and Compassion. Later goddesses often shared some of these representations: Arianrhod in the Celtic tradition wore a necklace of stars and was recognized as Queen of the Zodiac; the Egyptian goddess, Isis, was also worshipped as Queen of Heaven among other titles.

---

[170] Silvestra, "Inanna – Sumerian Mother Goddess, Queen of Heaven and Earth," in *Goddess-inspired Spirituality*, (June 10, 2012), accessed January 24, 2016, https://goddessinspired.wordpress.com/2012/06/10/inanna-sumerian-mother-goddess-queen-of-heaven-and-earth/; and Johanna Stuckey, "'Inanna and the *Huluppu* Tree': One Way of Demoting a Great Goddess," in *MatriFocus Cross-Quarterly for the Goddess Woman* (Lammas 2005, Vol 4-4), accessed January 24, 2016, http://www.matrifocus.com/LAM05/spotlight.htm.
[171] Silvestra, "Inanna – Sumerian Mother Goddess, Queen of Heaven and Earth."

In her role as Queen of Earth, Inanna wore a horned crown enclosing a cone, representing the sacred mountain. The owl and the lioness accompanied her and were respected as spiritually significant by association. She was also often represented with wings and worshipped as a Bird Goddess, or accompanied by a serpent-entwined staff. As Goddess of Natural Law and Justice, she showered humankind with gifts of civilization, wisdom, and prophesy. Again, goddesses of other cultures bore some of her characteristics. Isis was often represented with wings as Goddess of the Wind, and Cybele, a Great Mother Goddess in sixth-century BC Anatolia, shared Inanna's association with lions. In the patriarchal times that emerged centuries later, their connection with lions earned both Inanna and Cybele the title, Goddess of War.

As Queen of the Underworld, Inanna, like the Moon, cyclically journeyed into darkness. She traversed the depths beneath the earth just as the new moon blended into the dark of the night sky. Versions of her story evolved along with human consciousness, which at first perceived all things as one flowing unity, similar to the way our right brains conceptualize the *gestalt* of the world. Later, as the left brain slowly evolved into prominence with its capacity to notice details and markers of time, human stories expanded their focus from moon cycles to sun cycles. They described more specifically how Inanna took on a consort, a Sacred King whom she would choose yearly through her Sacred Priestess, her earthly, human representative. This priestess would rule with her king for one year during the growing season, during which time we may readily imagine not only crops but a human baby "germinated" and grew.

Once the growing season ended and the time for harvest approached, her king would be ritually killed so as to journey into the Underworld. The separation of priestess and king occurred only in the earthly realm, however, because he could rejoin Inanna in the Underworld where she also reigned. Regeneration of their relationship, the land, and the people took place during this dark time in the Underworld; when the next planting season approached, Inanna through her Sacred Priestess would choose a new consort (Sacred King) to rejuvenate all life once again.

The Underworld then served as a vital part of all life. People believed that the seeds for the next cycle of fertility would not be reborn without the journey to this dark, mysterious place, just as they would not regenerate without the cyclical new moon. At that point in human history, we did not fear the Underworld. That came later, accompanied and perhaps engendered by our increasingly evolving left brain and temporal lobe development. As our brains began to appreciate the details born of left brain discernment over the next few thousand years, humankind realized that physical death marked the finality of life in the body and mind. The Underworld, to which the dead departed, became a place to dread and fear.

Our human ancestors then evolved a new sense of the sacred in which they worshipped Inanna as Goddess of Life. They continued to revere her as Queen of Heaven and Earth, but relegated the position of Queen of the Underworld to her sister, a corn goddess named Erishkigal. She became the Goddess of Death, and our predecessors ascribed to her the torments and torture we have attributed to the Underworld ever since.

As Inanna's myth evolved over the centuries, she still journeyed to the Underworld cyclically for the three-day dark of the moon in her role as Moon Goddess. In some later versions of her story, her consort had been killed and she chose to rescue him to restore his life. She had to use her power to gain entrance to the Underworld by threatening her sister with violent entry. Erishkigal relented, but only on condition that Inanna enter stripped of her power. At each of the seven gates of "hell," Erishkigal demanded that Inanna successively release "her heavenly crown, earrings, necklace, brooches, belt, bracelets, and, lastly, the cross that 'covered her femininity.'"[172] These seven gates relate to the seven nights of the darkening, waning Moon.

During the actual three-day dark of the Moon, Inanna stood before her sister naked, derided by her, then bound and tortured with the "sixty miseries of eyes, heart and head."[173] She hung on a hook as a skeleton for three days until Erishkigal gave in to the demands of other gods, who complained about the death of the grain and vegetation above ground. Erishkigal reluctantly relented and had her sister sprinkled with the water of life and led to freedom. This permitted the restoration of growing vegetation upon Earth. In yet another version, Erishkigal's condition of release required that, once Inanna returned to Earth, she had to designate another to take her place. Upon her return, Inanna witnessed her lover, Dumuzi, deriving too much pleasure from the opportunity to rule as her alternate, so she sent him to the Underworld in her stead.

These differing stories of Inanna persist despite the conquest of one culture after another, traceable by way of mythological details despite name changes for both the culture and the goddess. Conquering peoples would often retain the qualities of the local goddess while

---

[172] Claire Gibson, *Goddess Symbols: Universal Signs of the Divine Female* (New York, NY: Barnes & Noble Books, 1998), 21.
[173] Ibid.

assimilating her features into those of their own deities to support a more seamless transition to the new civilization. When Babylonia conquered Sumer, for example, Inanna became Ishtar, and Dumuzi, her lover, became Tammuz. Later, Ishtar would become Astarte when the Assyrians took over the land. To this day, the Hebrew calendar reflects the season of Tammuz[174] in July when the crops dry up on the parched land.

Christianity has also incorporated various aspects of these myths, the most prominent being Mary's and her mother Anne's association with Inanna, whose name—in the forms of Nana and Anna—refers to the original Great Mother/Grandmother/Virgin Goddess.[175] In ancient days, the concept of virginity did not imply inexperience with the sexual act, but referred to a woman or goddess who "may not be compelled either to maintain chastity or to yield to an unwanted embrace… she is 'one-in-herself.'"[176] Many ancient mother goddesses were also considered virginal. We recognize this theme and its more recent modifications in the Christian description of Mary.

The Divine Feminine

Throughout the ages, the Divine Feminine has permeated the human psyche's quest to make sense of this earthly life in the context of the Divine. Even those religions whose primary God is masculine have their Divine Feminine counterparts to fulfill the human need for an accessible and relational Divinity. We find Her in the form of goddesses in ancient mythologies; as Shekinah in Judaism; as a

---

[174] Barbara G. Walker, *The Woman's Encyclopedia of Myths and Secrets* (New York, NY: HarperSanFrancisco, 1983), 970–971.
[175] Ibid., 429.
[176] M. Esther Harding, *Woman's Mysteries Ancient and Modern: A Psychological Interpretation of the Feminine Principle as Portrayed in Myth, Story, and Dreams* (New York, NY: Harper & Row, Publishers, Inc., 1971), 103.

Divine Mothering energy in Islam and Sufism; as Kuan Yin and Tara in Buddhism; as White Buffalo Woman in the Native American Oglala tribe; as Grandmother Spider for the Cherokee; and as Mary in Christianity, to name a few of Her faces.

Significantly, "She" is not just a *concept* to ease the suffering of our dualistic mind. Her power and presence have been palpable for centuries to those sensitive to it: some feel Her in the earth, some at sacred sites in stones, trees, and waters, and some as they gaze into the night sky. I especially felt Her at Chartres Cathedral. Interestingly for us, Mary's life (with which I am the most familiar) also poignantly embodied the dilemmas of the empath and their potential resolution. While what follows is in no way meant to evangelize a particular religious belief, I would like to suggest that as empaths we do need models and companions for our healing journey, and that the Divine Feminine, however we perceive Her, offers this gift.

My attempt to offer a model, of course, must rely upon my own experience. I readily admit that since childhood I have been drawn to Mary. I have studied and experienced other faces of the Divine Mother that seem to offer complementary aspects approximating the Divine All, including dark and fierce features as well as those that are gentle and loving. In the Christian tradition, Mary bears much resemblance to Inanna and other virgin mother goddesses, though tradition has stripped Mary of her fierceness and darkness. Like the later Inanna, Mary's shadowy side has had to find a home in a darker other: Erishkigal and Mary Magdalene, respectively. All these bearers of the Divine Feminine carry different aspects of Her nature; we can benefit from recognizing which of Her attributes resonate most with our uniqueness, and thus best assist us as spiritual beings coping with dualistic consciousness on the Earth plane.

Empaths in particular need a model for traversing the Underworld, where they can be met with love and meaningful discovery. As far as I know, no other goddess with a loving nature has reigned over the Underworld in the way Inanna did of old. Mary's reign over the centuries has only included Heaven and Earth (in keeping with the change in Inanna's designated role after the split in our consciousness), yet her story includes her Seven Sorrows as well as her Seven Joys. Her sorrows, which pierced her heart with a sword seven times, all involved the heartaches she bore from witnessing the trauma her son endured. Her joys included some of his celebrations, as well as her own. She clearly journeyed to hell and back as an empathic witness and participant in her son's journey. She knew his pain within the cells of her very being. Perhaps the Black Madonna has carried this deeper aspect of Mary's *knowing* and Inanna's roots into our present day.

In the Buddhist tradition, Kuan Yin,[177] Goddess of Compassion, also traveled to the Underworld after living a life of devotion to the Divine, which her father did not understand or support. In fact, he tried to manipulate, threaten, and harm her in his attempts to force his will upon her. While the stories about her do not stress her suffered feeling-response to her father's perversions of love, she remained ever sensitive to his suffering, such that when he finally appealed to her for help and forgiveness she gave it readily in the form of her own eyes and arms. The stories also include her journey to the Underworld, depicted as our version of hell; while there, wherever she stepped, roses bloomed.

---

[177] "Kuan Yin," Religion Facts, last modified November 14, 2015, www.religionfacts.com/kuan-yin; and "Guanyin," Wikipedia, last modified January 4, 2016, https://en.wikipedia.org/wiki/Guanyin.

Kuan Yin, Mary, and Jesus brought love to our consciousness of the Underworld. They offered a transformed vision of Erishkigal's domain. They have redeemed its torment with compassion and love, returning it to its primordial state of existence. They teach us that journeys to the Underworld need not be approached with so much dread. As Inanna's Sacred King modeled for us how to courageously face its darkness, we too can appreciate the Underworld as a place of surrender to regeneration and rebirth.

The Underworld and the Empath: Inanna or Erishkigal?

If we accept the Inanna of eight thousand years ago as a symbol of the Divine Feminine, we may more fully explore her significant contribution to the empath's spiritual experience. As Queen of Heaven, Earth *and* Underworld, she models how to move freely amidst these realms as we experience our many emotional states in the course of any given day and lifetime. Heaven, Earth, *and* Underworld lie along the Vertical Path. (Figure 17-1) The Underworld offers a dimension of human experience that we cannot avoid but which, under Erishkigal's reign, we learned to overvalue with fear, and either diagnose or ignore in our efforts to heal.

When we appropriately attend to our Underworld experiences along with those of Heaven and Earth, however, Inanna's three-tiered terrain offers greater clarity regarding many aspects of our human feeling life. Without judgement we may better understand ourselves, heal and grow. Her role as a sacred, evolving goddess also suggests a way for us to embrace spirituality as a dance with Mystery in an unceasing process of "becoming." In her capacity to traverse the three Worlds of the Vertical Path she has much to teach us, while she also fully embraces oneness in herself and all of life. No longer do we need to dissect and disconnect. She offers an opportunity to appreciate the totality of our feeling life with compassion, meaning, and purpose.

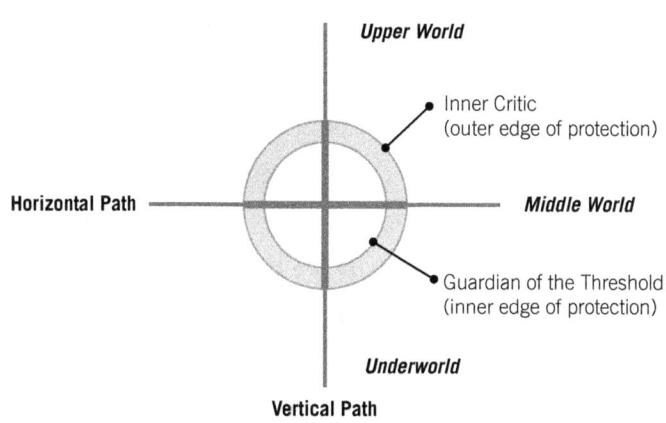

Figure 17-1: The Three Worlds of the Vertical and Horizontal Paths

As empaths who so readily feel the inner states of others, we recognize that it is the tumultuous, painful inner states that give us the most difficulty. These states immediately introduce us to an Underworld experience in that they lie hidden beneath the surface of the Earth realm's day-to-day expectations. Caregivers for those with chronic illness know this well, especially if the one they care for naturally struggles with his or her own inner fears, sadness, anger, and hopelessness. These painful feelings register in the belly brain of the caregiver's body and resonate with a broken heart. Our culture's tendency to relegate the caregiver's physical and emotional reality as secondary to cognitive definitions of "the good caregiver" further imprison the caregiver's physical and emotional experiences in the Underworld domain.

Our social expectations define good caregivers as those who supposedly provide their service willingly and graciously, without complaint. Additionally, good caregivers would never refuse to care for their loved one, particularly as their loved one would want it. How then do they manage the natural feelings that arise as they experience their life upended while also having to witness the same thing happening to their loved one, for even more devastating reasons?

How can a caregiver for someone so ill speak of her fear that perhaps she is not doing enough? Or that what is expected or required feels like too much? What can the caregiver do to protect herself from the expressed anger or sorrow of the one suffering? Or from the empathically perceived host of feelings that so naturally accompany the other's loss of function and ongoing distress? How does a caregiver seek personal assistance for her own feelings of hopelessness when the duration of caregiving seems endless? Or for her desire that it all be over, especially when that implies the death of her loved one?

Often those empathically caring for others bury these feelings, not realizing that some of them come from the one they love, and some are their own natural responses to a difficult situation. When buried beneath the surface of conscious expression, they live, perhaps even fester in the Underworld, potentially out of reach unless we have learned to journey there like Inanna.

Most empaths in my experience are all too familiar with the existence of the Underworld, and have developed habitual ways of coping with it. Some, for example, maintain "a good face" for the outer Earth world, yet *live* in the "in-between." This liminal space of "not here, not there," yet both and neither, is dark, shadowy, invisible. It marks the place where consciousness ventures when the insula is not able to hold life's contradictions simultaneously in one's body and mind.

On the continuum of this avoidance of the Underworld's domain—and Earth's as well—we recognize the roots of addiction. Denial or dissociation may also occur when vital aspects of life, such as passions, intuitions, alerts for danger, and dislikes, slide quietly into the dreaded domain below, unavailable for conscious experience or recognition. Add to this all the "beastly" reactions, like anger, desire, the right to ownership of one's space and time, coupled with shame and guilt for feeling and wanting these things, and the Underworld becomes a huge, dark, hidden, and dreaded vagueness dwelling below consciousness itself. Silenced in this way, the Underworld can only communicate with the caregiver through dreams, projections onto others, cravings, unpredictable outbursts or moods, and/or eventual physical illness.

In contrast, rather than avoid the Underworld, some fight it. Yet anger at God or at life for being unfair, cruel, filled with suffering, does nothing to alleviate the pain. Another alternative, pride, may be subtler in its social effects, especially when couched in a snide "you should have known better—like I do" attitude. But pride can resort to arrogance in its attempts to keep the Underworld at bay. These dynamics give those who use them a false sense of power while actually interfering with their ability to heal. That interference may even ultimately lead to chronic illness, plunging those susceptible into the very Underworld they worked so hard to avoid.

Whether we try to avoid the Underworld or fight it, we may feel like we're drowning in it when those coping mechanisms fail us. Without a connection to the mending heart, the ego's descent to the Underworld will likely elicit despair: let's remember that Erishkigal's rule over this domain began when the developing ego recognized the eventuality and significance of its own death. Thus, when Erishkigal reigns over a heartless Underworld, we feel stripped of our power, derided, hopeless, perhaps even lifeless at times. Yet one other option exists—surrender. Not resignation, not despair, but surrender in the Vertical Path, heart-centered sense of the word. This brings us back to the Sacred King and the ancient Inanna as Queen of the Underworld, to her role as Goddess of Compassion, and to the experience of love.

In his book, *Gift of the Body*, Jonathan Goldman describes several qualities of the Heart Chakra[178] that can guide us here. He maintains that surrender lives in the spiritual body of this chakra, suggesting that the Presence to which we surrender holds divine intention for us and our healing. This kind of surrender involves active living, sensing, and feeling—no avoidance. No argument. No drowning. How can we possibly endure such pain as can be suffered in the dark Underworld and still engage in this experience of surrender? We must recognize other equally important qualities of the heart and learn how to develop them further.

The quality of endurance springs from the heart and teaches patience. While pride may keep us from experiencing the shame of Underworld descent, humility lives purely and freely in the center of the heart and in this darkened place. There is no place lower to go,

---

[178] Goldman, *Gift of the Body*, 264–326.

and humility accepts this darker awareness with grace. In the process, we discover that our wounded heart has descended and hidden itself in the Underworld; all the parts of us that have never known love have been relegated to Erishkigal's shadowy home.

If Inanna reigns here instead, she will lovingly reveal herself as Goddess of Compassion. In her healing presence regeneration becomes possible, but we must first dare to ask for assistance and notice her response. As Goddess of Natural Law and Justice and Goddess of Compassion, Inanna will step forward and offer a new way of perceiving, describing and owning ourselves through embracing our broken heart. She invites us to be virginal: at one in ourselves, consciously. For most of us, this offers a whole new way of "becoming."

This requires us to hone the qualities of the heart—as in fact we have been doing while the wounded part of our heart dwelt in her dark domain. Embracing our wounded heart reveals the calm depth and truth that naturally reside there. That truth resonates with all that is True on the Horizontal and Vertical Paths. We consciously register this resonance through the heart's intuition and a sense of inner peace. Compassion, which naturally resides in the emotional body of the Heart Chakra,[179] awakens—and not just for others, as it flourishes in the Earth realm. In the darkness of the Underworld, our former sense of isolation recognizes the company of Inanna. We can receive her invitation to direct the compassion of our heart toward ourselves without distraction.

We can also ask the spiritual force of Forgiveness[180] to come our way, so that we may release shame and guilt. These feelings, which never knew love, and all the behaviors we thought made us deserve

---

[179] Ibid., 299–304.
[180] Ibid., 308–313.

that shame and guilt, can finally benefit from Inanna's understanding of justice. All that comes to the Underworld is meant to spark regeneration; the Underworld is for healing, not punishment. The Natural Law of cosmic movement and "becoming" would have what descends to the Underworld transform and rise again.

If we choose to surrender to the lessons of the Underworld and embrace our tender heart as it resides there, we must first notice which goddess we *expect* to find there. Which goddess do we *call*? If we call Inanna, we will find an ancient goddess who welcomes her lover in his sacrificial offer of self for the greater good of the community. All our rejected anguish, received in love and tended with compassion, rebalancing and regeneration, can instill renewed power within us, so as to enliven what might grow upon "the earth plane" of our life. In this dark place the beast can transform into the prince. Life changes for the better. In this mysterious, powerful place, healing happens.

In astrology, symbolically the planet Pluto (a Roman name for the Greek God of the Underworld, Hades) holds an archetypal association with the power of transformation and healing when used consciously, and with destruction and manipulation when not.[181] The victim role holds an unspoken power that often provokes and manipulates the behavior of others based on shame and guilt: both victim and responder must deal with these feelings. If we care to rid ourselves of those likely unintended yet destructive tendencies, we have to move from the victim role into one of empowerment. The Underworld offers private space within which to do this deep inner work. Here we may attend to our heartaches, heal old wounds,

---

[181] Steven Forrest, *The Book of Pluto: Finding Wisdom in Darkness with Astrology* (Borrego Springs, CA: Seven Paws Press, Inc., 2012).

and find renewed capacity to process the painful feelings of others in such a way as to transform, rather than destroy. Inanna as Divine Feminine can accompany us with guidance, justice, and compassion.

This healing process stimulates the root of faith, another quality that has always lived within our heart, though we may have lost sight of it amidst the wounding. Faith that love and healing triumph; faith in the unity of creation even if feelings of isolation overwhelm us; faith that our surrender to the soul's call and longing will always guide us to the intended destination. These aspects of our heart can only develop when we begin to heal our wounded trust. We must learn to discern what and who can be trusted, the heart's resonance with Truth serving as guide.

Our heart descends to the Underworld for a reason. When we embrace our wounded heart and regain our faith, the Underworld truly becomes the healing home to a spiritual force that loves us, and in which we know we are loved. On the Horizontal Path of the Earth realm, we experience the wounds, but lose sight of their purpose. When we approach the Vertical Path, at some point we must deal with the Underworld. Our work is to descend, to redeem our shadowed heartbreak, and to manifest its redemption in the Earth realm. Fortunately, the Earth realm is also Inanna's domain.

The Upper World and the Empath

If the caregiver described earlier allows her consciousness to descend into Inanna's Underworld, she will find that all her feelings, even if not socially sanctioned, are welcomed there, and that she is loved and not alone. She will experience compassion for herself, deepen her trust that a loving presence holds her even in her darkest moments, and find forgiveness for her vulnerability to the feelings she would rather not feel. She will know her heart's faith, and sense some higher purpose, despite her inability to name it in the darkness of her Underworld consciousness. She will not resist this dark place. Rather, as she befriends the Divine Feminine, she will find that the Underworld offers a calm respite and place to regroup amidst the flurry of activities, opinions, and heartaches along the Horizontal Path.

Unlike our encounters with the Underworld, our first exposure to the Upper World often comes in the form of a mystical, awe-struck moment when beauty overtakes us, usually by surprise. Some experience this in the dark stillness of a moonlit sky, the glorious colors of a sunset, the innocent smile on a child's face, or the exquisiteness of a vista or flower. This inspired awe transports us into the *Chayah* level of soul awareness, in which we feel at one with the Divine and everything around us. Time stops and our boundaries blur; we merge with "the eternal now." Remembering these heavenly moments serves us well in the Underworld darkness. These are the seeds that blossom into patience, mercy, tenderness, and compassion when fertilized by life experiences and nurtured with love in the deep Dark. These are the seeds of our faith.

For most of us, when our hearts have been broken and we have not yet embraced the wounded part in the Underworld, the healing part of our heart still resonates well with the Higher World teachings about oneness, harmony, and joy. Unfortunately, these heavenly qualities cannot penetrate the fullness of the heart when the wounded part is seemingly lost. Sadly, in such cases the unredeemed Inner Critic's protection of the wounded heart receives these teachings about oneness, mercy, compassion, and harmony as impractical, impossible goals, while using them to fuel additional venomous finger-pointing and reproach. Even if we serve as did Mother Teresa on the Earth plane, the unredeemed Inner Critic would never recognize that worth.

When our heart has been broken and we have not yet ventured past the Guardian of the Threshold to embrace our tender heart and its direct access to the Vertical Path, our ego's relationship with the Underworld may be fraught with despair and perceptions of evil. Similarly, persecution of self and/or others may arise as the ego prematurely affiliates with Upper World values. These ego-acquired Upper World teachings provide rationale for all sorts of treachery: the Inquisition and the Holocaust serve as painful reminders of this outer reality. Thus, authentic Vertical Path spirituality must be lived from the ego's embrace and relationship with a mending heart.

Once we respectfully approach the Vertical Path through the heart, Inanna, as Queen of Heaven, helps us appreciate that our fantasies and love of story, our longings and quests for understanding, and our capacity to conceive of realms beyond the physical, all play a guiding role in our healing and our daily walk through life. Our dreams matter and once we stop distracting ourselves with victimization, avoidance, or anger *at* the Underworld we can appreciate the Upper World and actualize those dreams, perhaps for the first time. From a refreshed spaciousness within, we can be open to sudden inspiration. We can evaluate our heart-based intuitions with respect for their not-always-logical perspective, while finding a realistic way to manifest them in daily life. When our heart is on the mend, these intuitions speak the truth of what the heart knows. Through the heart we can experience "heaven on earth."

As spiritual beings whose "holy sparks"[182] find release from the dense "husks"[183] of duality, we can sparkle like stars, radiant with our unique energy. Both in time and out of time, the heavens mark the passage of planets and stars relative to Earth, as well as a sense of eternity, in the seemingly motionless twinkling of celestial lights. In the heavenly Upper World of Inanna's reign, creativity happens. Not only may we perceive what others feel, but we may conceive of ways to assist them and ourselves as we negotiate life's challenging rough spots. In this place of "both/and," giving form to these inspirations does not deplete us. Instead, these spiritually guided activities enliven us *and* the other. We recognize the Light of Divine Essence for what it is, in ourselves and in the other, and for what it calls us to. We appreciate that the "waters of the deep" Upper World are perhaps not dissimilar to the depth of the Underworld. We may even recognize that both worlds have provided a familiar home for us all along.

The Middle World and the Empath

Surprisingly, we may find that living in the realm of Earth poses the greatest challenge for empaths. In this realm, opposites do not transform from one into the other as readily as they do in the Underworld. They do not swiftly and easily present as complements forming a whole, as they do in the Upper World. On earth we must live bodily in duality, manage the frustrations of living one moment after the next, and move in one direction to the exclusion of all others. Words spoken cannot be taken back. Fear of pain, loss, and death can make boxes of our mind, which would otherwise live and breathe. As we and others struggle with these challenges, information overload takes its toll.

---

[182] Cooper, *God Is a Verb*, 28–29.
[183] Ibid.

While engaging with others in this domain of Inanna's queendom, empaths learn how the Horizontal plane of existence works. In fact, we often move outward from our center and forget how to return. Guidance back to the Vertical Path calls us by way of our soul's longing as it flows through the heart-center of our being. When we are ready, the Vertical Path opens its access to both healing and creativity, to the Dark and Light of the "deep." Once we partake of these fruits, we can return to the Horizontal plane and manifest them with full expression.

The caregiver who acknowledges her own anger, sadness, and fear can move into the Underworld experience of her soul and feel the healing of divine comfort. She may also more fully appreciate the struggles of the one for whom she cares. Her capacity to appreciate the oneness of all creation, as it opens to her awareness in the Upper World, can bring inner peace in knowing that everything is unfolding in the Love of the cosmic web. Creative ideas may come to mind, offering better methods of caring for herself and her loved one in a way that honors them both in the process of "becoming." Bringing these two worlds together and into the realm of Earth can promote greater expression of patience, creativity, healing and care. The very feelings she brought to the center of these two paths transform, and she brings a renewed sense of self to her Horizontal activities on earth.

Thus, our journeying between all these worlds has value. Our walk within Earth's dualistic reality continually challenges us, providing new input for our next visit to the heart at the center of our being, where we can once again traverse the Vertical Path to the Upper World and Underworld. The rich healing and creativity we experience can then be heart-fully lived and shared along the Horizontal Path of our daily life. Each time we return to center, to the heart, and to each of these paths in turn, we gain an ease with the flow between them. Thus—as highlighted in the Kabbalah's Tree of Life—a continuous cycle of movement, back and forth, down and up, and back again, between these Horizontal and Vertical Paths marks our journey of continual "becoming." In the Kabbalistic sense, if we attend to this with wakeful consciousness, we have the potential to release holy sparks of Divinity from the dense husks of earthly life that conceal them. In this process we bear witness to the Divinity within us all.

The Heart at the Crossroads

It struck me with the surprise of the obvious that the Vertical Path carries our true essential nature, the levels of our Holistic Model, the five levels of the soul, the alignment of the chakras, and the ladder between the Upper, Middle, and Lower Worlds. Our life, our purpose, our meaning, all find their source along this Vertical Path. Yet we live on Earth amongst other beings, affected by them, and affecting them in turn. My surprise resulted from the simple recognition that we, as human beings on the Horizontal Path and as empaths especially, do not heal anyone or create anything. We *experience* the healing and creativity on the Vertical Path and we *express* what we've been given on the Horizontal earth plane. This realization confirms that the Empath Contract of childhood, with its primary focus on attending to the needs of others, completely missed the point.

In our engagement with others we can offer "presence," but we really don't "fix" or "heal" those in our familial and social constellations. That healing comes from the other's willingness to find her own center and to traverse her own Vertical Path to the Underworld and Upper World of her soul. As souls commune, we can meet them in these soul places and even support their ego as they decide to make the journey, but it is never our task or responsibility to make the journey on their behalf. The Christian myth seems to promote this fallacy with the *imitatio Christi,* but Jung and other theologians offer an alternate view.[184] Jesus lived his own Vertical Path, and by modeling "the Way" he invited us to find and traverse our own Vertical and Horizontal "cross"—which we can most easily access by embracing our tender heart. In pursuit of our unique path we too might then continually discover, appreciate, and share in some *becoming* aspect of the Divine.

Figure 17-2: The World Tree

[184] Dourley, *The Psyche as Sacrament,* 66.

This process reminds me of the World Tree, whose roots interweave downward and whose branches interweave upwards, such that as they spread they converge into an outer circle embracing the whole tree. (Figure 17-2) In our daily consciousness we live at the trunk of that tree, standing straight with direct access to the Upper and Underworlds. We know that, unlike a tree, we can move in any direction along the Horizontal Path. When we come into contact with other "trees," our limbs and roots may interweave with theirs, but our trunk remains distinctly separate—at least in a physical way.

As empaths we may sense what others feel inside their trunk, but we cannot directly change it; we can only bear witness with love in our heart. This image may offer guidance to the empath: we can journey to the Dark roots of the Underworld *with* others and serve as guide; we can rise to the limbs and Light of the Upper World and pray *with* them, at least at the soul level. On the earth plane, we can speak the truth of what we know with our heart, but we cannot live their earth plane/trunk experience *for* them. In the Middle World, we are separate and meant to live our own life.

From this image of the World Tree's periphery, we see that the Upper World and Underworld have much in common, despite their contrasting directions and focus. Healing can happen in the Dark of the Underworld because we bring our sorrows and all the discarded, repressed, rejected and abandoned parts of ourselves there and find Love. Creativity can emerge from the Light in the Upper World because we look to the heavens or pray for inspiration, for something new and unknown to influence or change a situation on the earth plane. Healing and creativity have much in common: they are dynamic; they change things; we do not control them, yet we can be conscious of both. From some Mysterious Source beyond this plane of existence, energy moves, comes and goes, runs and returns, and in so doing fuels our healing and our creativity. One transforms into the other. Healing requires a creative spark, and creativity is healing.

Knowing this, we can reconsider our purpose and meaning in the Earth realm of existence. Love emanates from the center. In our dualistic consciousness, we experience it and long for it as the lover or the loved. Yet if we transcend this consciousness, we have access to another experience. In the words of Osho:

> "When I say, 'Love yourself,' this is for those who have never gone inside, because they can always.... They are bound to understand only a language of duality. Love yourself—that means you are dividing yourself into two, the lover and the loved. You may not have thought about it, but if you go inside you will not love yourself, you will be love."[185]

This quote highlights beautifully how unitive and dualistic consciousness flow into and out of one another, like the yin and yang of the Tao. While we have no choice but to discuss the Vertical and Horizontal Paths, the three Worlds, our experiences of Light and Dark, our energy fields, and the contrasts and contradictions of daily life as if they were separate (and from a dualistic viewpoint they are), from the unified consciousness of higher soul these all become parts of the whole.

This places significant focus on the Vertical Path, despite the fact we've been taught to place priority on the Horizontal way of being

---

[185] Osho, "Discourses," in *The Quotable Spirit,* 157.

in the Middle World. In actuality, we are called to journey in consciousness between these two Paths so as to feed the one with the other. Duality merges into unity when we eventually find a way to walk the Vertical world in our Horizontal daily life. In truth, we *are* Vertical Path beings who have *incarnated* into a Horizontal Path world. Once we realize this, we can make the effort to reclaim our essence.

This reclamation requires focused attention amidst daily life distractions, the courage to be true to one's unique path, and a commitment to practice whatever is needed to maintain this deeper connection with one's soul, with one's Vertical essence. The fragmented, wounded aspects of *Ruach* (our personality) and *Nefesh* (our body) provide the doorways through which we approach the center. Healing these two lower levels of the soul, by learning to love ourselves unconditionally, and by honoring the body with appropriate care for its vulnerabilities and strengths, is both a necessity for and a benefit of this journey.

Over the course of centuries, many have identified methods for achieving this kind of Vertical Path consciousness. In my experience, meditation offers a means to set aside the daily distractions of Horizontal Path living so we may more easily access our heart center. Psychotherapy helps us develop the witness who can free the personality of its identification with intense emotions, old ways of thinking and outmoded beliefs. Focusing directs our consciousness to experiences in the body that may hold memories, emotions or old traumas, allowing them to release and share their knowing with us.

The Jungian practice of Active Imagination allows deeper dialogue with the archetypal images that arise from these emotions or traumas, so as to promote conscious integration and healing. The combination of any or all of these methods with Energy Medicine promotes quicker access to Vertical Path "knowing." These practices not only align our three brains with our cortex, they can facilitate Underworld and Upper World connections. Prayers can be uttered toward the Upper World from the two lower worlds; responses issue from the Upper World to complete the circle of "becoming."

The Empathic Heart

Empaths come into this incarnation uniquely poised to read the tensions in our universal web. We receive this information through the vessels of our body and our heart. If we wish to further the development of human consciousness, we must begin with our own states of awareness, and learn how to discern the information we receive. This requires that we relinquish the understandable but ineffective victim stance, and embrace who we are and what we have come to know. The spiritual aspects of this journey offer the guidance and sense of purpose for which our souls long. We are here to *really* learn about Love. Should we dare to accept this challenge, we will discover Love and come to know it again and again as we traverse the Worlds. We will share it with others as we traverse the Earth. Just as importantly, we will experience it for ourselves. Healing and Creativity meet in Love.

This chapter possibly invites more questions than it answers. It may also shed light on more potential pathways, rather than narrowly defining one specific way of being. Each empath is a unique person with her own particular soul path, her own energy patterns, her own personality style. How we each decide to explore and use the gifts we've been given and have further developed is up to us.

As we approach the conclusion of our journey of "feeling our way," some final thoughts about ethics and our responsibilities for these gifts remain to be shared. The next chapter focuses on the ethics of care for ourselves. The recognition that we each have our own way of living as empaths in the world invites us, I hope, to consider this with respect for discovering our own purpose and gift, each one valuable and essential to the integrity of the larger web.

CHAPTER 18

The Ethics of Care for Self

A BIBLICAL STORY tells of two women who gave birth within three days of each other while living in the same home.[186] One of the infants died in the night, and the next day one of the mothers accused the other of swapping the children. Tearfully, they presented their case to Solomon, a wise king whose reign covered an extensive kingdom surrounding Jerusalem from circa 970 to 931 BC. Solomon had to resolve this dilemma with little information. He had no access to DNA testing nor, apparently, to any disinterested witnesses. He rendered his decision by trusting the nature of mother-love: that a biological mother would rather surrender her child alive than possessively witness his death.

Solomon ruled that the child must be cut in two, like a log, to be equally divided between the two women. This decree effectively treated the child as an object, a "thing" for the workings of simple

---

[186] 1Kings 3:16-28, in *The Jerusalem Bible: Reader's Edition,* ed. Alexander Jones, L.S.S., S.T.L., I.C.B. (Garden City, NY: Doubleday Company, Inc., 1968).

mathematics, and the human heart of the real mother revealed itself. Did Solomon's own heart weigh in on the matter? Did his decision reflect the logic of a higher level consciousness? Ultimately we see that his "calculation" had nothing to do with math. He seems to have counted upon the complexity of the situation to reveal its own simplicity of love. Was this an ethical solution to the dilemma? We know it worked, but what made it right or wrong?

Ethical boards frequently must render a simple decision regarding a complex, seemingly impossible situation. What are their criteria? Do they rely upon the wisdom of the heart, as did Solomon? And/or upon rules and evidence-based data? The dictionary offers this basic definition of ethics: "That branch of philosophy dealing with values relating to human conduct, with respect to the rightness and wrongness of certain actions and to the goodness and badness of the motives and ends of such actions."[187] Complex feelings and thoughts often contribute to equally complex motives that funnel through relatively simple actions to produce multi-faceted, intended and unintended consequences. What criteria determine "rightness and wrongness... goodness and badness" of motives and their results? What level of discernment guides this decision-making process?

The subject of ethics leads anyone into very murky territory, especially empaths who so readily feel the emotion-laden motivations of others. How does the empath interpret those emotions, particularly when they are not spoken? How does that interpretation condition the empath's behavioral and/or verbal response? What responsibility does the empath bear, based upon that interpretation, to herself and to the other people involved?

---

[187] "Ethics," Dictionary.com, accessed January 6, 2015, http://dictionary.reference.com/browse/ethics?s=t.

THE ETHICS OF CARE FOR SELF

The "values relating to human conduct" used for ethical considerations suggest a set of standards upon which to base ethical decisions. These standards readily apply to some planes of consciousness, such as the physical, behavioral, and mental/verbal, but not so much to the emotional and spiritual. Additionally, ethical standards were designed for Horizontal Path living—but what about Vertical Path influence? Solomon found a way to bring Vertical Path wisdom to bear upon a Horizontal Path dilemma. While this topic may prove challenging to explore, its importance for the empath necessitates the effort.

Now that we have invested considerable time and attention in understanding our inner workings neurologically and psychologically, in appreciating and working with our energetic systems to promote balance and resilience, and in exploring potential spiritual paths of integration and meaning, the question remains: what do we do with all this information on a day-to-day basis? How do all these insights play out when we are confronted by a complex situation requiring a simple decision? Most importantly, when care for ourselves seems to conflict with care for another, how do we proceed?

We are more than a body and personality moving through life like a robot: we are souls on a spiritual path, living in a physical body, with feelings serving as the major source of information about our internal and external worlds. The basic questions to explore in these next two chapters are: Do we care for self *or* other? If so, which? Or do we care for self *and* other? If so, how? And why?

You will recall from Chapter 7 that the soul's capacity to engage with life extends from the unified Vertical field of *Yehidah* at our center, through our mystical awareness of *Chayah* and our purest character of *Neshama*, into our Horizontal world of duality, where

Ruach, the soul of our personality, and *Nefesh*, the soul of the body, engage in the recognizable dance of life. We know our thoughts range along myriad pathways, and our emotions can follow those thoughts in similar complexity. *Ruach*, the container for our thoughts and emotions, responds to our interior soul's call (Vertical Path) as well as to the external events and people around us (Horizontal Path). And yet we have only one body that can move in only one direction at a time, engaging in behavior which, on the Horizontal plane, is judged by some or by many as "right" or "wrong." Can the dualistic Horizontal Path dilemma of self *vs.* other shift to a unified Vertical Path agenda of self *and* other? If so, how might this happen? If not, can we make peace with duality's limitations and frustrations?

Examples for Ethical Consideration

Suppose an empath awakens one morning in a perfectly fine mood that persists throughout the first few hours of preparing for the day. Upon arrival at work, she meets a co-worker whose tense posture, constrained facial expression, and unspoken angry mood suddenly claim the empath's attention in not just visual, but visceral ways. In the absence of self-awareness, the empath may find herself feeling tense and trying to avoid that person throughout the workday. Or she may compulsively try to figure out what is troubling her co-worker and attempt to soothe her in some way. She will likely live into the terms of her original Empath Contract with little awareness or hesitation.

If the empath recognizes that her co-worker's mood has affected her own inner state, she may additionally become preoccupied by her own inner disturbance or perhaps feel guilty for using avoidance as a strategy. If she surrenders to the guilt and tries to shift the co-worker's anger without being asked to intervene, she risks eliciting a more demonstrable expression of that person's anger, or perhaps a polite, distancing acknowledgement but no shift in the co-worker's mood. Self-judgments likely result, coupled with ongoing exposure to her co-worker's smoldering anger and her own reactive "mud" within. In this situation, how does one ethically deal with the co-worker's right to be angry and the empath's right to feel peaceful?

Often in life one dilemma leads to another. Taking the above situation one step further, let us imagine that our empath has done considerable inner work and now has a clearer sense of her inner sensitivities. The above situation invites her to acknowledge what she does best—feel! Let's say she honors her feelings and uses the tools she has acquired to better understand how her own inner state may be resonating with that of her co-worker. She acknowledges that information to herself and finds a way to transform those feelings absorbed from her co-worker into other feelings more authentically aligned with who she is "becoming." Especially if she happens to care about her co-worker, will a return to her former peaceful state incite conflicted feelings within? Do we lose or surrender our sense of inner peace when those we love cannot share it?

Most empaths, myself included, have lived with so much inner turmoil that initially we may find the experience of inner peace quite foreign. We might even struggle with feeling unworthy to live peacefully, quickly comparing it to the tumultuous states of others and wondering how we might selfishly think we can feel peaceful while others cannot. This question derives from the belief that life entails suffering and that we are all in this together.

While these aspects of life are clearly real, focusing *solely* upon them means we ignore other aspects, such as healing, love and joy. If a previously suffering individual finds healing and joy in her life, she will gradually disengage from her identification with past suffering and from all those who insist she maintain her suffering sense of self. This growth dynamic will likely create significant conflict, especially with family members; developmentally we've been primed for guilt to emerge whenever we leave loved ones behind. Will our empath surrender to guilt and return to suffering, or find a way to deal with her guilt and continue to heal? And how will either choice impact her relationships? This poses another ethical dilemma.

In my work with clients over the years I have witnessed this conflict between care for self and care for others numerous times. It becomes particularly problematic for those with chronic illness when they begin to extend some effort toward their own healing. In many instances I have noted how the life patterns that support their illness also support a long-standing family dynamic. Unfortunately, these same life patterns significantly interfere with their healing. When a client marshals the courage to recognize these habitual ways of engaging in her family constellation, her struggle only intensifies. Often she has maintained these destructive patterns in order to save a family member from even more self-destructive behaviors, or so she believes. The intensity sparked by this kind of dilemma can take an additional toll on one's health.

For example, an empath may subject herself to enormous stress—and dissociate to some degree to cope with it—in order to spare herself the consequences of saying "no" to a previously accepted way of engaging with her loved one. She perhaps anticipates that her family member might experience or express significant anger or despair in response to her "no." That loved one might also be at significant risk of relapsing on drugs or alcohol or engaging in destructive behavior toward self, the empath, or others. In a situation such as this, what is an empath with a chronic illness to do? If she does not say "no" to her loved one, she will likely never heal. If she does say "no," she must live with whatever inner experiences and outer consequences that decision sets in motion. How much does the empath matter to herself? How much control does she truly have over her loved one's chosen response?

Mechtild of Magdeburg, a noted woman mystic of the thirteenth century, is quoted as saying: "The fish cannot drown in the water, the bird cannot sink in the air, gold cannot perish in the fire, where it gains its clear and shining worth. God has granted to each creature to cherish its own nature. How can I withstand my nature?"[188] In many respects, this becomes the quest of the empath. On this journey, empaths benefit from guidance that includes validation of their feeling state and greater discernment as to how feeling, thought, and worth weave their complexity into the simpler, four-dimensional actions of daily life.

This chapter may again pose more questions than it answers, but my hope is that these questions will provide a stepping stone for greater self-awareness and guidance as we each make the very personal choices and decisions impacting ourselves, our loved ones, and the larger world. I would like to begin with another myth from the ancient Greeks, demonstrating that we have inherited centuries-old dilemmas, as well as attitudes about their resolution. This provides a springboard from which to dive into new reflections and

---

[188] Mechtild of Magdeburg, "The Flowing Light of the Godhead," in *The Quotable Spirit*, 188.

opportunities. Perhaps it is quite fitting that we explore the story of Cassandra: no one listened to her then—let us redeem her efforts by listening to her now.

The Myth of Cassandra[189]

As the beautiful mortal daughter of Priam, the king of Troy, Cassandra attracted the eye of Apollo, a god of light and healing. His fame as one of the Olympian gods spread far and wide, particularly in his role as the Oracle at Delphi, where many would go to ask questions, understand their dreams, and find a new sense of wholeness. One version of the myth suggests that Cassandra had gone to the temple to consult with the Oracle when Apollo first gazed upon her. As a courting gift to Cassandra he gave her the power of prophecy, so she could see into the future and predict upcoming events. When she refused his romantic advances he cursed her, because he could not rescind his gift: "Divine favors once bestowed might not be revoked."[190] While Apollo could not take away her sight, his curse dictated that no one would ever believe her.

It is easy to imagine how the disbelief of others gradually undermined Cassandra's confidence in her own knowing. At the very least, she felt a profound sense of isolation from her social and familial circles, especially when they refused to heed her warnings. She foresaw the plotting of Paris, the wooden horse filled with armed Greeks penetrating her city, and the demise of her father's kingdom, but no one would listen to her premonitions. In the course of her social ostracism and the witnessing of these many tragedies, depression born of helplessness overcame her.

---
[189] Hamilton, *Mythology,* 202–203; 242–243.
[190] Ibid., 240.

As the Greeks bombarded Troy, Cassandra ran to the temple of Athena, Greek goddess of wisdom, and clung to the statue of the goddess while imploring her protection. Ajax, a Greek soldier, ripped her from the sanctuary—without protest from anyone—a serious violation of the deity. He then gave Cassandra to Agamemnon, the leader of the Greeks, as part of the spoils of the Trojan War. Agamemnon returned to his home with Cassandra after these battles.

Athena, enraged, appealed to Poseidon, god of the sea, to visit retribution upon those who had violated her sanctuary. Ajax, for his arrogance, fell overboard and was drowned. Agamemnon nearly lost all his ships, and his brother, Menelaus, was blown off course to Egypt. Odysseus fared a little better, but his journey homeward became an epic of its own. As for Agamemnon, upon returning with his company to his homeland, the distraught Cassandra predicted his death and her own. She ran toward his castle, which he had already entered with his vengeful wife, and both he and Cassandra were slain.

Cassandra and the Empath

The details of this tale reveal the cultural conditioning to which empaths have been exposed across the centuries. Consider, for example, that this myth describes Cassandra initially as beautiful, protected by family, stature and supposed wealth—in other words, she has resources. Despite these advantages, something motivates her to seek counsel from the Oracle at Delphi: a troubled inner state, perhaps? There she attracts the attention of the god who might facilitate her healing and because of that attraction, the tale says, he gives her the gift of prophecy. Viewed more realistically, she may have had this gift all along, but her contact with Apollo awakens her consciousness to this fact: with this awareness also comes the recognition that he will exact a price from her.

By current social standards, Cassandra is well within her rights to refuse Apollo's demand. She does not wish to merge with him, yet she foresees that refusing him will lead to some dreadful consequence. Courageously, she refuses him anyway. He curses her to live a life of "knowing," while simultaneously feeling disbelieved, condemned to social isolation, disconnected from her personal relationships, and ultimately dissociated from her own worth and very life. Her one noted appeal to a sensitive divine protector—a goddess of the intellect—ends in extreme violation of her sanctuary and of the divine's sacredness as well. The myth goes on to indicate that Athena did not passively tolerate this heinous crime. She sought revenge on those who committed this transgression through an alliance with the god of the sea, the watery domain of emotions.

With appreciation for this tragic tale's multiple levels of meaning, professionals from various backgrounds have coined the phrase, "The Cassandra Complex." As early as the late 1940's, writers have described social, economic, environmental, and political situations in which the seer is not believed. Empaths who sense the inner state of others, yet do not have those sensations confirmed by those others, often find themselves in a similar circumstance. Consider the angry co-worker, for example: the empath politely enquires about what may be troubling her, only to be told, "I'm fine!" In addition to these superficial denials, the myth taps into underlying themes of treachery and betrayal, isolation and despair. It also conveys an attitude or belief about what happens to those who perceive life differently, more deeply, and against the grain of accepted social beliefs.

THE ETHICS OF CARE FOR SELF

While this can occur for both men and women, Laurie Layton Schapira focused on women as she aptly described the inner state of those in such situations:

> "What the Cassandra woman sees is something dark and painful that may not be apparent on the surface of things or that objective facts do not corroborate. She may envision a negative or unexpected outcome; or something which would be difficult to deal with; or a truth which others, especially authority figures, would not accept. In her frightened, egoless state, the Cassandra woman may blurt out what she sees, perhaps with the unconscious hope that others might be able to make some sense of it. But to them her words sound meaningless, disconnected and blown out of all proportion."[191]

Hopelessness pervades this myth. Cassandra's gift causes her considerable grief and isolation. Family and friends withdraw their respect for her as a sensitive, resourceful, and potentially wise individual. Soldiers violate the terms of engagement in war and desecrate a designated sanctuary. The divinities of that age exact their revenge, but not with Cassandra in mind or heart. What she foresees she takes as destined: her mind conceptualizes everything in the context of doom—the perspective of a depressed person. The ultimate message of her experiences, and of this myth, presents as follows: better to be like everyone else, do what they want, keep quiet and invisible, than to live into one's truth, express it fully, and hope to shine forth like a guiding star. In other words, live authentically and suffer, or

---

[191] Laurie Layton Schapira, *The Cassandra Complex: Living With Disbelief: A Modern Perspective on Hysteria* (BookSurge, LLC, 1988), 65.

"dumb it down" in order to socially and relationally survive.

If survival is to take precedence, the lesson continues: surrender any care for self and live with a purpose solely focused on the gratification of others. Press forward with attention to *their* needs as the only meaning for one's life. And when the inner voice of personal desire or social protest arises, find a way to punish the body, efface the personality, and subdue and overcome the wild life surging within. This was the path of the stoics of old, of many revered persons in our human history, of many "saints." How might anyone counter the weight of this precedent and feel good about themselves as a caring person?! Should we even try? Here lies an ethical question—how do we balance the care for self with the care for others, especially when the two conflict? We now consider in turn the facets of this question, with the hope of redeeming Cassandra and the empath's experience.

The Ethics of Self-Care

This topic pervades the literature these days as we cope with shifting paradigms. The pendulum is swinging away from the extreme forms of patriarchy that over-emphasize efficiency, productivity, assertiveness, logic, and evidence. We witness the impact of these excesses in the destruction and violence affecting all sectors of the globe, directed toward people, animals, rain forests, the environment, and the Earth itself. Even technology loses its benefit when we forget the human feelings, limitations, and dreams that lie on the receiving end of the key stroke. Except for the earliest version of Inanna, the myths and fairy tales I cite throughout this text originated in the milieu of patriarchy; the dilemmas, solutions, and values all stem from patriarchal themes and agendas.

THE ETHICS OF CARE FOR SELF

From an evolutionary perspective, the matriarchal focus of oneness, community, and cooperation with the Earth and her rhythms shifted long ago to patriarchy's valuing of individual identity, competition, and dominance. In Chapter 17 we noted this shift through the changes incorporated into the Inanna myth over the centuries. But patriarchy has also provided gifts of discernment, exploration, and expanding consciousness. A true marriage of matriarchal and patriarchal values held in balance might advance the gains of both paradigms, while our consciousness evolves into a third, more respectful, more integrated point of view.

So how might these reflections inform our questions about self-care? Considering that we, as part of our culture, have been schooled in the patriarchal evolution of an individual sense of self, it logically follows that taking care of oneself has developed into a priority. Narcissists have accomplished this evolutionary task well, yet for some reason, others have incarnated into this "age of the individual" with empathic abilities and an over-focus on care for others. Might this serve a balancing function in our evolutionary story?

We have already gleaned from the fairy tale, *Beauty and the Beast*, that if left unevolved and unconscious, neither character will find fulfillment or redemption. Belle's books and the Beast's riches do little to help them fulfill their own deep desires for connection and release from their polarized agendas—care of other versus care of self, respectively. As islands of individual consciousness, without the trigger of the "other," their intra-psychic states remain static, even while the Beast's clock is ticking via rose petals as they fall.

Belle and Beast each have a longing that goes unsatisfied until, at the instigation of the other, they do their inner work. They each must recognize the opposing tendencies within their own psyche and harmonize those oppositions internally. Only then, with longing fulfilled, does their behavior in the outer world change, and by extension, the prince's servants and people of the kingdom also benefit. This tale aptly suggests that the empath can serve a wondrously meaningful purpose in supporting the swinging pendulum of the current paradigm shift. To engage in this process, however, requires significant unlearning, followed by new learning. We must apply intention and effort.

Many of us, having grown up immersed in the mindset that the "other" comes first, find it very difficult to shift our focus to include our own needs. This has historically been accentuated along gender lines in that the patriarchal, individualistic priority of our current paradigm has supported the advancement of men and masculine values, while subjugating women and feminine values to the service of the masculine. Consequently, female empaths who grew up prior to the mid-twentieth century (and later, as these ancestral effects shift slowly) received "the double whammy" of cultural expectations combined with the empathic prioritization of others. Sensitive men have experienced significant impact as well. In their attempts to restore the balance between the needs of self and other, those affected by these paradigmatic teachings often struggle with enormous guilt. I certainly did and continue to do so to some degree each time another opportunity to unlearn the old and open to the new confronts me. Fortunately, I now recognize this as just one more chance to evaluate and redefine my Empath Contract. It is clearly a work in progress!

We steadily receive invitations to shed outmoded beliefs and expectations so as to welcome a broader, more loving experience of ourselves and the world. Yet this process cannot happen all at once:

too much too soon can significantly destabilize a person. In the 1980's, Christina and Stanislav Grof described these destabilizations as spiritual emergencies.[192] Fortunately we now have tools, many of them, to support us in this evolution. We have already identified the value of several healing modalities: cognitive understanding; Eden Energy Medicine techniques; psychotherapeutic insights; exploration of one's inner story; Energy Psychology; development of an ego/soul connection to better appreciate one's longings as meaningful; and a deep relationship with Spirit, however one experiences it. All these pathways support care for self. I trust that each person can find her own way and I encourage everyone to do so as they feel called. Cassandra's myth offers additional suggestions.

The Deeper Aspects of Cassandra

We have already seen how perspective offers the emotionally overwhelmed empath a tremendous gift. Cassandra pursued this path at the Temple at Delphi, searching for a new point of view on whatever dilemma concerned her at the time. In this process, Apollo, a god of light and healing, reportedly gave her the gift of prophecy. At a high level of metaphor, this gift of sensitivity to the intangible may be associated therefore with a divine quality. As Cassandra became aware of her own abilities and sensitivities, she recognized that the Source of this gift wanted to merge with her.

Taken literally, the tale suggests that Apollo expected Cassandra's agreement to a romantic liaison as repayment for the gift he bestowed on her. We will discuss this from the perspective of culture and the collective unconscious later, but first let us continue this

---

[192] Stanislav Grof and Christina Grof, editors, *Spiritual Emergency: When Personal Transformation Becomes a Crisis* (New York, NY: Jeremy P. Tarcher/Putnam, 1989).

exploration at the more abstract level of metaphor. If we move beyond the literal description of Apollo wanting her sexually, we see that Cassandra reacted with fear, refusing the threatened penetration of her integral sense of self.

We recognize that the physical body and the personality struggle against anything that might threaten their familiar sense of intact separateness and safety. We also saw in Chapter 7 how the two lower levels of soul enliven the body as *Nefesh*, and the personality as *Ruach*. Because these lower levels of soul have been muddied by life and separated in consciousness from their three higher levels, they too come to experience themselves as discrete entities. Thus, these soulful aspects simultaneously stir within the body and the personality a longing to return to their former wholeness, while also trying to manage the body's and ego's fear of eventual mortality.

Without reconnection with their higher counterparts, these lower levels of soul do not have the resilience to bear the spiritual intensity that higher levels of soul can hold as receptive vessel for the Divine. Consequently, anything—even the most spiritually pure and loving— can destabilize these lower aspects of soul in their state of separation, causing their bearer to feel even more disconnected and groundless. Since Cassandra's consciousness lived at the levels of *Nefesh* and *Ruach*, she opted to maintain her tentatively grounded sense of self; she refused Apollo as divine light. In a similar state, so might we.

Ethics and the Vertical Path

If we continue this line of metaphor, we see from the story that, unless we engage the higher levels of soul consciousness, denying the spiritual aspects of our gift can leave us feeling bereft. Something deeply important continues to stir within, but no one on the grounded earth plane understands it. Similarly, when an empath senses the inner states of others but only acknowledges this ability from a body and personality perspective, she can feel misunderstood, isolated, and depressed, as perhaps did our empath with her co-worker. Appealing to Athena, goddess of wisdom (in other words, our intellect), for perspective does provide a needed, alternative point of view, but sometimes life has a way of ripping us from this sanctuary as well.

Not all explanations help us feel better. If the intellect has not considered or encountered the spiritual realm as a vital resource, the only recourse may be re-immersion in the emotional upheaval of the sea god, Poseidon. This, as we have seen, really resolves nothing. Cassandra survived this tumultuous sea journey and her stormy emotions, only to arrive on land where she foresaw her own demise. Her decisions and actions were guided by her emotionally overwhelmed perception, and her view of the situation lacked appreciation for the spiritual Source of her gift. Without that, she had no option but to experience it as a curse.

While this may seem like a discourse on the value of the spiritual, I offer it as an ethical consideration as well. As already noted, ethics is described as "that branch of philosophy dealing with values relating to human conduct, with respect to the rightness and wrongness of certain actions and to the goodness and badness of the motives and ends of such actions." This suggests that the value of our actions, their "rightness and wrongness," derives merit, or lack thereof, from a "philosophy," literally, "a love of wisdom." Wisdom exceeds the logic of things literal and tangible. Kabbalah offers an avenue of deeper exploration regarding this.

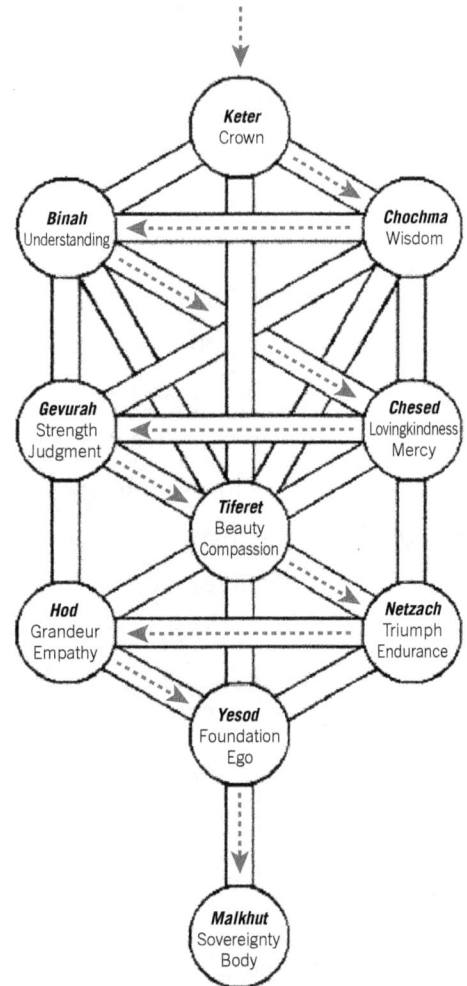

Figure 18-1: The Ten *Sefirot* of the Tree of Life

This is a derivative work of Morgan Leigh's "File: Tree of life wk 02.jpg" by Regina Bogle. M.D., 2016.

According to Rabbi David Cooper,[193] Divine Light pours through the receiving Void and enters the Tree of Life at the Crown. (Figure 18-1) Wisdom receives its Light directly from the Crown, the highest

---

[193] Cooper, *God Is a Verb*, 84.

Light on the Tree of Divine Radiance, and from Wisdom flow forth successively the Lights of Understanding, Lovingkindness/Mercy, Strength/Judgment, Beauty/Compassion, Triumph/Dominance,[194] Grandeur/Empathy, Foundation/Ego, and Sovereignty/Body. The Tree of Life in Kabbalah directly speaks of these Radiances, or *Sefirot*, as an emergence from *Ohr Ein Sof* (*Endless Light*) into Its first creation, the *Tzimtzum* (Void). *Kabbalah* means "to receive." Divinity flows into Its creation as Light and energy. Each Radiance, or *Sefira*, dances with the other nine to receive and source the endless "becoming" of creation.

Relevant to Solomon's decision, *Gevurah*, or Strength/Judgment serves as a receiving vessel for Lovingkindness.[195] The better word for Judgment here is Discernment. Judgment, or logic, quickly becomes sterile and potentially even destructive in the absence of Wisdom, Understanding, and Lovingkindness. When Judgment is not informed by these qualities, Compassion, Endurance, Empathy, and the remaining Radiances cannot manifest. Empathy, when exposed to cold, calculating logic in the absence of Compassion, cannot flourish, nor can it nourish the human personality or physical body in a positive way.

Solomon's prominence in biblical and historical literature suggests that he drew upon the gifts of the entire Tree of Life, not just that of Judgment: his "wisdom" included more than mathematical logic. His rendered decision in the case of the dispute over motherhood incorporated an understanding of human nature, discernment regarding the issues, mercy upon the child and his true mother, and compassion for what would unfold. We may infer that his ability to

---

[194] This *Sefira*, *Netzach*, has been interpreted by others in various ways, to include: Eternally-repeating Cycles (Halevi, *Psychology & Kabbalah,* 11), and Endurance (Edaina, "The Ten *Sefirot*," https://commons.wikimedia.org/wiki/File:The_one_tr%C3%A4d.jpg , accessed August 8, 2016).

[195] My thanks to Barbara Sussman for this insight.

hold all this, spiritually, intellectually, emotionally, and physically, was derived from a Source greater than his ego/personality. His love of Wisdom issued from his soul's longing and the essence of his Spirit. He surrendered to this Wisdom without losing himself.

Myth and Gender Implications for the Empath

We now address the gender issues involved here. Solomon, as a man, could surrender to Spirit without losing his center or sense of self, without being and feeling violated. A man surrendering to such Spirit-given Wisdom received then, and still receives the support of a patriarchal culture. A woman's surrender to Spirit in the context of patriarchy should be no different, yet cultural role definitions often subjugate that surrender by insisting on obedience to men and male-given rules. This has on numerous occasions, tragically, been extended to situations of extreme violation, such as inappropriate sexual advances, rape, and murder, followed by blaming the female victim for instigating and deserving her plight.

While his community revered Solomon for his wise "view" of the situation, Cassandra was cursed by Apollo for not using her vision in the way he desired. As she maintained a seemingly "virginal" stance in the face of his advances, he cursed her. This would not have been the case in the earlier period of matriarchal culture, when priestesses served the goddess by engaging in sexual acts with men so as to heighten the man's consciousness of the goddess herself. The man recognized his role in honoring the goddess, and thereby reverenced the priestess in the goddess's name. These priestesses were also "virginal" as each remained "at one in herself," choosing freely when and with whom to share her sacred feminine gifts.

THE ETHICS OF CARE FOR SELF

Unfortunately for Cassandra, for women in the not so distant past, and even today for women in many countries, patriarchal culture has defined the feminine sense of self as "less than," able to be given away in marriage and subjugated to the priorities of the masculine "ethic." For the modern empathic woman whose collective unconscious holds Cassandra's tale, learning that merger with the divine does *not* include violent dissolution of self may pose a tremendous challenge, especially for those who have experienced violations not just emotionally but physically as well.

While attempts to avoid this seemingly dangerous receptivity to the Divine are understandable, one significant risk of this dissociation is an excessive reliance upon left brain logic. Without the spontaneity of right brain input, the left brain loop tells an old tale over and over again. Unfortunately, left brain memories of violation often correlate with the outcome of Cassandra's story and the patriarchal definitions of life. In the absence of right brain inspiration, life may offer little hope or meaning.

Mindful access to the Cosmic Divine resides in the right brain, but its diffuse consciousness may seem threatening to some, even more overwhelming than the emotions stirred by empathic receptivity. Yet our right brains formerly knew a matriarchal "ethic" of oneness and continue to hold a collective memory of the sacred "virginal" priestesses of the goddess. If we remain locked in our left brain, the forces of Apollo threaten to overwhelm an empath's consciousness. If we dare to embrace the ancient memories of our right brain, in an earlier time Apollo would have bowed to the goddess as well.

From our exploration of these evolving tales, we can appreciate how the current cultural paradigm significantly impacts the ethical view of the "rightness and wrongness of behavior" and "the goodness and badness of the motives and ends of such actions." This understanding compounds the enormous complexity of our already challenging ethical considerations.

Self-Care for the Empath

Returning to the basics of self-care, we see that patriarchal ethics may value quite different choices and actions than those of a matriarchal time. Marrying the two paradigms allows for a more balanced third option to arise, should we dare to evolve, thereby creating a whole new set of ethics—a process similar to rewriting the Empath Contract. Yet paradigms do not shift because something huge, powerful and magical whips one paradigm into another: they happen slowly, one person at a time.

Living a life of meaningless suffering serves no one. Fears do arise in the process of growth, but we know that surrendering to them leaves us stagnant, with only the illusion of safety. Daring to care for ourselves must begin with our recognition of the need to do so and a willingness to try, even a little. When I first ventured into this territory, I managed this fear by telling myself that if it got too difficult I could always turn back. Fortunately, it never did, and I didn't feel a need to give up the journey. Each step I took supported me, giving me the fuel and courage needed for the next step. I cannot guarantee anything for anyone else, not even for myself really: I only know what lies on the side of not trying. Only when one becomes totally "fed up" with "the same old story" can the journey really begin.

Self-care starts with the basics: eating well, sleeping enough, ex-

THE ETHICS OF CARE FOR SELF

posing oneself to meaningful ideas, people, and activities that stir the heart into a feeling of safety and love, little step by little step. Eventually, old traumas and wounds need healing, and professional assistance may prove helpful. Spiritually, working to align our personality with the higher levels of soul will do much to support our receptivity to the Divine graces available to us. This deeper reunion of soul also strengthens us as vessels for processing the inner feeling states of others more meaningfully.

Yes, there will be setbacks and each time we need to decide: retreat back to the known, to the familiar; or rally and venture again into the unknown. In this self-caring context, we may need to develop a new attitude about life, perhaps beginning with a new attitude about exploration. Culturally we have inherited Cassandra's way of seeing the world, but we now have so many other options. Dare we take advantage of them? Doing so treads an unknown path!

Ultimately, self-care involves seeking and discovering a way to synchronize one's essence with one's actions. This may lead to a totally new way of living life, perhaps changing one's relationships, work, social and environmental circumstances, and commitments. At first this may seem daunting, yet empaths spend their life negotiating blurry boundaries and tumultuous emotional waters. Consider too that what we fear may be an inherited illusion, not a fact. Self-care involves reclaiming one's truth as held in one's essence, not as passed down through the story of generations. The plots of our ancestors, even of our own past lives if one conceives of life that way, require some acknowledgment, but they need not define the future.

Cassandra did not have the wherewithal to recognize that her "vision" of the future was only a sense of one possibility among many—and very highly conditioned by her past. She did not have the support to envision different alternatives, derived from the same greater Source that spawned the one vision she happened to notice first. Unlike Cassandra, we live in a time of quantum physics, expanded consciousness, and shifting paradigms. Possibilities are endless: failure to consider those options limits the paths we can take. Self-care invites us to tap into all of its riches. In this way we serve the paradigm shift of which we are a part.

Before we focus on the ethics of care for others in the next chapter, it is important to note that for empaths, any attempt to differentiate between the well-being of self and that of others proves fruitless. Deciding how to best manage the situation with the angry co-worker, for example, requires giving attention to both parties in this dance. As we shift our focus from either/or to both/and, I hope it is becoming clear that care for self provides positive effects for others, and that care for others also means care for self.

CHAPTER 19

The Ethics of Care for Others

WHEN HUMANS GATHER IN COMMUNITY, we face the potential for all sorts of conflict unless we operate from a high vibration of consciousness. This is why we develop and rely upon laws to avoid disputes and to settle them when they arise. Ethics followed as a means to evaluate the rightness and wrongness of those laws. Given the divergent interests arising in any group, the field of ethics provides some overarching guidelines regarding our behavior toward one another.

We can now appreciate how that guidance has received its direction from an evolutionary trajectory informed by past agendas and consequences. If empaths have incarnated to help move the paradigm shift along, it follows that their intrinsic ability to sense the inner states of others might best serve the advancement of a new sense of "rightness and wrongness." Empathic sensitivities processed through the heart may better guide our decisions about other people, other life forms, the environment, and the needs of the planet itself.

As mentioned in Chapter 1, some empaths more naturally "tune in" to the inner states of other beings, such as dolphins, the rain forest, or the earth, than to people. From an energy perspective, this has to do with our neurons' sensitivity to specific frequencies and the notion that each entity likely has its own energetic signature. The topic of care for others extends to a vast number of beings, and therefore any ethical consideration of "rightness and wrongness" can only be generally addressed at best. Although I limit this discussion to our interaction with people, it is still my hope that the needs of other beings will be recognized and honored with the same attention, best given by those who understand them most sensitively via their empathic gifts.

We now focus on the empath's ethical stance in relationship to others. How empaths can best respond to the inner states of people in their world while honoring their own needs often poses considerable challenges. First, when the inner state of another internally impacts the empath, it is often uncomfortable. What is the empath to do in these situations when the needs of self may conflict with the needs of the other?

We discussed the Empath Contract in Chapter 12: how it was formed during childhood, unconsciously; and how each encounter in our everyday world invites us to re-evaluate its current applicability to our life. What new terms we establish depend upon how we envision and value the balancing of care for self and others. In my practice, I often use the following analogy to describe this inner dilemma so common for empaths.

THE ETHICS OF CARE FOR OTHERS

The Dragon and the Queen

Imagine a queen at court ruling over a moderately sized queendom. She lives in a castle in the midst of her people, all surrounded by a moat, and with guards at the gate—usually wide open. There might even be holes in the castle walls. Let's also imagine that in a not so distant kingdom, the people are beset by a fire-breathing dragon. Their ruler sends a messenger riding at a furious pace to our queen. The messenger flies past the guard and over the bridge, runs up the steps, and stands before our monarch sweating and out of breath with a written message in his hand. The queen now has a decision to make.

Let's consider some of her options. Does she "shoot the messenger" to be free of his stress-inducing presence? Does she toss the message, unread, into the fire? Maybe she reads the message: now she has more choices to make. Does she absorb the information into her being, as if pasting the paper onto her forehead, and feel panic in response to the messenger's inner state? She may personalize the information received, fearing that a dragon might threaten *her* queendom at any moment. Having read the letter, she could throw it into the fire in an attempt to ignore it—but she can't seem to forget there's this dragon... She might fortify her walls to provide greater protection for herself and her people, and command that no one enter or leave through the castle gates. She could order some of her troops (or every last one of them) to assist the king in his defense against the fire-breathing foe, thereby leaving her queendom unprotected.

She has other options as well. Might she give the messenger some food and a place to rest? Or banish him along with the message he brought? Or perhaps the queen simply takes to her bed with a headache. Or pours herself a glass of wine… and then another… All these possibilities rest in that pivotal moment when she makes her decision. Upon what criteria does she base her choice? Does she react from a place of empathically induced fear? Will her own history of past invasions condition her response? Does she have a compulsive need to "fix it" for the king? Or can she react from a heart-filled space of compassion for the turmoil of his people as well as her own? Can she access a solid wisdom that fortifies her queendom, keeps her people safe, and honors the neighboring king and his realm? What ethical ground guides her as she makes this weighty decision?

Sometimes it helps to see things from afar, even with a little humor. It allows us to realize that we have options and choices. I find that giving myself permission to image something completely ridiculous offers more freedom to actually make the better choice! In this analogy, fortifying the walls to exclude further in-coming information will not permit the queen to know if the king has succeeded in subduing the dragon, or even if the dragon has overcome them and is *en route* to her queendom. While some stabilization of the perimeter makes sense, total enclosure does not. "Shooting the messenger" and ignoring the contents of the message will not keep the queen and her subjects safe. Becoming as anxious as the king facing the dragon or as worried as the messenger will not rally her current resources and power, and could effectively paralyze her.

Maintaining perspective while acknowledging the dire circumstances facing them—imminently for the king; potentially for the queen—offers the best chance for a successful resolution to this dilemma. She must be able to feel anxious without losing her capacity to think (her insula needs to serve as an adequate bridge in her brain). For best outcome, the queen will have processed and healed from any past experiences of invasion so she can face this potential without succumbing to panic or victimization. She must be free of addictions and other forms of escapist behavior. She must do her best for the messenger, for her subjects, for the other kingdom if she is able, and ultimately for herself. This all becomes possible if she has cared for herself. With regard to the other kingdom, "if she is able" is a key phrase worthy of further attention.

The Queen and the Co-worker

To make this scenario more practical and applicable, let's return to the example of the empath who awakens to a beautiful morning only to later encounter an energetically/emotionally angry co-worker. The co-worker is both a messenger of distressing tidings (cause unknown for the moment), and a potential dragon who may flare at the empath and/or others at any time. If this co-worker is willing to discuss her inner state with the empath, she may impart useful information, even if laden with emotional intensity. This is represented by the clearly written message in our analogy. Our empath can then determine if her co-worker's distress is personal—an upset at home, for example—or due to a situation at work that may directly involve or impact the empath.

The empath's response to this situation will derive from her "ethic" regarding personal and professional commitments, as well as the value she places on the relationship with her co-worker. Are they in this together? Is the co-worker over-reacting based on unresolved issues from her past? Does the co-worker respect our empath's input? Is

FEELING OUR WAY

there opportunity for mutual resolution and growth here? Or perhaps the whole situation is none of our empath's business at all! Perhaps compassionate support is all she can offer.

What if the co-worker will not speak to the empath about the source of her difficulty? Now there is no written message to provide information: the distraught, sweating messenger is mute. The empath has only her intuitive, inner sense of how the situation feels. Her response depends upon how clear she is about her own past experiences, some perhaps bordering on traumatic if not actually so. Has our empath worked to uncover and understand her own unconscious, knee-jerk responses to situations like this?

For example, what if this kind of sullen anger pervaded our empath's childhood? Perhaps one of her parents reacted to stress with this kind of coping style, and these incidents flooded her with feelings of abandonment, shame, and empathic as well as retaliatory anger. Then her co-worker's smoldering anger will likely trigger an old, habitual response pattern that leaves our empath feeling like a child again, unless she has developed other ways to process her internal reactions to this kind of stress.

If our empath has done her inner work, she may recognize that her internal state potentially resonates with the information received. She may feel the uncomfortable feelings stirred within her and recognize the fear of abandonment, the sting of shame, and the flare of anger, all the while knowing that nothing in her personal sphere has sparked these feelings. Having healed these wounds from her past, she may wonder if the same dynamics are now in motion.

Her former options, such as ignoring the messenger, "shooting the messenger," or trying *not* to shoot the messenger—while feeling guilt for wanting to—are unnecessary. With discerning sensitivities, our empath may even sense if and when the dragon's fire will flare. This kind of inner monitoring in order to stay safe—constant hypervigilance—exhausts a person, however. While energy medicine techniques offer tools to support resilience, a deeper, more direct resolution for this situation is needed for the longer term.

Opportunities for Discernment

We have given considerable attention to the many ways empaths experience healing in their life, as well as to the importance of this inner work. We can apply the fruits of that healing journey to our relationships in the world, since the actions, feelings, and thoughts of others react to our input and also invite our response. When feelings play a significant role in any exchange, acknowledged or not, discerning what is being communicated, by whom, from what cause, and to what end, helps clarify the best response for the greatest good. With this in mind, we return to the empath's experience with her angry co-worker as she tries to resolve this issue of care.

If the cause of her co-worker's emotional state has not yet been revealed, might the empath ask directly what is troubling her? Some relationships lend themselves to such intimate questioning; others obviously do not. If this co-worker happens to be the empath's supervisor, this could become a very delicate and stressful situation indeed. Even if not, the empath's experience of inner tension in response to the co-worker's way of coping may feel difficult to bear. An empath might be tempted to analyze the situation and to share that analysis with other co-workers, partly to gain perspective and partly to vent. But is that analysis correct? And is it anyone else's business?

As discussed in Chapter 3, empathically derived information usually has no words. The application of words to our body/heart understanding must filter through our cortex and consequently through all the stories we've been told and continue to tell ourselves. Any analysis derived from information gained through our three wordless brains and our empathic neurons will be colored by our personal slant on life and our experience in similar situations. The more inner work we do, the clearer the picture we receive, yet it will always have some degree of personal tint.

In fact, when sensing the unseen and the unspoken, some empaths like to think they are psychic. While they may be, I tend to see empathic resonance and psychic foretelling as two different gifts. From my own experience and perspective, empaths certainly pick up intangible information as do psychics, but does that predict the future? I don't think so. Like Cassandra, we risk deciding that the future is dictated by our present feeling—if I feel bad, it is bad, it will be bad, we're doomed.

If instead we recognize that what we receive simply carries information, we have options for how to interpret what we sense. Like the queen who receives a note about the neighboring kingdom beset by the dragon, we can realize that the current feeling tells us about the current situation, albeit laced with threads from the past. It offers valuable information; what we do with that information is up to us, and it is our *choice* that affects the future.

From an ethical perspective honoring both oneself and the other, we need to check with the person whose inner state we have experienced, when we are able. I always preface such inquiries with a statement like: "I'm not sure if this is true for you—and if it doesn't feel right, it isn't—but is there any chance...?" To the degree that the individual is conscious of his or her own inner workings or willing to become so, we will receive the needed validation or adjustment. This may open a door for further soulful and heart-felt discussion.

If those we encounter are not conscious of their inner state or not willing to share, we are left with incomplete information. Their denial may be a needed correction for us, or it may reflect information they cannot process consciously at the time. Either way, pursuing it and insisting on the correctness of our assessment violates them and solves nothing. Do we need to be "right" or relational? Do we take on a "more knowing than thou" stance in relationship to such individuals? Might we resort to self-doubt or self-compromise? Or might we hold what we feel with discretion and wait for further clarification, respecting them as they are in that moment?

To fully consider these many options, we must first acknowledge the response of our internal state to the situation. Then we must work with the empathically derived information, using all the tools of insight we have acquired as they relate to our past personal experiences. We can search for common themes among these feelings of past and present whenever a less-than-desirable emotional state has been reactivated by the situation at hand. This search may require an internal descent to the Underworld, where old feelings stir, partially healed wounds clamor once again for attention, and we receive the opportunity to apply another spiraling layer of love and healing. Back on the Horizontal plane, we can then speak to the issue with newly gained relevant insight.

If welcomed, this additional information may bring clarity to otherwise muddy circumstances. If unwelcomed, our own vision of the situation may never approach that of the other. We have to take responsibility for our own definition of reality regarding this issue, while also recognizing that our analysis of the information does not predict the future. If we have made the effort to consciously connect with our soul, the home of our free will, we maintain that freedom of choice in every moment—and this applies equally to all parties involved. Infinite possibility beckons. On the other hand, for those who have never consciously developed that soul-connection, their capacity for free will sleeps in the unconscious until they are ready to awaken it. In such cases, at least for the short term, the past will likely repeat itself. Predictions based on old familiar patterns may then come true.

If we do opt for a new story we tap into the infinite creativity of the Upper World, where we may pray for the situation and the people involved in it, which impacts the web in unseen ways. Additionally, we can request the spiritual resources needed to harmonize our own internal state and radiate a more peaceful energetic frequency into the situation. This may affect the other by what I've come to call "reverse empathy." I witnessed this process many years ago during a video demonstration by Daniel Hughes, Ph.D., a well-recognized attachment therapist.[196] This highlighted for me that empaths are not just receptive vehicles for feeling-toned information; we also transmit feeling-toned messages to others, and with consciousness we can do this for the good of all.

In this video, recorded during one of his healing sessions, Dr. Hughes engaged with a raging child, gently and respectfully meeting, sharing and reflecting the child's rage back to him. By doing

---

[196] Daniel A. Hughes, Ph.D., *Building the Bonds of Attachment: Awakening Love in Deeply Troubled Children* (Northvale, NJ: Jason Aronson Inc., 1998).

so, he invited the child's inner state into resonance with his own, in one sense abolishing the child's sense of isolation. Dr. Hughes then progressively altered his own internal feeling level, gradually shifting to a more peaceful energetic and emotional state. The child, having engaged with this therapist like one gear interlocking with another, followed the more dominant energetic lead of Dr. Hughes and became quite calm. This kind of work obviously requires a great facility with one's own range of emotional intensity and expression. These kinds of ability can only develop in response to considerable intention, effort, and practiced journeying along the Vertical Path.

Jonathan Goldman's discernment regarding the difference between sympathy, empathy, and compassion[197] brings further clarification to the practical application of Vertical Path wisdom. To paraphrase his descriptions, imagine walking along a path and finding someone who has fallen into a great big hole. A sympathetic person will recognize the other's difficulty and harness all her strength to pull the person out of the hole. This effort implies a belief that the hole is bad and that nothing good can come from being in it. Perhaps we may detect in this sympathy-driven dynamic some formative aspects of the Empath Contract. In any case, the sympathizer winds up exhausted from the effort, having exerted considerable personal energy to pull the person out of the hole. Furthermore, the one who was in the hole now finds another hole to fall into because she wasn't really ready to climb out.

An empathic person, on the other hand, will feel the pain of the other living in the hole and metaphorically jump in the hole to keep the person company. And an evolved empath whose actions spring

---

[197] Goldman, *Gift of the Body*, 304–308.

from compassion will not need to enter the hole at all. Instead, she will feel the distress of the person in the hole, acknowledge that person with respect for her soul path and, if it is her call to do so, be there at the right time to lend a hand as that person climbs out of the hole. No exhaustion here. Vertical Path gifts flowing through the heart offer patience, respect, humility, truth, compassion, faith, and trust. I suspect these qualities guided Dr. Hughes in his work, as they can also guide us.

Care for Self while Caring for Others

Let's return to our empath's dilemma as she tries to cope with her angry co-worker, who has thus far not validated the empath's sensitivities to this situation. Fortunately, with Energy Medicine techniques the empath has a means to release the associated tensions that may arise in these circumstances without violating anyone's privacy or confidence. She can privately hold her tentative analysis for a later time, for confidential processing with a trusted other, or for personal decision-making relating to this relationship. Avoidance, circumvention, confrontation, and compassionate engagement all present themselves to the thoughtful empath as possible responses in any given situation.

Our level of consciousness and relationship to soul and Spirit can guide the eventual choice. This again relates to the Vertical Path: alignment with Underworld and Upper World consciousness affords us an opportunity to connect with the Love and Essence at the center of our being. Acknowledging with acceptance and patience that we can fix nothing for anyone allows us to peacefully wait for the right moment, should the issue be ours to address at all. If we can remember that each person has a soul path which invites them to their own Underworld and Upper World experience, we may meet them in consciousness when they are ready. Thus, our connection with the Vertical Path can provide the guidance we need in many of these challenging situations.

Consequently, the empath must address some key questions as the care of self and the care of others converge into one decision, one path of action, within the confines of one body.

- How much pain is an empath to bear?
- Does it ever make sense to take on more than one's center can hold with integrity?
- For what purpose does an empath take on the pain of others?
- In the absence of "fixing" does "witnessing" have a value? What purpose might it serve?
- For how long does an empath expose oneself to the pain of a particular other?
- Does the process of *waiting* for "the right moment" dictate the duration of contact and endurance, or does one strategically become available when the other is ready to shift?
- Who and what is served by the empath's willingness to resonate with and experience the pain of others?
- Do we take our cues from what other people *want* or from what they *think they need*?
- And is that need defined by their Horizontal walk in the world or by their Vertical descent, transcendence, and growth?

Once empathic individuals have considered these questions in any given situation, there may come a time when their response to someone's request for assistance is, "No." A friend once modeled for me a phrase to which I had never been exposed, yet which in its simplicity was both to the point and kind: "No, that doesn't work for me." This expression offers a bit more elaboration and relational engagement than the humorous quip of other friends: "The word "No" is a complete sentence!" In either case, saying "No" at times is the soulfully, ethically "right" response. The empath may find using it takes courage at first, but the freedom accompanying its appropriate implementation nicely reinforces further use.

This brings us to the dilemma posed by the second example at the beginning of the last chapter. What if our empath realizes that her co-worker's anger and upset, although triggered by the current situation, are really rooted in the past? And what if her co-worker does not feel ready to resolve the issues contributing to her feeling state? If this co-worker also happens to be a friend, the empath has to make a decision about her own inner experience in the context of her friend's ongoing distress. Does she believe that loyalty to her friend demands she maintain her own state of misery?

The old expression, "Misery loves company," holds power at a certain level of consciousness. In this case, our empath would need to remain "held in place"—potentially a very miserable place—until her friend finds a solution to her dilemma. There is no freedom in this, except perhaps in the initial choice to accompany her friend in this way, assuming that this "choice" was consciously made. If the empath is unconsciously operating under the terms of her original Empath Contract, her compulsion is *not* a choice.

Alternatively, the empath could consciously move into her heart, her center where the Horizontal and Vertical Paths cross, then descend to the Underworld with her resonating pain. There she might learn something of healing value for herself, perhaps also for her friend if her friend is ever willing to journey there along her own Vertical Path. Our empath might also take the lesson of the Underworld to the Upper World where she can bless it and pray for the soul of the other, trusting that something larger than herself can bring healing to her friend. In this way, our empath may find contact with her friend less stressful, even while her friend continues to suffer. If her friend feels disturbed by the empath's ability to move through life peacefully, the empath may learn something about the value of that friendship as well.

Family Loyalties and the Empath

Issues of loyalty and commitment do arise whenever our dilemmas involve relationships with loved ones; these become especially troublesome when they tap into old wounds. The degree of disturbance depends on the intensity of the double-bind imposed during childhood, and the degree of inner reconciliation achieved thereafter. To elaborate, consider that during the formation of the original Empath Contract, when we unconsciously learned about life's terms of engagement, we were taught lessons about loyalty. When a relationship situation reconstructs our childhood's familial milieu, we may feel thrust back in time and find ourselves resorting to old, painful, and no longer useful responses.

For example, what happens within a person's psyche if their family's teaching expressed something like this? *Loyalty to family is most important. In our family we require that you, child, sacrifice yourself, your needs, your desires, the fulfillment of your essence for the sake of the family. If you dare to place yourself first, you will be disloyal to the family. So, ultimately, live loyal and invisible/unfulfilled, or live disloyal/disowned and fulfilled.* This is a set-up for emotional paralysis, with its roots in childhood, but extending far into adulthood.

Evolution and neurology have wired human beings for social engagement. In Chapter 3 we discussed the work of Stephen Porges, Ph.D., who outlined the importance of the Vagus Nerve and its evolution for the very purpose of social interaction and attachment. Chapter 7 discussed how, spiritually, we long for connection among all five soul levels, between soul and Spirit, between soul and ego, between soul and soul. A family message such as the one in the preceding paragraph violates one aspect or the other, ultimately both, of our human nature. This double-binding message makes it impossible to live at the center where the Horizontal (family belonging) and Vertical (soul connection) Paths meet.

The intense physiological and emotional distress engendered by such a no-win family message reflects not only the degree of wounding it caused, but also suggests the amount of constructive attention and effort required to bring about a healing resolution. Fortunately, some wise individuals have already trodden these waters and shared their wisdom so we may negotiate these pathways more confidently. The transcendent function, as described by Carl Jung and supported by Eden Energy Medicine and Energy Psychology, offers pathways of healing and inner integration. The resolution they offer for these energy-sucking no-win situations releases that energy for our use and makes possible the dramatic shifts needed in one's outer life to accommodate this interior growth.

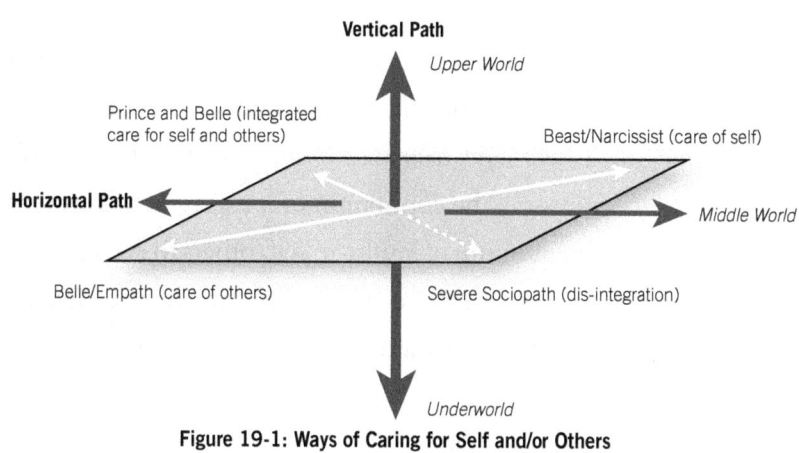

Figure 19-1: Ways of Caring for Self and/or Others

This healing is not a simple process for linear consciousness. To elucidate this point, let's begin with a diagram showing a line to portray this dilemma of tension between two opposites. At one end of the line we find the unevolved Narcissist (our friend, the Beast), and at the other end the unevolved Empath (Belle). (Figure 19-1) The Narcissist has taken the relatively exclusive path of care for self, often seeking fulfillment outside of family with all the tribally abandoned, neurological, and unconscious desperation implied here. The Empath has followed the path of prioritizing care for others, sacrificing self for the sense of belonging to family and community, with all the soulful desperation that accompanies this loss of connection to self.

In our diagram, another line crosses the continuum between loyalty to self and loyalty to others, revealing at one end the option of being loyal to nothing. Here resides potential sociopathy. In its very darkest aspects, the sociopath may become completely disconnected from any caring sense for self or others. At the opposite end of this continuum, we have the wedding of Beauty and the Prince. Such a person can maintain loyalty to self *and* others in a balanced way, as discussed in Chapter 15. This integration of loyalties reflects one aspect of the transcendent function: *I choose to be loyal/committed to anyone and anything that is also loyal/committed to me.* Some would describe this as healthy narcissism. The continuum of integration/dis-integration intersects the continuum of loyalty to self/others to create a plane on the Horizontal Path. Here we find options for how to live our Middle World relationships inwardly with ourselves and outwardly with others.

In Chapter 17 we noted how healing and creativity happen along the Vertical Path. Therefore, the horizontal plane of this diagram must now be intersected by a vertical line to represent a higher realm and a lower realm, the Upper World and the Underworld, respectively. This Vertical Path taps into infinity, so its point of intersection with the Horizontal Path can shift at any time (thus explaining our access to the transcendent function from any point on the horizontal plane).

Here on the Vertical Path we may also consider the polarity of fullness and emptiness. The mystic, for example, at the soul level consciousness of *Chayah*, experiences a tremendous, indescribable oneness in which all is full and complete. Awareness of self and other merges into oneness. In contrast, those who have experienced the Dark Night of the Soul have known the profound desolation of emptiness. I suspect that those occasional times when I sense something like the emptiness of a receding wave within me correlate with the Dark Night. The sucking power of the ocean as all things succumb to its retreating waters resonates with the painfully perceived, pervasive, empty space within.

With perspective and respect for the feelings involved, the Dark

Night offers balance to the mystical sense of "all-ness" by engendering its counterpart, "no-thingness." The reader may recall that both these qualities are attributed to the Divine in Kabbalah, where first the Void was created "to receive" (the meaning of the word *Kabbalah*) the All-ness of *Endless Light*. These experiences of fullness and emptiness also resonate well with our experiences in the Upper World and the Underworld, respectively. Both lie on the Vertical Path; creativity and healing happen here in the constantly changing cycles of "becoming." The wounded experience of the Underworld receives the creative spark of the Upper World and responds with healing and the creative birth of something new.

When this newness emerges onto the Horizontal Path, our left brain, linear consciousness, lower mind must pause. What has occurred defies logic: instead of the repetition of old patterns producing a known consequence, the Mystery of the Vertical Path has produced a new beginning.

Loyalty and Disloyalty in the Larger World

We began to explore this diagram as a way of understanding complex issues such as loyalty and disloyalty as they relate to the subject of ethics. In the context of individual and family dynamics and the painful conflicts that ensue, these issues may best be addressed by a psychotherapist or spiritual director. Once they extend beyond family, say to neighborhood, town, or country, discussion of loyalty and disloyalty finds its way into ethical debates about war, religion, race, social structure, euthanasia, and so many other important agendas currently confronting us. As the field of ethics attempts to discern the "rightness and wrongness" of behavior and the "goodness and badness" of motivation and its effects, does it not make sense that a sensitivity to the soul of the matter might offer a solution more encompassing than logic? What kind of place might the world be if respect for the feelings of all people and beings became a priority?

Of course, not everyone can be satisfied by any decision, but considerate communication that meets people "where they live" in consciousness, and offers to make allowance for their needs over time, does much to minimize conflict and violence. The value of empathy cannot be overstated here. As the potential for violence in our world increases, so must our sensitivity to the issues at hand, and our willingness to address the needs of ourselves and others from a broader perspective. The ethics behind these decisions, the discernment underlying the "rightness and wrongness" of behavior and the "goodness and badness" of motivation and its effects, derive their ultimate guidance from the heart-centered wisdom and soulful consciousness developed on the Vertical Path.

From this broader perspective, we have noted how the many conflicts described in this chapter spark painful feelings that typically invite the seeker to first exhaust Horizontal Path options for resolution, and then explore Vertical Path possibilities. Repeated trials and course corrections move us into recurring cycles of emptiness and fullness, with each cycle expanding our consciousness and deepening the vessel of our heart. Every conflict marks the doorway to awareness of greater unity—if we dare to cross its threshold seeking love.

Feelings are not the same as the heart but they can certainly lead us to that loving destination if we but recognize their invitation and choose to accept it. If we do, the Vertical Path transforms us; Cassandra will have a new story to tell and so will we. In the next chapter we explore these life-changing possibilities as they specifically affect the empath.

CHAPTER 20

The Spiraling Path Continues

HOW DOES ONE CONCLUDE A JOURNEY such as this? Paying dedicated attention to our feeling life, we have spiraled from the microcosm of our DNA, with its antennae for electromagnetic energy, out to the world of our cells and neurological hardwiring, further out to the way we've come to psychologically appreciate life and our place in it, and further still to a deeper awareness of our souls and spirits in the macrocosm—and microcosm—of the Divine Unknown. We have acknowledged energy as a vehicle for information exchange within our physical being, between us via our emotions and emotional energy bodies, and beyond us through our consciousness of the everyday and the other-worldly. We have recognized the power of Love in its many manifestations, and the importance of our heart in witnessing, negotiating, expressing, and dwelling in that Love, body and soul. Still, while abstract affirmations and their wisdom offer some guidance for our daily walk through life, our empathic receptivity can sometimes overwhelm even the most inspired among us. So where do we go from here?

In so many ways, throughout this book we have directly and indirectly addressed the bitter-sweet qualities that often penetrate our awareness in any given situation. An empath deals with this duality of bitter-sweet quite intensely every day. I may have at times over-emphasized the "bitter," primarily because it can be so difficult to deal with—but we know that the intensity of the "sweet," while often wonderful, can be just as difficult to bear at times. That difficulty not only relates to its intensity, but also to our expectation that it will not last. The fairy-tale notion of "happily ever after" captures our attention and our longing but, truth be told, that's not how it works on Earth. Even in that moment when the pendulum has swung to its maximum, it prepares for its next descent. Like our breathing, that simple pause between the inhale and exhale is pure—fullness or emptiness—but all the other moments are process, filled with both, the empty filling and the full emptying, mixing the sweet with the bitter whether we notice these cycles or not.

We know, realistically, that if we were to freeze our breathing in its phasic motion at some desirable point, we would die. Like the constant motion of our breath, life's Wheel of Fortune must keep turning, or stagnation and psychological paralysis will ensue. Never-ending cycles of becoming beckon us if we can muster the courage to change and grow. In this process, our feelings descend from the heights then rise from the depths, only to descend and rise again, all in four-dimensional time and space. This relative slow motion, compared to the warp speed of our current science fiction, affords us an opportunity to notice details along the way.

Our feelings carry information and they can transform us if we let them. When honored in the heart, they deepen our capacity for love. But what also keeps us going in the midst of life's hardships involves the awakening and strengthening of our heart's faith. As noted in Chapter 17, this faith is not dogmatic or religious, but it *is* energetic and spiritual. A broken heart may lose its connection with faith, but we have seen that with the heart's mending, faith can guide and support us anew. Through the well-known fairy tale, *Sleeping Beauty,* we now delve more deeply into these challenging cycles to appreciate how they can impact our growth.

"And they lived happily ever after." Really?

I will never forget my dismay when I realized that the fairy tale glow at the conclusion of *Sleeping Beauty, Part I* really only served as preamble to the nightmare of *Sleeping Beauty, Part II.* In *Part I,*[198] Maleficent, the uninvited witch at Aurora's christening, retaliated by dictating that Aurora would prick her finger upon a spinning wheel at the age of sixteen, and by doing so she would die. Rather than allow their daughter to live fully for her sixteen short years, the King and Queen chose to have all spinning wheels in the kingdom burned. They also agreed to seclude Aurora away from the joys of the castle and even their presence, to prevent her having any contact with Maleficent.

Flora, Fauna and Merriweather, three sweet fairies, did their best to soften the curse, but no one would know their effectiveness until the tell-tale moment. Aurora, in her boredom and loneliness, did find the dreaded instrument on her sixteenth birthday. She fell into a deep sleep that could only be undone when the desire and

---

[198] Jane Werner Watson, *Sleeping Beauty: Based on the Walt Disney Motion Picture* (New York: Simon and Schuster, 1957).

persistence of her true love would lead him to overcome the thorny thicket surrounding the castle where she lay. According to the fairies' spell, she could only awaken after he gave her the redeeming kiss. He did, of course, and they enjoyed a royal wedding. According to the conclusion of *Part I*, they lived happily ever after.

As *Part I* of the tale ends, everyone breathes a sigh of relief. *Part II*[199] never became popular, which says something about our psyche's wish for the eternal longed-for reunion and joyful celebration—as we also found in *Beauty and the Beast*. In *Part II* Aurora meets a different fate, as she now must live with the prince's mother, a dowager queen who has no room in her heart for any competitor for her son's affection. The queen mother fabricates a war, sends her son off to deal with it, and plots to devour Aurora's two children and eventually, the heart-broken Aurora as well. Fortunately, the cook swaps an animal for the child each time the queen mother orders her "stew," and he serves it to her with a life-saving lie. Eventually the prince returns—just in time, of course. With the family reunited, Aurora's ogre mother-in-law disappears, never to threaten them again.

Upon reflection, we notice in *Part I* that our heroine's fate is determined by others: Maleficent curses her; her parents restrict her exposure to potentially deadly stimuli and much joy as well; and the fairies send her into a long, protective sleep. For the first part of her life, Aurora is numbed and lonely until the Prince's kiss initiates her into the fullness of her feeling life.

In *Part II* she has awoken, but her fate is still determined by others: her mother-in-law plots her demise; the cook secretly saves her children; her husband rescues her and saves them all from the

---

[199] "Sleeping Beauty," Wikipedia, last modified January 20, 2016, https://en.wikipedia.org/wiki/Sleeping_Beauty.

queen. In contrast to *Part I*, however, Aurora *feels* the horror of loss when she thinks her children have been killed and eaten. We may even imagine that she misses her husband—and has a feeling or two about her mother-in-law. Such painful and challenging experiences sometimes send an empath retreating into the metaphorical sleep of *Part I*. If the empath maintains focus, however, and allows herself to face her feelings squarely, new options arise.

Perhaps if there were a *Part III* to this tale, Aurora would become the mistress of her own fate, feeling fully and finding her way to joy. Even so, she would continue to experience periods of struggle and growth, followed by a happy ending leading to the next challenge, as the Wheel of Fortune continues its ever-turning motion. Unlike Aurora whose life is confined to the printed page and movie screen, we fortunately have the opportunity to live into our own *Part III*. We can consciously take up our own spinning Wheel and live into the fullness and emptiness of feeling, its sweetness and its bitterness, over and over again. Empaths know this cycle well if they have not closed themselves to life. The heart bears this ebb and flow if we dare to let it. And if the painful tension sometimes becomes impossible to bear and breaks our heart, we now have ways to mend it.

Spirit, the Heart, and the Seesaw

Two years ago I came upon a prayer two lines of which really speak to this issue: "O Blessed One, keep my heart forever open to fully feel life's pain and delight. Help me to not turn away from those things that are difficult to witness, or those that cause me to be fearful."[200] These lines come in the form of a prayer because we humans can only hold so much alone, without assistance.

---

[200] Reynolds, *Ink and Honey*, 142.

Empaths will always feel to some degree the sadness, anxiety, anger and distress of our current world and those we love—and the delights and gladness also. I do. Feeling deeply is not a diagnosis or a disorder: it's a life lived fully with passion in its guises of heartache and joy. As we mature along this path, we may come to realize how strong and deep the heart truly is. We also, one hopes, come to trust it and to trust that the spiritual forces flowing through the heart will respond to our request for support at any time. As our heart mends over and over again, our heart's faith deepens. The turns of the Wheel eventually become part of a welcomed universal flow.

As noted by Jonathan Goldman, faith links us with spiritual forces and lives in the front mental body of the Heart Chakra.[201] Faith is an energetic part of who we are, of our *essence*. Yet difficult or painful experiences challenge this faith that healing abounds and that all will be well. These trials send us into an Underworld experience if we have ventured onto the Vertical Path, and though we may not be able to see love, hear it, feel it, or know it, if we descend there looking for Love we will find it.

I have come to realize that faith is one of Love's many faces. And we need it most during our Underworld experiences. Like Sleeping Beauty, faith may lie hidden in the background or seem to be sleeping, or it may be sorely tested and eventually rewarded. Ultimately, faith must be awoken and strengthened by our intentional attention and prayer, and by meeting the very challenges that test it. We must become like the Aurora of the yet-to-be-written *Part III*, who recognizes she needs her loving center restored to fullness, and who makes the active effort to reunite the healing and wounded parts of her tender, precious heart.

---

[201] Goldman, *Gift of the Body*, 316–322.

When we are overcome by the sorrows, turmoil, tedium, and cruelty of our days, our struggle lies in remembering to search with commitment for the joys, peace, wonder, and beauty of life as well. This is not easy. These polarities of feeling can pull hard at one another across a potential divide within our tender heart. Insight, stamina, and all sorts of support—spiritual, human, and furry—matter here and can make a huge difference regarding how we handle this tension.

The image of a seesaw comes to mind. Does the seesaw move back and forth such that we focus on painful feelings when one side of the seesaw is up, only to have it fall into the unconscious, after which we give our complete attention to the other side, newly lifted and happier, forgetting the pain we once felt? Or is the tilted seesaw stuck, so that we split our consciousness and live into only one of these polarities, either feeling the ongoing pain of a broken heart, or working hard to pretend nothing is wrong? Or do we experience the seesaw from its center? Can we manage to hold these tensions within our tender heart while seeking a way to love all aspects with compassion, forgive what is necessary, and bless what needs to move on? I myself am still on a significant learning curve regarding this, challenged always to remember the importance of the heart. The heart is our integrator, and in its mending we simultaneously bridge all sorts of divisions within.

Long ago, while in the midst of my own depression, I read Jung's *Answer to Job*.[202] I remember reflecting upon the tension between the opposites, and how Jung encourages the integration of these polarities within us in order to experience wholeness. Prior to my engagement in this work, I wondered what holds these opposites together in the first place. What IS that tension, taut like a rubber

---

[202] Carl G. Jung, *Answer to Job*, in *The Collected Works of C. G. Jung*, Volume 11, Bollingen Series XX, trans. R.F.C. Hull (Princeton, NJ: Princeton University Press, 1969).

band about ready to snap at times? Is it potential energy? Is it an ingredient of stubbornness, or better, determination? Is that tension an aspect of the Divine? Does the Kabbalistic understanding—that Ultimate Divinity initiated creation to behold Itself—have something to do with these opposites and the tension between them? If so, how would such a concept relate to my pervasive feelings of sadness and occasional despair when their counterparts of joy and hope were little more than fleeting shadows in my psyche? Might I count on that tension to hold these long-awaited feelings, even if hidden, for my future discovery?

I now realize that once I made the decision to *acknowledge* those darker, overwhelming feelings without letting them *define* me, I had to find a way to understand and deal with them. An opposing challenge arose: not to let any newly learned *cognitive* understanding critically define how I "should feel." Just a day or so before writing about this topic I awoke from a dream, a nightmare really, which reminded me that "ascent" in consciousness without living from the heart is meaningless.

The heart loves us wholly, lower chakras as well as upper. Sometimes, on the spiritual path, we forget that Sacred Love applies to the whole of us, the fullness of our humanity: all our gifts, talents, and achievements; all our cares, longings, and strivings; all our vulnerabilities, failings, and feelings about them. The disembodied "head," the intellect producing logic and "good ideas" without connection to Love for the whole of us, is intelligence devoid of wisdom. In the sometimes quoted words of *Star Trek*'s Mr. Spock: "Logic is the beginning of wisdom, not the end."[203]

---

[203] "Great Star Trek Quotes," Great Sayings, accessed March 8, 2016, http://greatsayings.blogspot.com/2009/05/great-star-trek-quotes.html.

Spirit, the Heart, and the Spiral

As noted throughout this work, questing into the realm of the Spirit has offered me a way to redeem my own feeling life, as well as the feeling life of those who sensitively experience the inner states of others. In my search I have gratefully discovered that the wisdom communicated by many seekers shares a similar message, though they traveled very different paths. For example, in the words of Rabbi Laura Duhan Kaplan: "Our mystical tradition of Kabbalah teaches that God is everywhere, including in our thoughts and feelings."[204] This is echoed by Rudolf Steiner, the founder of Anthroposophy: "All that dwells within each human being, including thoughts and feelings, must be considered holy and inviolable. We must be filled with a profound awe for everything human, even in our memories and recollections."[205]

Listening to their shared wisdom, we may further wonder about the purpose of the feeling experiences that arise when our tender heart strains to contain the tensions of opposing concerns. What follows has emerged from my own quest to give meaning to these painful conflicts within.

The Divine is Love. Love desires relationship to experience and share Itself. Love creates Duality: Darkness and Light, Night and Day, Underworld and Upper World, Feminine and Masculine, to name just a few. Each partner of each pair offers clarity and complementarity to its mate. Because these pairs are born from Love, they dance together in Love. When they comingle, the Two create a Third. Creativity swells from the union of these Divine Opposites; they

---

[204] Rabbi Laura Duhan Kaplan, "Isaac and Ishmael," *Sophia Street: Walk with Wisdom* (October 29, 2015), 3/4, accessed January 14, 2016, http://sophiastreet.com/2015/10/29/Isaac-and-Ishmael.
[205] Steiner, *How to Know Higher Worlds*, 64.

love the process of creating and continue to do so. Thus, Diversity emerges. Love remains at the center of it all, so that Unity pervades the Diversity. As Diversity continues to create more diversity, the human heart evolves so we may consciously embody Love and its flow: "Even in loving, it is Love that loves through us."[206] The heart also provides an abode for the soul's longing, as well as its guidance for how to return to this knowing of Love should the complexity of progressive diversity obscure the way home.

So as we venture into the experience of Love's created life on earth, our feelings and sensitivities speak to our consciousness, offering us a steady stream of information about all its diversity and our place in it. Our heart intrinsically and intuitively understands these feelings and how to integrate their flow with the soul's longing and guidance. When our heart is broken by any of the mind's messages that distort or violate this natural flow, we have to expand our consciousness to better understand the cosmic and earthly creation Love made for us. Fortunately, Love's creation includes healing options. We have been created in Love, destined to experience and share Love, and blessed to know Love. When we live into the full purpose of our creation, Love's desire for experience and sharing is fulfilled.

So, as creations of Love who have been muddied by life's diversity, we must first attend to our feelings as prompts for consciousness. It is often said that information is power: once we properly discern our feeling-information, we can make choices. Power can be used for Love. This, our spiraling journey, often has us revisiting old wounds as the resonating "tuning forks" within us vibrate with every exposure to all the lower and higher frequencies we have

---

[206] Blum, *The Book of Runes*, 140–141.

ever experienced. The lower ones in particular (fear, shame, rage, anger, jealousy, criticism, guilt) need love no matter what person, place, thing or situation "pings" them into our awareness. Unless we actively choose to love these problematic emotions and the whole of ourselves with a mending heart, we will feel stuck on a merry-go-round of endlessly wounding repetitions.

If instead we actively choose to heal, even while inertia tends to drag our feeling life in seemingly meaningless circles, other possibilities await discovery. Whenever the vibrations of those inner tuning forks resonate with some lower frequency in our midst, learning to love those uncomfortable pings a little more each time means we experience our spiraling consciousness shifting into a unified field of Love. We can redeem and co-create: our feelings, no matter how bleak, become sources of information; our hearts, no matter how wounded or broken, receive opportunities to mend; the people we meet and the experiences we share with them offer possibilities for deeper love and greater consciousness. Ultimately, the world benefits from increasing numbers of intentional humans working to restore the conscious manifestation of Love that resides in all of creation at all times. In our redeeming and co-creating, we are "becoming." We live into the Love that we are.

The Day-to-Day Spiraling of Love

My appreciation for Love's gifts during sessions transforms my massage table and my office into a sacred space. When I work with someone, they agree to partner with me and together we appeal to the creative, loving Presence in our midst. I trust that we are held in a Divine embrace of Love, whose agenda isn't always gratifying to our ego, but whose intentions are for the greatest good of ourselves and the world at large. I also trust that each person carries worth, beauty, and blessing within, and that our partnering mission is to better understand these gifts in the context of hurtful patterns. Recognizing the love that fueled the initial response to the wound—and its habitual repetitions, which have grown ineffective and more hurtful over time—becomes an essential aspect of the wound's and love's redemption.

Acknowledging the wisdom attained in living the wound, and finding the love that has carved one's heart into a deeper vessel, permits a "letting go" of those hurtful patterns. After releasing these old habits as energy (now available for use elsewhere and for other intentions), one needs to receive and "install" a new pattern, a new way of being. This involves the integration of opposites in a transcendent way to become more whole. To do so requires blessing that which has previously been rejected, appreciating its essence, redeeming its potential to enrich one's life, and finding a way to make positive use of it. Ultimately, these perspectives draw upon the premise that Love holds everything in a unity, that Power can be used to promote balance, and that Consciousness fulfills the desire of the Kabbalistic Divine, to behold Itself knowing and sharing Love.

During a recent workshop, I experienced the opportunity to integrate my own empathic abilities into my developing sense of self and service. As writing this book would soon come to an end, I wondered, *how will I know what to do next? What is my purpose?* The answer came in the form of a *Star Trek* metaphor that continues to make me smile. (I hope avid Trekkies will forgive my inclusion of characters from two different series!) I began the workshop with the sense that I had developed my inner Deanna Troi (empathic sensitivities), Mr. Spock (ability to logically process them), and Dr. McCoy (capacity for utilizing numerous healing tools, including reliance upon Spirit, for healing self and others). But I had not yet consciously developed my inner Captain Kirk.

During the workshop, I realized that I do indeed have a strong James Tiberius Kirk. I love adventure and have enormous curiosity. I care deeply about my inner crew members and willingly follow the dictates of Starfleet Command (my soul) to explore and honor newly discovered life forms and civilizations (creatures and people). I simply had not allowed Captain Kirk (my heart) to consciously serve as the active captain of my inner life. I still believed it was safer to play it small and to hide in the shadows. I found myself more keenly afraid of Starfleet Command's (my soul's) next mission, "to boldly go where... [I have never] gone before."[207]

I realized in the course of my healing weekend (thanks to Jonathan Goldman) that my Captain Kirk needed to learn some humility. He was part of my broken heart, eclipsed by the shadows of my low self-esteem. The Empath Contract of my childhood had skewed his sense of capacity and responsibility. Like the unconscious Beast, he made an occasional appearance, but he had definitely not matured enough to assume his leadership role. For this, my long-ago broken heart needed more mending. Paradoxically, it was during my preoccupation with feeling small and invisible that the captain developed a more balanced sense of his limits and strengths.

From the shadows he witnessed my Inner Critic transform into Spock, as criticism shifted toward discernment. He noted how my inner Deanna came to appreciate the value of my sensitivity's

---

[207] "Where no man has gone before," Wikipedia, last modified February 22, 2016, https://en.wikipedia.org/wiki/Where_no_man_has_gone_before.

contribution to the whole. He witnessed the McCoy within me exploring many healing interventions and making them my own. As my heart has been mending, he has also observed how I learned to appreciate and fully inhabit my body (Scottie) and to communicate more effectively (Uhura). From his place in the shadows of my psyche, Captain Kirk observed each of these crew members in action and learned to value them and their gifts. As he is now ready to resume command, he respectfully includes them all—and their input—in his decision-making process.

Now, Scottie reports on the state of my body: the amount of fuel available; maintenance required; the impact of stressors and need for repairs. Deanna acknowledges the people and situations that attract my attention and how they make me feel. She also tells the captain when someone or something feels amiss. Spock assesses the data offered with discernment, not criticism, and shares it with Captain Kirk. Uhura communicates with all parties involved: with Starfleet Command to receive instructions and ask for help; with the crew via the intercom system; with the captain, to relay all this important information; and with the people external to my energy vehicle at the captain's request. McCoy assesses the health of those who come to me with his Tricorder (my Third Eye) so I can facilitate healing when possible, in coordination with the captain and crew. Starfleet Command appreciates the value of my Enterprise in the cosmic scheme, and cares about the condition of this and all its starships and staff. Captain Kirk, the heart of my operating system, respectfully listens to all this input, makes sacrifices when necessary, and leads the way toward fulfilling the sacred mission entrusted to me. Some missions are more perilous than others. Healing tools and miracles become available as needed, gifted by the Mysterious Unknown.

In keeping with this metaphor, I also realized during the workshop that I had to consciously cut the tethers holding me to the past, so that my Starship Enterprise can boldly depart into the starlit darkness of space for the adventures that await me. I (Captain Kirk and crew) will receive our missions from Starfleet Command, visiting planets and situations where one or more of us may be challenged. We will work as a team, helping one another and whoever may need our assistance in accord with our mission, without interfering in that planet/situation's evolution or the soul path of its people. My inner team will repair our damages if necessary and move on to the next assignment, respecting our limits and needs. And Captain Kirk, my heart, will lead the way and have the final say.

From a heart perspective, my inner aspects will confer as we live from a heart-centered humility, acknowledging our smallness in the vast cosmos while honoring the importance of our soul's assignment. We will do our best to remain calm in the face of adversity. We will extend compassion for Captain Kirk (my mending heart) for having to make weighty decisions in the face of the Unknown, for all of us (all my chakras) as his crew, and for all those impacted by our decisions. We recognize that we have no control over whether others perceive our firings as Genesis pods or destructive phasors. We can only hold the most compassionate intentions for all as we do our best in each and every circumstance. In faith we will trust the guidance of the Love that links us to the All, even in the direst of moments. We will surrender to the Mystery with gratitude for the opportunity to "explore strange new worlds."[208] And we will

---

[208] "Where no man has gone before," https://en.wikipedia.org/wiki/Where_no_man_has_gone_before.

always return to center, to humility, changed by the experience on our spiraling journey of becoming.

Appreciation for the Gift of Feeling

So, unlike the ancient Cassandra, we have discovered that it is a divine gift to be an empath. We have been granted an opportunity to consciously experience an aspect of Divinity, to feel life fully in all its movement and intensity. As empaths we are invited to heal, to grow, to help our world transition into its next level of becoming. It is not an opportunity offered to the faint of heart.

With faith we can embrace our tender heart, trusting that tomorrow's realized truth will be greater than today's. We must forgive ourselves for yesterday's inadequacies so as to embrace tomorrow's wisdom. These engagements with life require courage to face what is "difficult to witness," compassion for the human frailties and limitations handed to each of us on this journey, forgiveness for ourselves and others as we blindly try to negotiate an untrodden course, and blessing for our efforts past, present, and future.

May our ever-expanding consciousness, prompted by the information offered through our feelings and compassionately understood in our heart, propel us into a greater awareness of Love. May we trust that when we are truly searching, the timing of our discoveries is perfect—not only for ourselves, but for our community and the larger web. And may we never forget: "In the life of the Spirit, you are always at the beginning."[209]

May we attend to each new beginning as we spiral outward in our process of "becoming" the fruitful blessing of Love that we are!

---

[209] Blum, *The Book of Runes*, 94.

CONCLUSION

A New Story for the Empath

CULTURAL INFLUENCES SHAPE our myths, and as life evolves so do our stories. If Cassandra were to live into the next paradigm, her story might be different. She would then have access to all the scientific discoveries, academic literature, and accumulated wisdom afforded by the passage of time. Dismissal, social isolation, fear and depression would permeate neither her life experience, nor that of those who envision life differently than others. We have benefitted from the lessons of her story, and as we live into the current shifting paradigm we have an opportunity to write and enact new stories. These modern tales will endure if they resonate with something intrinsic and profound within the human psyche. They will survive the "test of time" if they support attitudes that ensure the survival of our species and our planet. They also need to honor healing and to redeem the world, ourselves and all life as sacred.

With some trepidation, but with a clear sense that we must begin sometime, I offer an alternative narrative for the sensitive Cassandras of our world. It may sound like a fairy tale but we have already seen what power fairy tales convey. I invite each of us to consider what tale we might like told about us as we age. In so doing, we may offer future generations new guidance on how to honor sensitivity, empathy, and healing. We may develop new dynamics for the expression and use of power. We can support and further develop our daily engagement with Love. With all this in heart and mind, I offer the following tale.

A New Story for Cassandra

Once upon a time there lived a beautiful young girl named Cassandra. She grew up on the outskirts of a large city with her family, who loved her dearly. Even while Cassandra was quite young, her parents realized how sensitive she was to all the sights and sounds, fabrics and foods, even the moods of others in her day-to-day world. These sensitivities sometimes made her appear awkward to others, unpredictably moody, and difficult to engage. Sometimes, in frustration, her parents would change their plans to avoid her inevitable "meltdown" in crowded situations. All the while, they also recognized the beauty of her delicate nature.

The thoughtful care her parents provided, which gradually included avoidance of unnecessary over-stimulation, fostered Cassandra's inner sense of safety and the development of her natural inquisitiveness and intelligence. Her family members also enjoyed her creativity and sense of humor, and they appreciated the caring sensitivity Cassandra expressed toward them, their friends, and even strangers who respectfully entered their social circle. Her uncanny awareness of their moods often surprised them. They learned to respond gently and wisely to their daughter's sensitivities, guiding her as best they could during her early childhood years.

Not all unfolded perfectly in her family's home, however. Being human, Cassandra's parents occasionally experienced momentary slides into stress and anger. Her siblings sometimes fought with each other and with her. People they cared about died or became ill, so feelings of grief occasionally pervaded their home. Conflicting schedules sometimes placed extra stress on family members. In addition, city life offered its own collection of exciting stimuli and relational strain. As a child, she experienced many ups and downs because she was so vulnerable to the energies and moods around her, but her family loved her and each member grew to appreciate the gentler, less chaotic, more peaceful life created by tending to her needs.

Over time, Cassandra learned more about her physical and feeling responses when she sensitively internalized the intense and subtle reactions of others, whether expressed outwardly or not. As her parents began to recognize patterns, they not only learned how to ease Cassandra's upset, but tried to give appropriate words to her feelings, as well as their own, so she could learn to discern the source of the many feeling-responses within her. Her parents even worked hard to react differently to their own life challenges as time went on. As she grew, Cassandra felt a warm sense of belonging in her family. They taught her about her unique soul path of sensitivity as they came to more deeply understand this sacred aspect of their own lives through personal explorations and discoveries. They responded to her with respect, and discovered their own empathic responses increasing as well.

Despite her family's best efforts, Cassandra's sensitivities led to deep hurts and anger, especially once she went to school and engaged with peers in the larger world. Her parents could not protect her from this, or the news, or the preoccupations of her social circles. They had no helpful explanation for why suffering, violence, and bullying in its many guises pervaded mainstream thinking. Her family members were more than willing to listen to her feelings when she came home from school, but they couldn't make her hurts go away. Especially during her adolescence, relationships and situations with other teenagers and sometimes with her teachers became progressively more painful and confusing. In response, she sometimes wished she could disappear. She tried several things to ease her emotional pain, but none brought any significant relief. Some were even unhealthy, self-destructive, or addicting. Her confusion intensified, as did her loneliness. She believed that no one really understood how she felt inside. She worried that she would always feel this way.

In time, the resilience instilled in her youth sparked her search for deeper healing and understanding. She remembered the soulful connections and conversations she sometimes had with her parents and a few special adults in her life. Her sensitivities also offered her information about the painful experiences of others, and the healing ways they learned to deal with their heartaches. She read voraciously, exploring spiritual perspectives and potential opportunities for healing and growth. She came to understand that the pain of the world had broken her heart, her heart needed mending, and love in all its many manifestations would supply the needed ingredients. She began to embrace her tender heart.

Cassandra's childhood memories of loving acceptance, along with her present-day encounters with caring others, sparked her search for avenues of deeper soul connection within herself, though she might not have named it as such at the time. One or two significant adults in her world seemed to resonate with this quest within her; they were able to recognize it and to validate her path. Now that she had reached adulthood, Cassandra could make the personal decision to heal. She pursued the healing avenues that resonated with her feeling state and intuition. She studied what felt important to her. She made the needed commitment to gradually ease the suffering of her inner world and to explore its potential value for her life.

Once Cassandra began to focus on what mattered for her own healing and growth, she then understood and trusted her gifts of sensitivity and intuition. She learned to listen well to the messages from her body, her intuition, and her visions, and she honored them. Cassandra became adept at interpreting the information she received, all the while humbled by its implications. She discovered increasing support in her social circles and offered her wisdom in turn to those who asked for it. She actively developed and made time for her own spiritual unfolding, as she increasingly lived from the center of her mending heart. She learned to access the healing and creativity of the Vertical Path for the benefit of herself and others who might value it.

Cassandra recognized that not everyone wanted the information she could share. She respected her gifts and her needs while acknowledging that each person has her own soul path and her own unique timing for its unfoldment. She developed the strength to "witness" without the compulsion to "fix." When what she witnessed on the Horizontal Path brought sorrow to her heart or a sense of emptiness to her core, she knew to attend to herself lovingly while journeying along the Vertical Path to the Underworld. There she would wait for the emptiness in her to recede. There she experienced a loving Presence and trusted that a rejuvenating fullness would eventually carry her to the Upper World, where new inspiration and hope would restore her sense of balance and purpose. Once refreshed, she would return her focus to the Horizontal Path if she felt called to partake in its activity and to receive input anew.

As Cassandra developed her capacity to move freely and lovingly between the Vertical and Horizontal Paths, she experienced greater inner peace. She recognized that on the Horizontal Path she would be challenged to deepen her capacities for love, courage, endurance, forgiveness, compassion, faith and gratitude. Life there did not frighten her much anymore. The Vertical Path's safety and freedom remained readily available, and the Guardian of the Threshold welcomed her every time she approached. She came to realize that no "shoulds" exist along the Vertical Path, only the freedom and the response-ability[210] of choice. Cassandra experienced increasing sovereignty of Spirit as she marked the sacred passage of her days. She lived to be an old, loving and wise woman, consulted by many. She died as she had lived, a blessing to all whose hearts she touched…

…and slowly, one person at a time, the world became a better place. Blessings to you! So may it be.

---

[210] Osho, *Tarot in the Spirit of Zen: The Game of Life* (New York, NY: Osho International Foundation, St. Martin's Griffin, 2003), 11.

REFERENCES

Book References

Alexander, Eben, M.D. *Proof of Heaven: A Neurosurgeon's Journey into the Afterlife*. New York, NY: Simon & Schuster Paperbacks, 2012.

Anonymous. *Meditations on the Tarot: A Journey into Christian Hermeticism*. Translated by Robert Powell. New York, NY: Jeremy Tarcher/Penguin, 1985.

Blum, Ralph H. *The Book of Runes. A Handbook for the Use of an Ancient Oracle: The Viking Runes, Tenth Anniversary Edition*. New York, NY: St. Martin's Press, 1993.

Brennan, Barbara Ann. *Hands of Light: A Guide to Healing Through the Human Energy Field*. New York, NY: Bantam Books, 1987.

Cooper, Rabbi David A. *God Is a Verb: Kabbalah and the Practice of Mystical Judaism*. New York, NY: Riverhead Books, 1997.

Dourley, John P. *The Psyche as Sacrament: A Comparative Study of C.G. Jung and Paul Tillich*. Toronto, Canada: Inner City Books, 1981.

Eden, Donna with David Feinstein, Ph.D. *Energy Medicine: Balancing Your Body's Energies for Optimal Health, Joy, and Vitality*. New York, NY: Jeremy P. Tarcher/Penguin, 2008.

Eden, Donna, and David Feinstein, Ph.D. *The Energies of Love: Using Energy Medicine to Keep Your Relationship Thriving*. New York, NY: Jeremy P. Tarcher/Penguin, 2014.

Feinstein, David, Donna Eden, and Gary Craig. *The Promise of Energy Psychology: Revolutionary Tools for Dramatic Personal Change*. New York, NY: Jeremy P. Tarcher/Penguin, 2005.

Forrest, Steven. *The Book of Pluto: Finding Wisdom in Darkness with Astrology.* Borrego Springs, CA: Seven Paws Press, Inc., 2012.

Fox, Everett. *The Five Books of Moses: Genesis, Exodus, Leviticus, Numbers, and Deuteronomy.* The Schocken Bible: Volume I. New York, NY: Schocken Books, 1995.

Friedman, Robert Lawrence. *The Healing Power of the Drum: A Psychotherapist Explores the Healing Power of Rhythm.* Reno, NV: White Cliffs Media, 2000.

Gellert, Michael. *The Way of the Small: Why Less Is Truly More.* Lake Worth, FL: Nicolas-Hays, Inc., 2008.

Gerber, Richard, M.D. *Vibrational Medicine: The #1 Handbook of Subtle Energy Therapies, Third Edition.* Rochester, VT: Bear & Company, 2001.

Gibson, Claire. *Goddess Symbols: Universal Signs of the Divine Female.* New York, NY: Barnes & Noble Books, 1998.

Goldman, Jonathan M., M.Ac. *Gift of the Body: A Multi-Dimensional Guide to Energy Anatomy, Grounded Spirituality and Living Through the Heart.* Bend, OR: Essential Light Institute, 2014.

Grof, Stanislav, M.D. *Beyond the Brain: Birth, Death and Transcendence in Psychotherapy.* Albany, NY: State University of New York Press, 1985.

Grof, Stanislav, and Christina Grof, editors. *Spiritual Emergency: When Personal Transformation Becomes a Crisis.* New York, NY: Jeremy P. Tarcher/Putnam, 1989.

Halevi, Z'ev ben Shimon. *Psychology & Kabbalah.* York Beach, ME: Samuel Weiser, Inc., 1986.

Hall, John E., Ph.D. *Guyton and Hall Textbook of Medical Physiology, Twelfth Edition.* Philadelphia, PA: Saunders Elsevier, 2011.

Hamilton, Edith. *Mythology: Timeless Tales of Gods and Heroes.* New York, NY: Mentor Books, 1942.

REFERENCES

Hanson, Rick, Ph.D., with Richard Mendius, M.D. *Buddha's Brain: The Practical Neuroscience of Happiness, Love & Wisdom*. Oakland, CA: New Harbinger Publications, Inc., 2009.

Harding, M. Esther. *Woman's Mysteries Ancient and Modern: A Psychological Interpretation of the Feminine Principle as Portrayed in Myth, Story, and Dreams*. New York, NY: Harper & Row, Publishers, Inc., 1971.

Hawkins, David R., M.D., Ph.D. *Power vs. Force: The Hidden Determinants of Human Behavior*. Carlsbad, CA: Hay House, Inc., 2002.

Hillman, James. *The Soul's Code: In Search of Character and Calling*. New York, NY: Random House, 1996.

Hughes, Daniel A., Ph.D. *Building the Bonds of Attachment: Awakening Love in Deeply Troubled Children*. Northvale, NJ: Jason Aronson, Inc., 1998.

Jones, Alexander, L.S.S., S.T.L., I.C.B., editor. *The Jerusalem Bible: Reader's Edition*. Garden City, NY: Doubleday Company, Inc., 1968.

Jung, Carl G. *Answer to Job*. Translated by R.F.C. Hull. In *The Collected Works of C. G. Jung*, Volume 11, Bollingen Series XX. Princeton, NJ: Princeton University Press, 1969.

Jung, Carl G. "The Practical Use of Dream-Analysis." In *The Essential Jung: Selected and Introduced by Anthony Storr*. Princeton, NJ: Princeton University Press, 1983.

Jung, Carl G. "On the Psychology of the Unconscious." In *The Essential Jung: Selected and Introduced by Anthony Storr*. Princeton, NJ: Princeton University Press, 1983.

Keyes, Daniel. *Flowers for Algernon*. Orlando, FL: Harcourt Brace & Company, 1966.

Lipton, Bruce H., Ph.D. *The Biology of Belief: Unleashing the Power of Consciousness, Matter & Miracles*. New York, NY: Hay House, Inc., 2005.

Lorie, Peter, and Manuela Dunn Mascetti, compilers and editors. *The Quotable Spirit: A Treasury of Religious and Spiritual Quotations, from Ancient Times to the 20th Century.* New York, NY: Macmillan, 1996.

Moore, Thomas. *Care of the Soul: How to Add Depth and Meaning to Your Everyday Life, The Illustrated Edition.* New York, NY: HarperCollins Publishers, 1998.

O'Donohue, John. *Eternal Echoes: Celtic Reflections on Our Yearning to Belong.* New York, NY: Perennial, HarperCollins Publishers Inc., 1999.

Osho. *Tarot in the Spirit of Zen: The Game of Life.* New York, NY: Osho International Foundation, St. Martin's Griffin, 2003.

Porges, Stephen W., Ph.D. *The Polyvagal Theory: Neurophysiological Foundations of Emotions, Attachment, Communication, and Self-Regulation.* New York, NY: W.W. Norton & Company, 2011.

Reynolds, Sibyl Dana. *Ink and Honey.* Chandelles Press, 2012.

Roman, Sanaya. *Soul Love: Awakening Your Heart Centers.* Tiburon, CA: H J Kramer, Inc., 1997.

Schapira, Laurie Layton. *The Cassandra Complex: Living With Disbelief: A Modern Perspective on Hysteria.* BookSurge, LLC, 1988.

Steiner, Rudolf. *How to Know Higher Worlds: A Path of Modern Initiation.* Translated by Christopher Bamford. Hudson, NY: Anthroposophic Press, 1994.

Taylor, Jill Bolte, Ph.D. *My Stroke of Insight: A Brain Scientist's Personal Journey.* New York, NY: VIKING, Penguin Group, 2006.

Thie, John, D.C., and Matthew Thie, M.Ed. *Touch for Health: A Practical Guide to Natural Health with Acupressure Touch, The Complete Edition.* Camarillo, CA: DeVorss Publications, 2004.

Tompkins, John, Jr., *Mastering Reiki: A Practicing and Teaching Primer.* St. Paul, MN: Llewellyn Publications, 2002.

Von Franz, Marie-Louise. *The Inferior Function.* In *Lectures on Jung's Typology.* Dallas, TX: Spring Publications, Inc., 1971.

Walker, Barbara G. *The Woman's Encyclopedia of Myths and Secrets.* New York, NY: HarperSanFrancisco, 1983.

Watson, Jane Werner. *Sleeping Beauty: Based on the Walt Disney Motion Picture.* New York, NY: Simon and Schuster, 1957.

Whitmont, Edward C. *Return of the Goddess.* New York, NY: The Crossroad Publishing Company, 1984.

Whitmont, Edward C. *The Symbolic Quest: Basic Concepts of Analytical Psychology.* Princeton, NJ: Princeton University Press, 1969.

Wickes, Frances G. "Chapter 2: Influence of Parental Difficulties upon the Unconscious of the Child." In *The Inner World of Childhood: A Study in Analytical Psychology.* New York, NY: Signet Books, 1966.

Educational Training References

Eden, Donna. "Advanced Practitioner Class." Presented at The Second International Gathering of Eden Energy Medicine, Orlando, Florida, September 18–22, 2013.

Eden, Donna, with David Feinstein. *Eden Energy Medicine Certification Program Class 1 Handout.* Ashland, OR: Innersource, Spring 2012.

Eden, Donna, with David Feinstein. *Eden Energy Medicine Certification Program Class 2 Handout.* Ashland, OR: Innersource, Summer 2012.

Eden, Donna, with David Feinstein. *Eden Energy Medicine Certification Program Class 3 Handout.* Ashland, OR: Innersource, Fall 2012.

Eden, Donna, with David Feinstein. *Eden Energy Medicine Certification Program Class 4 Handout.* Ashland, OR: Innersource, Winter 2013.

Eden, Donna, with David Feinstein. *Eden Energy Medicine Certification Program Class 5 Handout.* Ashland, OR: Innersource, Spring 2012.

Eden, Donna, with David Feinstein. *Eden Energy Medicine Certification Program Class 6 Handout.* Ashland, OR: Innersource, Summer 2012.

Eden, Donna, with David Feinstein. *Eden Energy Medicine Certification Program Class 7 Handout.* Ashland, OR: Innersource, Fall 2012.

Eden, Donna, with David Feinstein. *Energy Medicine EM101: Introducing Energy Medicine Class Handouts.* Ashland, OR: Innersource, 2015.

Web References

Aron, Elaine, Ph.D. "The Highly Sensitive Person." Accessed July 13, 2016. http://hsperson.com/.

Ashman, Howard, lyricist, and Alan Menken, composer. "Beauty and the Beast" song. *Beauty and the Beast.* Walt Disney Pictures, 1991. Accessed March 8, 2016. http://www.disneyclips.com/lyrics/lyrics74.html.

Blank, Martin, and Reba Goodman. "DNA is a Fractal Antenna in Electromagnetic Fields." *International Journal of Radiation Biology,* Vol. 87, No. 4 (April 2011): 409–415. Accessed February 10, 2015. http://informahealthcare.com/doi/abs/10.3109/09553002.2011.538130.

Blausen.com staff. "Blausen gallery 2014". *Wikiversity Journal of Medicine.* DOI:10.15347/wjm/2014.010. ISSN 20018762.

BrainyQuote.com. "Albert Einstein Quotes." Xplore Inc, 2015. Accessed March 11, 2015. http://www.brainyquote.com/quotes/quotes/a/alberteins130982.html.

CBS Evening News. "On The Road with Steve Hartman." Published August 7, 2015. https://www.youtube.com/watch?v=OCPc2RlMTII.

Dictionary.com. "Ethics." Accessed January 6, 2015. http://dictionary.reference.com/browse/ethics?s=t.

REFERENCES

Edaina. "The Ten *Sefirot.*" Accessed August 10, 2016. https://commons.wikimedia.org/wiki/File:The_one_tr%C3%A4d.jpg.

Eden, Donna. "Donna Eden's Daily Energy Routine [OFFICIAL VERSION]." Youtube. Last modified November 24, 2015. https://www.youtube/Di5Ua44iuXc.

Eldringhoff, Stephanie, M.A., L.M.F.T., and Victoria Matthews, N.D. "Frozen and Irregular Energies: Hidden Energy Stumbling Blocks." Innersource Handout Bank. http://innersource.net/em/resources/free-handout-bank.html#WorkSp.

Grant, Adam. "Helicopter Managers: The Helping Hand Strikes Again." Accessed March 13, 2015. https://www.linkedin.com/pulse/20130421122648-69244073-helicopter-managers-the-helping-hand-strikes-again.

Great Sayings. "Great Star Trek Quotes." Accessed March 8, 2016. http://greatsayings.blogspot.com/2009/05/great-star-trek-quotes.html.

HeartMath Institute®. "The Energetic Heart Is Unfolding." Accessed February 12, 2015. http://www.heartmath.org/free-services/articles-of-the-heart/energetic-heart-is-unfolding.html.

Innersource. www.Innersource.net.

Kaplan, Rabbi Laura Duhan. "Isaac and Ishmael." *Sophia Street: Walk with Wisdom* (October 29, 2015), 1–4. Accessed January 14, 2016. http://sophiastreet.com/2015/10/29/Isaac-and-Ishmael.

Kelly, Matthew. "Everybody is a Genius." In *The Rhythm of Life: Living Every Day with Passion and Purpose.* New York, NY: Simon & Schuster, 2004. *Quote Investigator: Exploring the Origins of Quotations.* http://quoteinvestigator.com/2013/04/page/2/.

Martens, Willem H. J., M.D., Ph.D. "The Hidden Suffering of the Psychopath." *Psychiatric Times* (October 7, 2014). Accessed January 18, 2015. http://www.psychiatrictimes.com/psychotic-affective-disorders/hidden-suffering-psychopath#sthash.TW1e3Og0.dpuf.

Mayo Clinic. "Vasovagal Syncope—Definition." Mayo Clinic Staff. Accessed February 9, 2015. http://www.mayoclinic.org/diseases-conditions/vasovagal-syncope/basics/definition/con-20026900.

McCraty, Rollin, Ph.D., Director of Research. *The Science of the Heart: Exploring the Role of the Heart in Human Performance.* HeartMath Research Center. https://www.heartmath.org/resources/downloads/science-of-the-heart/#user-content.

Merriam-Webster. "Sacrifice." Accessed March 8, 2016. http://www.merriam-webster.com/dictionary/sacrifice.

Religion Facts. "Kuan Yin." Last modified November 14, 2015. www.religionfacts.com/kuan-yin.

Sachs, Gerardo. "Ehyeh-Asher-Ehyeh." In *The Jewish Bible Quarterly*, 38:4, October-December 2010, 244–246. jbq.jewishbible.org/assets/Uploads/384/384_Ehyeh.pdf.

Silvestra. "Inanna—Sumerian Mother Goddess, Queen of Heaven and Earth." *Goddess-inspired Spirituality* (June 10, 2012). Accessed January 24, 2016. https://goddessinspired.wordpress.com/2012/06/10/inanna-sumerian-mother-goddess-queen-of-heaven-and-earth/.

Stuckey, Johanna. "'Inanna and the *Huluppu* Tree': One Way of Demoting a Great Goddess." *MatriFocus Cross-Quarterly for the Goddess Woman* (Lammas 2005, Vol 4-4). Accessed January 24, 2016. http://www.matrifocus.com/LAM05/spotlight.htm.

REFERENCES

Wikimedia Commons. "A Schematic of the 'Chinese' or Human Body Meridians." Figures 5-3 and 6-2 adapted from the work of KVDP, January 2010. Accessed May 20, 2016. https://commons.wikimedia.org/wiki/File:Chinese_meridians.JPG.

Wikimedia Commons. "Autonomic Nervous System." Figure 3-1 adapted from the work of Geo-Science-International, March 2016. Accessed May 19, 2016. https://commons.wikimedia.org/wiki/File:The_Autonomic_Nervous_System.jpg.

Wikimedia Commons. "Gray's Anatomy Plates." Figures 3-3, 3-4, 3-6, 3-8, 4-1, 8-1 adapted from Plate Numbers 501, 591, 717, 720, 724, 726, 970, by Henry Gray, *Anatomy of the Human Body*, 1918. Accessed April 19, 2016. https://commons.wikimedia.org/wiki/Gray%27s_Anatomy_plates.

Wikimedia Commons. "Kabbalistic Tree with Flaming Sword." Figures 16-1 and 18-1 adapted from the work of Cronholm144, a derivative work of Morgan Leigh's "File:Tree of life wk 02.jpg," 2007. Accessed July 20, 2016. https://commons.wikimedia.org/wiki/File:Tree_of_life_wk_02.jpg.

Wikimedia Commons. "The Human Atmosphere, or, The Aura Made Visible by the Aid of Chemical Screens." Figure 6-1 adapted from the work of Walter John Kilner, 1911. Accessed June 1, 2016. https://commons.wikimedia.org/wiki/File:The_human_atmosphere,_or,_The_aura_made_visible_by_the_aid_of_chemical_screens_(1911)_(14762852712).jpg.

Wikimedia Commons. "The Kabbalistic Tree of Life." Figures 16-1 and 18-1 adapted from the work created by PuckSmith with LView Pro 1.D2 and ACDSee 3.1, January 2006. Accessed July 20, 2016. https://commons.wikimedia.org/wiki/File:Tree_of_life_bahir_plain.png.

Wikimedia Commons. "The Seven Major Chakras with Descriptions." Figure 10-1 adapted from the work of xxglennxx, February 2010. Accessed July 1, 2016. https://commons.wikimedia.org/wiki/File:ColouredChakraswithDescriptions.jpg.

Wikimedia Commons. "Triple Warmer." Figure 5-2 adapted from the work of Depak Muniraj, June 2012. Accessed May 31, 2016. https://commons.wikimedia.org/wiki/File:Triple_warmer_meridian.jpg.

Wikimedia Commons. "Wu Xing Five Elements." Figure 13-2 adapted from the work of Don Reynolds, March 2007. Accessed August 7, 2016. https://commons.wikimedia.org/wiki/File:FiveElements-CycleBalanceImbalance.jpg.

Wikipedia. "Beauty and the Beast." Plot summary adapted from Jeanne-Marie Leprince de Beaumont, *La Belle et la Bete,* in *Magasin des enfants,* 1756. Accessed September 29, 2014. https://en.wikipedia.org/wiki/Beauty_and_the_Beast.

Wikipedia. "Guanyin." Last modified January 4, 2016. https://en.wikipedia.org/wiki/Guanyin.

Wikipedia. "Sleeping Beauty." Last modified January 20, 2016. https://en.wikipedia.org/wiki/Sleeping_Beauty.

Wikipedia. "Where no man has gone before." Last modified February 22, 2016. https://en.wikipedia.org/wiki/Where_no_man_has_gone_before.

Wikiquote. "Talmud." Mishnah Sanhedrin 4:9; *Yerushalmi Talmud,* Tractate Sanhedrin 37a. Last modified February 28, 2016. https://en.wikiquote.org/wiki/Talmud.

INDEX

A

Active imagination, 213, 374
Addiction, 35, 71, 73,184, 335, 361
Adrenal glands, 184
Advanced Star Diagnostics protocol, 282, 289
Aggression, 175, 274
Amygdala, 55, *59*, 60, 86, 126, 158, 159, 176
Anger, 66, 70, 136, 200, 210, 253-54, 268, *275*, 276, 361, 380-82, 405-07, 431
Anxiety, xxv, 131, 198, 200, 244-45, *273*, *274*, 276
Appearance management, 267-68
Apollo, 384-86, 391-92, 396-97
Arianrhod, 351
Astarte, 355
Attachment, 155-56, 158
Attractor energy fields, 127, 135-37, 140, 210-11
Aura, 86, 103-25, *106*, 221, 250, 261-64, 268, 302
  detached, 110
Autism, 34
Autonomic Nervous System, *44*, 45

B

Beauty and the Beast, 342, 350-51, 364, 389-90, 417
  analysis, 311-14
  tale, 307-11

Beliefs, 23, 36, 103, 107-08, 118, 120, 156, 162, 172, 183, 199-200, 213, 218, 232, 238, 239, 242, 244-46, 248-49, 336-37, 343-44
Belly brain, 46-50, 70, 74
Big Bang theory, 332
Black Madonna, 357
Blessed Mother, Mary, 355-58
Brainstem, 55, *56*, 56, 153

C

Caregiving, 359-66, 369
Cassandra, analysis, 385-88, 391-93, 396-98, 436
  myth, 384-85
  new story, 438-42
Cassandra Complex, 386-87
Central Meridian, *87*, 111, *112*, 113, *273*
Central Nervous System, *44*, 45
Cerebral hemispheres, 57, 185, 191-92, 203
Chakras, 86, 196, *197*, 239, 302, 370, 432-36
  Crown Chakra, 204-05
  Heart Chakra, 109, *197*, 200-01, 206-10, 318, 321
  Root Chakra, 111, 198, 206, 210, 319
  Sacral Chakra, 198-99, 319
  Solar Plexus Chakra, 199-200, 206, 218, 319, 321

Third Eye Chakra, 175, 203-04, 434
Throat Chakra, 201-03
Chronic illness, 382-83
Circulation-Sex Meridian, *87*, 88, 272, *273*
Cleansing the Aura, exercise, 116-18, 264
Compassion, 25, 36, 75, 140, 148, 201, 215, 238, *273*, 274, *275*, 277, 333, *334*, 363, 395, 411-12, 436, 442
Consciousness, 25, 83-85, 157, 191-92, 302
  and chakras, 198-206
  and choice, 144, 414
  dualistic vs. unitive, 209
  in healing, 220, 223-27, 232-33, 238-39, 242-44, 292-93, 305-06
  and holistic model, 131-46, 432
  and spirituality, 326-28, 346-48, 373-75, 409-15
Corpus Callosum, *56*, *59*, 191
Cortex of the brain, 57, *59*, 60, 70, 164, 177, 221, 244, 274
  frontal lobe, *49*, *56*, *59*, *67*, 68, 127, 138, 269-70, 276
  temporal lobe, *49*, *56*, *59*, *67*, 68
Cover the Eyes, exercise, 96-97
Courage, 136, 169, 210-11, 213-14, 246-50, *273*, 374, 435-36, 442
Crossover Homolateral Repatterning, exercise, 266
Crossover Shoulder Pull, exercise, 265
Cybele, 352

D

Daily Energy Routine, 112, 115, 119, 261-62
Dark night of the soul, 418-19
Darwin, Charles, xxiv-xxvi
Depression, xxvi, 33, 131, 200, 245, 254
Despair, *273*, 362, 367
Discernment, 174, 187, 200, 214, 243, 276, 395, 407-12, 434
Dissociation, 71, 73, 177-78, 184, 277-78, 361, 386
Divine Feminine, 355-358, 366
DNA as a fractal antenna, 84-85
Dorsal Motor Nucleus of the Vagus, *49*, 52, 58, 71, 92, 154
Dragon and the Queen, The, 403-05
Drumming, 192
Ducks and sponges, 22-25, 27-28, *37*, 116, 125, 162, 167-68, 250
Dumuzi, 355

E

Echo and Narcissus, analysis, 32-33
  myth, 31-32
Eden Energy Medicine, xxxv, 78-80, 93-101, 110-16, 119, 121-23, 218, 231-34, 239, 246-47, 258, 264-66, 269-78, 280-86, 391, 416
Eden Energy Medicine exercises:
  Cover the Eyes, 96-97
  Crossover Shoulder Pull, 265
  Daily Energy Routine, 112, 115, 119, 261-62
  Homolateral Repatterning, 266
  Hook Up, *112*, 113-14
  Insula-Triple Warmer Hold, 277-78

INDEX

massaging the feet, 115
Neck Flow, 79, 280
spooning the feet, 115
smoothing behind the ears, 91
tracing Triple Warmer backwards, 91
Triple Warmer/Spleen Hug, 98
walking on wet grass, 115
Zip Up, 113
Ego (Personality), *132*, 143-46, 157-61, 164, 168, 226
   ego-soul relationship, 147, 204-05, 298-99, 302, 304, 329-30, *334*, 342, 347, 392-93
   and chakras, 199, 202-05
Ehyeh-Asher-Ehyeh, 341
Emotions and meridians, 272, *273*
Empath Contract, 250-258, 284, 317, 370, 380, 411, 414, 415, 433
Empath, definition, 13-14, 19, *37*, 36-38
Empathy, definition, 10
Empathy, reverse, 410-11
Empathy and intimacy, 63-64
Emptiness, 326-27, 418-20, 422, 441
Endless Light, 143, 238, 333, 395, 419
Energy, kinetic and potential, 80-82
Energy bodies, 105, *106*, 116-18
   emotional, 105-07, 108, 135, 302
   etheric, 105, 107, 108
   mental, 107-08
   spiritual, 108-09, 111
Energy Psychology, xxxv, 9, 234-39, 258, 280-86, 289, 391, 416
Entrainment, 55, 200
Erikson's Stages of Psychosocial Development, 151-53

Autonomy vs. Shame and Doubt, 157-63
Ego Integrity vs. Despair, 171
Generativity vs. Stagnation, 170-71
Identity vs. Role Confusion, 169-70
Industry vs. Inferiority, 168-69
Initiative vs. Guilt, 163-68
Intimacy vs. Isolation, 170
Trust vs Mistrust, 153-57
Erishkigal, 353-54, 356, 358, 362-63
Eros, 333-34; myth (as Cupid), 142
Ethics, definition, 378-79, 393
Extraversion, 25-29, *37*

F

Faith, 201, 238, 329, 365, 366, 423, 426, 436, 442
Fear, 136, 199, 210, 274, *274*, 276, 431
Feeling vs. emotion, 133-34
Feelings, as messengers, 163, 164, 195, 423, 430, 434; as sacred, 429, 436
Fight, flight, freeze, 29, 43, 45, 60, 71, 116, 126-27, 136, 158, 160-61, 176
Fisher King, The, 299-300
Five Elements/Five Rhythms Model, 270-273, *271*, 282
Five Rhythm Neurovascular Reflex Points, 274-77
   Earth, *275*
   Fire, *274*
   Metal, *275*
   Water, *274*
   Wood, *275*
Flowers for Algernon, 188-89
Focusing, 374
Forgiveness, 36, 165, 201, 215, 238, 248, 357, 363-64, 436

Free will, 144, 195, 410
Freeze response, 29, 43, 46, 65, 71-72, 75, 92, 158, 160-61, 172, 184
Fullness, 418-20, 422

G

Governing Meridian, 87, 111, *112*, 113, 153, *273*
Grace, 145-56
Grandmother Spider, 356
Gravity, 83-84, 333-34
Grief, 16, 134, 136, 184, 210, *273*, 274, *275*, 276, 298, 311
Grounding Techniques: massaging the feet, 115
   spooning the feet, 115
   walking on wet grass, 115
Guardian of the Threshold, 101, *345*, 346, 347, *359*, 442
Guilt, 136, 163-67, 169, 202, 210, 214, 245, *273*, 363-64, 380-83, 431
Guilt vs. shame, 163

H

Hades, 364-65
Heart, brain, 50-55, 70, 74
   chakra, 109, *197*, 200-01, 206-10, 318, 321
   electromagnetic center, *53*, *54*, 54-55, 183, 200-01, 248
   endocrine organ, 51, 200
   at the crossroad, 371, 415
   broken/wounded, xxiv, 16, 148, 175, 182-93, 206-07, 248, 365, 367
   healing/mending, xxiv, 148, 208, 215, 239, 248, 322, 342, 348, 367, 426, 431-36, 441-42
Highly Sensitive Person, 19
Hippocampus, 55, *59*, 69, 184-85
Holistic Model of Human Consciousness, 131, *132*, 146-47, 187, 223-25, 292, 370
   behavioral level, 133
   emotional level, 133-37
   mental level, 137-41
   physical level, 131-32
   soul level, 141-46
Holy Grail, 299-300
Hook Up, exercise, *112*, 113-14
Hopelessness, *273*, 274, 276, 387-88
Horizontal Path, 339-48, *345*, *359*, 365, 369, 370-75, 380, 418-20, 441-42
Hormones, 46-48, *47*, 60, 132, 176, 225
Humility, 174, 201, 293, 305, 363, 435-36, 441-42
Hypothalmus, 55, *59*, 60, 86, 126, 176, 184
Hysteria, *273*, *274*, 276

I

Inanna, and Divine Feminine, 356-59
   myth, 351-55
   and Vertical Path, 362-64, 368
Inner Critic, 173-93, *345*, *359*
   effects, 140-41, 176, 179-86, 207, 209, 221, 241, 252, 299, 318-19, 344, 366-67
   formation, 161, 176-78
   healing, 180-82, 242-47, 284, 319-21, 344-47, 433

Inner Witness, 244
Inspiration, 191, 276, 293, 367-68, 372, 397, 442
Insula, 56, *59*, 65, 68, 70, 74, 176-78, 183, 221, 277-78
    Insula-Triple Warmer Hold, exercise, 277-78
Intelligence, 188-89
Intention, 67-78, 82, 99, 116, 120, 122, 145, 182, 233, 244, 246, 280, 299, 328
Introversion, 25-29, *37*
Intuition, 24, 70, 121, 146, 192-93, 196, 201, 231, 259, 361, 363, 367, 441-42
Irregular energies, 79, 92-93, 114, 115-16, 262, 266-68
    correction, 79, 93-94, 115
Ishtar, 355
Isis, 351, 352

J

Jesus, 299, 357-58, 371
Joy, 68, 99, 136, 189, 198, 204, 211, 256, *273*, 276, 292, 337-38, 366, 427
Judgment, 43, 122, 174-75, 200, 221, 395

K

Kabbalah, 130, 143-45, 208, 238, 333, 370, 393-96, 419
Kidney Meridian, *87*, 114, 272, *273*
Kinetic energy, 80-82, 85
Kuan Yin, 357-58

L

Light, healing with, 238
Limbic system, 55-57, *59*, 60, 70, 74, 164, 177, 221, 269-70
Love, xxvii-xxviii, 136, 185-88, 211, 216-18, 332-36, 342, 346, 349-51, 369, 373-75, 412, 426-36, 442
Lovingkindness, 333, *334*, *394*, 395
Loyalty, 414, 415-420

M

Main Neurovascular Reflex Points, *269*, 269-70, 274-77
Mary, Blessed Mother, 355-58
Mary Magdalene, 356
Meditation, 140, 184, 213, 374
Medulla Oblongata, *56*, 56, *59*
Memory, cellular, 70, 132
Memory retrieval, 69-70, 185, 244, 328
Meridian Flow Wheel, *87*, 87-88, 112
Meridians, 86-88, *87*
    and emotions, 272, *273*
    see specific meridians
Middle World, *359*, 368-75
Mind, higher and lower, *132*, 139-40, 187-93, 293, 349
    higher, 203, 210-14, 331, 335, 346
    lower, 138, 177, 199, 202, 209-10, 212-13, 330
Mirror neurons, *67*, 67-68, 70
Multiple Personality Disorder, 184
Myelination, 68, 153, 155
Mystery, xxxv-xxxvi, 141-42, 163, 181, 212-13, 281, 299, 323, 330, 338, 341-44, 348, 349-51, 358, 419, 435

N

Narcissism, healthy, 30, 418
  imbalanced, 30-31, 249-50, 312, 319, 389, *417*
Neck Flow, exercise, 79, 280
Nervous System, *44*, 45
Neurotransmitters, *47*, 48, 60, 132, 225
Neurovascular Reflex Points, 269-70, 274-77
  Earth, *275*
  Fire, *274*
  Main, *269*
  Metal, *275*
  Water, *274*
  Wood, *275*
Normality, definition, 13
Nucleus Ambiguus, *49*, 52, 58, 71, 155

O

Ohr Ein Sof, 395

P

Panic, 89, 274, *274*, 276, 289, 305, 403, 405
Paradigms, matriarchy, xxv
  patriarchy, xxiv-xxv, 390
  shift, xxv, 4, 220, 388-89, 398, 401-02, 437
Parasympathetic Nervous System, *44*, 45, 48, 155, 199
Peripheral Nervous System, *44*, 45
Pineal gland, *56*, *59*, 192, 204
Pituitary gland, *56*
Pluto, astrological planet, 364-65
Polarities, emotional, 427-428
  energetic, 79, 92-94, 114-15, 264-65
  paradigmatic, xxiv-xxv
  physical, 422
  sacred, 429
Polyvagal Theory, 57-60, 71, 154-55, 158, 416
Porcupine Theory, 63-64
Potential Energy, 80-82, 428
Power Point, 153, *154*
Prayer, 327, 375, 410, 415
Pride, 136, 174-75, 203-04, 210, 362
Psyche, definition, 129-31
  myth, 142
Psychic ability, 408
Psychopath, see Sociopath

R

Radiant Circuits, 99, 113-14, 153, 272
Reiki, 77-78, 227-234, 239
Religion, 343
Resilience, 23, 110-11, 119-20, 258, 260-64, 267, 290, 392
Resistance, 78, 290
Resonance, 66-67, 70, 74, 201, 301, 306, 316, 327, 331, 430

S

Sacred King, 352-55, 358, 362
Sacrifice, 316, 336-39, 434
Sefirot, 238, 333, *334*, *394*
Selective mutism, 73
Self-care, 398-400, 441-42
Sensory types, 121-25
  digital, 123
  kinesthetic, 121-22, 123-34, 126
  tonal, 122, 124
  visual, 122-23, 124

INDEX

Serotonin, 46, 50
Sino-Atrial Node, *53*, 53-54, 183
Sleeping Beauty, analysis, 424-25, 426
    tale, 423-24
Shame, xxvi, 21, 32-33, 127, 135,
    163, 169, 202, 214, 221, 245,
    282-83, 342, 363-64, 431
    and freeze response, 43, 71-72, 75,
    158-161
Shekinah, 355
Sociopathy, 34-35, 319, *417*, 417
Solitary Tract Nucleus, *49*, 52
Solomon, king, 377-79, 395-96
Soul, 4, 125, 129, 131, 433-34
    five levels of soul, *132*, 143-46,
    302, 330-32
    relationship with the heart, 304,
    348
    longing of the soul, 300, 303-06,
    322, 329-32, 347, 416
    reunion of the soul's levels, 330-32,
    347
Soul levels, 143-146, 379-80, 391-92
    also, *Chayah*, 418
    Nefesh and *Ruach*, 374
Spirituality, 8, 283-85, 289, 293,
    330-36, 392, 398, 436, 441-42
Spleen Meridian, *87*, 94-98, *95*, *271*,
273
Star Trek references, 10, 219, 225,
    428, 432-36
Surrender, 205, 231, *273*, 281, 339,
    362-64, 396-98
Survival of the fittest, xxiv- xxvi
Survival vs. growth, 57, 70-71, 99, 164
Sympathetic Nervous System, *44*,
    45, 53-54, 71, 86, 126, 155, 161

Sympathy, 411
Synchronicity, 78

T

Tammuz, 355
Tenderness, definition, xxiii-xxiv
Thalamus, 55, *56*, *59*
Theory of Mind, 34, 68, 70
Transcendent function, 225-26,
    350-51, 416, 418
Trauma, primary, 41, 65
    secondary, 42-43, 65
Tree of Life, *334*, 370, *394*, 394-95
Triple Warmer, 116, 119-20, 152-56,
    160-62, 181, 184, 186-87, 216-17,
    221, 243-46, 249, 261-63, 278,
    279-80, 290, 299, 336, 346
    as Guardian of the Threshold, 101,
    345, 346, 347, *359*, 442
    as meridian, *87*, 88-92, *90*, 95,
    161, 216-17, *271*, *273*
    as Radiant Circuit, 99, 346-47
    as system, 100
Triple Warmer balancing exercises:
    Cover the Eyes, 96-97
    smoothing behind the ears, 91
    tracing Triple Warmer backwards,
    91
    Triple Warmer/Spleen Hug, 98
Tzimtzum, 333, 395

U

Underworld, 351-54, 357-65, *359*,
    370-75, 409, 418-19, 426, 441-42
Upper World, 351, *359*, 366-68,
    370-75, 410, 418-19, 441-42

V

Vagus Nerve, 40, *44*, 48-50, *49*,
   52-53, 57-60, 86, 126, 153-56,
   154, 158, 183, 199, 221
   DorsalMotor Nucleus of the
      Vagus, *49*, 52, 58, 71, 92, 154
   Nucleus Ambiguus, *49*, 52, 58, 71,
      155
   Solitary Tract Nucleus, *49*, 52
Vasovagal response, 91
Vertical Path, 339-48, *345*, 358, *359*,
   365, 369, 370-375, 380, 411-12,
   417, 418-20, 426, 442
Victim mentality, 195, 222, 251, 293,
   327, 364, 375, 405
Virgin goddess, 355
Vivaxis, 152-53
Void, 247, 394, 419
Vortex, 103-04, 110-11

W

Wisdom, *334*, 393-96, *394*, 428, 432
World Tree, *371*, 372
Worry, 134, 249-50, *273*, 274, *275*,
   277, 304

Y

Yin and yang meridians, *87*, 88, *271*,
   273

Z

Zip Up, exercise, 113

ABOUT THE AUTHOR

Regina Bogle, M.D., was born in Philadelphia, PA, and received her medical degree from Jefferson Medical College in 1980. After completing her psychiatric residency in 1984, she worked in various mental health settings, including inpatient hospitals, residential programs for children, outpatient clinics, foster care agencies, partial hospitalization programs for children, adolescents and adults, and more recently in private practice for the past sixteen years. Since completing the Eden Energy Medicine Certification Program, the Clinical Practicum, and the Advanced Practitioner curriculum in 2014, she has devoted her practice to the combination of Energy Medicine, Energy Psychology and psychotherapy. In addition, she is a Bach Foundation Registered Practitioner and a Reiki III Level Practitioner. She also provides workshops for empaths, and teaches classes integrating psychology, spirituality, mythology and energy medicine for mental health professionals, physicians, nurses, spiritual directors, life coaches, body workers, and interested others.

www.ingramcontent.com/pod-product-compliance
Lightning Source LLC
Chambersburg PA
CBHW060447170426
43199CB00011B/1120